TRANSPORT IN A UNIFIED EUROPE
Policies and Challenges

Studies in Regional Science and Urban Economics

Series Editors

L. ANSELIN
M. FUJITA
P. NIJKAMP
J. THISSE

Honorary Editors

Å. E. ANDERSSON
W. ISARD

Volume 24

NORTH-HOLLAND – AMSTERDAM • LONDON • NEW YORK • TOKYO

Transport in a Unified Europe

Policies and Challenges

Edited by

DAVID BANISTER
Planning and Development Research Centre
The Bartlett
University College London
London, U.K.

JOSEPH BERECHMAN
The Public Policy Program
Faculty of Social Sciences
Tel Aviv University
Ramat Aviv, Israel

N·H

1993

NORTH-HOLLAND – AMSTERDAM • LONDON • NEW YORK • TOKYO

ELSEVIER SCIENCE PUBLISHERS B.V.
Sara Burgerhartstraat 25
P.O. Box 211, 1000 AE Amsterdam, The Netherlands

ISBN: 0-444-81702-6

This book is printed on acid-free paper.

Printed in The Netherlands

INTRODUCTION TO THE SERIES

Regional Science and Urban Economics are two interrelated fields of research that have developed very rapidly in the last three decades. The main theoretical foundation of these fields comes from economics but in recent years the interdisciplinary character has become more pronounced. The editors desire to have the interdisciplinary character of regional sciences as well as the development of spatial aspects of theoretical economics fully reflected in this book series. Material presented in this book series will fall in three different groups:

- interdisciplinary textbooks at the advanced level,
- monographs reflecting theoretical or applied work in spatial analysis,
- proceedings reflecting advancement of the frontiers of regional science and urban economics.

In order to ensure homogeneity in this interdisciplinary field, books published in this series will:

- be theoretically oriented, i.e. analyse problems with a large degree of generality,
- employ formal methods from mathematics, econometrics, operations research and related fields, and
- focus on immediate or potential uses for regional and urban forecasting, planning and policy.

The **European Science Foundation** is an association of its 54 member research councils, academies and institutions devoted to basic scientific research in 20 countries. The ESF brings European scientists together to work on topics of common concern, to co-ordinate the use of expensive facilities, and to discover and define new endeavours that will benefit from a co-operative approach.

The scientific work sponsored by ESF includes basic research in the natural sciences, the medical and biosciences, the humanities and the social sciences.

The ESF links scholarship and research supported by its members and adds value by co-operation across national frontiers. Through its function as a co-ordinator, and also by holding workshops and conferences and by enabling researchers to visit and study in laboratories throughout Europe, the ESF works for the advancement of European science.

This volume arises from the work of the ESF Network for European Communications and Transport Activities Research (NECTAR).

Further information on ESF activities can be obtained from:

European Science Foundation
1 quai Lezay-Marnésia
67080 Strasbourg Cedex
France

Tel. 88 76 71 00
Fax 88 37 05 32

FOREWORD

Europe now forms the largest free trade area in the world with a market of over 400 million consumers, and a Gross Domestic Product which is greater than that the United States of America and more than twice the size of that in Japan. At Europe's core are the 12 European Community nations, but this number is likely to be increased with additions from Scandinavia and other countries (eg Austria). With the dismantling of the Iron Curtain, new opportunities have arisen with the countries of Central and Eastern Europe now providing additional markets for European goods. Underlying the political and economic changes in Europe has been a consistent growth in income levels and car ownership; this in turn has led to unprecedented levels of mobility, particularly by car and more recently by air. There has been a similar growth in the movement of freight by road and rail. The quality and capacity of the transportation network must be adapted to meet this increase in demand and new links are also required between peripheral regions and the center, and between the West and the East.

It is against this background that significant problems and challenges concerning the future of transportation systems in the new wider Europe are being faced by policy makers, planners, economists and engineers . First, it is far from clear how present demographic, mobility, life-style, technological and logistical trends will shape future transportation needs. Second, in many cases (such as freight movement or railways), national policies tend to supersede global European interests thus making the operation of unified transportation markets inefficient and costly, both in economic and environmental terms. Third, it seems to be difficult to obtain agreement at the European level on priorities and actions concerning major issues such as capital investment, liberalization of markets, linkages within peripheral regions, abolition of administrative and physical barriers to free movement, and action against environmental destruction. Fourth, neither the present EC countries nor those of the wider Europe form a closed economy. All of these changes will combine to fundamentally alter the political, economic and social maps of Europe and the implications for travel by all modes of transport will be substantial over the next decades. Although our focus is primarily on the 12 EC countries, experiences crucial to the development of a unified Europe are also drawn from Scandinavia and the Eastern European countries.

This book explores all of these major changes in the context of Europe. The chapters each take a particular theme and this is developed with examples taken from a range of different European situations, with the intention of seeking common themes, policy issues and possible solutions to perceived problems. This reflects the trend towards unification within Europe with key decisions being taken at the supranational level as well as at the national and local levels. Transport is one sector within the European economy which affects all people and industries, and solutions are now being assessed on a European scale.

The book is split into two parts. The first reviews European transport by the various modes of transport - including highways and travel, the bus industry, high speed rail, air transport, waterways and freight. In each case background trends have been reviewed, and the key issues have been determined together with the means by which they can be resolved. This part is essentially modal and scene setting, with each author(s) adopting particular theoretical positions from which arguments for change can be based. The first part also acts as a context for the specific themes taken up in Part Two.

In Part Two, policy issues and challenges are selected which integrate all modes as real progress towards integration of transport in a unified Europe must depend upon clear strategic policy objectives. The key themes selected include missing transport networks, the links between mobility and environmental sustainability, regional issues in peripheral countries, regulatory reform in local transport, the crucial need to develop new links between Eastern and Western Europe, financing transport and investing in the transport infrastructure. If these challenges can be met, the ability of the transport system in a unified Europe to meet political, economic and social objectives can be realized. However, the difficulties in terms of financing, reconciling transport priorities with the environment, the integration of old and new systems (particularly in Eastern Europe), the problems of balanced development between the core and the periphery, and the operation of the market in transport cannot be underestimated. The agenda is a challenging one.

The final chapter (Chapter 16) places the European passenger transport scene in a wider context and draws comparisons with developments in the USA. Many of the issues outlined in the 14 central chapters of the book have direct parallels in the U.S., providing an opportunity to learn from each other's experiences.

The achievement of this book is to bring together 22 authors from 16 different countries to present an international perspective on the problems facing transport planners, economists and policy makers in Europe. Each author, either alone or in collaboration, has been asked by the editors to prepare a contribution on a specific topic in his/her area of expertise, and, although there may be substantial differences in views and priorities, we trust that the output is an authoritative statement on transport policies, issues and challenges facing Europe at the threshold of the 21st century.

ACKNOWLEDGEMENTS

This substantial book has required the cooperation of many individuals and organizations and we would like to thank them all for their participation in this venture. We are grateful for the support of the European Science Foundation who have both encouraged this project and provided essential support for collaborative work, in particular the enthusiasm of Dr. John Smith (Scientific Secretary for the Social Sciences). Most of the contributors have been involved with the European Science Foundation's Network for European Communication and Transportation Activities Research (ESF-NECTAR) which for the past seven years has brought together some seventy researchers from nineteen countries to participate in collaborative research. The original motivation for this particular book has arisen from papers published in a special issue of Transportation Research on Transportation Policy in Europe (1992, Vol. 26A, 2), edited by Joseph Berechman. Many of the authors of those papers agreed to contribute completely revised, lengthened and new chapters to this book.

We would also like to thank all the contributors for their hard work in meeting the editors' impossible deadlines, in maintaining a high level of quality in the chapters, in producing text to machine compatible guidelines, and in responding to referees' comments. The problems of international collaboration have been accommodated with authors from different countries combining to produce chapters, and with representatives from the majority of European countries participating in the book.

On the production side, we would like to thank our respective Institutions for their support -- The Bartlett School at University College London and The Faculty of Social Sciences at Tel Aviv University. Dr. Paulo Camara in the Bartlett School at University College London helped with preparing the computer based diagrams in the text and Mrs. Nina Reshef in the Public Policy Program at Tel-Aviv University edited the basic text and tables into a consistent form for publication. Finally, we would thank Mrs. Lilian van der Vaart, the Publishing Editor at Elsevier, for her support in producing this book.

LIST OF AUTHORS

Dr. Bjorn Andersen
More and Romsdal College
PO BOX 308
N-6401 MOLDE
Norway

Dr. David Banister
Planning and Development Research Center
The Bartlett
Wates House
22 Gordon Street
LONDON WC1H 0QB
England

Dr. Sean Barrett
Department of Economics
Trinity College Dublin
DUBLIN 2
Ireland

Professor Joseph Berechman
The Public Policy Program
Faculty of Social Sciences
Tel Aviv University
RAMAT AVIV 69978
Israel

Professor Dr. Ulrich Blum
Faculty of Economic Sciences
Technical University of Dresden
Fakultaet Wirtschaftswissenschaften
Mommenstrasse 13
O-8027 DRESDEN
Germany

Professor Kenneth Button
Department of Economics
Loughborough University
LOUGHBOROUGH
Leicestershire, LE11 3TU
England

Dr. Vlasta Dugonjic
Transport Division
UN Economic Commission for Europe
Palais des Nations
CH-1211 GENEVA 10
Switzerland

Mr. Bernard Gerardin
European Investment Bank
100 Boulevard Konrad Adenaur
L-2950 LUXEMBOURG

Professor Maria Giaoutzi
Department of Geography and Regional Planning
Zographo Campus
National Technical University of Athens
GR-15710 ATHENS
Greece

Professor Gerold Hauser
The Socioeconomic Institute
Universitat Zurich
Raemistrasse 71
CH-8006 ZURICH
Switzerland

Dr. Veli Himanen
Technical Research Center of Finland
Road, Transport and Geotechnical Laboratory
Sahkomiehentie 3
SF-02150 ESPOO
Finland

Dr. Ira Hirschman
Parson Brinkerhoff, Inc.
One Penn Plaza
NEW YORK, NY 10119
United States

Mr. Dimitri Ioannides
Department of Urban Planning
Rutgers University
Livingston Campus
NEW BRUNSWICK, NJ 08903
United States

Professor Peter Jones
Transport Studies Group
University of Westminster
35 Marylebone Road
LONDON, NW1 5LS
England

Dr. Jörgen Kristiansen
Department of Development and Planning
Aalborg University
Fibigerstraede 11
DK-9220 AALBORG
Denmark

Dip. W. Ing. Frank Leibbrand
Faculty of Economic Sciences
Technical University of Dresden
Fakultaet Wirtschaftswissenschaften
Mommenstrasse 13
O-8027 DRESDEN
Germany

Dr. Rico Maggi
Socioeconomic Institute
Universitat Zurich
Raemistrasse 71
CH-8006 ZURICH
Switzerland

Professor Gines de Rus Mendoza
Faculty of Applied Science and Economics
University of Las Palmas
Saulo Toron, 4 (Urb. Zurbaran)
TARIFA BAJA
Grand Canaries
Spain

Professor Peter Nijkamp
Department of Economics
Free University
PO BOX 7161
1007 MC AMSTERDAM
The Netherlands

Professor Juraj Padjen
Institute of Economics and Faculty of Economics
University of Zagreb
Trg JF Kennedy-a
41000 ZAGREB
Croatia

Professor John Pucher
Department of Urban Planning
Livingston Campus
Rutgers University
NEW BRUNSWICK, NJ 08903
United States

Professor Jose Viegas
CESUR
Instituto Superior Tecnico
University of Lisbon
Avenida Rovisco Pais
P-1096 LISBON
Portugal

TABLE OF CONTENTS

PART TWO: POLICY ISSUES AND CHALLENGES IN EUROPE

TRANSPORT IN A UNIFIED EUROPE. Policies and Challenges.
D. Banister and J. Berechman (Editors)

Chapter One

TRANSPORT POLICIES AND CHALLENGES IN A UNIFIED EUROPE: INTRODUCTION

David Banister
Joseph Berechman

1. Introduction

During the last 20 years there have been massive changes in the structure and nature of society, resulting in an unprecedented growth in the demand for road, rail and air transport. This growth in demand cannot simply be examined just on the basis of extrapolation of past trends but must now include a wider range of demographic, economic, social and structural factors, all of which contribute to the demand for travel. In the next ten years these factors are likely to increase in their importance as the more advanced countries move towards post-industrial society. National statistics show the increase in living standards, the rise in car ownership levels, the increase in owner occupation, the rise in leisure time, the increase in the number of women at work, and the growth in the service sector and technologically based industries. All these factors are likely to increase passenger transport demand and to change existing patterns.

This book examines the key policy issues and challenges facing Europe. The definition of Europe used is much wider than the 12 countries of the European Community (EC) as it includes the other countries in Western Europe as well as the countries of the former East European. In total, the population of Unified Europe amounts to between 400 and 500 million, which is greater than the U.S. and the Pacific Countries. The EC 12 countries are second only to the U.S. in wealth creation (1986); over the 20-year period 1970-1990, annual economic growth in the EC was 2.6 percent per annum in real terms. Although the focus of the book is primarily on Western Europe, examples are taken from all Europe and comparisons are made with the other major economic powers in the world.

European Community	12 Countries	$3463 Bn	2630 Bn ECU
Western Europe	18 Countries	$4163 Bn	3160 Bn ECU
East & West Europe	25 Countries	$4763 Bn	3600 Bn ECU
United States		$4185 Bn	3180 Bn ECU
Japan		$1988 Bn	1510 Bn ECU

In this introductory chapter, a broad perspective of social and economic issues in Europe is presented. The first part reviews the changing demographic structure of the population and its implications for travel demand. This review is then complemented by one that explores the changing economic structure of society with the move away from a manufacturing base towards service and high technology industries. Again, the implications for travel demand are assessed. Social and environmental issues also feature high on the political agenda as transport decisions have important distributional implications and because transport is both a major consumer of non-renewable resources and creator of significant levels of pollution. The final section discusses the problems of the periphery and questions of regional development. It does not attempt to make predictions but tries to identify the main areas of certainty and uncertainty, possible beneficial and undesirable outcomes, and some of the critical policy choices that may have to be made. As such it provides the basic context to the remaining contributions to the book.

2. Demographic Change

Population growth across all Europe has gradually stabilized over the last decade and it is expected that change in the next decade will range between a loss of 2.5 percent (FR Germany and Denmark) and a gain of 4.5 percent (Netherlands and Portugal, see Table 1). The main exceptions are Turkey (+22 percent), Ireland (+11 percent), Yugoslavia (+6 percent) and Switzerland (-4.5 percent). However, it is the changing composition of the population that raises the most interesting questions in terms of travel demand. There has been a decline in birth rates across all advanced countries, with the average number of children per woman falling from about 2.5 in 1950 to about 1.5 in 1990. A fertility rate of 2.1 is normally assumed to maintain a stable population. This means that the number of young adults entering the workforce will continue to decrease until 1995 and then increase. Overall, the number of people of working age will continue to increase, but at a much slower rate than over the last decade, peaking in 2010. Beyond that time, there will be a marked downturn in the number of people of working age and, within the EC, it is expected that population growth will have ended. The population of the EC is expected to stabilize at 330 million in the year 2000. These figures do not take full account of possible international migration, the projections being based on current fertility

TABLE 1

Population Trends in European Countries (Thousands)

	1983	1990	2000	% Change 1983-2000
Belgium	9,855	9,977	9,972	+1.2
Denmark	5,114	5,147	4,940	- 3.4
Germany[a]	61,423	79,701	77,740	- 3.7
Greece	9,847	10,200	10,435	+6.0
France	54,729	56,540	58,573	+7.0
Ireland	3,508	3,512	4,247	+21.1
Italy	56,836	57,739	57,966	+2.0
Luxembourg	366	381	373	+1.9
Netherlands	14,367	15,010	15,643	+8.9
United Kingdom	56,377	57,478	57,902	+2.7
Spain	38,173	38,994	41,117	+7.7
Portugal	9,946	10,393	11,053	+11.1
Norway	4,129	4,225	4,325	+4.7
Sweden	8,329	8,109	8,098	- 2.8
Switzerland	6,505	6,168	5,889	- 9.5
Austria	7,552	7,579	7,625	+1.0
Finland	4,840	4,955	4,964	+2.6

Note: [a]Germany covers the Federal Republic in 1983 and unified Germany in 1990 and 2000.

Source: Eurostat (1992).

rates. It should also be noted that the decline is likely to be most pronounced in those countries which currently have the lowest fertility rates -- FR Germany, Italy, and Sweden.

The most significant growth in population will be among the elderly. This growth is attributed to the increase in life expectancy and the tendency to retire earlier. It is estimated that in Western Europe the proportion of persons over 65 years will increase from 13 percent in 1985 to more than 20 percent in 2020. For OECD countries, the number will increase by 50 percent from 98 million in 1990 to 147 million in 2020, peaking in 2040 with 175 million people over the age of 65. Growth is particularly significant in the age group 80+, which is projected to triple in the next 50 years. Taking these two changes in population together, namely the decline in fertility rates and the growth in the elderly population, means that not only does the absolute number of the elderly double, but the proportion of the elderly increases due to the relative decline in the younger population (OECD, 1989). By the year 2020, the elderly population in most European countries will exceed 20 percent of the total population, with the highest rates in FR Germany, France and Sweden.

These changes are likely to have significant impacts on demand patterns for all kinds of activities, including travel. A considerable increase will be required in health and social services to meet the needs of the elderly; there is likely to be a decline in the demand for school places and a surplus in the number of jobs available for school leavers. The implications for travel demand will be tremendous, particularly among the elderly. Today's elderly is the first generation of retired people that has experienced mass car ownership and so can be expected to continue to be car-oriented. With the tendency towards earlier retirement, a significant new group is emerging within the population, namely Peter Laslett's third age of personal fulfillment (Laslett, 1990). This group (aged 60-80) no longer has the complex responsibilities of earning a living and raising a family, it is reasonably affluent, and so has the money and time to spend on personal fulfillment. Much of these activities could involve travel, and it is here that one major growth area in travel can be expected to develop over the next decade (see Table 2).

It is only when people reach the age of 80 that full retirement and dependency is expected to take place. This group of people, which accounts for about 21 percent of the elderly, will require special facilities and transport services which can accommodate many particular requirements, for example, wheelchair accessibility or room for a person to accompany them. This group will not be able to drive and so will require public transport services, taxis, or chauffeur-driven private cars such as the service currently provided by many voluntary sector organizations. One possible development might be a vehicle designed specifically for the elderly to give them some degree of independence, perhaps similar to the battery-operated tricycles which are already available or cars with voice-activated functions to ease the physical requirements of driving. Special routes could be provided for low performance vehicles which could be used by the elderly and perhaps

TABLE 2

Summary of the Main Population Trends, 1980-2000

Group	Laslett's Ages	Trend	Comment
School Leavers and Young Adults	1st Age: 0-20	Growth of 10 percent in the longer term	Decline has already taken place in 1980s and up to 1995
Working Age Adults	2nd Age: 20-60	Small increase of 2 percent	Decline in 20-40 year age group in the 1990s, but growth in the 40-60 year age group
Age of Personal Fulfillment	3rd Age: 60-80	Stable over the next decade	Growth expected in this group in the longer term
Full Retirement and Dependency	4th Age 80+	Growth of 25 percent	Major growth in the next 50 years

Sources: Various.

children. With the age of consent being reduced (it is now 12 in the Netherlands if there are no complaints), the age at which young people can drive a low performance vehicle may also be reduced, particularly if there is a novice period for newly qualified drivers such as that which operates in Australia. Such a change would allow greater independence for young people and reduce the need for parents to perform complex escort functions.

In addition to greater mobility of young people and the growth in the elderly population, the age of retirement is also being reduced, to 55 years or less. This means that apart from the natural growth in the elderly population, the number of people in the retired age group will increase through early retirement and Laslett's third age will now cover the age range of 55-80, not 60-80.

The changes outlined so far assume that the stabilization of population in most European countries will not be offset by any major increase in international migration. The number of guest workers in most European countries has declined but the international movement of labor is still considerable. Most of the movement in the EC is from one member country to another, but movement may increase from East Europe to the West. Migration may alleviate some labor shortages, but it will not reduce the growth in the elderly population.

Over the last 30 years, the average household size has fallen in all European countries by about 20 percent. In Britain, the level has declined from 3.1 persons to 2.6 persons (1961-1986), in FR Germany from 2.8 to 2.3, and in Italy from 3.6 to 2.8. This decline can be explained in part by the fall in the fertility rate and the increase in the proportion of elderly people in the population, but family structure has also changed. In Britain, 14 percent of dependent children live in one person families, there has been an increase in the divorce rate, more people now cohabit (7.7 percent of women aged 18-40 cohabit), and there is a larger number of births outside marriage (25 percent of all births in 1988). Similar trends are apparent in other EC countries where divorce is permitted. During the 1970s, divorce rates doubled in Belgium and France, and trebled in the Netherlands. By 1986, births outside marriage accounted for nearly half the total births in Denmark and Sweden (Masser, Sviden and Wegener, 1992). These trends have an impact on the housing market, with an increase in the demand for small housing units which could be located either in the city centers through the subdivision of existing larger properties or in the suburbs in purpose-built units. In each case it is likely that the ratio of car parking spaces to homes will be near unity and, if location is in the suburbs, the number of trips generated and the length of trips will both increase.

The dynamics of change in population means that the geographic distribution of growth is not uniform. It seems that the link, argued in classical location theory, between home and workplace has been broken as many people now move for reasons not directly associated with work (Champion et al., 1987). For retired people, access to a job is not a consideration, but there has also been a growth in the number of people working from home, the proportion of households with two or more people working in different places, a growth in the number of self-employed, and the attractiveness of long distance commuting.

The pattern of work journeys need no longer be fixed by time of day or by day of week. Destinations may vary as individuals visit the head office once a week, regional offices on other days, or are involved with site visits or overseas trips. Time for travelling may also vary. Regular patterns may be established, but not on a daily basis. Commuting patterns have become more complex with cross-commuting becoming more important than commuting to city centers.

There have also been fundamental changes in occupation and work status with the move away from semi- and unskilled jobs in manufacturing towards information and service-based employment. The increased participation of women in the labor force is well known, and this trend is likely to continue, e.g., 90 percent of the expected one million increase in the labor force in Britain will be women (1988-2000). Associated with this increased participation of women has been an increase in part time working and, to a lesser extent, job sharing. Some of this growth may result from women rejoining the labor force after they have raised their families, and from those mature women who have gained new skills through retraining. In Britain, the growth in professional, technical and managerial occupations is expected to average 1.7 percent (1988-2000), more than twice the average for the economy as a whole (0.7 percent per annum).

In most European countries, labor force participation has increased over the last 15 years due largely to the increase in the number of working women. In the UK, female participation rates have increased by 12 percent to 48 percent (1976-1985) while male activity rates have remained constant, at 73 percent (see Table 3). The increase in female labor force participation has been particularly marked in the Mediterranean countries such as Italy, where there has been an increase of 14 percent to a total of 34 percent (1976-1985). However, national differences between countries are apparent (see Table 3). The explanation may be due to cultural attitudes and traditions which are not likely to disappear (Masser, Sviden and Wegener, 1992).

As these changes take place, travel demand patterns will also respond. Women often have considerably greater constraints on their activities as they have a multi-function role: to get the children to school, to do the shopping, and to carry out other domestic activities. If employment is added to this list, the number and range of trips generated will also increase. If men take on more family responsibilities, more traffic will again be generated. Lifestyles are becoming more complicated for all members of the household, not just the adults. Children, too, are evolving complex social patterns based around school and home activities (Grieco, Pickup and Whipp, 1989). However, increased participation in the labor force has to be balanced against the shortening of the working week and increased levels of affluence. The number of economically active people now having to support a growing number of pensioners is decreasing; also, the labor force participation of people over 65 (as Table 3) decreases as the level of affluence increases. Again, these trends are likely to generate more travel both nationally and internationally.

Three major changes in lifestyle are all likely to increase the demand for travel and they will reinforce the demographic changes outlined here. In the UK, 40 percent of households take no holidays at all (Government Statistical Service, 1992), over 25 percent take two or more holidays (1988), and expenditure on leisure now accounts for 17 percent of all household expenditure. Nearly all those in full time employment have over four weeks of paid vacation and 24 percent have more than five weeks (1988). The number of overseas holidays taken by UK residents has trebled from 7 to 21 million (1976-1988), and holidays within the UK now number 73 million (1988). The package holiday and changes in air transport have revolutionized the way in which the world is viewed.

TABLE 3

Labor Force Participation Rates in 1985 (Percentages)

	Male	Female	65+	Total
Belgium	62.5	36.2	1.7	48.9
Denmark	73.6	60.1	7.7	66.7
Germany FR	69.9	41.0	3.2	54.6
Greece	67.8	34.0	10.3	50.1
France	67.3	46.2	2.5	56.2
Ireland	71.2	32.6	10.6	52.0
Italy	66.8	33.5	4.9	49.5
Netherlands	66.6	34.5	2.4	50.4
United Kingdom	72.5	48.4	4.8	60.0
Spain	66.6	27.1	3.6	46.0
Portugal	72.2	45.0	12.3	57.8
Austria	70.6	40.6	1.5	54.6

Source : Eurostat (1988).

Europe is the most popular tourist destination in the world. It accounts for 64 percent (1990) of all tourist arrivals. This figure represents an increase of 3.5 percent per annum over the last decade (1980-1990). Income from tourism has increased by 8.3 percent per annum over the same period and accounts for about 5 percent of EC GNP (Eurostat, 1992). Italy has 63 million foreign visitors (1987), Spain 51 million, Yugoslavia 26 million, Portugal 16 million and Britain 15 million (OECD, 1988). All modes are used, with road tourism accounting for over 80 percent of visitors to Italy, Portugal and Yugoslavia, while arrival by air accounts for two-thirds of visitors to Britain; Spain's tourists are split between road and air.

Instead of taking only one holiday each year, families and individuals are taking two or three holidays -- a main summer holiday overseas, a winter holiday skiing and a third holiday based in their own country. In addition, days are taken off, often at weekends, to create short bridging breaks or long weekends. These changes are likely to continue and increase. It has been estimated (Masser, Sviden and Wegener, 1992) that by 2020, leisure activities may account for as much as 40 percent of all land transport (in terms of kilometers travelled) and 60 percent of air travel across all European countries.

The second lifestyle change is the increase in affluence and the importance of self-development and achievement. Apart from the activities of the mobile early retired groups, there are many other groups involved in a wide range of activities either of a social or a voluntary nature, or of a challenging (e.g., sporting achievement) or of an environmental nature. In each case time, skill and knowledge is applied to this activity and no payment is received. One reason for this self-development has been the growth in real income over the last 10 years and the increased levels of inherited wealth. As a result of the unprecedented increases in levels of housing prices over the last 20 years large amounts of capital are now being spent or passed onto ones children. Alternatively, when individuals trade down in house size or move to cheaper areas, capital is released so that more consumer spending can take place. Similarly, people are borrowing more against the actual or expected rises in housing prices. Wealth, together with income and available credit, has fuelled the increase in consumer spending which has been a feature of the 1980s. Increased rates of growth in car ownership, including a large increase in the provision of company cars, and increased levels of participation in a wider range of activities, have all contributed to the growth in the number of trips, the range of destinations, and the distances travelled. Although housing prices are at present falling as the gearing between prices and wages is gradually readjusted, the underlying increase in values is likely to increase.

The third change in lifestyles has been the function of the home as an office or workplace. Much has been written on working from the home, together with the dreams (or nightmare) or the electronic cottage (Nilles, 1988; Moss, 1987; Miles, 1989). It has been estimated that 20 percent of all urban trips makers and about 50 percent of skilled workers could telecommute, but that only 5 to 10 percent would actually make the change (Button, 1990). The hard evidence of such a significant change has not appeared in Britain or elsewhere. There has been very little change observed in the U.S. (Hall and Markusan, 1985). A more likely scenario could be of an individual spending a day a week working from home. This would reduce commuting and perhaps disproportionately long distance commuting as this is where the advantages of telecommuting are most apparent. However, it is also likely that the long distance commuting journey would be replaced by a series of short distance trips to alternative locations for different purposes. Overall, travel distance may be reduced, but not the number of trips. The evidence on the impact of telecommunications on travel is not decisive as to whether it acts as a substitute, a stimulator, or a modifier of existing patterns.

These changes in lifestyle identified here will not be felt by all societies equally. Some will not be directly impacted at all, while others will be, or have been, impacted by each change. It would seem that as with all social change, it is the affluent that will be impacted first. Those on fixed or low incomes, and those who do not have the knowledge to react to technological change, may only benefit in the longer term. The net result of lifestyle changes may be an increased polarization between different groups within society. On the one hand, there will be those affluent individuals with increasing leisure time who will be technologically literate -- these information-rich people will have increased mobility. On the other hand, there will be poor individuals on low or fixed incomes or those unemployed, with no resources or leisure time, who will not be technologically literate -- these information-poor people may possibly have reduced levels of mobility. The distributional impacts of social change may thus become even more significant in post-industrial society.

3. Economic Change

Traditional manufacturing industry has relied upon mass production and economies of scale (Fordism). In the era of Post-Fordism, economies of scope have become more important, and increased levels of vertical integration have developed at all stages in the production process. A greater proportion of manufacturing is contracted to outside suppliers, with a corresponding tightening of control through logistics to ensure a synchronization of operations and on-time delivery to minimize stock levels. Many more of the components required for manufacturing are in transit rather than stored at depots. Such logistic systems have resulted in significant savings for manufacturers and distributors as their costs and risks are minimized by taking full advantage of an efficient transport system and low transport costs. Employment has also switched from manual activities to those which require much greater levels of skill. Growth has taken place in supervisory jobs and in service activities, including the new high level financial, computing and consulting services.

Modern industry can now locate almost anywhere as it is not dependent on a single source of raw material inputs. Similarly, markets are national and international, not local, as the globalization of the world economy takes place. One of the results of this location flexibility has been an increase in travel demand. Investment in new infrastructure has improved productivity, reduced transport costs, and strengthened the attractiveness of particular locations thus creating considerable economies of scale and scope. The high speed rail network and the Channel Tunnel are two examples of major infrastructure investments which will open up new locations for industrial development. Even in Southern European countries where agriculture is still a relatively large source of employment, the growth in new markets and greater transport accessibility will change the production methods and increase efficiency and specialization.

Technological change has reduced the effects of physical distance and allowed further decentralization of lower-order back office functions where cheaper labor can be used; it is only the front office functions that need to be located in the city center with a highly skilled and expensive labor force (Goddard, 1989). Many inventory, financial and communication transactions can now be carried out remotely. However, the impacts of technology are not equal across all sectors because they relate to the functions of individual organizations and their links with high quality and expensive computer infrastructure networks.

Large multinational companies are using the highly differentiated European labor and skills market to maintain their international competitiveness. Companies are becoming transnational in order to exploit local labor cost differentials between individual countries and to compete in world markets (Roos and Altshuler, 1984). High level knowledge-based activities and skill-intensive tasks may be concentrated in a few core cities and regions, while low skilled standardized production tasks are carried out in the peripheral areas within individual countries as well as within the peripheral areas of Europe as a whole (Masser, Sviden and Wegener, 1992). Complementing these developments in the large multinational companies has been the growth in small- and medium-size firms which provide a specialist service or product. Many of these small companies are in the high technology area and form an integral part of the growth in science parks and technopolis programs. The implications for travel demand are unclear, but these changes are likely to substantially affect existing patterns of movement.

Q6

The level of interaction between organizations both nationally and internationally, and within spatially separated parts of the same organization, are likely to increase by using all means of communication, including transport. The greatest unknown at present is the impact of Eastern Europe markets both as opportunities for increased sales and as locations for peripheral factory locations in order to exploit cheaper labor costs. Growth and affluence may be concentrated in particular countries or in particular areas, such as "the Blue Banana" from Southeast England through Benelux, Southwest Germany and Switzerland to Northern Italy, or "the Sunbelt" along the northern part of the Mediterranean. The opening up of Eastern Europe will certainly move the center of activity from Western Europe to the East.

The uncertainty created by the move to post-industrial organization and the structural changes taking place in industry, together with technological innovation, make it difficult to identify the actual impact of these factors on transport demand. In addition to the economic and technological revolutions, there have been unprecedented changes in the political boundaries with the opening up of Eastern Europe and the Single European Market. The Cechini Report (1988) estimated that internal trade barriers in the EC were equivalent to 4 to 6 percent of Gross Domestic Product.

In the EC, the total amount of freight ton kilometers moved has increased by 17.6 percent (see Table 4). The real growth was in road freight (+34 percent in the EC), with compensating declines in sea transport (-24 percent) and pipelines (-14 percent). Rail increased by 5 percent and inland waterways by 14 percent. From an environmental and energy perspective these trends are disconcerting as the growth has taken place mainly in environmentally damaging road transport, which is road freight have been found in Belgium and Norway, followed by Spain, Great Britain, and Finland. The current proportions of intra-EC trade by tonnage (1990) are 40 percent by road, 30 percent by sea, 21 percent by also energy intensive. The greatest growth rates over the decade in inland waterway, 8 percent by rail, and 0.1 percent by air. For all types of traffic (both national and international) carried on land, the dominance of road is clear (86 percent), with 94 percent of national traffic being carried by road, where two-thirds of traffic is for journeys of less than 50 kilometers. The increasing dominance of road freight is expected to continue over the next 20 years, with a 74 percent increase in ton kilometers carried by road out of a total increase of 51 percent (Group Transport 2000 Plus, 1990). These levels may be underestimates after the Single Internal Market eliminates the barriers to movement and taxes between EC Member States become harmonized. It is expected that road freight traffic will rise by over 30 percent immediately following the Single Internal Market (Masser, Sviden and Wegener, 1992).

TABLE 4

Freight Traffic, 1980 and 1990 (Billion Ton-Kilometers)

	Road			All Modes[a]		
	1980	1990	% Incr.	1980	1990	% Incr.
Belgium	18.3	32.0	75	34.0	47.0	38
Denmark	7.8	8.0	3	11.0	14.0	27
Germany FR[b]	103.0	131.0	27	233.9	273.9	17
France	103.9	112.0	8	217.3	203.8	-6
Italy	119.6	165.0	38	180.5	232.1	29
Netherlands	17.7	22.1	25	59.6	65.8	10
Great Britain	89.7	130.6	46	166.0	199.5	20
Spain	98.9	145.0	47	144.2	191.5	33
Portugal	11.8	16.2	37	12.8	17.8	39
Norway	5.3	8.5	60	25.0	34.4	38
Sweden	21.4	23.0	7	48.4	50.9	5
Switzerland	5.9	7.4	25	14.5	17.6	21
Austria	7.9	8.0	1	27.6	28.8	4
Finland	18.4	26.3	43	30.3	37.8	25

Notes: [a]All modes includes road, rail, inland waterway, sea going and inland pipeline; [b]Figures for Germany include only the Federal Republic.

Source: UK Department of Transport (1992).

inc.

Travel mobility has increased dramatically over the last thirty years, primarily as a result of increases in car ownership levels. In Great Britain, traffic has increased by over 50 percent (see Table 6) and the number of cars and taxis by about 38 percent (1980-1990). In real terms, the costs of motoring have never been cheaper and some two-thirds of all households now have at least one car. Across all Europe, similar trends are apparent (see Table 5), with a 36 percent increase in the number of vehicles owned (1980-1990) while population has increased only marginally (see Table 1). Recent increases in car ownership are often in larger households already possessing one or more cars. It is likely that over the next 20 years car ownership will increase by a further 50 percent, with some 80 percent of the population (aged between 26 and 65) having a driving license (Department of Transport, 1992). This will bring car ownership levels in many European countries to about 550 cars per 1000 population, or similar to the 1979 level in the U.S. (Banister, 1979). This in turn will mean an increase of over 50 million cars in the 12 EC countries (+43 percent). As it is unlikely that the road capacity will increase by anywhere the same amount, congestion will increase over this period.

The car has become the dominant mode of travel as measured by passenger kilometers travelled. Over the last decade, passenger travel has increased by an average of 31 percent in Europe with the increase in travel by private road vehicles being more than the overall average in most countries (the average is 36 percent, see Table 6). However, these national averages conceal other important changes, such as the increase in trip lengths over that period as a result of decentralization, the reduction in trips to city centers, the growth in trips from suburb to suburb, and differences between various social groups within the population. As Goodwin (1990) notes, "there is a chain of relationships in which income determines car ownership levels, and car ownership dominates the amount of travel. Within this, there are important but smaller modifications due to employment status and family size" (p. 80).

Spatial factors such as the growing problem of suburban congestion are also important, particularly in the U.S. (Cervero, 1986; Prevedouros and Schofer, 1989), as is the interaction effects between the social and spatial elements. From the U.S. evidence, it appears that the explanation behind suburban congestion relates to household structural changes and the increases in affluence, which in turn lead to the development of a distinct lifestyle based on the car (Gordon and Richardson, 1989). The car is an essential precondition for people living in suburban and rural areas. But in more densely populated urban areas, the limitations of the car are becoming more apparent with increased congestion and heavy environmental and resource costs. It is here that public transport has a crucial role to play, especially for those without access to a car and for those who do not want to own or use a car.

The overall pattern has considerable variation, but this variation cannot be explained by population, size, area, density or economic factors such as Gross Domestic Product (GDP) or purchasing power alone. The greatest increase in private vehicle ownership (see Table 5) over the last 10 years has been in the peripheral EC countries with low levels of GDP per capita (Portugal, Greece, Spain and Finland). Growth has also been high in Italy and Luxembourg, but mainly from a higher base. Denmark and Ireland have the lowest levels of increase, followed by the Netherlands, Belgium, France, and Sweden. The other countries, including the UK, have above average growth (30 to 35 percent). Even in the U.S., the growth in car ownership has been about 20 percent; the assumed saturation level of 650 cars per 1000 was exceeded in 1989. The current level (1990) of vehicle ownership per 1000 population in the U.S. is 849, with the Japanese figure being 603. Both these levels are considerably higher than the European average of about 426. The increase in car ownership in the U.S. has been greater than that of many EC countries including the UK, France, the Netherlands, Spain, Belgium, and Denmark.

Growth in car use has also taken place, with Portugal, Italy, and Great Britain all recording increases in excess of 50 percent, well above the EC 12 average of 37 percent. All other EC countries had a growth in car use between 20 to 40 percent (see Table 6). The use made of each car has also increased in many countries, with Great Britain, Denmark, Luxembourg, Ireland, and Norway all recording more than 10-percent growth in annual kilometers travelled per private vehicle. The only country recording a major decline in the use of each car has been Portugal. The position of the car is dominant in all developed countries, with over three-quarters of passenger kilometers being made by car. The only exception is Japan (51 percent), where some 38 percent of travel is by rail. But it is in the UK that one of the largest increases in the use of the car (+52 percent), one of the highest increases in distances driven in each car figure (+13 percent), and one of the greatest increases in the proportion of total passenger kilometers by car (+5.6 percent) have been recorded. The EC averages for each of these three indicators is 37 percent, 6 percent and 3.5 percent, respectively. The importance of the transport sector in the EC cannot be underestimated -- it accounts for 7 percent of GDP, 7 percent of jobs, 40 percent of public investment, and nearly 30 percent of energy consumption. These figures only record its direct contribution and do not take account of transport induced activities nor its role in the overall functioning of a modern society (Group Transport 2000 Plus, 1990).

Congestion is probably the most talked about transport issue of the 1990s, with "gridlock" occurring regularly in city centers, suburban centers, and more irregularly in rural areas. In the U.S., the official view (Federal Highway Administration, 1988) seems to be that the key determinants of future demand are population, age and gender, percentage of driving age population with a license, and personal income. At present, nearly 90 percent of the adult population have driving licenses and there are, on average, nearly two vehicles per household. Distance travelled by residents averages at over 29,000 kilometers per household. These levels are much higher than those in European countries, and the consequences of the same trends occurring in Europe may be severe as population densities are much higher and the infrastructure is less well developed.

TABLE 5

Private Road Vehicles and All Vehicles in European Countries (Thousands)

	Private Road Vehicles	Private Road Vehicles	% Change	Vehicles per 100 Population
	1980	1990	1980-1990	1990
Belgium	3,159	3,864	22.3	47.1
Denmark	1,390	1,600	15.1	39.9
Germany	25,870	34,685	34.1	50.6
Greece	863	1,605	86.0	25.2
France	19,130	23,550	23.1	54.2
Ireland	736	798	8.4	27.7
Italy	17,686	25,000	41.4	57.1
Luxembourg	129	183	41.9	50.0
Netherlands	4,552	5,509	21.0	44.8
United Kingdom	15,619	21,485	37.6	43.6
Spain	7,557	12,011	58.9	39.4
Portugal	1,119	2,552	128.1	30.5
Norway	1,234	1,613	30.7	49.8
Sweden	2,883	3,601	24.9	46.1
Switzerland	2,247	2,994	33.3	59.5
Austria	2,247	2,991	33.1	48.6
Finland	1,226	1,926	57.1	47.3

Source: GB Department of Transport (1992).

TABLE 6

Passenger Traffic, 1980 and 1990 (Billion Passenger-Kilometers)

	Private Road Vehicles			All Modes		
	1980	1990	% Incr.	1980	1990	% Incr.
Belgium	61.8	75.0	21	77.8	91.5	18
Denmark	38.3	53.7	40	49.9	67.5	35
Germany FR	466.5	588.4	26	572.6	688.3	20
France	452.5	587.7	30	545.3	692.8	27
Italy	324.0	494.0	52	442.3	624.5	41
Netherlands	101.8	133.9	32	120.5	158.1	31
Great Britain	389.4	590.9	52	471.2	669.7	42
Spain	130.9	163.0	25	173.8	220.3	27
Portugal	40.1	65.0	62	54.0	81.0	50
Norway	31.4	41.0	31	38.1	47.1	24
Sweden	66.7	86.2	29	81.0	101.3	25
Switzerland	55.1	66.0	20	69.1	84.5	22
Austria	48.4	63.7	32	69.3	86.3	25
Finland	33.9	46.8	38	45.5	58.6	29

Source: GB Department of Transport (1992).

However, not all the evidence is negative. In a most interesting paper, Lave (1990) argues that trend-based analysis is an inappropriate generalization from a highly atypical period of history. As vehicle ownership in the U.S. reaches saturation and nearly all the driving age population has vehicle access, the growth rate of vehicle use will decline. He also suggests that the growth rate in vehicle travel will be much lower. While most analysts have been concerned with the consequences of demographic changes, they have missed the structural shift in the demographics of car ownership and car use. This shift has led to a disproportionate growth in the vehicle population but the transition has ended as the demand for cars is now saturated.

This optimism from the U.S. may not be appropriate in Europe as car ownership has not yet reached the levels found in the U.S. (see Table 5); even in the most affluent countries only between 50 and 70 percent of the assumed saturation levels of 650 cars per 1000 people has been reached. Secondly, there is a link drawn by Lave (1990) between car ownership and car use which he claims is a stable relationship: if there is no further increase in car ownership, he argues, there will be no increase in the use of those cars. Evidence from Britain and other European countries suggests that trip lengths have significantly increased, and that the lower mileage recorded by second cars in car-owning households is more than outweighed by the increased mileage recorded by households obtaining their first car. In countries where car ownership is still increasing and where structural changes in the economy are taking place, both the numbers of trips made and the distances travelled will continue to increase, leading to greater congestion.

Air travel has increased by about 6 percent per annum over the last 10 years, with air freight more than doubling (see Table 7). Again, problems of capacity may limit the growth in this sector, but with the expected growth in income, wealth and leisure time, that demand will still be present. European air traffic will more than double over the next 10 years (Banister and Button, 1991). Congestion occurs in the air due to the limited capacity of the current air traffic control systems, limitations of runway and terminal capacity on the ground, and problems of airport access. The airline industry itself is being restructured, with mergers taking place to compete with the global mega-carriers, the intense competition over the allocation of available slots at key airports, the tendency to hub operations through a few centers, and the introduction of more competition in European transport.

In the short term, airlines have used larger aircraft and have maintained fares at high levels, particularly when compared with equivalent distance flights in the U.S. This strategy is likely to change with the expected competition from high speed rail networks, the growth in low cost airlines, particularly from the East European countries, and the greater use of regional airports. More importantly, major changes will occur when the full effects of air deregulation are realized. The experience of 15 years of deregulation in the U.S. air market may provide some insights into the likely structure of the European air industry. There is considerable uncertainty over the long term future and structure of the European airline industry as policies are developed on mergers and acquisitions, competition, environmental concerns over night flights and noise, the dominant market position of a few large carriers, and a European air traffic control system perhaps using a greater amount of air space than is currently available for civil aviation.

TABLE 7

Air Travel

	Freight (Billion Ton-Kms)			Passengers (Billion Passenger-Kms)		
	1980	1990	%Increase	1980	1990	%Increase
EC 12	7.3	15.9	118	182.2	318.6	75
Europe 20	8.1	17.4	115	215.4	377.8	75
Japan	1.9	5.0	163	52.3	100.5	92
U.S.	8.4	14.5	73	427.7	751.5	76
Total for all ICAO States	29.1	58.9	102	1136.9	1975.4	74

Source: GB Department of Transport (1992).

4. **Social and Environmental Issues**

The social and environmental costs of transport are considerable. The human factors include the loss of life (see Table 8), protection from noise, nuisance and physical disturbance, the aesthetic quality of the human environment, and the quality of life in general. Twenty percent of the total developed area in European towns and cities is now taken up by transport-related land uses. With the construction of more roads, new rail networks and airport development, and the demand for more parking spaces, this figure is likely to increase, but not to the levels of over 30 percent as in some cities in the U.S. (Renner, 1989). Added to these factors is the consumption of non-renewable resources, principally gas, diesel, and aviation fuel. Nearly 30 percent of all final energy consumption is transport-related, and consumption has increased in absolute terms over the past 10 years. Even within Europe, the differences in energy consumption are considerable, with Germany consuming more than twice as much energy per capita than Greece or Spain (Masser, Sviden and Wegener, 1992). Price seems to have had little impact on consumption, and there seems to be little correlation between price and consumption. This may in part reflect the situation that the prices charged for transport are not related to their social and environmental costs.

TABLE 8

Road Deaths[a]

	No. of Deaths 1980	No. of Deaths 1990	Rate of Road Deaths per 100,000 1990
EC 12	75,666	64,628	18.1
Europe 20[b]	89,139	78,291	16.9
Japan	11,388	14,595	11.5
U.S.	51,091	44,529	17.8

Notes: [a]Deaths defined as those resulting in death from a road accident within 30 days; [b]Europe 20 includes the EC 12 plus Austria, Czechoslovakia, Finland, Hungary, Norway, Sweden, Switzerland and the states of the former Yugoslavia.

Source: GB Department of Transport (1992).

Transport-related pollution is a major contributor to global warming (transport accounts for about 20 percent of all carbon dioxide emissions), acid rain (transport accounts for about 60 percent of nitrogen oxide emissions and 4 percent of sulphur dioxideemissions), and to morbidity and fertility (transport accounts for 78 percent of carbon monoxide emissions). In all cases, with the exception of carbon monoxide, the levels are increasing (see Table 9 and Banister and Button, 1993). It is only through the introduction of tax advantages that unleaded gas has made an impact on purchase patterns (see Table 10). New EC Regulations require all new cars (as of January 1993) to be fitted with three-way catalytic converters which use only unleaded petrol, but they will remove only about 80 percent of carbon monoxide and nitrogen oxide emissions, while slightly increasing carbon dioxide emissions. There are substantial differences in petrol prices in EC countries (see Table 10), but the impact of the Single European Market (January 1993) will act to reduce these differences. The issue here is whether average effective prices are reduced, thereby encouraging more travel, or increased. The possibility of a carbon or energy tax is being actively discussed in Europe.

Other effects of transport on the environment include land consumption and impacts on plants and wild life habitats, water and soil quality, and the local ecosystem. The ecological effects are thought to be considerable, but little systematic research or monitoring seems to have been carried out.

TABLE 9

Transport Emission of Pollutants per Head[a] (Kilograms per Head)

		1980	1988	% Change
EC 12	Oxides of Nitrogen	16.3	19.8	+22
	Carbon Monoxide	93.6	90.4	-3
	Carbon Dioxide	1530.0	1860.0	+22
Europe 20	Oxides of Nitrogen	20.4	24.1	+18
	Carbon Monoxide	102.1	83.8	-18
	Carbon Dioxide	1747.0	2140.0	+22
U.S.	Oxides of Nitrogen	43.0	32.9	-23
	Carbon Monoxide	246.3	167.3	-32
	Carbon Dioxide	5400.0	5800.0	+7

Note: [a]Data are incomplete for some countries, so the figures are approximations.

Source: GB Department of Transport (1992).

Technological improvements through better engine design (e.g., lean burn engines) and vehicle design (e.g., weight reduction and aerodynamics) have helped, but any advance takes many years to impact on a market where the turnover in vehicles is about 12 years for cars and nearly 20 years for buses. The growth in traffic more than outweighs these energy savings. Alternative fuels might provide the main opportunity through a breakthrough in electric vehicle technology or through the use of hydrogen as a clean fuel.

Much discussion is now taking place to ensure that the polluter pays the full social and environmental costs of transport. The EC has been active in promoting the concepts of sustainable mobility (Commission of the European Communities, 1992) and the compact city (Commission of the European Communities, 1990). Clear links have been drawn between transport, development and land use to allow energy and environmentally efficient urban forms to develop. This would result in greater accessibility, reduced trip lengths, increased occupancy levels and the promotion of public transport. Restrictions would have to be placed on the use of the car in city centers through parking controls and access restrictions, and road pricing is being actively promoted as one possible alternative.

CONCLUSION

TABLE 10

Petrol and Diesel Prices[a] in EC Countries

	Petrol Prices (1991) and % Unleaded (1989)		Diesel
Belgium	97	9%	80
Denmark	101	37%	84
Germany FR	86	59%	71
France	101	8%	73
Greece	86	<1%	41
Ireland	108	<1%	99
Italy	131	<1%	97
Luxembourg	70		51
Netherlands	98	31%	68
Portugal	109	<1%	75
Spain	92	<1%	75
United Kingdom	86	24%	83

Notes: [a]1991 Prices in US$ per 100 liters.

Source: GB Department of Transport (1992).

5. Regional Development

Development in Europe has been focused at the center with most of the industrial, service and financial power being concentrated in the "Blue Banana", from London and Birmingham in the North, through the Benelux countries and the Rhine corridor to Switzerland and the Northern Italian cities of Milan and Turin. A second, more recent development, has been the "Sunbelt" region in the South extending along the Northern Mediterranean coast from Italy through Southern France to Barcelona and Valencia in Spain. The Ile de France region is the only major economic center in Europe to lie outside these two growth axes.

Unless regional policy positively discriminates against development in these corridors, growth will continue in these core areas at the expense of the peripheral regions in Europe. Notions of spread and backwash effects have been discredited (Masser, Sviden and Wegener, 1992). The EC has a strong regional development policy and regions can be classified as eligible for Community assistance if they fulfill one of the following conditions:

* Their per capita GDP is less than 75 percent of the EC average;

* Their rate of unemployment is higher than the EC average, a ratio of persons employed in industry to the total of those in employment is equal to or higher than the EC average, and there has been a decline in industrial employment; and

* The number of persons working in agriculture, their level of development assessed on GDP per head, and how near they live to the periphery of the EC.

Despite this policy of very positive intervention over the past 30 years, the differences in income, employment, infrastructure and provision of services between the regions of Europe are still enormous. "If the mean gross regional product of the EC is taken to be 100, regions vary between 218 (Hamburg) or 175 (Paris) and less than 50 in parts of Greece and Spain and less than 30 in most of Portugal" (Masser, Sviden and Wegener, 1992, p. 94). This picture is complicated by other factors. New axes may develop in peripheral regions as the EC is joined by new members. Links between the East and West are likely to be strengthened as are those with Scandinavia. It is here that infrastructure investment may have a major role to play in opening up new areas, such as the new links between Denmark and Sweden and the new airports at Munich and Berlin. Secondly, with industrial restructuring, a physical presence in the core axes is no longer essential. Provided that the skills are available, industry may move to the peripheral regions where the costs of land and labor are cheaper and there is a significant sunshine factor (as in Silicon Valley in California). The peripheral regions may also benefit from regional specialization and local advantages such as tourism, traditional rural activities, and wilderness areas.

Underlying all these factors is the importance of being accessible, whether through the transport or the communications infrastructure. The top 20 most productive regions in the EC are located in or adjacent to the "Blue Banana" or the "Sunbelt", and these corridors are served by the best ground transport infrastructures and contain the six largest airports in Europe (Masser, Sviden and Wegener, 1992). The lack of a modern infrastructure, urban amenities and a tradition in skill-based activities means that the peripheral regions have failed to attract enough high technology manufacturing and information-based service industries, and in many locations there is a net outflow of population. Where growth has taken place, it is in locations where high skilled labor, good environment, and resources are present together with quality national and international transport and communications networks. These sites are often located at major transport interchanges, particularly airports. These trends are already apparent, but more so in the core areas than in the peripheral regions.

References

Banister, D., 1992, *Demographic Structure and Social Behaviour*, Proceedings of the 12th International Symposium on Theory and Practice in Transport Economics - Transport Growth in Question, Lisbon, May, 109-150.

Banister, D. and Button, K. (eds.), 1991, *Transport in a Free Market Economy*, Macmillan, London.

Banister, D. and Button, K. (eds.), 1993, *Transport, the Environment and Sustainable Development*, Spon, London.

Button, K., 1990, Transport and Communications, Paper Presented at the Department of Transport Conference on Longer Term Issues in Transport Demand, July.

Cervero, R., 1986, *Suburban Gridlock*, Center for Urban Policy Research, Rutgers University, New Brunswick, NJ.

Champion, A. G., Green, A. E., Owen, D. W., Ellis, D. J., and Coombes, M. G.,1987, *Changing Places: Britain's Demographic, Economic and Social Complexion*, Edward Arnold, London.

Commission of the European Communities, 1990, *Green Paper on the Urban Environment*, Com (90) 218, June, Brussels.

Commission of the European Communities, 1992, *White Paper on Transport and Sustainable Mobility*, Com (92), December, Brussels.

Department of Transport, 1990, *Transport Statistics Great Britain 1979-1989*, HMSO, London.

Department of Transport, 1992, *Transport Statistics Great Britain 1992*, HMSO, London.

Duncan, S. S., 1990, Do Housing Prices Rise That Much? A Dissenting View, *Housing Studies*, 5(3), 195-208. European Conference of Ministers of Transport, 1990, *Statistical Trends in Transport*, 1965-1987, ECMT, Paris.

Eurostat, 1992, *Europe in Figures*, Brussels.

Fagani, J., 1987, Daily Commuting Time: The Stakes for Working Mothers in France, *Transportation Research Record*, 1135, 26-30.

Federal Highway Administration, 1988, *America's Challenge for Highway Transportation in the 21st Century*, Interim Report on the Future National Highway Program Taskforce, November.

Ferguson, E., 1990, The Influence of Household Composition on Residential Location and Journey to Work in the United States, Paper Presented at the Transportation Research Board's 69th Annual Meeting, Washington DC, January.

Goddard, J., 1989, *Urban Development in an Information Economy: Policy Issues, OECD Group on Urban Affairs - Project on Urban Imparts of Technological and Socio-Demographic Change*, UP/TSDC (89) 1.

Goodwin, P., 1990, Demographic Impacts, Social Consequences, and the Transport Policy Debate, *Oxford Review of Economic Policy*, 6(2), 76-90.

Gordon, P. and Richardson, H. W., 1989, Gasoline Consumption and Cities: A Reply, *Journal of the American Institute of Planners*, 55(3), 342-346.

Government Statistical Service, 1992, *Social Trends 1992*, HMSO, London.

Grieco, M., Pickup, L., and Whipp, R., 1989, *Gender, Transport and Employment*, Avebury, Aldershot.

Hall, P. and Markusan, A. (eds.), 1985, *Silicon Landscapes*, George Allen and Unwin, London.

Laslett, P., 1990, *A Fresh Map of Life: The Emergence of the Third Age*, Weidenfeld and Nicholson, London.

Lave, C., 1990, *Things Won't Get a Lot Worse: The Future of US Traffic Congestion*, University of California, Irvine, Economics Department, Mimeo.

Masser, I. Sviden, O. and Wegener, M., 1990, *The Geography of Europe's Futures*, Belhaven, London.

Miles, I., 1989, The Electronic Cottage: Myth or Reality?, *Futures*, 21(1), 47-59.

Moss, M. L., 1987, Telecommunications, World Cities and Urban Policy, *Urban Studies*, 24, 534-541.

Nilles, J. M., 1988, Traffic Reduction by Telecommunications: A Status Review and Selected Bibliography, *Transportation Research* A, 22A, 301-317.

OECD, 1988, *Tourism Policy and International Tourism in OECD Countries*, OECD, Paris.

OECD, 1989, *Comparative Socio-Demographic Trends: Initial Data on Ageing Populations*, OECD, Group on Urban Affairs, UP/TSDA (89)1, April.

Prevedouros, P.D. and Schofer, J.L., 1989, Suburban Transport Behaviour as a Factor in Congestion, *Transportation Research Record*, 1135, 47-58.

Renner, M., 1989, Rethinking Transport, *Transport*, 25/1989, Commission of the European Communities, Brussels.

Roos, D. and Altshuler, A. et al., 1984, *The Future of the Automobile*, George Allen and Unwin, London.

U.S. Department of Transportation, 1986, Personal Travel in the U.S. In *Nationwide Personal Transportation Study*, Vol. 2, November.

Part One

EUROPEAN TRANSPORT

TRANSPORT IN A UNIFIED EUROPE. Policies and Challenges.
D. Banister and J. Berechman (Editors)

Chapter Two

CONGESTION AND THE CAR

Peter Jones

1. Introduction

Probably more than any other issue, the ownership and use of cars highlights the contradictions and conflicts surrounding transport and wider economic policy within Europe. Car manufacturing and the extensive range of supporting services is a significant source of employment and wealth in many European countries, and one which few governments would wish to put at risk. Politically, too, the aspiration to car ownership is supported by most national parties as an important feature of individual freedom in the modern world; more and more, household lifestyles are becoming dependent on the car. Across Europe as a whole, the free movement of people and goods is seen as fundamental both to the democratic principles of the Community and to the efficient operation of a single European market.

Yet collectively, road traffic is increasingly seen as problematic and potentially destructive in a number of respects. For example, as summarised by the European Conference of Ministers of Transport (ECMT, 1990), these negative aspects include:

* *Traffic congestion (resulting in longer and less predictable journey times);*
* *Traffic accidents/road safety;*
* *Traffic noise;*
* *Vehicle pollution;*
* *Carbon dioxide emissions and global warming;*
* *The colonization of various public spaces by illegally parked cars;*
* *Severance of social networks;*
* *The general unpleasantness of using street spaces on foot.*

Traffic growth is closely linked to increases in GDP, and the bulk of such traffic is contributed by the private car. Surprisingly, given the importance of movement by car in Europe, there is very little comparable European-wide data available on this subject compared to movement by rail and by air, and by goods vehicles on the road network.

The aim of this chapter is to outline some of the general benefits and costs of car ownership and use, and to discuss three broad approaches that are being adopted to tackle the negative impacts of car use in Europe, namely, advances in technology, additional road infrastructure, and policies of traffic restraint.

While various technological developments are designed to address all forms of car travel, there is a marked tendency for the additional infrastructure option to be applied at the inter-urban level, and the restraint option to be focused on car travel in urban (and some ecologically sensitive rural) areas.

2. The Benefits and Costs of Car Ownership and Use

Across the European Community as a whole, transport represents around 5 percent of Gross Domestic Product, directly employs 5 percent of the workforce, and accounts for 28 percent of energy consumption (Eurostat, 1992); it is estimated that approximately one in ten workers in the Community depends directly or indirectly on the motor vehicle sector for his/her livelihood. Western Europe is the largest centre of car production in the world: in 1987, approximately 12 million cars were built in Western Europe, compared with 8 million in Japan and 7 million in the United States. Annual new car sales in Western Europe are now around 13 million units; in 1989 there were approximately 125 million passenger cars and 2.6 million kilometers of roads, covering 1.3 percent of the land area of the European Community.

On the negative side, it has been estimated that the total economic loss in the Economic Community through urban and inter-urban congestion and detours amounts to 500 billion ECU (European Currency Units) per year. Around 55,000 people are killed on Community roads and 1.7 million are injured annually, at an estimated economic and social cost of 70 bn ECUs per year. In addition, the contribution of vehicle emissions to environmental pollution (excluding the contribution to global warming) is estimated to cost the Community between 5 and 10 billion ECUs per year (Bielefeldt, 1989); the car is the major contributor to these figures, which are projected to increase substantially in the coming decades. A recent study of CO_2 emissions found that the transport sector was responsible for around 25 percent of the total Community emissions, of which, approximately 55 percent was generated by private cars (TNO, 1991). For more detailed discussion of the environmental impacts of transport, see Button and Rothengatter (1993).

During 1991, the International Union of Public Transport (UITP, 1992) and the European Commission sponsored a study of European attitudes concerning "access to city centres". The study was comprised of a public attitude survey using Eurobarometer (with approximately 1,000 adults in each member state), and a study of decision maker attitudes carried out in personal interviews with 157 individuals by Socialdata. Respondents were asked about the consequences of car traffic in the urban area in which they lived/worked/shopped; across Europe as a whole, 59 percent described these as "hardly bearable" or "unbearable", with this proportion ranging from a low of 27 percent in Denmark to a high of 84 percent in Italy, with a score of 49 percent in the UK. For political decision makers across Europe, 73 percent rated the consequences of urban car traffic as being hardly bearable or unbearable, and all mentioned some traffic-related problem in their city.

When specifically asked about what contribution they thought that car traffic in the city centre made to the deterioration in the quality of the air, 78 percent of the adults across Europe saw car traffic as the main cause or an important cause of the deterioration, with percentages ranging from a low of 57 percent in Ireland up to 95 percent in Italy; 74 percent of those interviewed in the UK held this view. Among decision makers, the mean percentage across Europe was higher (92 percent).

On the other hand, most car owners value their possession very highly. Public attitude surveys in the United Kingdom, for example, have found that 60 to 70 percent of drivers regard their lifestyle as being fully dependent on car ownership. In one survey (Hallett, 1990), 58 percent of all adults also agreed with the statement that "people without cars suffer because modern life is geared towards those with cars"; only 26 percent disagreed.

A recent report in the UK by the Automobile Association (1992) summarised the "Balance Sheet" of motoring in the following terms:

> The unquantifiable benefits and burdens of motoring are numerous. But the value of the benefits that a car gives to both individuals and society through increased freedom to travel, economic growth, tourism, employment and household tasks are a great deal more than the cost. The car is the most liberating mode of transport ever invented: to

constrain ownership and use in any unreasonable way will be impractical, expensive and politically damaging to whichever authority attempts to impose it.

However, these burdens have been, and increasingly will be, exacerbated by the relentless growth in road traffic. Car passenger kilometers doubled between 1970 and 1990 across the European Community as a whole, and are expected to increase broadly in line with growth in the GDP in the future. In a country such as the Netherlands, this translates into a projected increase in the costs of congestion (at current prices) from 1 billion guilders in 1990 to 4 billion guilders in 2010 (with a projected 70-percent increase in car use).

By the year 2010, road transport is expected to account for 30 percent of Community CO_2 emissions. Problems are expected to grow much more rapidly in Central and Eastern Europe, albeit from a much smaller base. It has been recognised that major action is needed to deal with the issue.

3. The Potential Contribution of Technology

Major programmes are now underway in Europe (such as DRIVE, see Keen, 1992, and PROMETHEUS) and in the United States (IVHS) to harness the latest developments in technology in order to reduce the impacts of traffic-related growth problems. These developments are designed to achieve one of two primary aims:

* *To reduce the environmental impacts of individual vehicles (through more fuel efficient engines, quieter systems, and cleaner exhausts).*

* *To increase the operational capacity of the available road network.*

3.1 Improving Vehicle Performance

Increased Engine Efficiency: The European car industry is already committed to increasing the fuel efficiency of new vehicles, from around 9 litres/100 kilometers to 7 litres/100 kilometers (an improvement of 28 percent), and a further 10-percent saving has been promised over the next ten years (ERT, 1992). However, because of the growth in the car fleet, the European Commission estimates show that even with a 40-percent increase in fuel efficiency by the year 2005, stabilization of CO_2 emissions will not be achieved by the year 2010 (European Commission, 1992, para. 172).

Diesel engines are, on average, 15 percent more fuel-efficient than petrol engines, and some countries such as France have encouraged the purchase of diesel-powered cars through high fuel tax differentials. However, there is rising concern about the pollution caused by diesel engines (especially particulates), and some authorities are now taking the view that diesel cars are less desirable than petrol-driven ones fitted with catalytic converters. There are suggestions in some cities that light vans should be converted from diesel to petrol for air pollution reasons.

Use of Catalytic Converters: In cities where air pollution is perceived to be a serious problem, it has been suggested that this can be addressed through technology rather than through traffic restraint by fitting catalytic converters to all vehicles. Experience in Stockholm has shown that this policy can lead to substantial reductions in air pollution -- for a time. However, this city has found that after a decade of improvement, although the technology diffused downwards through the ageing car stock, the growth in the overall number of vehicles has outstripped the reductions in pollution per vehicle, and the city is now having to consider explicit curbs on car use in areas of high traffic density.

Doubts have also been raised about the effectiveness of catalytic converters in cities, where many journeys are too short for engine temperatures to reach the required levels for efficient operation (Holman et al., 1990). In addition, this measure does nothing to address the problem of carbon dioxide emissions. Here again, it appears that the question of explicit traffic restraint will have to be confronted if traffic levels continue to grow.

3.2 Increasing Network Performance

Increased network performance can be achieved using three broad strategies:

* Better management of the network, using improved signal controls, both in the form of computer-linked traffic lights and the assignment of diversionary routes.

* Direct vehicle-to-vehicle communication and the use of electronic coupling procedures (particularly for inter-urban travel).

* providing drivers with up-to-date information on network conditions and options. This can be more easily achieved than better management of the network -- which focuses on rerouting -- if the information is available before the start of the journey, as drivers may choose to change destination, timing or even mode of travel and so relieve pressure on the general network.

All these technologies are likely to lead to some improvement in road capacity, but each has its limitations. By using the existing network more fully, the removal of redundancy may make the prospect of catastrophic network failure more likely in the event of a major accident or other blockage. In addition, there are doubts as to whether the expense of some technologies (e.g., electronic guidance and protection of vehicles) will make them inaffordable for the foreseeable future, except in very specific situations (e.g., by reserving a motorway lane for vehicles that can be coupled and driven electronically).

While the adoption of the simpler technologies based on Advanced Transport Telematics can be expected to result in worthwhile gains in road capacity and reductions in accidents and pollution levels, improved information and network optimization alone are unlikely to be sufficient to eliminate or even contain urban traffic congestion: in the short to medium term, such systems are expected to increase capacity by 10 to 20 percent, which could soon be absorbed in a network with high levels of suppressed demand. In addition, better information might encourage an overall increase in road traffic: it would enable using the capacity more efficiently, but would result in an overall increase in environmental pollution.

There is a growing recognition (for example, in the DRIVE 2 programme) that enhanced driver information systems can provide one component of an urban transport policy, but that policy needs to include improvements in public transport as well as some form of explicit restraint on road traffic in the more congested areas.

4. Infrastructure Improvements

4.1 Providing Additional Road Capacity

One means of tackling traffic congestion is to increase the amount of physical infrastructure through road widening or new road construction. The scope for doing so is severely limited in many urban areas; but for inter-urban traffic, the construction of additional road capacity is seen as an important response by most national governments in

Europe, although one which is circumscribed by growing environmental concerns in some of the most congested areas.

At the European Community level, major strategic road projects are encouraged as part of the development of a trans-European road network:

> The purpose behind the introduction of trans-European networks is to interconnect existing networks, fill in the "missing links" or unblock the bottlenecks between various national networks, overcome the problems of isolation in the peripheral regions and extend the Community networks towards northern, central, eastern and Mediterranean Europe. The trans-European network programme is primarily aimed at road transport infrastructures with the interconnection of cross-border roads or motorways, as well as the construction of a high speed railway network, the improvement of rail links between neighbouring networks in border regions and the completion of major trans-European railway routes (Eurostat, 1992, pp. 52, 54.)

While the development of trans-European networks is seen as central to the successful operation of the Single Market, there are worries that improvements in connectivity will lead to substantial increases in traffic which will both offset the capacity improvements and lead to further environmental deterioration. With regard to the latter, we can observe some differences in view between Transport and Environmental Ministries in several European countries regarding the issue.

In the UK, for example, the Department of the Environment is cautious about policies which encourage increases in travel, preferring instead to reduce trip lengths and facilitate modal shifts. The Department of Transport, on the other hand, is very positive about increasing inter-urban road capacity, citing the benefits of reduced congestion in terms of reduction in air pollution and CO_2 emissions, coupled with the CO_2 benefits of extensive tree planting alongside Britain's motorways.

In transport terms, two problems arise about the use of the additional capacity. First, how can we ensure that the benefits of the increased capacity are allocated mainly to journeys which directly benefit the economy (e.g., goods transport) rather than to longer car commuting trips or additional recreational trips? This is of particular concern in countries such as The Netherlands, which wishes to preserve Rotterdam as the major European transhipment port.

Second, how can we reconcile an increase in inter-urban capacity and trip making by car, with a limit on capacity in urban areas: what happens to all the additional traffic as it pours off the ends of the Euro-motorways? This clearly depends on the precise nature of any additional traffic: if it mainly represents an increase in trip lengths, then the load on the urban parts of the network will remain unchanged; if it is mainly additional car trips, however, there will be severe knock-on effects on the urban road network, with consequential congestion and environmental impacts.

4.2 Paying for New Road Capacity

One issue that has arisen in connection with inter-urban road construction and maintenance is how to devise an equitable means of meeting the costs of road provision, particularly with an increasing proportion of longer distance road traffic originating outside the host country. There is increasing talk of inter-urban road charges, to pay both for new road construction and the upkeep of the network. Although maintenance costs relate primarily to the damage done by heavy goods vehicles, new construction will generally be of greatest benefit to car drivers.

Such charges are already made on a limited basis in some parts of Europe. They often apply to all classes of traffic (although the charge level may vary by vehicle type), [such as for tunnel road passage under the Alps, or for the use of the auto routes in France]; or there may be targeted charges, such as the passenger-kilometer charge imposed on tourist coaches entering Germany. In Sweden as well as New Zealand and parts of the United States, heavy goods vehicles are already charged directly on a tonne/kilometer basis.

Given the perceived urgency of completing a trans-European road network, organizations such as the European Round Table of Industrialists (ERTI, 1991) have advocated the introduction of road user charges to ensure the provision of adequate road capacity. This is likely to reduce more economically marginal uses of the road network and so ease congestion pressures. Thus, until recently, the emphasis has been on charges to fund an increase in supply, rather than as a mechanism for restraining demand. However, this emphasis is gradually changing in the light of concerns to develop a sustainable transport policy.

Summing up the current position, the European Commission's recent White Paper on future common transport policy notes:

> The private car and lorry have thus emerged as the dominant means of transport causing congestion in main road corridors and urban centres. The present traffic situation in many city centres and conurbations is one of complete saturation or close to it. Further development of road infrastructure alone is unlikely to resolve the problem, necessary as it may be in some areas. In others, the construction of new capacity is in any case meeting significant obstacles, physical and political. Moreover, associated with a continuing increase of cars and lorries is an inevitable increase in pollution and in the number of dead and injured from accidents on the road, not always offset by technical or other improvements in the fields of environment protection and safety (EC, 1992, para 77, pp. 31-32.).

The clear view is that technological developments and new road building are not enough, and that some restraint on the growth in road traffic will be needed if conditions are not to deteriorate further.

5. Options for Traffic Restraint

To date, the most common mechanism for restraining traffic levels has been congestion itself, both on inter-urban and urban links of the network. However, although this is in some ways the politically "easy" restraint option as it may be superficially viewed as equitable -- with all road users being commonly affected -- it is neither economically efficient nor environmentally desirable. In addition to indiscriminate time losses, it results in excess consumption of non-renewable energy and excess production of various pollutants.

The focus in the remainder of this chapter is on traffic restraint mechanisms in urban areas. Here the basic options faced by local government involve controls either on *stationary* traffic (with a destination in the local area), or on *moving* traffic passing through the area. In both cases, there are three primary mechanisms that can be used to restrain traffic levels: physical, regulatory and pricing. Each situation is considered in turn.

6. Controls on Stationary Traffic

Controls on on- and off-street parking are the most common means by which vehicles are restrained in European cities and in some ecologically sensitive rural areas (e.g., parts of the Peak District and New Forest in England).

As noted, there are three general mechanisms that can be used to control car parking in an area:

* By *physically* limiting the total number of spaces available. This is very effective as an absolute constraint but does not enable priority to be given to one type of parker over another and may result in network congestion due to queuing or cruising as drivers search for an available space.

* By *regulating* the use of the available spaces, both in terms of who may park there (e.g., reserving spaces for disabled drivers or local residents), and for how long they may park (e.g., three-hour time limit to discourage car commuters). Although this enables more selective restraint to be introduced, it does not completely overcome the problems of insufficient capacity and search-generated traffic.

* By *charging* for parking spaces. This can be added to the controls provided by physical and regulatory parking restraint to ensure that the total demand is in balance with the local supply of parking spaces. In this way, most of the problems of queuing and cruising can be avoided.

Such controls can have two broad kinds of effect:

* They restrain the number of vehicle trip ending in an area by limiting the numbers of vehicles that can park there at a given time.

* In urban areas, on-street parking controls can be used to transfer more of the limited roadspace for use by through-traffic, resulting in some increase in capacity. This can be most readily achieved by banning parking at peak times on the approaches to major road junctions.

Although most cities do use parking controls as a means of regulating the flow and volume of traffic in some areas (particularly in city centres), there are limits as to how effective such measures can be by themselves as means of restraining car use. In particular, as pressures on roadspace increase:

* Non-compliance with parking regulations becomes a growing problem in most European countries as pressures for the limited parking space build up and the size of the penalty and level of enforcement fail to offer a sufficient deterrent. Non-compliance may result in drivers stopping in areas not reserved for parking, and thereby hindering through-traffic or the delivery of goods. Topp (1993) reports that in German cities, 40 to 50 percent of total parking is typically illegal.

* Restrictions on the size of the total parking stock in some areas are being relaxed in the face of pressure for more parking spaces from local residents, who are acquiring more cars, or groups with special needs, such as disabled drivers (increasing in number as the car driver population ages).

* As competition from out-of-town shopping centres increases, there are concerns that too much restriction on access by car to central shopping areas may lead to a terminal decline in the prosperity of the area. This leads to pressures from shopkeepers and local businesses wanting more of the available space for short term visitors (e.g., as in Inner Amsterdam). Such developments increase the volume of originating/terminating traffic: Topp (1993) estimates that an on-street visitor or shopper space is used on average five times more intensively than one reserved for residents or employees.

* In most cities, municipal authorities are only able to control a proportion of the parking stock in an area (typically well under half) because of the existence of residents private parking spaces and PNR (private non-residential, e.g., office spaces). As controls on public spaces are tightened, PNR spaces in particular tend to be used more intensively, thereby increasing the trip generation/attraction rates per space.

* Parking charges represent a higher proportion of costs for shorter journeys, and so provide less of a restraint on the longer distance journeys that contribute more to overall congestion and pollution.

* Parking controls cannot deal with the problem of through-traffic, which in central areas tends to take up any capacity released by parking restraint. In central

London, for example, 30 to 40 percent of vehicle traffic is passing through rather than terminating in the area.

* While effective parking controls may limit the amount of traffic penetrating inner city areas, use of Park and Ride facilities does not contribute to a net reduction in traffic levels outside urban areas.

Despite these limitations, parking controls are likely to form an integral part of a comprehensive traffic demand management strategy, although they cannot provide the prime mechanism. Many cities are recognising that some form of direct control on the movement of vehicles is also needed if traffic problems are to be alleviated.

7. Controls on Moving Traffic

As with parking controls, there are three main mechanisms for introducing controls on moving traffic:

* Physically, by using the capacity limitations of a link, junction or network as the restraining device, and by deliberately restricting the space or time available for vehicular movement in a controlled and selective way.

* Through traffic regulation procedures, by allowing only certain classes of road users to have access to a link or an area. The exemption may be defined either in terms of the class of vehicle or the type of driver.

* Through charging directly for the use of roadspace, i.e., using the "market mechanism" to allocate scarce roadspace on the basis of "willingness to pay".

In terms of practical applications of these measures, traffic restraint policies show significant variation from one European country to another. Germany and The Netherlands, for example, have been applying "traffic calming" measures in a number of cities to reduce accidents and environmental impacts (Keller, 1990) for many years, Italy has imposed access controls on entry to the centres of many of its historic cities, and Norway has introduced road charges in urban areas to finance environmental road schemes. Hence Europe provides a fascinating test site for assessing the effectiveness of a wide range of urban traffic restraint measures.

7.1 Physical Restrictions on Speed and Capacity

Traffic Calming Measures: The purpose of these physical measures is to "tame" rather than restrain, traffic by reducing speeds so that motorised and non-motorised traffic are more compatible while reducing noise levels and environmental pollution. This approach is now widely applied in many German cities, where the objective (Keller, 1986) is:

> All destinations in the area should be accessible using direct routes, roads should remain open for motorised traffic, but *obstacles to fast driving* should be increased, by narrowing roads, by slightly elevating road surfaces or by installing green areas, tree planters, etc.

Most applications of these measures have been in residential areas, often in conjunction with 30 kph/20 mph speed limits. In some countries, consideration is now being given to the application of traffic calming measures on through routes, for example, on inter-urban routes in Danish towns (Herrstedt, 1988).

Although these measures can lead to improvements in road safety and environmental conditions within the treated areas, Whitelegg (1990) has raised concerns both about displacement effects and the use of the policy as a "smoke screen" that, he argues, has hastened rather than retarded the increase in car traffic in Germany.

Traffic "Collars" or "Throats": Capacity can be restricted in one of two ways, either through limiting *space* (e.g., reallocating part of the carriageway to bus lanes), or *time* (e.g., using traffic signals to impose delays). In practice, the two are commonly used in combination, with bus lanes bypassing the traffic signals. The "zone and collar" scheme introduced in Nottingham for a short while (Vincent and Layfield, 1977) provided an example of the approach.

In terms of traffic, this can be a very effective means of regulating the traffic levels in an area; in practice, however, it can be difficult to implement and enforce (often meeting considerable local hostility at it also affects deliveries to the area). It can also have undesirable impacts on traffic and land use outside the controlled area. The main implementation problem is to find enough space on the road system to store the queuing vehicles without obstructing major junctions and unrelated local or cross movements; this severely limits the size of the delay that can be imposed on an urban network, usually to around 5 or 10 minutes, which is insufficient to have a major impact (see Cracknell et al., 1975, for an evaluation of the suitability of this measure in London).

Traffic Cells and Mazes: A traffic *maze* allows movement through an area, but only by using an indirect route, making it an unattractive option; traffic *cells* usually involve the creation of a contained area, with entry/exit from one side only (sometimes with exceptions for buses).

This type of measure has been applied in most European countries, and has had a significant impact on the pattern of vehicle movements over a wide area. One of the best documented examples is in Gothenburg (Sweden), where reductions of up to 50 percent were observed on some roads that had previously been main routes through the central area. However, it has been noted (Falk et al., 1988) that:

> ...traffic cells are primarily traffic rerouting rather than restraining techniques and therefore involve the transfer of traffic-induced problems to other locations. If these locations are better able to accommodate the traffic, or less sensitive to it, then there is likely to be a substantial net benefit.

Thus, none of these physical restrictions appear to lead, by themselves, to significant reductions in the use of motor vehicles, although they can be effective in redistributing the local pattern of movement. However, in some instances, they can result in an increase in vehicle miles travelled and in carbon dioxide emissions. Further, unless additional measures are taken, all road vehicles are equally subject to delay.

7.2 Regulatory Controls on Moving Traffic

Most countries identify various categories of road users when drafting traffic regulations, e.g., emergency vehicles, pedestrians, cycles, cars, light vans, heavy goods vehicles, buses and taxis. Regulations may be devised that either exclude specific groups (e.g., bans on heavy lorries, except for loading), or reserve links or areas for certain types of road user (e.g., bus only lanes, pedestrian zones).

Traffic regulations have been used in four different ways to restrict or exclude motor vehicles from parts of the urban road network:

* A complete ban on motor vehicles, through pedestrianization of links or areas.

* Designation of a hierarchical road network, with varying degrees of access to the network afforded to different categories of traffic.

* Restrictions on entry to certain vehicles throughout an area, based on some characteristic of the vehicle (e.g., the attributes of the number plate).

* A blanket restriction on all vehicles throughout an area, but with some exemptions based on the personal characteristics of the owner (e.g., local resident), driver, or vehicle occupant (e.g., disabled person).

The first and second options tend to be limited spatially to parts of the local road network, whereas the third and fourth have wider applicability. The latter are briefly described below.

Restrictions on Vehicle Types: Although cities may apply bans on heavy goods vehicles or large buses by link or by area, it is more difficult to differentiate between various types of car or light van. The only means by which this has been achieved in practice is on the basis of the numbers on the vehicle licence plate. In Athens, such a restriction operates in the central area, within the inner ring road; the enclosed area is known as the "dactylios" and is approximately 3.5 x 3.0 kilometer. The scheme was introduced in September 1982 and has undergone a number of extensions since then, although the basic principle remains the same. For most of the day, vehicle entry is regulated according to the last digit of the licence plate of the vehicle, such that each vehicle is banned on alternate days, Monday to Friday. Similar schemes operate in Lagos, Mexico City and Santiago.

The authorities introduced the scheme because of deterioration in environmental conditions, with the objective of reducing car traffic by up to 50 percent. Although early monitoring studies did find significant reductions in traffic (Matsoukis, 1985; Argyrakos, 1986), they were not as great as anticipated. Inside the dactylios, private car use decreased by around 22.5 percent rather than 50 percent (due to exemptions to certain groups such as doctors, rescheduling of journeys, etc.) and taxi use increased by 26 percent (before taxis became subject to restrictions) -- suggesting a major switch from car to taxi. Nevertheless, vehicle-kilometers decreased by around 15 percent and vehicle-hours dropped by 22 percent, showing worthwhile reductions. Beneficial reductions in some types of pollutants were also observed in the first year (NO_2 decreased by 38 percent and SO_2 by 16 percent).

Entry by Permit: A number of entry by permit schemes have been introduced in different Italian cities to reduce traffic levels in congested, polluted and/or historic central areas. Car access has been limited to those who are felt to have need of a car, or to have more "right" to be in the area. The Bologna scheme (which started out as a hierarchically regulated network), now restricts entry to most of the old city area only to commercial vehicles, residents and local businesses. The area is divided into four zones; around 40,000 permits have been issued (25,000 for residents and 15,000 for others).

Similar schemes are now in operation in a number of other cities, including Florence, Milan and Rome. Most schemes limit entry to residents and businesses in the area, plus goods vehicles and public transport, although the details vary. For example, in Bologna, the resident permit only allows parking in the designated zone, but the vehicle may pass through all four zones, whereas in Florence, the permit generally limits both parking and access to one of five designated zones (in effect, a traffic cell system operates inside the restricted area).

Both the licence plate and permit forms of area-wide regulatory restraint cover several square kilometers, thereby avoiding problems of gainers and losers at the level of the individual streets within the restricted area. However, there can be very major boundary problems just outside the area, in the form of congestion and heavy on-street parking, as people bypass the restricted area or bring their cars as close as they can to the city centre. To counter the problem, several Italian cities have introduced residents' parking schemes in areas bordering the controlled zone.

Limited evidence suggests that short term reductions in traffic levels of 10 to 30 percent can be achieved by using either the Greek or Italian form of regulation; but such measures are likely to become less effective over time, as car ownership increases. The Athens odd/even licence plate scheme is able to restrain only a portion of potential traffic and does not impose an absolute ceiling on demand such as that placed by a road capacity restriction. Permit systems also have their builtin difficulties, as more people belonging to eligible groups obtain cars over time and "leakage" occurs: there has been a 25-percent increase in the number of UK disabled driver "Orange Badge" holders in just two years. However, permit systems at least have the merit that benefits can be directly targeted at specific groups.

Both physical and regulatory controls are susceptible to the continuing growth in vehicle ownership and use. This is one reason why road pricing is being considered as a more realistic longer term solution to urban traffic problems.

7.3 Controlling Traffic Levels Through Pricing

There are strong theoretical arguments in favour of road pricing as a method of directly combating urban congestion and for making drivers face the various social and environmental costs of vehicle use (Goodwin and Jones, 1989). However, it is only recently that such arguments have entered into serious political debate. Among traffic engineers and transport planners, the phrase "road pricing" has taken on a wider, generic meaning, referring to the imposition of direct charges on road use; this is in contrast to economics, where the term is usually taken more specifically to mean the setting of price equal to the social marginal cost of a trip (primarily covering track and congestion costs).

Many countries have a tradition of using tolls on selected sections of road to pay for new road construction. But, as there are often legal impediments to charging for the use of a pre-existing urban road network, and in most countries new legislation would be required. Payment might then be based on a number of principles, such as link or junction charges, cordon pricing, supplementary licensing, or continuous pricing (see Jones, 1992, for a general review of these issues).

In its latest White Paper on future common transport policy, the European Commission set out two clear reasons for favouring road user charges over the other methods of traffic restraint that have been reviewed here:

> In conditions of scarcity it makes sense to ensure that demand management mechanisms including charges are imposed which will create an incentive for users to reflect on the value of a particular journey or to consider other alternatives. Second, to rely on cost imputation or even road pricing is to use a market mechanism which still leaves operators with choice while ensuring a better utilization in time and space of different transport modes. Some other possible techniques for dealing with these problems do not have these advantages. It makes sense to explore fully the possibilities for resolving problems on the basis of such a mechanism if it can avoid the need for more directive techniques substituting regulation for user choice, albeit a conditional one (EC, 1992, para. 100, p. 39).

Note that recognition is given (see para. 117) to the important role that parking controls and traffic management measures and restrictions can play in ameliorating traffic impacts at the local level -- provided that they do not discriminate against vehicles from other Member states.

Objectives Behind Road Pricing Proposals: A number of European countries are in the process of implementing, or are actively considering, some form of urban road charging, but often with very different policy objectives in mind. Three kinds of objectives lie behind these various proposals:

* *Infrastructure:* To raise money for new environmentally sensitive road construction (and, very recently, to finance public transport improvements). This has been the primary motive behind the existing urban toll schemes in Norway.

* *Congestion:* To regulate demand through the price mechanism, and so eliminate traffic congestion (the primary rationale behind the current debate and proposals.

* *Environment:* To reduce traffic levels in order to achieve environmental benefits (reductions in pollution, traffic noise, energy use, accidents). This has been a primary motivating factor in the Swedish debate.

Increasingly, the arguments for road pricing are being advanced on the basis of achieving multiple objectives. For example, in the Netherlands, the recent (now defunct) proposals for regional road pricing ("Rekening Rijden") were designed to achieve all three objectives, and debates on future schemes in Norway are taking this wider view. This means that difficult compromises sometimes have to be made in the detailed design of the schemes.

Behavioural Aspects: From the limited evidence available from the Area Licence Scheme in Singapore (Behbehani et al., 1984) and the comprehensive studies carried out in Hong Kong (Harrison, 1986), it is evident that road user charges can be very effective as a means of managing demand: many motorists can be deterred from making specific journeys by car if charges are set at a sufficiently high level.

In the case of Singapore, car traffic into the central area was cut by over a half during the morning peak. In contrast, the toll ring schemes in Norway have led to only marginal reductions in traffic levels. It should be emphasised that this was not their purpose: their aim in Norway has been to raise revenue for local transport infrastructure projects, and the maintenance of existing traffic levels -- rather than their reduction -- was an important politically stated aim of the schemes.

One of the main problems to be faced in introducing road pricing as a restraint mechanism in European cities is to identify what the appropriate charge levels, given the lack of European data on the responsiveness of motorists to direct road charges. The three-year (1992-1994) research programme for the Department of Transport in England aimed at assessing the feasibility and effectiveness of introducing some form of road pricing in London should provide valuable additional information about driver responses to road user charges in large urban areas.

Sociopolitical Aspects: Road pricing probably offers the most flexible tool for matching demand and supply, and provides the "fairest" way of paying for road use and for new road construction in a market economy. Paradoxically, however, it is usually the least popular form of traffic restraint in attitude surveys among motorists, who often view it as a measure of "last resort". Arguments against road charging include:

* The use of an AVI (automatic vehicle identification) technology, whereby vehicles are tracked in order to record and collect the charges, is an invasion of privacy.

* It is perceived as just another form of taxation, which governments would exploit when short of income (as has occurred in some countries with hypothecated revenues in the past); motorists already feel they pay too much.

* Roads are public goods that should be freely enjoyed by all.

* Pricing is inequitable because poorer motorists are forced off the road at the expense of the rich.

Governments have to find a way of addressing these issues if urban road pricing is to become publicly acceptable. The most pervasive arguments relate to the use of the money raised and the equity issues. In the Netherlands, the government has attempted to turn the equity argument on its head, and to say that road charging is a tax on the rich, to provide better public transport and cycle/pedestrian facilities for the majority of people -- but this would only apply where revenues are hypothecated.

A recent public attitude survey in the UK, reported in Jones (1991), found that support for road pricing doubled from 30 percent (as a standalone measure) to 57 percent when viewed as part of a package of complementary measures, where the money raised from road user charges was specifically allocated to improvements in public transport, road safety and the environment; similar findings were reported in London (NEDO, 1991). It seems unlikely, therefore, that road pricing will be successfully introduced as a traffic restraint measure unless it forms part of a package of measures to improve urban accessibility and the environment.

8. Conclusions

Movement by car dominates as the main form of passenger transport in most of Western Europe; based on current trends, this practice will extend more widely throughout Central and Eastern Europe in the future. Car travel brings great benefits to individuals, but at increasing costs to the economy and to society as a whole as the numbers of car travellers increase.

Serious attempts are now being made to address this problem through advances in technology (notably Advanced Transport Telematics) and an increase in the provision of road infrastructure. However, in the denser parts of Europe, they are unlikely to be sufficient. Some form of restraint and prioritization is seen as inevitable by many city councils, a practice which in time may extend to parts of the inter-urban network too. Increasingly, authorities are talking of providing for "necessary" rather than "desired" traffic levels.

However, the debate concerning these issues is at a very early stage. The slowdown in economic growth through much of Western Europe -- and hence a reduction in the rate of traffic increase in many countries -- may remove the pressure to make difficult decisions in the short term. In addition, it is likely that any major shifts in transport policy concerning car use will need to be agreed upon at the European level, to avoid putting less environmentally concerned cities at a short term competitive advantage, and to enact the common technical standards needed in any electronic payment systems that might be introduced. All this will serve to delay any widespread introduction of urban or inter-urban traffic restraint measures; consequently, targets for the stabilization of CO_2 emissions in road transport by the year 2000 are extremely unlikely to be met (unless there are very sharp increases in carbon taxes).

If car traffic is to be restrained on congested and environmentally sensitive parts of the road network without seriously affecting lifestyles or aspirations, it will be important to provide attractive alternatives, for many of the urban and inter-urban journeys currently made by car. The importance of an integrated, attractive transport alternative to the car is stressed in the Commission's White Paper *The Future Development of the Common Transport Policy*:

> Collective transport systems which offer a high quality service, traffic management schemes which provide easy passage and enhanced accessibility for collective transport as well as attractive pricing and payment technologies should encourage the user to opt for collective transport, particularly for urban and inter-urban journeys and more specifically during certain periods of the day and certain times of the week and year. This shift can be made easier by a proper linkup of the different stages of a journey: from point of departure (home/office) to metro/bus stop to train station/airport to metro/bus stop] to final destination. Such policy instruments could be supplemented by public information initiatives, providing the user with reliable information, if possible on line, about available services, fares, frequencies and special facilities] as well as by guaranteeing frequent, reliable and rapid services (EC, 1992, para. 175, p. 62).

And at the local level:

> Action to promote the use of environmentally friendly forms of transport, such as the bicycle and the electric car, can also make a useful contribution (EC, 1992, para. 176, p. 62).

As already noted, funds raised from road pricing could be used to finance these improvements and make a broadly based package approach both politically attractive and practical in today's financially stringent climate.

In relation to the traffic restraint elements of such a package, two important points need to be recognised:

* The objectives behind restraining traffic need to be clearly formulated; they will, to a considerable extent, dictate the appropriate form of measures.

* It would be wrong to assume that any single approach to restraint is the only way forward: pricing, regulatory and physical measures will all have a role to play within a given urban area, with the appropriate balance varying from one city to another.

While there is a tendency to see the aim of countering the disbenefits of car use (as measured in terms of congestion, road accidents, environmental damage, etc.) as leading to a common set of policies and outcomes, in practice improvements in one measure may not always be compatible with improvements in others. For example, reductions in urban congestion will reduce traffic delays and certain types of emissions, but may lead to increases in the number and severity of road accidents; similarly, a primary focus on minimising emissions will lead to pressure for a reduction in maximum inter-urban speed limits, which could significantly increase road journey times for longer distance journeys across Europe and might be seen as countering the aims of integrating the European market.

It is also important to avoid the temptation to see any one restraint measure as providing the "ideal" solution in any urban area. Here we can turn to parking policies as a guide: these have been evolving in many Northern European cities for the last thirty or forty years and represent a much more mature stage of application than in the case of controls on moving traffic. Here we find combinations of all three restraint mechanisms contributing to overall policy objectives: physical controls on the total size of the parking stock, regulatory devices to reserve capacity for certain groups (residents, disabled drivers, etc.) and the use of the pricing mechanism to allocate the remaining parking spaces according to willingness to pay. Over time, we may expect a similar coordinated, multi-measure approach to be adopted in relation to controls on moving traffic in urban areas.

Dealing effectively and fairly with the issue of the role of the car in cities will require more than targeted restraint policies and improvements to alternative modes (public transport, walking and cycling). Changes in land use policy will be needed, to reduce trip lengths and provide greater choice of access to facilities other than by car. This will mean not only spatial but temporal change in order to both reduce car trips and spread the load on the network more evenly in time, e.g., the greater introduction of flexible work hours, changes in shopping hours (as practised in Athens in the winter months), This recognition of the need for a much broader approach is reflected in a recent report produced by the Confederation of British Industry's London Region (CBI, 1992), which recommended a range of such measures to reduce the capital's dependence on travel by car.

One area where the scope for change is often underestimated is land use: while the stock of buildings may change slowly, the use to which they are put -- or, in some cases, their complete abandonment -- may occur very rapidly. It is probable that sharp increases in the costs of fuel, for example, would lead to a repatterning of the occupation of space that would shorten trip lengths quite quickly, although the physical change in the landscape would take much longer to appear. Rathery (1993) has suggested that changes in land use patterns and work practices may be forced on companies by deteriorating road conditions and rising costs, particularly in relation to industrial production and distribution. In a just-in-time culture, increasing unreliability may force a regionalization of production and distribution and a reduction in overall levels of goods transport.

In hindsight, there are several measures that could have been introduced in cities decades ago that would have reduced the scale of the current problems, but for which the time in Western Europe -- although perhaps not Central and Eastern Europe -- has now passed. For example, the imposition of a requirement for car owners to provide their own off-street parking (as operates in larger Japanese cities) would probably have slowed the growth in car ownership and certainly reduced the traffic problems found in many residential areas today. Similarly, had more cities reserved and retained exclusive rights of way for public transport vehicles, public transport could have become a much more reliable alternative to the car than it is today. In such circumstances, expectations about when and where cars should be used would have evolved differently, too.

Given, however, that most cities are now starting from a "car-dominated" base situation, a key aspect behind any attempts to limit car use -- and one which will largely determine the pace at which such changes can be implemented -- is public acceptability. Educating the public about the issues and options will form a vital component of change, creating a drive to lead rather than lag behind what has become in some countries an increasingly cautious political approach to this delicate subject. Over the last decade, major changes in driver attitudes and behaviour have occurred in many European countries in relation to drunken driving, seat belt use and, quite recently, excessive speeding, all on the basis of a heightened concern for road safety.

I personally doubt that growing traffic congestion per se will generate the same degree of pressure for change, except in special cases such as city centres -- unless conditions were to get much worse -- but related concerns about air quality and public health may well do so. Monitoring studies in some European cities are beginning to show pollution levels well above WHO and EC guidelines, which is arousing public concern. It is only when a more fundamental aspect of the lifestyle and well-being of a sufficient number of people is threatened by continued growth in car use that collective action will be effect the necessary modifications in the use of cars. A greater emphasis on public education and a more informed political debate will thus need to be encouraged as an important element of strategic transport policy development in Europe in the coming years.

References

Argyrakos G., 1986, *The Influence of Private Car Restrictions on Commuting - The Case of Athens*, International Conference on Commuting, Rome, May.

Automobile Association, 1992, *The Balance Sheet of Motoring*, Automobile Association, Basingstoke, England.

Behbehani, R., Pendakur, V.S. and Armstrong-Wright, A.T., 1984, *Singapore Area Licensing Scheme: A Review of the Impact*, The World Bank, Water Supply and Urban Development Department, July.

Bielefeldt, C., 1989, Europe's DRIVE on Streets and Highways, *PTRC Summer Annual Meeting, Seminar A*, University of Sussex.

Button, K. and Rothengatter, W., 1993, Global Environmental Degradation: The Role of Transportation, in D. Banister and K. Button (eds.), *Transport, the Environment and Sustainable Development*, Spon, London.

Confederation of British Industry (CBI), 1992, *Interim Report*, London Region Transport Task Force, London.

Cracknell, J.A., Martin, B.V., May, A.D. and Pickering, D., 1975, Physical Restraint: Greater London's Cordon Restraint Study, *Traffic Engineering and Control*, 16(9), 368-372.

European Commission, 1992, *The Future Development of the Common Transport Policy: A Global Approach to the Construction of a Community Framework for Sustainable Mobility*, Commission of the European Communities, Brussels.

European Conference of Ministers of Transport (ECMT), 1990, *Transport Policy and the Environment*, ECMT, Brussels.

European Round Table of Industrialists (ERTI), 1991, *Missing Networks, A European Challenge: Proposals for the Renewal of Europe's Infrastructure*, ERTI, Brussels.

European Round Table of Industrialists (ERTI), 1992, *The Efficient Use of Energy: Looking into the Future*, Discussion Paper, ERTI, Brussels.

Eurostat, 1992, *Europe in Figures*, Third Edition, Office for Official Publications of the European Communities, Luxembourg.

Falk, S., Bendixson, T. and May, A.D., 1988, Gothenburg, in *Cities and Transport*, OECD, Paris.

Goodwin, P.B. and Jones, P.M., 1989, *Road Pricing: The Political and Strategic Possibilities*, Round Table 80, ECMT, Brussels.

Hallett, S., 1990, Drivers; Attitudes to Driving, Cars and Traffic - Analysis of the Results of a National Survey, Discussion Paper No. 14. In R. Jeffreys (ed.) *Transport and Society*, Transport Studies Unit, University of Oxford, Oxford.

Harrison, B., 1986, Electronic Road Pricing in Hong Kong: 3. Estimating and Evaluating the Effects, *Traffic Engineering and Control*, January 13-18.

Herrstedt, L., 1988, Environmentally Adapted Through Road in Vinderup: Effect Evaluation, *Proceedings of Seminar B*, PTRC, September.

Holman, C., Fergusson, M. and Robertson, T., 1990, The Route Ahead. Vehicle Pollution: Causes, Effects, Answers?, World Wildlife Fund, Zurich.

International Union of Public Transport (UITP), 1992, *Assessments of Mobility in Europe*, UITP, Brussels.

Jones, P.M., 1991, Gaining Public Support for Road Pricing Through a Package Approach, *Traffic Engineering and Control*, 4, 194-196.

Jones, P.M., 1992, *Review of Available Evidence on Public Reactions to Road Pricing*. Report to the London Transportation Unit, Department of Transport, London.

Keen, K., 1992, European Community Research and Development on Advanced Road Transport Telematics, 1992-1994, Traffic Engineering and Control, 4, 263-267.

Keller, H.H., 1986, Environmental traffic restraints on major roads in the Federal Republic of Germany, *Built Environment*, 12, 44-59.

Keller, H.H., 1990, Recent Developments in German Traffic Calming. Paper Presented at the PTRC Summer Annual Meeting, University of Sussex, Environmental Issues Stream.

Matsois, E.C., 1985, An Assessment of Vehicle Restraint Measures, *Transportation Quarterly*, 39(1), 125-133.

National Economic Development Office (NEDO), 1991, *A Road User Charge? Londoners' Views*, NEDO, London.

Rathery, A., 1993, Traffic Flow Problems in Europe, *Transport Reviews*, 13(1), 1-23.

TNO, 1991, *Possible Community Measures Aiming at Limiting CO_2 Emissions in the Transportation Sector*, TNO Policy Research, Delft.

Topp, H.H., 1993, Parking Policies to Reduce Car Traffic in German Cities, *Transport Reviews*, 13(1), 83-95.

Vincent, R.A. and Layfield, R.E., 1977, *Nottingham "Zones and Collar" Study - Overall Assessment*, Report No. 805, Transport and Road Research Laboratory, Crowthorn.

Whitelegg, J., 1990, Traffic Calming: A "Green" Smokescreen?, Paper Presented to the Conference on Traffic Calming - Ways Forward, London Borough of Ealing.

TRANSPORT IN A UNIFIED EUROPE. Policies and Challenges.
D. Banister and J. Berechman (Editors)

Chapter Three

CONTESTABILITY AND ENTRY DETERRENCE IN THE BUS INDUSTRY

David Banister
Joseph Berechman
Gines de Rus Mendoza

1. Introduction

Faced with severe fiscal crisis, many European countries are presently considering regulatory reforms of their public transit sectors. These reforms range from regulation with extensive tendering (e.g., in France) to partial deregulation where transit operators are free to set service levels and frequencies (e.g., in Finland) to complete deregulation (e.g., in Portugal outside Lisbon and Porto). While the primary factor motivating these reforms is a substantial reduction in public funding of transit operations, there are some trepidations concerning additional consequences from these reforms. In particular, it has been argued that the market structure that will emerge from these deregulatory policies may not be competitive or even contestable[1]. The main reason given is that incumbent transit firms erect entry barriers in order to create a monopolistic market position. If this is indeed the case, then the likely results of transit deregulation will be declining output, higher prices and, in general, an inefficient industry.

Given these concerns regarding the consequences from deregulation, the main objectives of this chapter are, first, to examine entry deterrence strategies which, at least in theory, are open to incumbent transit firms. Second, based on results from actually implemented deregulation policies, an assessment is made of the effectiveness of these strategies. Since the UK bus transit deregulation is, to date, the most comprehensive change introduced in Europe, experience from this reform constitutes a major part of this analysis. Finally, conclusions are drawn from experience of bus deregulation in other European countries and the implications of different forms of regulatory regimes are assessed in terms of the future of the bus industry.

2. Regulatory Reform Policy Regimes and Market Entry

In general, the regulation of transit services involves a large number of economic and operational parameters which together demarcate the economic environment of transit operations. In evaluating results of deregulation policies, specification of which of the above parameters fall within the regime of a particular policy is critical. We define a policy of *complete deregulation* as one that does not impose any restriction on the key decision parameters of transit firms. These include fare level and structure, use of input factors, type and quality of services supplied, route network organization, economic investment in rolling stock and fixed facilities, and freedom of market entry and exit.

A policy regime of *partial deregulation* is defined as one that imposes some restrictions on a subset of the above major decision parameters. As more regulatory constraints are imposed, we move from a policy regime of partial deregulation to a constrained regulatory regime and, at the extreme, to a policy regime of *complete regulation* where all these parameters are under public control.

Assuming a policy regime of complete deregulation, the cardinal question with which we are concerned here is whether or not the market will become competitive. It does not become competitive but, rather, monopolistic or oligopolistic, a major objective of the regulatory reform will not be accomplished. To explore this issue we first examine the case of market contestability, where a single transit firm (usually the incumbent firm) supplies the greatest portion of the demand but, for fear of attracting entry, sets prices and quantities approximately at the levels of a competitive market. Subsequently, we examine alternative strategies which an incumbent firm can actively pursue in order to deter entry by erecting entry barriers.

3. Transit Market Contestability

The production of transit services is subject to several types of economies, including density, scope and network economies[2]. It has also been found that transit firms operate under conditions of excess capacity of rolling stock. Following deregulation, a likely result of these production characteristics is the emergence of a monopolistic or oligopolistic market structure, one in which a transit firm has a natural monopoly position in a given market. This, in turn, leads to a misallocation of resources as manifested by prices charged and output produced.

To prevent this situation from actually occurring, the theory of contestable markets claims that these distortions will not materialize if conditions of market contestability prevail. These include free entry to and exit from transit markets; similar demands for incumbent firms as well as newly entrants; a possibility of "hit-and-run" type entry; an active secondhand market for capital assets, particularly buses; time lags to prevent sudden changes in prices or withdrawal of services by the incumbent firm; and insignificant sunk costs relative to fixed costs. If these conditions indeed prevail, contestability theory predicts that, following deregulation, there might be just one firm supplying transit services. However, this firm (the incumbent firm) will be engaged in average cost pricing which, in turn, implies zero monopolistic profits. If positive monopolistic profits were earned, potential competitors would enter this market by undercutting the incumbent firm's prices and profits. Thus, according to contestable market theory, the mere threat of entry will be extremely effective in forcing the incumbent transit firm not to behave as a monopoly despite the intrinsic production properties which enables it to do so.

Given the known cost and production properties of transit, it is not certain that genuine contestable transit markets will emerge following deregulation. In particular, hit-and-run and sunk cost conditions are unlikely to prevail, especially if a policy of partial deregulation is enacted, thus making entry threats by potential entrants non-credible. The results from the British transit deregulation experience seems to support this conclusion, although no direct empirical test of the contestability hypothesis was reported[3].

The next question, discussed below, relates to the strategies of entry deterrence that incumbent firms can exploit to maintain their market position.

4. Theories of Entry Deterrence Strategies

A number of studies (e.g., Schwartz, 1986) have pointed to several potential barriers to the formation of genuinely contestable transportation markets despite the enactment of a deregulation policy which removes all restrictions on entry and exit, prices charged and level of services offered. Yet the possibility that such barriers may exist does not, in itself, preclude the possibility that some forms of entry into the deregulated market will still take place.

In general, a potential entrant firm will move into a new market only if it expects to make positive profits -- by undercutting the incumbent's prevailing price -- and to serve at least some portion of the market demand at the lower price. If, in response to this entry attempt, the incumbent firm lowers its price below the entrant's price, the latter firm can exit the market without any substantial loss, provided that no sunk costs were involved. Under such conditions, new entrants are undeterred by prospects of retaliatory price cuts by incumbent firms; they are deterred when *existing market prices* leave no room for profitable entry. Therefore, the purpose of creating entry barriers is either to make some of the entrant's costs sunk or greatly lower the entrant's expected profits (preferably zero), or both. Thus, the principal question which needs to be examined is whether or not, in a deregulated transit market, an incumbent transit firm can successfully impede entry attempts by making the entrant's potential profits trifling. To answer this question, it is necessary to consider the conditions which enable an incumbent transit firm to charge substantially reduced prices in the market where entry has occurred. These conditions underlie the incumbent's deterrence strategy. As we shall see, a major determinant enabling transit firms to devise such strategies is the spatial nature of transit services supplied. We have already argued that due to the production structure of transit services, it is not quite clear if transit markets can genuinely be contestable. Here we examine other barriers to potential entry.

One major strategy is that of *product differentiation*, defined as the case when consumers do *not* regard products as perfect substitutes. Thus, a new entrant who wishes to minimize the risk of entry deterrence must provide a service which is markedly distinct from the one currently being provided (i.e., a poor substitute). For example, because of the spatial dimension of transit output, alternative services are viewed by consumers as being *imperfect substitutes*.

The incumbent firm, on the other hand, will attempt to build consumer loyalty, and thus their propitious preference for its service, mainly by increasing its reliability and its reputation for operational dependability. That is, the most important factors in this strategy seem to be product quality and information. Product quality and information cover such issues as access to terminals, a comprehensive network of established services, and coordination of services and fares. This creates customer loyalty based on the knowledge that reliable information on a particular service can be obtained by one enquiry.

Competition on roadways has therefore been restricted to high density corridors where the market is large enough for several operators to provide services in direct competition with each other and where the necessity to provide particular service information is reduced because of the high service frequency. Operations on other routes are restricted to one operator who has a local monopoly, either through deterring entry as the route does not generate sufficient demand or through local monopoly rights as distributed through the tendering process. Minibus services have provided the other main opportunity for market entry as these services can open up new markets in suburban areas. Where the frequency of service is high, detailed timetables may not be required (Banister and Mackett, 1990).

Another entry deterrence strategy is *anticipatory action*. This occurs when the incumbent operator has the means and the incentive to take strategic action to deter entry using a range of anticipatory moves. For example, market share can be best maintained through an established reputation for toughness, through maintaining a presence in the market, and through an established product reputation. Those barriers are likely to have been intentionally erected both to reduce the possibility of entry as well as a means for profit maximization (Salop, 1979).

A major entry deterrence strategy in the transportation market is that of *network reorganization*. With this strategy, the incumbent firm redesigns its service delivery network in a way which enables it to exploit network economies and, as a consequence, makes potential entry by rival firms rather unprofitable. As shown by several studies (e.g., Berechman and Shy, 1991) the principal mechanism which enables the use of this entry deterrence strategy is the ownership of and access to fixed facilities. In the past, the major British Coach Company (National Express) had exclusive access to Victoria Coach Station in Central London. But with its privatization (as part of the restructuring of the National Bus Company into 72 smaller companies) in 1988, this monopoly was broken as its control over the coach station was ended. However, National Express still managed to maintain its dominant position on the basis of product quality, including brand name and market outlets, and because effective competition was eliminated before this barrier was removed. The long purse arguments which favor the incumbent, their local knowledge of the market conditions, and product loyalty from customers should not be underestimated in a deregulated market. It is not easy for a new entrant to enter the bus market, even if many of the perceived barriers are eliminated.

5. Is the Market Contestable? The Experience from Britain

Bus deregulation in Britain took place on inter-urban routes in 1980 and in urban and rural areas in 1985, and the subsequent events followed a similar pattern to airline deregulation in the United States. Kahn (1988) has itemized the process of turmoil and subsequent reconcentration through the explosion of entry, lower fares, the restructuring of routes, price wars, labor-management conflicts, bankruptcies, consolidations, and dismal profit levels in the U.S. airlines over the last 10 years. The intention in this section is not to give a detailed account of the experience in Britain but to extract some of the principal lessons as they relate to the market structure and organization of the bus industry[4].

Radical change in the organization and regulation of the British bus industry has long been overdue. Public transport patronage has more than halved from peak levels in the early 1950s. The bus and coach share of the total passenger-kilometers travelled has declined from 42 percent to 8 percent. The principal reason for the drop has been the increase in car ownership over the same period (2.5 million cars in 1952, the figure in 1982 was 15.7 million). Other important changes have taken place, such as increases in standards of living, the decentralization of homes and workplaces, and the development of high technology industries. These changes have resulted in fundamentally different types of travel patterns, many of which are car-based.

All this has taken place against an expanding market for all forms of transport (passenger-kilometers travelled has increased by 2.5 times over this 30 year period). Within the bus industry, the picture is one of declines in levels of service, increases in the costs of operations, and increases in fares, which have risen by 30 percent in real terms during this period (1972-1982). Revenue support has also grown from £10 million (1972) to £520 million (1982), a thirteen-fold increase in real terms (GB Department of Transport, 1984).

Prior to deregulation, the structure of the bus market in Britain was characterized by local monopoly operations with standard fares, internal cross-subsidization between routes, and external subsidy. Often, the profitability of a particular company was dependent upon one or two high density routes which earned excess profits. The political rationale behind deregulation was to end this local monopoly control and to introduce competition, particularly on these highly profitable routes. There was also a strong desire to reduce the levels of subsidy to the bus industry and to make it cost-efficient.

The Conservative Government introduced the first stage of their bus deregulation plan in the 1980 Transport Act. Restrictions were lifted on minibus operations, road service licenses were no longer required on long distance bus services (a minimum journey length of 48 kilometers), and local areas could be designated as 'trial areas'. In these trial areas, road service licenses were no longer required and operators could run services on any routes they wished. For other services, road service licenses were now granted provided that the new service was not against the public interest and operators had more freedom to charge market fares. The 1985 Transport Act has effectively made all of Britain (outside London) a trial area. The provision of bus services in Britain (outside London) thus provides a laboratory for *complete deregulation* as defined earlier in this chapter.

6. Evidence on Entry Deterrence

6.1 Anticipatory Action to Deter Entry

Contestable market theory assumes that each operator has complete information, but it is evident that this assumption is not valid. It is not in any operator's interest to publicize its own commercial information to competitors. It is more likely that operators will release limited information to potential competitors to deter entry. Entry can still take place even if perfect information is not available. The Austrian School of Economics argues that entrepreneurs exploit ignorance to create profits and that opportunistic action can only take place in situations where there is incomplete information. Opportunistic action exploits price differences in the economy created by ignorance of the actual situation. Littlechild (1986) takes this even further and argues that all action is taken in the light of imagined future conditions; this in turn results in creativity and uncertainty. The dynamic element is crucial in that an equilibrium situation is never created, as that would mean no market opportunities for entrepreneurs.

As the deregulated bus market in Britain stabilizes, it seems that most competition takes place off the road for tendered services. Contracts are for three years. With the renewal of these tenders, it appears that the incumbent has advantages as he has full operating information. For prospective competitors, that information is not available and they have to rely upon secondbest estimates if they are to successful participate in the bidding process. In the longer term this may result in the market being less competitive, even for the tendered services, than was at first expected.

Entry is further deterred in Britain by the requirement for a 42-day notice of entry to or exit from the market. This registration information, which is supplied to the traffic commissioners, allows the incumbent to take immediate action (such as increasing frequencies on the same route), which will deter entry. To make the market more contestable, this requirement should be reduced, but this would result in greater uncertainty to the customer. Perhaps different notice periods could be specified for entry to the market, and for exit from the market. Such an arrangement could still create problems as the incumbent does not need to give notice of fare changes and can [threaten to] reduce fares to deter entry. It seems that any arrangement works to the disadvantage of the new entrant. This is one problem facing the competitive market which has not been successfully resolved.

As part of the process of deregulation, the National Bus Company has been restructured into 72 separate private companies and sold off. At the time of the sale there was heavy criticism of the tendency to undervalue the asset of these companies, particularly the value of city center bus stations. Even though a claw back procedure was included in the legislation, it has not been extensively used. The Government claims that the sale was successful as no parts of the NBC could not be sold. The net receipts to the Exchequer from the sale was £385 million (1991 prices), but the net surplus was only £45 million after debt repayments, interest and taxation charges, and provision for pensions had been made (Committee of Public Accounts, 1991). These privatized companies are now reforming themselves into larger units through mergers, holding companies, and other forms of horizontal agreements. Agreements allow the sharing of information, the joint marketing of services, and the pooling of resources (such as buses and maintenance facilities). This presents an even more formidable, although indirect, deterrent to entry.

6.2 Predatory Action After Entry

Despite these arrangements, some entry may take place. It may then become necessary for the incumbent to eliminate that competition or at least to minimize the threat. The Chicago School of Economics would argue that predation is irrational as no one gains except the passenger in the short term (Stigler, 1975). The strategy of the incumbent on a particular route would be to price-, service- and schedule-match, and use customer loyalty and intensive marketing to ensure that any entry is short lived. It is unclear whether any predatory pricing has taken place in the UK as cost data are sparse. Prices have risen significantly (see Table 1), but most of the increases have taken place in the initial unstable period of deregulation when there was a readjustment of fares which were too low prior to deregulation. By definition, predation is difficult to detect, and the entrant has often been forced to leave the market before any official action can be taken.

New forms of regulation may be the only means to ensure that predatory actions are minimized. Rule-based approaches, such as that proposed by Areeda and Turner (1975), may only have limited impact, as short term losses can be recouped in the longer term. Beesley (1990) suggests remedies including the possibility of adopting the U.S. sanction of triple damages to a party shown to have been injured by anti competitive behavior. Even with such a sanction it is difficult to prove anti-competitive behavior. However, more research is needed on the means of proof of the existence of a crime rather than on the scale of the punishment. It may be in no one's interest to impose exemplary fines, particularly if it bankrupts the company involved.

6.3 Comment

The most important changes (1985-1990) are summarized in Table 1. The pattern of services has changed little as local monopolies have survived, sometimes even after a short period of intense competition. Patronage in Britain has fallen by a further 13 percent in line with trends prior to deregulation, but in the Metropolitan Counties this decline has amounted to 26 percent. Fares have risen substantially, but most of this increase took place immediately after deregulation and may be seen as part of the readjustment process to low fares policies. More vehicle-kilometers of services are being run, particularly by minibus, but passenger receipts have fallen in all areas. Operating costs have been reduced by 25 percent, with reductions in labor costs, new working practices and increases in productivity. The substantial reductions in revenue support (see Tables 1 and 2) are partly offset by rises in concessionary fare payments. In this respect, deregulation can be seen as a success as its primary rationale was to reduce levels of subsidy.

White (1991) argues that the profitability of the bus industry is poor and declining, yielding an average return of only 5 percent in 1988. Given this situation, the expected renewal of the bus fleet is not taking place as only half of the required 5000 replacements of large buses per year is being made (the actual figure for replacements in 1990 was 2,630). If minibuses are included, this figure falls even further[5]. The average replacement cycle for large vehicles is now 25 years, reflecting high interest rates and low rates of return in the industry. There is a buoyant market for second hand vehicles as the capital costs and risks are much lower, but this market will gradually become exhausted as fewer new buses are bought and as the oldest buses are scrapped. Unless new forms of leasing are introduced including high standards of maintenance as a condition for tendered services, the quality of service as reflected in the age of the vehicle will decline. This may lead to greater control of the industry by those companies owning the vehicle fleet, which in turn may reduce opportunities for small operators to enter the market. Membership in a holding company may effectively become a condition of market entry.

Imperfect competition seems to be the long term outcome of deregulation in urban areas as the market is too small to sustain many operators. With market concentration and collusion between operators, the outcome of competition may be higher prices and poorer service to the user (Banister, Berechman and de Rus Mendoza, 1992). Competition is now limited to high density radial routes from city centers and between cities. Evans (1991) suggests that urban bus routes are natural monopolies, as competition increases average user costs and that despite the removal of legal barriers to competition, there is usually one operator on each route. This is explained by the value that passengers place on integration of services; integration is difficult to achieve if a route has more than one operator.

TABLE 1

Summary of Changes over the First Five Years of Deregulation in London and the Metropolitan Counties

	Full Deregulation: Metropolitan Counties (%)	Competitive Regulation: London (%)
Passenger Journeys	-26.2	+3.9
Vehicle Kilometers	+12.9	+11.4
Fares[a]	+31.8	+12.0
Proportion Tendered	14.0	40.0
Staff Employed	-26.0	-23.0
Passenger Receipts[a]	-12.2	-9.1
Revenue Support[a]	-61.3	-18.0
Concessionary fares[a]	+19.3	+8.3
Operating costs[a]	-40.0	-20.0

Note: [a]Changes denoted in real terms from 1985 to 1991.

Source: Department of Transport (1991).

Different forms of action to deter effective entry can be taken prior to market entry. These barriers to entry include economic factors such as pricing but also cover access to terminals, marketing and coordination of services and tickets, the restructuring of the industry into larger units, and even the availability of suitable vehicles. It is very difficult for a new operator to compete effectively, and even if it were possible, the returns in the short term would be limited by a strong response from the incumbent.

In addition, although operators may be making profits on high density routes and on tendered services with some cross-subsidization of thin routes, the overall financial position of most operators seems precarious. Short term gains may have been made through the sale of assets (principally property) and through delaying the replacement of vehicles, but in the longer term, profitability does not seem to be guaranteed, particularly when set against falling patronage levels. The initial savings in revenue support are no longer being maintained, and there has been a consistent increase in the levels of concessionary fares payments (see Table 2). Cost savings through greater efficiency and local wage agreements have also stabilized, and so the only potential for further savings would be through a reduction in route-kilometers. All the evidence cited here points to the conclusion that further substantial gains in cost efficiency must be obtained through concentration on the profitable high density routes. As in the airline network, the thin routes will gradually be phased out and the bus network will become focused on a hub and spoke configuration, both within urban areas and between urban areas.

TABLE 2

Revenue Support and Concessionary Fares Reimbursement for Local Bus Services in Great Britain.

	Revenue Support[a]		Concessionary Fares[a]	
	Metropolitan Areas	All Great Brit. (excl. London)	Metropolitan Areas	All Great Brit. (excl. London)
1985/86	292	465	140	280
1990/91	113	219	167	309
Change	-61%	-53%	+19%	+10%

Note: [a]£ Million in 1990/1991 prices.

Source: GB Department of Transport (1991).

7. Lessons from Britain and the European Experience

Britain is the only example in Europe of *complete deregulation* in the commercial network with a tendering process in the non-commercial network. Apart from this exception, two main common characteristics appear in the different regulatory regimes for the provision of public transport in Europe (see Table 3). First, public and private operators act as

TABLE 3

Regulatory Regimes in Public Transport in Europe

COUNTRY	Exclusive Rights to Public Companies	Tendering Contract Periods	Free Entry or with Qualitative Restrictions	Free Entry with Quantitative Restrictions Depending on Local Assessment of Necessity
BELGIUM	U Exclusive Rights for 4-6 Years			
DENMARK		U Contracts: 5 Years		
FINLAND				U,I (Contracts of 5 Years)
FRANCE		U,I 5 to 7 Years (Average), All Lengths are Possible		
GREECE	U (Public Co-operative) Unlimited in Practice.			I
IRELAND	U Licensing Only (no limit)			I Licensing (No Time Limit)
ISRAEL	Regulated Monopoly (U,I)	Licensing (No Time Limit)		
ITALY	Unlimited in Practice		I (Unlimited in Practice)	I
NETHERLANDS	U			U, I[a]
NORWAY		U,I 10 Years Formally, No Time Limit in Practice		

Continued

TABLE 3 (Continued)

Regulatory Regimes in Public Transport in Europe

COUNTRY	Exclusive Rights to Public Companies	Tendering Contract Periods	Free Entry or with Qualitative Restrictions	Free Entry with Quantitative Restrictions Depending on Local Assessment of Necessity
NORWAY		U,I 10 Years Formally, No Time Limit in Practice		
PORTUGAL	U License Length: Still to be Regulated	U	I	
SPAIN	Unlimited in Practice	I 20 Years before 1987 8-20 Years in New Transport Act (1987)		
SWEDEN	No Longer Use Licensing	U,I Minimum 3 Year Contracts through Tendering or Agreement		
SWITZERLAND	U, I	Licenses 3 Years Trial + 10 Years Railways 50 Years		U, I
TURKEY		Licenses: 1 Year	U, I	U
UNITED KINGDOM		3 Years. Being Reviewed	U, I	
WEST GERMANY	Licenses: 8 Years			U, I

Key: U = Urban; I = Inter-city/Inter-urban.

Note: [a]Unsubsidized services which may not compete with existing subsidized services.

Source: Survey of 18 European Countries carried out in 1990 by the European Science Foundation's Network for European Communication and Transportation Activities Research (NECTAR).

statutory monopolies providing transport services protected by absolute barriers to entry; second, public agencies control the size of the network, level of service, price structure and the level of subsidy.

In the majority of European cities, the type of ownership is private, with public operators having responsibility for the provision of services in the largest cities (see Table 4). The regulatory regimes for public transport in Europe combine the following systems: exclusive rights to public companies, franchising, and quantitative restrictions depending on local assessment of needs. Table 3 summarizes the situation in 18 European countries (including Israel) with respect to bus regulations on urban and inter-urban services. It can be seen that the urban bus services in most countries are still regulated, with some tendering in Scandinavian countries (see Andersen, this volume); it is only within the inter-urban services that competition can take place.

The impact of eliminating barriers to entry in local bus transport markets in Europe could dramatically affect the average cost levels of the industry. The reduction of 20 percent in costs as a consequence of deregulation in Great Britain is not the only reference. Recently, competitive tendering has permitted reductions of 20 percent in the U.S., 25 percent in London and Israel, and 10 to 15 percent in Sweden. In Australia, private operators are 11 to 24 percent more cost-efficient than public operators. In Spain, productivity costs are lower in the private sector and labor costs are, on average, 20 percent higher than in public companies in similar operating conditions in other countries (e.g., Andersen, 1992; de Rus Mendoza, 1989; Glaister and Beesley, 1990; Hensher, 1987).

The present regulatory framework in European cities does not present a strong incentive to minimize costs. The absence of competition, the lack of commercial objectives, and the presence of network subsidies as the main form of public support do not create a suitable environment for the achievement of productive efficiency. The possibility of new entry in the industry depends on the probability of obtaining profits above normal returns on capital. There are several reasons which justify the belief that new entry would be an immediate consequence of deregulation even in the case of incumbents breaking even or suffering losses (the usual situation in local bus transport):

- There is technical inefficiency and x-inefficiency in many cases so an opportunity for cost reduction exists;

* Subsidies are given for the whole network and this is compatible with different degrees of profitability as routes and services vary in their average speed and load factors;

* Flat fares (the usual price scheme) lead to cross-subsidization and the possibility of making profits is real in some parts of the network or at some times of the day;

* Product quality or variety. The present pattern of regulation may not favor the supply of frequencies or the services (for example, minibuses) that users are willing to pay for, so profits are possible in those market segments.

8. Summary

The objective of creating a fully contestable bus market in Europe has not yet been achieved. The experience of Britain suggests that it would be extremely difficult to create such a market: the size of the market is too small and there are too many opportunities for concentration and collusion between operators, even if the bus companies themselves are broken up into small units. As can be seen from Table 4, there is a wide range of bus company sizes across Europe. The general pattern is for urban operators to be publicly controlled with non-urban and inter-urban services being run by private operators.

The question of optimum bus company size and the most appropriate structure for the bus industry has yet to be resolved. Mergers have taken place in Britain and in Norway, permitting economies in management and greater flexibility in the use of the vehicle fleet. However, mergers may take place for other reasons, such as the maintenance of market share and in order to deter entry. One interesting development is the possibility of international mergers and an increased interest in bus companies from multinational organizations not traditionally associated with the bus industry. For example, bus operations are only a small part of the Johnson Company activities, which include contracting and real estate, industrial activities, shipping, and transport. This Swedish company has registered subsidiaries in Norway and Denmark, and is running bus services in Copenhagen.

One of the main innovations that deregulation in the UK has fostered is the reduction in bus size and the extensive use of minibuses. The main reasons for this decision are the

TABLE 4

Ownership and Size of Public Transport Operations in Europe

BELGIUM	Monopoly rights to public operators in six major cities. Other services run by regional units of the nationally owned bus company. Some services subcontracted to private operators.
DENMARK	Outside Copenhagen: 2,097 buses, average size: 5 public/private ratio 40/60, one large operator (600 buses). Copenhagen area: 1,446 buses of which 1,210 owned by HT (The Copenhagen area publicly owned operator). Public/private ratio: 72/18 (1987), but to be changed to 55/45 (1994) through privatization.
FINLAND	Private 425. Public: 10. Local operators provide inter-city and charter services.
FRANCE	Urban: 150 (franchising). Non-urban: 2,762 private + 16 public.
GREECE	Urban: 30 cooperative, 1 private, 2 public. Inter-city: 59 cooperative.
IRELAND	Large towns: public monopolies - Small operators, very small fleet size.
ISRAEL	1 large private cooperative society (3,700 buses, country-wide). 1 local public operator (110 buses). 1 large private cooperative society (1,400 buses, metropolitan) 3 local small private operators. (Urban + Inter-city 35 buses average). 10 very small private operators: (10 buses average).
ITALY	Private: 27 operators (average fleet: 10 buses). Public: 2 operators (average fleet: 1,908); 112 (average fleet: 28-200)
NETHERLANDS	25 public operators (9 urban and 16 regional). No companies operating specific inter-city; fleet size: from 300 to 50. 3 small private operators.

Continued

TABLE 4 (Continued)

Ownership and Size of Public Transport Operations in Europe

NORWAY	441 operators (10,871 buses), average size: 25 buses. Public/private ratio 50/50 with an increase in public ownership. The 29 largest companies own more than 100 buses and have 40% of all vehicles.
PORTUGAL	Private: 50. Public: 9.
SPAIN	185 operators: 157 private; 28 municipal. The largest cities: municipal but there is medium size cities with municipal and private.
SWEDEN	1,043 operators (600 are private). Average company size is 9 buses. The 10 largest companies own 50% of the total fleet. Average size of private companies is 4 buses. The one large public operator (>2,000 buses).
SWITZERLAND	Urban traffic: 16 operators (2,600 vehicles: buses, trams and trolley buses). Regional traffic: 171 operators (2,796 buses, of which 1,540 buses belong to public operators).
TURKEY	Urban: Municipal + Private operators. Istanbul: 1,526 buses (municipal); 793 private buses. Size of private operators 1-10 buses. Inter-city: 600 companies (mostly private) 24,000 buses.
UNITED KINGDOM	Post-deregulation - public: 132 operators (average fleet size: 292 buses); private: 5,819 (average fleet size: 5.3 buses)
WEST GERMANY	5,650 operators (66,558 buses, private/public ratio of 51/49). If non-scheduled transport is eliminate, the ratio is 42/58; but if we take into account subcontracting of private operators, the ratio changes to 70/30. Of the number of operators 5,426 are private with average bus size of 6 buses.

Source: Survey of 18 European Countries carried out by the ESF's NECTAR, 1990.

reduction in labor costs due to differences in wages paid to drivers of buses of different sizes, together with lower capital and maintenance costs. It is nonetheless difficult to assess the effect on the average bus size in Europe if deregulation were introduced. Differences in labor markets in different countries could affect the choice of vehicle size in different ways. Although it is possible that the pattern developed in Great Britain could also develop in other countries, we should not rule out the possibility of a limited effect in countries where wages are not as sensitive to size of vehicles.

Although tendering appears to be widespread in European cities, the length of the exclusive right in many cities seems too long to speak of real competition for the road. In practice, the unlimited length of contracts seems to be a common system of regulating the industry. Some countries are introducing a more market-oriented system through contracts and tendering with a significant impact on costs. This more cautious approach of competitive tendering, similar to that operating in London, permits the reduction in barriers through freedom of access to terminals, common ticketing systems, shared information, and the maintenance of a common standard of service. In some countries, the terminals are normally owned by the municipalities and not the operators, so access is available to all operators. Similarly, the timetable information is coordinated by the transport authority for all services provided by all operators on a country-wide basis, including details on rail as well as bus services.

In those European countries which are introducing competitive tendering combined with the public control of the network, the results are promising, with objectives and funding being modified. Well-defined commercial objectives are being stated for inter-urban services and increasingly for urban services. Subsidies for complete networks are being replaced by more selective subsidies for individual routes. Capital subsidies are being reviewed, as are concessionary fares and fuel tax rebates. The consequence of this reassessment has been an increase in the revenue cost ratio, particularly in those countries which have begun to use tendering procedures (see Table 3) and, by implication, subsidy levels have been reduced.

The future of the European bus industry is in a state of transition. The example of Britain will not be followed in its entirety as other European countries have a different tradition of public service provision with less priority being given to cost efficiency. However, changes are taking place in allowing for some competition on densely used routes, in permitting different types of vehicles, in using new forms of contracting out, and in encouraging the private sector to play a major role in service provision. Market contestability may be questioned but regulatory reform in different degrees of severity is affecting the bus industry across the whole of Europe.

Notes

1. The intense debate on this issue that took place in the literature prior to the British deregulation of public transit illustrates these concerns (see Beesley and Glaister, 1985a, 1985b vs. Gwilliam, Nash, and Mackie, 1985a, 1985b).

2. On the other hand, in the empirical literature, constant or even decreasing economies of scale were found to characterize bus transit firms with fleet size exceeding 300-400 buses (Berechman and Giuliano, 1985).

3. Morrison and Winston (1987) report the results of empirical tests on contestability theory in the context of the U.S. domestic airline industry. Their findings indicate that this industry is imperfectly contestable, i.e., potential competition may have an important effect on consumer welfare. Based on data from the deregulated transit bus markets in the UK, Evans (1991) argues that the intra-city and metropolitan markets are contestable.

4. For detailed descriptions of the inter-urban position, see Robbins and White (1985); for an analysis of rural and urban areas, see Evans (1988 and 1991); for the experience in the metropolitan areas, see Tyson (1990); for a general overview, see Cloke and Bell (1990); and for an economic analysis, see Glaister (1990) and Gomez Ibanez and Meyer (1990).

5. In Great Britain (1990/1991), there are 22,000 double-decker buses which currently cost £90,000 and have an assumed life of 15 years. There are also 42,000 single-decker buses (over 17 seats), costing up to £70,000 and having an assumed life of 10-15 years. The numbers of minibuses has increased to 8,000, with each costing about £30,000 and having an assumed life of 7 years.

References

Andersen, B., 1992, Factors Affecting European Deregulation and Privatization Policies in Local Public Transport, *Transportation Research* A, 26A(2), 179-191.

Areeda, P., and D.F. Turner, 1975, Predatory Pricing and Related Practices Under Section 2 of the Sherman Act, *Harvard Law Review* 88, 697-733.

Banister, D.J., Berechman, J. and G. De Rus Mendoza, 1992, Competitive Regimes Within the European Bus Industry: Theory and Practice, *Transportation Research* A, 26A(2), 167-178.

Banister, D.J., and R. Mackett, 1990, The Minibus - Recorded Experience and Their Implications, *Transport Reviews* 10(3), 189-214.

Banister, D.J., and L. Pickup, 1990, Bus Transport in the Metropolitan Areas and London, in, Bell, P. and Cloke, P. (eds.), *Deregulation and Transport*, Fulton, London.

Baumol, W.J., 1982, Contestable Markets: An Uprising in the Theory of Industry Structure, *American Economic Review*, 72(1), 1-15.

Beesley, M.E., 1990, Collusion, Predation and Merger in the U.K. Bus Industry, *Journal of Transport Economics and Policy*, 24(3), 295-310.

Beesley, M.E., and S. Glaister, 1985a, Deregulating the Bus Industry in Britain -- A Response, *Transport Reviews*, 5, 133-142.

Beesley, M.E., and S. Glaister, 1985b, Deregulating the Bus Industry in Britain -- A Reply, *Transport Reviews*, 5, 223-224.

Bell, P. P. and Cloke, eds., 1990, *Deregulation and Transport*, Fulton, London.

Berechman, J. and G. Giuliano, 1985, Economies of Scale in Bus Transit: A Review of Concepts and Evidence, *Transportation*, 12(4), 313-332.

Berechman, J. and Shy, O., 1991, *Airline Deregulation and the Choice of Networks*, Working Paper No. 2-91, The Sackler Institute of Economic Research, Tel Aviv University, Tel Aviv.

Committee of Public Accounts, 1991, *Sale of the National Bus Company*, Ninth Report of the Committee of Public Accounts, House of Commons, Session 1990-91, HC 119 (London, HMSO).

de Rus Mendoza, G., 1989, El transporte público urbano en España: Comportamiento de los costes y regulación de la industria, *Investigaciones Económicas,* 13(2), 207-225.

Evans, A.W., 1988, Hereford: A Case Study of Bus Deregulation, *Journal of Transport Economics and Policy*, 22(3), 283-306.

Evans, A.W., 1991a, Are Urban Bus Services Natural Monopolies? *Transportation*, 18(2), 131-150.

Evans, A., 1991b, Bus Competition: Economic Theories and Empirical Evidence, *Transportation Planning and Technology*, 15, 295-313.

Glaister, S. (1990) *Bus Deregulation in the U.K.*, Paper Prepared for the World Bank, May, Washington, D.C.

Glaister, S., and M. Beesley, 1989, *Bidding for Tendered Bus Routes in London*, Mimeo, Conference on Competition and Ownership of Bus and Coach Services, Thredbo, Australia (mimeo).

Gomez Ibanez, J.A., and J. Meyer, J., 1990, Privatizing and Deregulating Local Bus Services: Lessons from Britain's Buses, *Journal of the American Planning Association*, 56(1), 9-21.

Great Britain, Department of Transport, 1984, *Buses*, Cmnd 9300, HMSO, London.

Great Britain, Department of Transport, 1991, Bus and Coach Statistics, Great Britain 1990/91, *Transport Statistics Report*, November, HMSO, London.

Gwilliam, K.M., Nash, C.A., and P.J. Mackie, P.J., 1985a, Deregulating the Bus Industry in Britain - The Case Against, *Transport Reviews*, 5, 105-132.

Gwilliam, K.M., Nash, C.A., and Mackie, P.J., 1985b, Deregulating the Bus Industry in Britain: A Rejoinder, *Transport Reviews*, 5, 215-222.

Hensher, D., 1987, Productive Efficiency and Ownership of Urban Bus Services, *Transportation*, 14, 209-225.

Kahn, A.E., 1988, Surprises in Airline Deregulation, *American Economic Review*, 78(2), 316-322.

Morrison, S., and C. Winston, 1987, Empirical Implications and Tests of the Contestability Hypothesis, *Journal of Law and Economics*, 30(1), 53-66.

Robbins, D., and P.R. White, 1985, Deregulation of Express Coach Services: Has the 1980 Act Worked? in Harrison A.J. and Gretton J. (eds.), *Transport UK 1985: An Economic, Social and Policy Audit,* Newbury, Policy Journals, 65-72.

Salop, S., 1979, Strategic Entry Deterrence, *American Economic Review*, 69(2), 335-338.

Stigler, G.J., 1975, *The Citizen and the State: Essays on Regulation*, University of Chicago Press, Chicago.

Tyson, W.J., 1990, Effects of Deregulation on Service Coordination in the Metropolitan Areas, *Journal of Transport Economics and Policy*, 24(3), 283-294.

White, P.R., 1991, *Three Years' Experience of Bus Service Deregulation in Britain*, Paper Presented at the Second International Conference on Privatization and Deregulation in Passenger Transport, Tampere, Finland, June.

TRANSPORT IN A UNIFIED EUROPE. Policies and Challenges.
D. Banister and J. Berechman (Editors)

Chapter Four

HIGH SPEED RAILWAYS IN EUROPE

Jose M. Viegas
Ulrich Blum

1. Introduction

Much has been written and discussed about the existing High Speed Railway (HSR) lines and their generally good technical performance and market acceptance, as well as about the configurations foreseen for the global European Network of HSR. This chapter begins from the recognition of those merits, and tries to focus attention on the process building towards that global network. It tries to identify the motives and consequences of the network expansion priorities that will be defined along the way, as well as the main difficulties and contradictions likely to be encountered.

The global political environment is favorable for the expansion of the European HSR network because the HSR is perceived as providing a good competitive advantage for the cities and regions served (Harris Research Institute, 1992), as well as being an environmentally sounder transport mode than the airplane and the private car, which are its direct competitors.

To a significant extent, the market potential of the HSR in the lines already built is reinforced by the fact that although high speed is only achievable in the purpose built sections of the track, the same trains can travel in the "normal" tracks. This flexibility allows specific terminals sections of a long distance service to be served with great advantage (without any transfer for the passengers), even if those sections have not had their infrastructure rebuilt.

Nevertheless, the cost of building the new infrastructure for the HSR is so high that several countries (such as Sweden, Italy, and Portugal) have opted for an intermediate speed system, using tilt trains on the previously existing infrastructure, with only relatively cheap track improvements. Although the speed range on these systems is around 200 to 250 kilometers/hour, compared to the 300 to 350 kilometers/hour of the HSR, their competitiveness with the private car is already firmly established for distances above 200 kilometers, and the investment cost is substantially lower than that needed for a real HSR system. The cost ratio between these two options varies strongly depending on whether there is a previously existing track (and on what condition) or whether a new right of way that has to be established.

According to information directly supplied by ABB (one of the major suppliers of this technology), an existing track in good condition (such as the Goteborg-Stockholm line in Sweden) can be upgraded at a cost of US$ 0.2 million per kilometer, which represents only 5 percent of the cost of the Paris-Lyon TGV HSR line (US$ 4.0 million per kilometer), itself a very favorable case for a new construction. More generally, the upgrading of an existing line would probably cost around 30 to 40 percent of the cost of a line built to HSR standards. This improved standard would allow tilting trains to operate.

In the meantime, several HSR lines have been built, first in France, then in Germany and Spain, and the Channel Tunnel about to be completed as a vital link in the connection between Great Britain and the Paris-Brussels-Cologne-Amsterdam (PBKA) line, making a high speed system. Only a relatively small part of this system will be built to HSR standards at the expected opening date of the tunnel (1994).

Technical progress has been substantial: energy consumption per seat kilometer at 300 kilometers/hour is now the same as in the early 1980s at speeds of 160 kilometers/hour; top speeds in operation go as high as 350 kilometers/hour seating capacity has been increased significantly with doubledecker trains; command and control systems now allow headways of 3 minutes at 300 kilometers/hour (Couvert, 1992).

In parallel with this progress on the "wheel on rail" systems, magnetic levitation has also shown great advances, both at overcoming some technical problems and at reaching very high top speeds. This system is still under active investigation in Germany and seems capable of greater efficiency at higher speeds (around 500 kilometers/hour), with lower energy consumption and a smaller curve radius. Even if its introduction is hampered by a total incompatibility with the existing tracks, the technical and financial strength of its developers and of the German government may be capable of assuring it a significant presence, probably associated with a feeder role in the network of larger airports.

2. The Current Position with Respect to the Expansion of the Network

In the preparation process, the UIC (Union Internationale des Chemins de Fer) and the CCFE (Community of European Railways) have been natural and strong advocates of this innovation, establishing study groups and committees in order to address the main problems identified. Two major issues have emerged: the financial problem -- how are the enormous costs to be covered, and the technical problems -- mainly related to issues of compatibility.

In the financial area, the problem is simply that the investment costs for the network are too high to be supported by government budgets alone, and the expected traffic related revenues are insufficient in all but a small number of lines to cover running costs and repayment of the investment. This implies the creation of public-private partnerships, but the dimension of the projects, the project development risks (particularly those associated with construction delays, referred to later), and the fair competition policy of the EC may create substantial difficulties for the establishment of such partnerships.

In any case, it seems obvious that, with very different expected returns on the investment and very different risk profiles for the various lines, an array of financial solutions must be developed to ensure construction under the very different circumstances.

In January 1990, the European Commission created a high level working group, with representatives of the member countries of the European Railways Community, the rolling stock industry, Eurotunnel and the European Round Table of Industrialists. The mission of this group concerned the following issues (Commission of the European Communities, 1990):

* Draft a Master Plan for the European Network of High Speed Railways;
* Identify priorities for project development; and
* Select appropriate measures to ensure the necessary degree of compatibility of infrastructures, equipment and rolling stock.

Three subgroups were formed, dedicated to:

* The definition of the network and priority links;

* The technical compatibility questions; and

* The development of an integrated control and command system.

The Master Plan for 2010 was completed, including 9,000 kilometers of new lines, 15,000 kilometers of refurbished lines, and 1,200 kilometers of connecting lines. In addition, the whole of the electrified railway track of the EC will be accessible to the high speed trains. Fourteen main corridors were identified, and the group recommended a deeper study of the economic and financial feasibility of 15 key links, considered critical for the functioning of the network. These links, mainly located at border regions, were thus considered priority projects (see Map 1).

The questions of technical compatibility required a great level of attention from the group. As is known, national railway networks were developed independently of each other, with different standards, for historical reasons. The result has been a great diversity of both infrastructure and equipment. The whole system has been decomposed into over 100 basic elements, and for each the importance in the harmonization process has been established. Efforts have been made to ensure the convergence of legal, regulatory and administrative procedures which apply to the circulation of high speed trains.

The control and command system for the high speed trains must be capable of ensuring that trains from one member country will be able to circulate in another without the interruptions which might result in a loss of service quality. Since national systems were also incompatible, a three-step transition process was agreed upon:

* The onboard systems from the various countries will be present in all trains (this will take place immediately);

* After a period of about three years, partially harmonized systems will be adopted through adaptation of common or compatible elements in the national systems; and

* Over a longer term (7 to 11 years), a unified European system of control and command (ETCS, European Train Control System) will be defined and adopted by all new trains.

This transition process is seen as a pragmatic approach to solving the problem of uninterrupted services when crossing borders, but the cost it imposes on the trains is considerable. There will be strong opposition among the producers of the national systems of the main European countries in adopting their systems as a European system, and this can cause delays in the harmonization process. Only pressure from the transport suppliers can be effective if the above-mentioned timetable is to be respected.

Inter-operability of high speed trains is a major concern of the European Commission and of the railway companies in general. It addresses the issue of regulations, technical, and operational conditions that must be satisfied to assure the uninterrupted circulation of these trains in the whole HSR network without limitation by their design specifications. Work is still going on towards the approval of an inter-operability EC directive (Mourareau, 1992).

Another important problem area that must be dealt with is related to the substantial increase expected in international traffic. To a large extent, "border effects" have been identified in the relations between most European countries. It is expected that the suppression of administrative borders and the increase in the quality of supply given (among others) by HSR will be instrumental for the elimination or strong attenuation of those effects. But this increase of international traffic will create difficult problems, among which are those related to the setting-up of timetables and to the working conditions of the drivers and train masters.

The difficulty with timetables arises from the fact that international trains will be much more prevalent, so that the importance of finetuning of their frequencies and departure times will be much more crucial for their commercial success that they had been. This will create tension with domestic trains (particularly inter-city trains), which up to now always had first choice in picking their preferred time slots.

As for drivers and train masters, the usual practice in international trains was to change crews at the borders. The train is always allocated to a national crew of the country where it was travelling. But high speed trains will not stop at the borders, and so this practice will have to change. Apparently, the favored solution is one of interpenetration of the crews in the networks of the different countries along a line, which not only signifies great changes in habits and attitudes, but also raises other types of problems. These include thorough training so that drivers will be perfectly familiar with the signalization and safety rules of the other countries; personnel qualifications must be harmonized; and languages must be learned.

Since working conditions and corporate relations are very different in the various countries, it was decided in the Tunnel services to keep them differentiated by nationality (Southgate, 1992). This is probably the easiest solution at the start of the service, but it will inevitably raise problems in the future when crews with similar qualifications, performing identical jobs in the same trains, face different pay levels and social security benefits. A unified scheme must be perceived as inevitable, even if that means that those crew members are considered as temporarily detached from their national railway companies.

3. The Environmental Question

One of the key arguments in favor of HSR is its benign relation with the environment, at least when compared with its competing modes, the airplane and the private car. Still, even if the balance seems clear when questions are considered globally, construction of HSR tracks has aroused strong resistance from the inhabitants of the regions it crosses.

A comparison can be made among HSR, air transport and road transport with respect to the benefits and costs that each mode generates for the inhabitants of the regions crossed. Air transport is only perceived as relevant by inhabitants in the vicinity of the airports. Road transport can be seen as harmful (especially due to the noise created in high volume roads), but it can also provide a strong increase in accessibility when a new motorway is built across a region that previously had none. Therefore, claims against these modes come mostly from people with a more global view of their impacts. The exception to this principle relates to cases of regions where one existing motorway is congested and a new motorway is proposed. Local inhabitants have their access problems solved, but at the cost of some delay if they choose to travel at certain hours. They are already suffering the costs of a constant heavy traffic presence, so it is understandable that they do not want more of the same.

However, in the case of HSR, with the long distances between stations, most of the local communities close to the tracks running will feel that they have nothing to gain but a lot to lose in terms of their tranquillity, together with disruption of property rights and landscapes. Financial compensation for the expropriation of the land needed for the track will not satisfy their sense of loss in many cases. From a local point of view, HSR is probably the least acceptable of the three modes, and it is not realistic to expect that local interests will fade when people are informed of the great global benefits (for whom, they will ask) brought by this new system.

This issue probably presents one of the major difficulties preventing fast development of the HSR network in Europe, as it has an indirect effect in addition to the direct delay it imposes on the construction. The uncertainty it raises over the construction delay for new lines will strongly increase the financial risk for private investors who might be considering investment in HSR projects. Since the claims and objections to the construction of new infrastructure are normally raised by grassroots movements, they are out of the control of the Government, which cannot offer any valid guarantees that they will not occur on a given line. As private financing might be essential for the construction of the network over a reasonable time horizon, without proper management of this type of risk it is unlikely that implementation will take place.

The key problems for HSR in this area are noise and physical separation. Noise is a transitional problem, mainly due to rolling (up to about 300 kilometers/hour) and to aerodynamic pressure (above that threshold). Progress has been made, and ICE trains in Germany now produce the same noise at 300 kilometers/hour as their predecessor IC trains were producing at 200 kilometers/hour (Barsikow, 1992). But the best that can be said in this respect is that in spite of the increase in speed, the level of noise has not increased (or decreased). Physical separation is a permanent effect, and sensitivity is high particularly in agricultural areas. Solutions cannot be expected from technological progress and problems must be dealt with on a case-by-case basis, with a flexible attitude towards the access questions posed by the people involved.

The recent trend in the design of new lines has been to route them along the same corridor of another significant transport channel, in most cases a motorway. Even if the total width of this barrier expands, there will be only one barrier, and zones of little or no permanent activity because the noise levels will be the same for both transport modes. The best solution seems to be the construction of new HSR lines along the axis of an existing motorway, since the marginal impact will be very low.

4. Serving the Interstitial Regions

The only approach that seems likely to succeed (apart from systematic tunnelling to avoid problems) is to develop a strategy in the development of the projects that includes some real benefit for a much larger portion of the populations in the regions crossed by the HSR tracks. This can include a denser pattern of stations along the HSR line (with each train stopping only at one out of three or four stations), or the development of convenient feeder services along a traditional railway line, with a good interface to the high speed service.

Smaller neighboring cities might first compete and then collude to get this kind of skip-stop service (Blum et al., 1992). But, even if each train stops only at a small number of stations, the fact that the following train does not stop at the same stations increases the headway between them, and this lowers the capacity of the line. This will only be acceptable if demand does not require full use of existing capacity; otherwise, severe strains could build up (i.e., if those smaller cities were located between two very large metropolitan areas).

The repeated occurrence of these situations may lead to the future development of a train composed of ejectable modules (in essence, passenger wagons) that can be released in motion from the main body of the train to an exit station. Alternatively, these module could be started from an entry station into the main line, where they would be attached to the main body of the train (Costa Lobo and Viegas, 1992). When approaching an intermediate served station, the last module in the train would detach, decelerate a little, and take the ramp to that station, whereas the train would go on through the main line (without any need for proximity to the station). At more or less the same time, a starting module would be leaving from that same station along the exit ramp towards the main line, where it would be attached to the train as its new last module. This approach-and-attach maneuver is certainly delicate and requires the definition of safety concepts that are new for the railway world (where two running trains should never touch). Nevertheless, the potential it opens for new patterns of service seems worth exploring. It must also be noted that the use of this principle in a trip serving several stations would imply the displacement of passengers (with their baggage) within the moving train, at least for those not boarding at the initial station. This is certainly an inconvenience, but the advantages of the added connectivity seem to considerably outweigh them. Control and command technologies already exist to make this feasible, and the gain in service quality would be very significant, as all travellers would have a nonstop journey at almost constant (high) speed.

For the regions and cities without a station in the HSR system, traditional railways and motorways must play a very important feeder role. For this reason, it is essential that the criteria for the choice of location of new stations in the HSR system not be exclusively internal to that system, but incorporate the need for its interface with these two other modes.

Apparently, however, the need for an interface of the HSR system is currently being considered mostly by "looking up". This means that the HSR systems are exploring links with air transport rather than "looking down" to lower speed modes but with greater territorial cover. As regions with smaller concentrations of population start being considered, the need to capture more traffic in those regions will inevitably change this perspective on interface needs.

5. Regional Development and High Speed Railways

The quality of the accessibility provided by the HSR is undeniably seen as a plus by the political and business leaders of all regions in Europe. But some of them may admit that their region does not have the population or the location to justify connection to the network. If one looks at the map of Europe with the HSR network proposed by the Master Plan (see Map 1), it is clear that as long distance connectivity increases for the cities directly served in the network, the risk arises that economic activities and populations in the interstitial zones will be subject to "suction" forces into those nodes. Some activities and populations will subsist out of those nodes, but they will be only local players.

This applies not only to regions that are not expected to be served according to the Master Plan but also to those waiting to be served, although only at later stages. At a time when industrial strategies are being reviewed and relocations are systematically considered, being on the waiting list may be worse than not being on the list at all, as the latter possibility will certainly try to develop alternative accessibility strategies. This is an important point that must be considered by the EC in its regional policy. Over the next decade, this new transport mode will probably be a major factor in creating imbalances in accessibility across European regions.

Regions not (yet) served must be capable of developing their own accessibility profiles based on other modes, either alone or in conjunction with HSR. They must argue that these infrastructures should be given the same level of financial support that will be given for HSR lines in competing regions. Multi-modal articulation is vital, not only for the correct and timely construction of new HSR lines, but also to ensure a minimum level of balanced accessibility to the regions left out (or left for later) in the Master Plan.

6. Competition with Other Modes

For the ranges where HSR is seen as most effective (from a few hundred to almost 1000 kilometers), its competitors are the private car and the airplane. The discussion about competition often tends to be rather vague as there are, for this specific distance range, clearly different market segments, each with different prevailing reasons of mode choice.

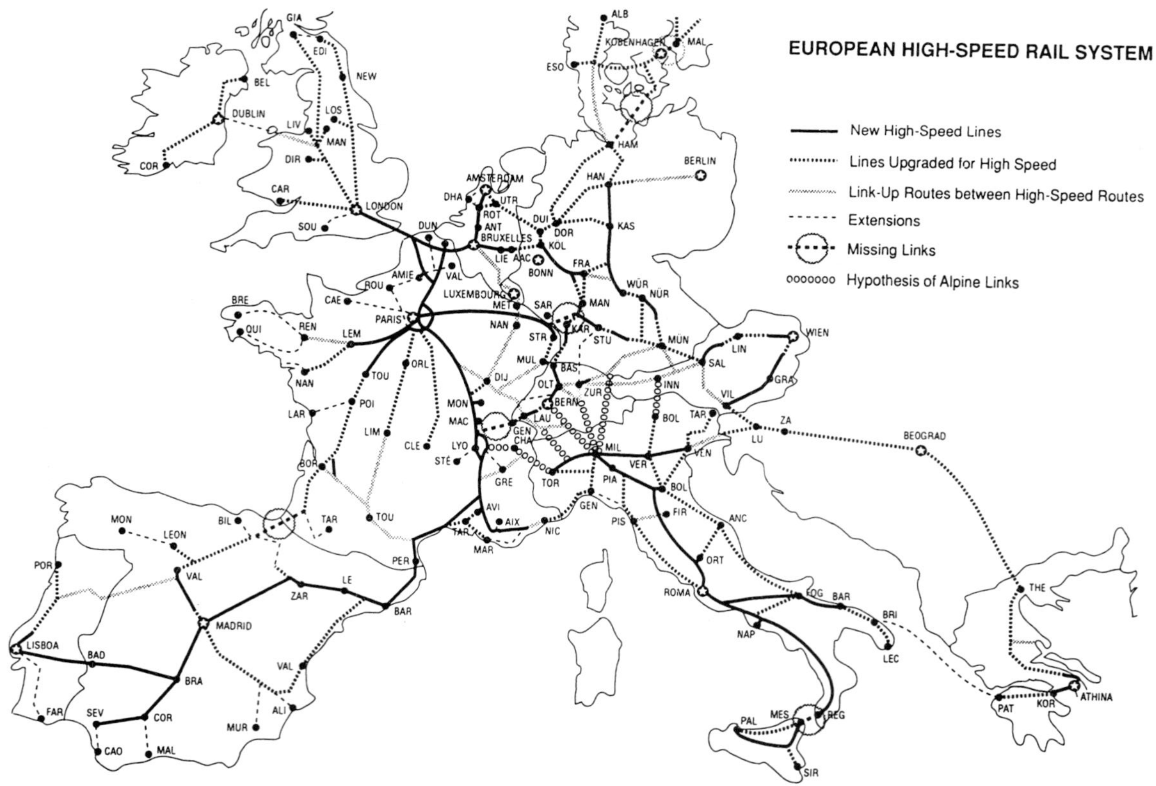

FIGURE 1 Master Plan for 2010

Source: European Conference of Ministers of Transport (1992).

In spite of this difficulty, and putting price aside for a moment, key attributes for most segments in this competition seem to be:

* Journey time (advantage airplane);

* Flexibility of departure times on the original and the return trip (the private car advantage); and

* Ease of access to final destination (the private car advantage); reliability of arrival time estimates (the train advantage), safety (the train advantage).

From this short list, it is possible to see that the attributes in which the train ranks first are connected to its low risk profile, both in terms of accidents and of time deviation. But to reach a successful presence in the market, it must be a close second in most domains where it cannot be first.

By approaching the journey times for the airplane, the HSR has gained market share. But in order to compete with the private car in the time flexibility dimension, it must ensure high frequencies of service throughout the day, without which its advantage on journey time over the car can be lost. Also, to compete with the car in its advantage on local access, the HSR networks must be connected to very good quality urban public transport networks, namely underground networks.

Other attributes exist which can be decisive for some travellers, particularly when choosing between rail and air. These include: the ease of reservation and purchase of a seat, and the quality of service on board, both of which are important "second level" factors. Railway companies in many countries must make an effort to match the service levels of the aviation world, which is much more accustomed to a competitive environment.

Price is a more complex issue when a comparison is made between the private car and collective transport modes. Not only is there the well known fact that private car users usually under-perceive the real cost of their car trips but, in this distance range, many of the trips will be family trips. Very often the pricing policies of railway companies for the higher speed services (i.e., inter-city and high speed) focus too narrowly on the business traveller in comparing the cost of the train, the plane and the car for the individual traveller. But a family of 3 or 4 travelling together has a marginal cost which is practically nil on the car yet rises almost linearly (for most cases) in the two other modes. Capturing family traffic will certainly imply not only some imaginative price setting, but also the design of inclusive packages that allow the family to retain its mobility on destination (i.e., car rental, local public transport subscriptions, etc.). A possible scheme for cost minimization and rational resource utilization would be to induce the family to have their own car available for local use by other tourists (with full insurance), and a deduction on the price of their own vacation.

Competition with the airplane should be based on trying to outdo that mode on all aspects except journey time, with a particular emphasis on the frequency of service and connections with the urban transport networks, as well as the ease of booking and quality of service on board. The key message that the train can transmit to its advantage is "no time need be lost" (in waiting lounges, in connections, or even on board).

In a study commissioned by the EC and the CCFE, the market of long distance passenger transport by all modes in Western Europe has been analyzed. The key results are presented in Morellet and Mueck (1992) and include an interesting picture of the situation in 1988, as well as a projection for 2010. The main points of the 1988 situation are the following:

* Air transport has a significant market share (13 percent), a good part of which is due to the charter flights to southern Europe as part of holiday traffic;

* International traffic within the 14 CCFE countries, the Balkans and Scandinavia accounts only for 30 percent of total passenger-kilometers made on long distance journeys; and

* The market share of railways is 18 percent for domestic traffic in CCFE countries; it declines to 10 percent in international traffic for the same market.

For the estimation of the 2010 situation, demographic and employment data have been projected, in parallel with the evolution of motorization, economic growth, and transport supply conditions. The main changes found in the scenario without the HSR network are an increase in the difficulty (and cost) of travel by the private car, and thus a relatively small increase in global mobility as measured in passenger-kilometers (+1.9 percent). Market shares change little, with only a small transfer from the private car to the airplane. When the construction of the HSR network is considered, the models described in that study predict only a small increase (2 percent) in total mobility compared to the 2010 scenario without this network but a strong transfer of passengers between modes. The total number of passenger-kilometers per year by train in this distance range will increase from 188 to 286 billion (52 percent), the gain being due to transfer from the private car (41 percent) and the airplane (32 percent), and only 27 percent due to induced traffic or choice of farther destinations. The final market share of the train thus becomes 22.6 percent instead of the 16 percent it had been in 1988 or the 15.2 percent for 2010 without the HSR network. In all cases, the private car clearly remains the dominant mode.

When these traffic volumes are separated by motive (professional versus personal), it is seen that the main growth in relative terms is due to professional traffic. For this sector, the construction of the HSR network implies a growth in passenger-kilometers in 2010 (between the scenarios with and without the HSR) of 103 percent, against 42 percent for personal traffic. The latter group is more difficult to entice out of the private car; this is explained mainly by the price factor referred to above.

7. Financing the Construction and Operation of the HSR Network

As outlined above, financing of most of the lines proposed in the HSR Master Plan will be difficult, not only because of its cost dimension, but also because of the industrial and commercial risks involved. The cost dimension of the projects and the low flexibility of government budgets jointly imply that if public financing alone was to do the job, the timetable for completion of the network would be much longer that anticipated. Private capital has to be enrolled to increase the amount of financial resources available and quicken the completion of the network. But the engagement of private capital must be done on a voluntary basis (i.e., driven by market competition with other investment possibilities). This means that private capital will only be mobilized for projects that appear to offer an acceptable return on investment. This involvement can provoke additional imagination on the project design and with it a marginal gain in profitability, but it will not perform the miracle of turning unprofitable projects into profitable ones.

The role of the state in such cases must be that of sponsor of the project; it must be responsible for the clear definition of the rules of the engagement of private money. It may have to underwrite some of the risks, namely those related to delays in the project caused by political arguments (related to ecological impact disputes) or economic hazards not under the control of the private partner (for instance, those related to inflation or interest rates).

The private partners can be made responsible for the detailed configuration of a project financing scheme. Part of this would involve a critical assessment of all financial aspects of the project, and the careful measurement of the risks and rewards in addition to the actual mounting of that scheme. Circumstances will vary according to location and institutional rules and habits. Frequently, the "project" being financed will have to involve more than the simple construction of the railway line and stations. Building the infrastructure is of little use if there is no HSR service on it; the investment cost on the trains is so high that they should be kept running. This means high quality regular maintenance of the track, associated infrastructure and rolling stock.

A striking characteristic of the lines that are operating presently is that a new type of train was developed for each of them. This is probably inevitable in the first stages of the expansion of the system as technical innovation is still very strong, and there is a strong desire for exact matching of the anticipated market requests between the different types of systems available. But, as the network grows and profitability of the marginal lines goes down, it is essential that some "prêt-a-porter" train designs are used so that costs can be reduced through economies of scale.

For the provision of transport services, high hopes are being placed in the engagement of private companies. But they will only appear (on an unsubsidised basis) if they see the market potential for the return on their investments, and that is not easy to expect in some of the proposed lines. Here, too, some risk sharing might be necessary, possibly accompanied by partial participation of the state in the cost of leasing of the rolling stock.

Costa Lobo and Viegas (1992) have developed the idea of a "peace dividend" at the end of the cold war, by suggesting the conversion of Europe's heavy industry (mainly in the East) for construction of the HSR network and rolling stock. If this is accepted, part of the cost will be absorbed by the state as the equivalent of what they would have to pay if this conversion was not made. The traffic threshold for project feasibility would come down and the pace of construction of the new network would accelerate. It must be remembered that this conversion should be started now, not in 20 years time, when all the social problems (namely huge unemployment) will have materialized and the actual worth of the factories will be nil.

8. Conclusions

It seems that High Speed Railways will not have an easy time in the construction of a European Network, at least in the short term. Traffic forecasts in several of the corridors described in the Master Plan will be under the minimum levels considered sufficient to justify the investment. The "obvious" links are the ones already built or underway. The rest of the network will certainly be subject to closer scrutiny for the following reasons:

* Some countries will develop transition strategies based on tilting trains;

* Cars continue to diminish their environmental pollution levels and their use of resources;

* The real environmental damage caused by airplanes will be investigated and reduced; and

* Europe is developing a new unified air traffic control system that will strongly contribute to diminished congestion in European skies.

Given the high investment costs of HSR and all these trends, the most likely scenario probably is one in which some links will be made in cases where the demand for travel is too great for the existing roads and where distance provides a significant advantage for the HSR over the airplane. But a decisive push for the construction of the HSR network as a collectively assumed goal is probably under risk of being postponed for many years unless it is collectively seen as the only alternative that allows governments to refrain from imposing too strong constraints on our habits of (unconstrained) mobility.

References

Barsikow, B., 1992, Une Stratégie Visant à Réduire le Bruit Ferroviaire à la Source, Actes Eurailspeed 1992, *Rail International/Schienen der Welt*, 6-7.

Blum, U., Gercek, H. and Viegas, J., 1992, High Speed Railway and the European Peripheries: Opportunities and Challenges, *Transportation Research 26A*, 2, 211-221.

Couvert, J., 1992, Le TGV: Un Système Techniquement Optimisé, Actes Eurailspeed 1992, *Rail International, Schienen der Welt*, 6-7.

Costa-Lobo, M. and Viegas, J., 1992, *Transport Policies for Regional Development in Europe*, Paper presented at the ISOCARP World Congress, Cordoba.

Harris Research Institute, 1992, *European Top Cities*, London.

Morellet, O. and Mueck, R., 1992, La Place d'un Réseau Ouest-Européen de Trains à Grande Vitesse dans le Marché du Transport de Voyageurs à Longue Distance, Actes Eurailspeed 1992, *Rail International/Schienen der Welt*, 6-7, 1992.

Mourareau, R., 1992, Harmonisation Technique pour la Grande Vitesse: Proposition de la Commission, Actes Eurailspeed 1992, *Rail International/Schienen der Welt*, 6-7.

Southgate, M., 1992, Adapter les Systèms d'Exploitation aux Exigences d'un Service International, Actes Eurail-speed 1992, *Rail International/Schienen der Welt*, 6-7.

TRANSPORT IN A UNIFIED EUROPE. Policies and Challenges.
D. Banister and J. Berechman (Editors)

Chapter Five

AIR TRANSPORT MARKETS

Sean Barrett

1. Introduction

Air transport in Europe has been highly regulated, based on national sovereignty and non-competing national airlines. Air transport between European countries was typically confined to the national carriers of the countries concerned, with independent airlines excluded from the market as were third-country airlines. The fares charged were agreed upon by the airlines in advance and ratified by governments. Market capacity was also decided in advance, as was its division between the airlines. This regulatory system was frequently criticized because it resulted in high fares and high cost airlines. The fares charged by European scheduled airlines have traditionally been the highest in the world and approximately three times those charged by Europe's charter airlines, which operated under a more competitive regulatory system.

Liberalization measures were introduced between Britain and the Netherlands in 1984 and between Britain and Ireland in 1986. In the remainder of the EC, gradual liberalization has been under way but the results have not been dramatic. Liberalization of the EC market is scheduled for completion in 1997. Agreement with the EFTA countries has also been reached for a free trade area in aviation encompassing both the EC and EFTA members.

Serious difficulties have nonetheless presented themselves in the way of a contestable market in European aviation. These include a series of mergers between airlines which might have been expected to otherwise compete; difficulties in achieving slots at hub airports for new airlines; predatory pricing; computer reservation system bias; ground handling monopolies; frequent flyer programs; and state subsidies to national airlines.

While aviation is not currently included in GATT negotiations, countries with large service sectors such as the United States have argued for its inclusion in future trade liberalization rounds. The competitive position of a unified European aviation system, compared to regions such as North America and the Asia-Pacific region, is important in any future liberalization of the sector worldwide. In addition, the economies of Eastern Europe have the potential to play a significant part in a deregulated aviation market because of their lower labor costs.

2. The Efficiency of European Airlines

2.1 Europe in World Aviation

Table 1 shows that the share of world aviation performed by European airlines has declined from 36.1 percent in 1971 to 31.9 percent in 1990. It American share of world aviation has declined 48.1 percent to 38.5 percent although its share increased slightly during the 1980s. The fastest growing airlines are those in the Asia-Pacific region, whose growth of the industry worldwide was 10 percent and in the 1980s it was 8 percent.

Passenger traffic generates two-thirds of international airline revenues, with freight accounting for one-third. Freight grew rapidly in the 1960s. While it's growth rate declined in the 1980s, it remained ahead of the growth in passenger traffic. Increasingly, freight is carried on passenger aircraft. All cargo operations have declined. Air freight is particularly suited to the long distance transport of goods with a high value-to-weight ratio. The increased location of world manufacturers in the Asia-Pacific region and the growth of product markets such as computers, cameras, videos, and medical and pharmaceutical goods have favored the development of air freight.

In the last 20 years, integrated carriers such as Federal Express and DHL have grown rapidly. They provide door-to-door service and specialize in carrying small items and documents. The development of just-in-time (JIT) production methods has focussed attention on the high cost of holding goods in stocks in warehouses and in transit. Air transport's speed over long distances and its reliability are important JIT advantages.

Doganis (1992) points out that "within Europe, most regional air freight is trucked by road. Europe's motorways are criss-crossed nightly by heavy lorries carrying 'air' freight!" (p. 318-319). The development of better road and rail networks in a unified Europe is likely to induce some further diversion of air freight over short distances but in a global economy with a liberal trade environment, the market for long distance road freight will remain buoyant.

TABLE 1

Regional Distribution of Scheduled Airline Traffic by Percentage of Total Ton-Kilometers Performed by Airlines Registered in Region, 1971-2000

	1971	1981	1990	2000
North America	48.1	37.5	38.5	41.0
Europe	36.1	34.6	31.9	24.6
Asia/Pacific	8.2	16.5	19.8	26.1
Latin America/Caribbean	3.9	5.4	4.7	2.5
Middle East	1.7	3.1	2.9	4.1
Africa	2.0	2.9	2.2	1.7
World	100%	100%	100%	100%

Sources: ICAO Annual Reports (1989): Forecast from ICAO Circular 222, The Economic Situation of Air Transport.

2.2 European Air Fares

Air fares in Europe have traditionally been the most expensive in the world. ICAO surveys international air fares each September in 17 regional markets and estimates a world average fare for eight journey lengths ranging from 250 to 16,000 kilometers. Table 2 shows that in September 1990, the average fare for a 250-kilometer flight was 70 cents per kilometer in Europe compared to a world average of 45.1 cents. The fares for the 250-kilometer journey in the Asia-Pacific and North American regions were 20.8 and 39.7 cents, respectively. The European fare was the most expensive of nine regions and the Asia-Pacific fare the least expensive. The ICAO survey in the 1990 covered 10,281 city pairs of which 3,098 were "local Europe" services. The rates of exchange used in converting the fares to US dollars were £0.52 sterling, 5.25 French francs and 1.56 DM per dollar. The margin of excess of European air fares over the world average for three decades is shown in Table 3.

TABLE 2

Comparison of Average Economy Class Normal Fares[a] for Passenger-Kilometer by Route Group and Distance, 1990

	Distance[b]				
Route Group	250	500	1000	2000	4000
World (Average)	45.1	35.5	28.0	22.1	17.4
North/Central America	46.3	32.2	22.5	15.6	10.9
Central America	34.5	25.3	18.6	13.6	
North America	39.7	27.9	19.6	13.8	9.7
North/South America		21.2	18.4	16.0	13.9
South America	22.9	19.6	16.8	14.4	12.3
Europe	70.0	51.8	38.4	28.4	21.0
Middle East	33.2	26.4	21.9	16.7	15.4
Africa	31.1	26.1	21.9	18.4	15.4
Europe/Middle East		27.3	25.0	22.8	20.9
Europe/Africa		26.2	23.6	21.3	19.2
Mid-Atlantic					20.7
South Atlantic					14.5
Asia/Pacific	20.8	19.1	17.5	16.1	14.7
Europe/Asia/Pacific			13.7	13.9	14.0
South Pacific					15.7

Notes: [a]US cents per kilometer; [b]Kilometers.

Source: ICAO, Annual Survey of Air Fares (1990).

In addition to being above the world average, European air fares are significantly above fares in North America and the Asia-Pacific region. In 1990 the fares for a 500-kilometer journey were 51.8 cents in Europe, 27.9 cents in North America, and 19.1 cents in Asia-Pacific. The European fare was therefore 46 percent greater than in North America and 171 percent greater in Asia-Pacific.

TABLE 3

Index of European Air Fares as Proportion of World Average, 1977, 1985 and 1990[a]

Distance (Km)	1977	1985	1990
250	129	126	155
500	122	118	146
1,000	116	111	137
2,000	109	104	129
4,000	115	96	121

Note: [a]World average = 100.

2.3 Productivity

Tables 4 and 5 show the ton-kilometers performed per staff member in 17 European and 15 North American airlines in 1990. North American productivity was on average 36.7 percent higher than in Europe. The ton-kilometer measure covers freight, mail or passengers carried for one kilometer. Passenger ton-kilometers are obtained by multiplying the number of passengers by 90 kilograms, which allows for the weight of the passenger plus luggage.

Measures of physical productivity per person employed should, however, be used in conjunction with wage costs. Doganis (1992) points out that:

> many of the Asian carriers now come into their own with labor productivity levels double or triple those of their European or North American counterparts. Airlines like Air India or Pakistan International Airlines (PIA), the least efficient users of labor in physical terms, are now among the most efficient in terms of resource costs. Conversely, among U.S. airlines, the high ATKs (available ton-kilometers) per employee are substantially eroded by the relatively higher wage levels so that their ATK's per $1,000 of labor cost do not look so impressive (p. 134).

Table 6 shows the available ton-kilometers per US$ 1,000 labor cost for five North American, five European, and five Asia/Pacific airlines in 1988. The Asia-Pacific average is 2.07 times, and the North American 3.15 times the European. In an analysis of the total factor productivity of 41 airlines in 1983, Windle (1991) found that the U.S. airlines had a 19-percent productivity advantage over European airlines and that a sample of East Asian airlines had a 155-percent productivity advantage over the U.S.

TABLE 4

Staff Productivity of European Airlines, 1990

Company	T-km Performed (Millions)	Staff (No.)	T-km per Staff ('000)
Austrian	316	4,128	77
Sabena	1,045	7,340	142
Finnair	981	7,127	138
Air France	6,873	39,810	173
UTA	1,146	6,787	169
Lufthansa	8,211	47,619	172
Olympic	829	11,906	70
Aer Lingus	402	5,945	68
Alitalia	2,933	19,348	152
KLM	4,328	24,247	178
TAP	794	9,711	82
SAS	2,564	22,180	116
Iberia	2,587	28,843	90
Swissair	2,542	19,296	132
British Airways	5,769	50,008	115
Dan Air	499	3,843	130
Virgin	492	1,399	352
Total	36,037	300,545	120
Average of 17	2,120	17,679	120

Source: ICAO, Civil Aviation Statistics of the World (1991).

TABLE 5

Staff Productivity of North American Airlines, 1990

Company	T-km Performed (Millions)	Staff (No.)	T-km per Staff ('000)
Air Canada	3,362	22,622	149
American Airlines	12,845	85,915	150
Canadian	2,712	17,832	152
Eastern	2,653	19,075	139
Delta	9,829	64,791	152
Continental	4,857	33,533	145
Alaska	459	5,822	79
Northwest	10,019	35,775	282
Pan American	5,873	28,823	204
American West	1,769	12,764	139
Hawaiian	498	2,808	177
Midway	732	5,171	142
TWA	6,019	33,189	181
United	13,186	70,179	188
US Air	5,559	50,464	110
Total	80,372	488,763	164
Average of 15	5,358	32,584	164

Source: ICAO, Civil Aviation Statistics of the World (1991).

TABLE 6

Available Ton-Kilometer per $1,000 Labor Cost for Major Airlines, 1988

Region	ATK/$1,000 Labor Cost
North America	
Pan Am	10,800
Northwest	8,300
TWA	7,600
Air Canada	7,500
United	6,700
Europe	
British Airways	7,000
KLM	6,500
Lufthansa	5,300
Alitalia	4,000
Swissair	3,600
Asia/Pacific	
Thai	24,000
PIA	23,500
Singapore	20,900
Quantas	10,300
JAL	6,500

Source: Doganis (1992), p. 136.

2.4 European Airline Regulation and Economic Rent

The ban on new entrants coupled with output pre-determination and price collusion by airlines generated surpluses, or rents, for producers above the revenues necessary to supply air services in a free market. Rent is an allocatively unnecessary payment, not required to attract resources to a particular employment; it is a receipt in excess of opportunity cost (Buchanan, 1980).

Economic rents in aviation could have been eroded by competitive tendering for route licenses (Demsetz, 1968). With revenues determined exogenously, competitive tendering would have eroded supernormal profits for efficient carriers, increased productivity, and reduced costs. The rent to airlines from the operation of air services in Europe has a number of alternative uses. It might, for example, result in increased profits, increased pay, reduced productivity or the operation of non-commercial services.

TABLE 7

Average Wage Per Airline, 1989

Region	US$
Europe	
Sabena	36,785
Finnair	30,714
Air Inter	30,269
UTA	45,204
Lufthansa	46,393
KLM	37,869
TAP	24,786
SAS	47,554
Iberia	37,819
Swissair	48,435
British Airways	19,238
British Midland	19,232
Dan Air	25,657
Air UK	16,530
Virgin	17,727
Average (15)	32,280
North America	
American	44,526
US Air	51,176
America West	27,833
Alaska	47,550
Continental	37,094
Delta	54,219
Eastern	50,404
Hawaiian	43,447
Midway	25,336
Northwest	53,681
Pan Am	46,912
TNA	50,075
United	49,836
Average (13)	44,776

In European aviation, there is evidence that the economic rents of airlines resulted in higher wages for airline employees. Table 7 shows that airlines average wages in 1989 were lower in airlines which faced more competitive markets, such as those serving the United Kingdom. In markets where new entrants are blocked, "there will be no dissipation of rents... output will not be forced above monopoly limits and price will not fall" (Buchanan, 1980, p. 7).

In North America, deregulation has brought a two-tier wage structure. Wages in the established airlines reflect economic rents earned before deregulation while the lower wages paid in new airlines, such as America West and Midway, reflect the more competitive deregulated markets. In the established airlines, the two-tier wage structure links the wages of staff recruited since deregulation to those of the new airlines, thus creating a two-tier wage structure.

The OECD (1992) noted that "a study by Lehman Brothers Kuhn Loeb Research has shown that during the pre-deregulation era in the United States, the combined effect of government intervention in all its forms, permitted labor costs to increase at a rate which, within the productivity gains made possible by technological advances, was far in excess of the market for comparable skills."

3. Pricing and Cost Structures in European Airlines

3.1 The Causes of High European Airline Costs

Tables 8 and 9 show two studies of the excess of European costs over North America in 1981 and 1983, based on research by the Civil Aviation Authority and the Association of European Airlines.

In the CAA study (CAA, 1983), European costs were 98.5 percent higher than in North America. Five cost headings accounted for almost four-fifths of the excess costs in Europe. These were: Sales costs (22.9 percent); Route and Landing charges (18.3 percent); Station and Ground (13.8 percent); Fuel (13.4 percent), and Crew (11.2 percent).

In the AEA study (AEA, 1984), European costs were 74.0 percent higher than in North America. Five costs headings also accounted for almost four-fifths of the excess costs in Europe. These were: Ticketing, Sales and Promotion (26.8 percent); Landing and Enroute charges (24.2 percent); Station and Ground (12.3 percent); Cabin Services (9.7 percent); Maintenance and Overhaul (9.0 percent) and Aircraft Fuel and Oil (8.7 percent).

TABLE 8

US and European Airline Cost Levels, 1981

	Passenger Cost[a]			
Cost Item	Local Europe	U.S. Domestic Trunk	European Cents	Excess Cost (%)
Crew	0.99	0.47	0.52	11.20
Fuel	1.98	1.36	0.62	13.40
Maintenance	0.80	0.46	0.34	7.30
Depreciation	0.46	0.28	0.18	3.90
Route & Landing Charges	1.05	0.20	0.85	18.30
Station & Ground	1.36	0.72	0.64	13.80
Passenger Service	0.50	0.43	0.07	1.50
Sales	1.63	0.61	1.02	22.00
Other	0.58	0.18	0.40	8.60
Total	9.35	4.71	4.64	100.00

Note: [a]U.S. cents per seat/kilometer.

Source: Civil Aviation Authority (1983), Table 7.

Higher sales costs were the leading cost difference in both the CAA and AEA studies. Higher sales costs in Europe reflect the lower productivity of sales staff in European airlines. Barrett (1987) found that the number of passengers per airline ticketing, sales and promotion staff in Europe in 1984 was only 47 percent of the North American level (p. 45).

The second most important cost difference in both studies are landing and enroute charges. Since these are services bought by the airlines they will be examined separately later.

Station and ground crew and cabin costs reflect the lower productivity of European airlines. The Association of European Airlines study concluded that "the result of the significantly different route network, fleet structure and social environment in the USA compared to Europe is a systemwide rate of personnel productivity, measured in available ton-kilometers per employee, almost twice that achieved by AEA airlines" (1984, p. 13).

Fuel costs per liter in Europe in 1987 were 114 percent of those in North America (Doganis, 1992, p. 138). Fuel costs per passenger-kilometer are also a function of the aircraft type used.

TABLE 9

US[a] and European[b] Operating Costs, 1983

Operational Area	Average Cost[c] per ATK for 15 AEA Airlines	Average Cost[c] per ATK for 11 US Major Airlines	European Excess Costs Cents[c]	European Excess Costs %
Aircraft Fuel & Oil	12.8	10.1	2.7	8.7
Maintenance & Overhaul	6.7	3.9	2.8	9.0
Landing & Enroute Charges	8.1	0.6	7.5	24.2
Cabin Services	7.3	4.3	3.0	9.7
Station & Ground	10.6	6.8	3.8	12.3
Ticketing, Sales & Promotion	14.9	6.6	8.3	26.8
General & Administration	3.1	1.5	1.6	5.2
Unexplained Residual[d]	9.4	8.1	1.3	4.2
Total	72.9	41.9	31.0	100

Notes: [a]US Data: CAB Form 41 costs for American, Continental, Delta, Eastern, Northwest, Pan-American, Republic, TWA, United, US Air and Western; [b]AEA Operating data for 1983 for Air France, Finnair, Alitalia, British Airways, AER Lingus, Iberia, KLM, Lufthansa, Olympic Airways, Austrian Airlines, SAS, Sabena, Swissair, Turkish Airlines and TAP-Air Portugal; [c]U.S. cent; [d]Not examined in AEA study.

Source: Association of European Airlines, Comparison of Air Transport in Europe and the USA (1984), Table 2.

3.2 Airport and Enroute Charges

These charges account for a quarter of the cost difference between North American and European airlines according to the AEA and slightly under a fifth in the CAA study. Graham (1992, p. 201) estimates that the average airport cost per WLU (Work Load Unit) in North America in 1989-1990 was $3.86 compared to $11.37 in Europe. Table 10 breaks down these costs and shows that labor costs are the chief source of extra costs in Europe.

TABLE 10

Airport Costs[a] in North America and Europe, 1989/90

Cost Item	Europe	North America	Index
Staff	4.77	0.85	561
Other Operating Costs	3.87	1.31	295
Capital	2.73	1.70	135
Total	11.37	3.86	295

Notes: US$ per WLU (Work Load Unit).

Source: Graham (1992), p. 201.

The cost differences between North American and European airports reflect the different ways in which airports are managed and financed. Many airport facilities in the US are built and managed by the airlines themselves. US airports raise a higher proportion of their incomes from concessions for commercial activities such as shops, car parks and car rental desks. Since their customers, the airlines, did not engage in price competition in the past, European airports have had less market incentive to control and reduce costs. Higher airport charges to airlines were easily recouped in higher airline fares where airlines did not engage in price competition.

4. Dismantling Protectionism in European Aviation

Three major barriers to competition in European aviation have been in place for almost 50 years. These are the bans on new entrants, price competition and capacity competition. In addition, the industry has many anti-competitive practices which restrict the possibility of competition even if the major barriers were removed.

The Compass Report (1981) by the European Civil Aviation Conference revealed the lack of competition in European aviation. Only 2 percent of routes had more than one airline operating per state. On 93 percent of routes there were limitations on the number of flights per airline. Up to 85 percent of ton-kilometers were performed under revenue-sharing arrangements.

In the first phase of EC liberalization in December 1987, market access for new airlines was increased by provision for multiple designation of carriers on routes with 250,000 or more passengers. As of 1 January 1993, any EC airlines may operate any international route in the Community. Full access to air markets within other member states will be permitted in April 1997. Fares charged are to be decided by the airline from January 1993, subject to intervention by the EC and Member States in cases of excessive fares or predatory pricing. The 1987 policy reducing the safety net market share to 40 percent for the protection of weaker airline is abolished in the 1993 policy.

TABLE 11

Barriers to Contestability in a Deregulated European Aviation Industry

Structural	Strategic
Hub Airport Dominance	Mergers
Ground Handling Monopolies	Pricing Policy
Computer Reservation Systems	Frequent Flyer Programs
CRS Bias	State Aids

The results of EC liberalization measures have been limited. Airlines have successfully held the high unrestricted fares that they traditionally charged. Sorensen (1991), reviewing the period 1987-1989, states that "the take-off point for real competition has not yet been reached." Doganis (1992) also doubted that there would be real competition in European aviation because of infrastructure deficiencies at airports and in air traffic control, the likely dominance of the market by the larger European airlines, and the inability of liberal national regimes [in aviation] to transfer their policies to conservative states. Pryke (1991) stated that "if liberalization is not to turn out a monopolistic damp squib, it is vital that governments and the EC should do everything possible to foster competition and make airline routes as contestable as possible". Therefore, serious obstacles remain to a fully competitive aviation market in Europe. These are shown in Table 11.

4.1 Hub Airport Dominance

Hub airport dominance is the control of major airports by incumbent airlines via restriction or exclusion of new entrants. The allocation of airport slots is controlled by committees of airlines rather than by airport management. Allocations are made on a grandfather rights system and new airlines may be allocated slots at unsuitable times or be excluded from hub airports. This occurred at Heathrow between 1977 and 1991. All of the increase in passengers (from 22 to 40 million) was allocated to the incumbent airlines by administrative decision.

It has also proved difficult to promote both new airlines and new airports, such as Luton, Stansted or London City, which in 1989 attracted only 6 percent of air passengers in the London area compared to 61 percent using Heathrow and 33 percent using Gatwick. Airlines lose the possibility of attracting interlining traffic at the hub. It may also be difficult to develop surface transport links between city centers and smaller airports.

Established airlines can earn economic rents at the hub airports in their control. These rents may be used to fund predatory pricing elsewhere. To tackle the problem of hub airport dominance, Bailey and Williams (1988) recommend that "airport authorities need to make airport access available on fair and reasonable terms that give all carriers an equal opportunity to compete and that conform to the rights of private citizens to enforce these duties. Antitrust authorities need to look at carriers' abilities to extract rents based on local monopoly positions at hub airports, not just at national monopoly characteristics".

The first step in ensuring the efficient allocation of airport capacity between established and new entrant airlines is to transfer the slot allocation function from scheduling committees of established airlines to airport management, thus ending the grandfather rights of established airlines.

Slots could also be allocated by:

* Buying and selling slots with and without grandfather rights;
* Slot lotteries;
* Slot lotteries with ring fences for categories such as regional services, new entrant airlines, or other target categories; and
* Administrative allocations of current capacity.

The attraction of selling slots would be the allocation of these slots to more efficient users. For example, Heathrow and Gatwick had 31,000 general aviation movements in 1984. If a market transferred these to airlines carrying 100 passengers per plane, an extra 3.1 million passengers could have been handled.

Slot auctions would, however, place low cost airlines in competitive markets at a disadvantage compared to airlines operating in monopolistic markets. The auction system would also give airport management the incentive not to invest in extra airport capacity where it might drive down the price of the slots at auction.

Slot lotteries would distribute airport capacity in a random way between established and new entrant airlines. Constraints on the randomness, such as a share for new airlines, domestic feeder services, or particular international services, could be imposed.

Administrative intervention to allocate airport capacity has included the removal of charter airlines from busy airports, removal of small domestic services with low interline content, curbing general aviation and capping the frequency of services on a route per carrier.

In 1992, American and United Airlines acquired the slots of Pan Am and TWA at London Heathrow. The UK government allocated slots at Heathrow to Virgin Atlantic, thus eroding the advantage enjoyed by British Airways when Virgin operated from Gatwick. In the liberalization of UK-Ireland services, the competitive position of Ryanair was improved by the allocation of slots at Stansted instead of Luton because of easier surface access and more interlining traffic at Stansted. Nonetheless, the carriers with Heathrow access, Aer Lingus and British Midland, enjoy a considerable market advantage in attracting business traffic.

Airlines with grandfather rights regard slot reallocations as confiscation. In economic terms, the airlines are the customers for, rather than the owners of, airports slots.

4.2 Ground Handling Monopolies

Aircraft and passenger handling costs accounted for 12.2 percent of total airline costs in the EC in 1984. These services are typically provided by authorized airlines only. Since the authorizations are frequently restricted, a new entrant airline may face the prospect of having its ground handling carried out by a competing airline. The option of self-handling requires that a new airline has a sufficient scale of market entry to justify investment in ground handling equipment and staff.

An example of problems facing airlines in this area is the case of British Midland at Heathrow. In providing evidence to the Monopolies and Mergers Commission (1985) the airline stated that

> from its experience of handling at Birmingham, it thinks that it could have provided the services itself at just over half the amount paid... It believes that this difference is a substantial element in its competitiveness, and that it should be able to pass on the benefits of lower handling charges to its customers".

An open market in handling at airports should be permitted. The Monopolies and Mergers Commission (1985) proposed that "any airline without rights to handle its own traffic has a choice of at least two handlers neither of whom is an airline with which it is in direct competition".

This falls short of a full competitive market. The avoidance "of unnecessary duplication of share and handling facilities" is the case made against competition. The case is weak because the number of ground vehicles required to handle each aircraft will not necessarily change, and competition will increase the overall efficiency of the system. Parking areas for vehicles not in use could be financed by a type of "road tax" on such vehicles.

Ground handling in Europe varies from monopolies to duopolies and more competitive arrangements. It is currently under examination by the Competition Policy Directorate of the EC. An illustration of the problems remaining in the area is the award, in 1992, by the Spanish Government of a seven-year monopoly at all Spanish airports to Iberia. In 1993, the Competition Policy Directorate of the EC began an investigation of ground handling under Article 90 of the Treaty of Rome.

4.3 Computer Reservation Systems (CRS)

Travel agencies use CRS to access information from airlines on flights and fares available and to make reservations. Since deregulation in the United States, the proportion of seats sold through travel agents has increased from 50 to 80 percent (Boorstein, 1988). An airline owning a CRS can use it to supply information biased in its favor. It may also earn economic rents for use of the CRS by other airlines. Saunders (1985) found that "the return on investment for a CRS ranges from 24 percent to 95 percent" (p. 176). Despite attempts to achieve neutrality in the presentation of CRS information by the US Civil Aeronautics Board in 1984, complaints have continued (OECD, 1988).

The EC regulations for CRS require neutrality in their operation. CRS vendors must rank flights by departure or arrival time for non-stop direct flights; for non-direct flights, they must add the elapsed journey time for stopping and for connecting flights by order of departure or arrival time and/or elapsed journey time. Fees are to be non-discriminatory and cost-related. There is to be no discrimination on the basis of different airports serving the same city.

The EC code of conduct for CRS is policed by an Article 85.3 exemption from the Treaty of Rome. The CRS owners would risk loss of this exemption by a breach of the code of conduct. In addition to EC protection for the consumer, it is important that there be two CRSs in Europe. Pelkmans (1991) notes that "the new CRSs are owned by groups of airlines and hence would not seem to generate problems of market power (via control of information about competitors) as might be the case in the United States". In early 1993, however, British Airways admitted that it had used CRS access to approach the customers of Virgin Atlantic. Stricter safeguards or divestiture may be required in order to ensure contestability.

4.4 Mergers and Concentrations

The tradition of price collusion among Europe's national airlines means that new market entrants have a vital role in increasing the contestability of European aviation. In recent years, however, national airlines have increased their share of home markets by absorbing their domestic rivals. Borenstein (1992) found that in the U.S., "the short run welfare effect of mergers between direct competitors was probably significantly negative" (p. 58).

The acquisition of UTA and Air Inter by Air France in 1989 reduced the independent airlines to 3 percent of scheduled aviation performed by French airlines. UTA had been refused permission by the French government to operate European services. The contestability of European aviation was thus reduced by removing two independent airlines, potential entrants to international routes currently operated only by colluding national airlines. Within France, Air France had total dominance over its remaining small competitors on busy routes such as Paris-Nice. Airlines from other countries will thus find it difficult to enter the French market when the right of cabotage within France is opened up under the third EC liberalization package.

There are several other examples of increasing mergers and concentration in European aviation. KLM acquired an 80-percent controlling interest in Transavia; the contestability of the market was further reduced when Air Holland collapsed. In Belgium, TEA collapsed. In Britain, British Caledonian (1987), Air Europe (1991), and Dan Air (1992) have left the market, thus increasing the dominance of British Airways. In Germany, the collapse of German Wings in May 1990 gave Lufthansa a 98-percent share of German aviation. The remaining German independent airlines are confined to small regional services and charter routes. In Scandinavia, the SAS takeover of Linjeflyg in 1992 reduced contestability. However, potential competitors such as Maersk, Transwede and Sterling remain.

4.5 Pricing Policy

Airlines with large networks can selectively lower fares in response to new market entry and raise fares on uncontested routes. Kahn (1988) describes this process in the case of Capitol Airways as follows:

> I take perverse satisfaction in having predicted the demise of price-cutting competitors like Capitol Airways if we did nothing to limit the predictable geographically discriminatory response of the incumbent carriers to their entry, and in having rejected the conventional wisdom that predation would not pay because any attempt to raise fares after the

> departure of the price-cutting newcomers would elicit instantaneous competitive re-entry (p. 319).

Europe also provides examples of geographically discriminatory responses of incumbent airlines to new market entrants. The European Commission (1989) found that while the average economy fare between Dublin and major European cities other than London increased by 3 percent between 1987 and 1989, the London fare declined to 51.9 percent of the 1987 level. The Dublin-London route had new market entrants while the other routes did not.

The EC liberalization package of 1992 gives the Commission powers to investigate fares which are either too high or too low. The former provision seeks to protect the consumer while the latter examines cases where pricing is predatory in order to eliminate a low cost producer from the market. A study prepared for the Commission found that "there have not been detailed formal investigations of predation in the airline industry" (Dodgson et al., 1991).

4.6 Frequent Flyer Programs

Frequent flyer programs give passengers free air mileage or other gifts. Airlines with a large route network enjoy an advantage over smaller airlines. Frequent flyer programs are thus a barrier to entry. Humphreys (1991) notes that:

> A passenger maximizes his benefits by concentrating his flying on a single airline, thereby increasing the difficulties of a new entrant in competing with a price-matching incumbent. Incumbent airlines can also vary the bonus awards, for example by increasing them on routes operated by a new entrant, or even before a new entrant starts a service.

Levine (1987) proposes that the frequent flyer program benefits be treated as taxable income of the recipients. He states that "it is difficult to defend as efficient those practices which reward undisclosed distortion of choices by agents at the expense of principals. The principal risk is intervening to control them in a way that does more harm than good. Regulating these programs in detail would entangle the regulatory agency in a morass of complicated marketing decisions about which it possesses little information...". There are at present no EC plans to regulate frequent flyer programs.

4.7 State Aid

Two schemes of state assistance for national airlines has been approved by the EC in 1991-1992. These include US$ 2 billion aid for Sabena from the Belgian government and US$ 2 billion for Air France from the French government. The EC is also examining a US$ 1.2 billion recapitalization of Iberia while Aer Lingus has also sought assistance.

Subsidies to state aviation companies distort competition between the recipient and non-recipient state and private sector airlines. The subsidies to state airlines have supported the economic rents of producers. Lower cost airlines are placed at a competitive disadvantage compared to the assisted airlines. The protection of state airlines from the consequences of mistakes in investment, labor policies, pricing and resource allocation, reduces overall economic efficiency.

5. The Gains from Liberalizing European Aviation

The large margin between scheduled air fares in Europe and the world average indicates significant potential gains from liberalizing the market. The first major liberalization was the UK-Netherlands market in 1984. Doganis (1992, p. 104) found that "on London-Amsterdam the club and economy fares were only marginally higher than they had been in 1983 before deregulation. This means that in real or constant value terms they actually declined". He also noted "a dramatic proliferation of low promotional fares". In 1983 the lowest promotional fare was £82 return and there were only three other reduced fares available. By 1989 there were around 30 fares, and the cheapest return fare was £62.

In 1986 the Ireland-UK routes were deregulated. Average yields dropped by a third. Traffic on Dublin-London grew only 2.9 per cent between 1980 and 1985 but doubled between 1986 and 1988 (Barrett, 1990 and 1992). Significant new traffic was generated and about 6 percent of the growth was at the expense of sea carriers. Elsewhere in Europe, road and rail transport are strong competitors with the airlines. Doganis (1992) feels that "it is unlikely that deregulation elsewhere in Europe will have such a profound effect as the doubling of traffic in two years" (p. 105).

6. EFTA Countries

The European Civil Aviation Conference (ECAC) incorporates both the EC and EFTA states. As of 1987, the EFTA states have participated in ECAC agreements to liberalize capacity and fare-filing arrangements. They also participated in the ECAC code of conduct for CRS. The EFTA states also sought negotiations with the EC to have the 1987 package of reforms applied to EFTA as well in 1993.

Switzerland and Austria have obvious geographical reasons for wanting to participate in EC liberalization. Since SAS is jointly owned by Denmark (an EC member), Sweden, and Norway, these countries also wish to be associated with the development of EC policy.

Sweden deregulated domestic routes in 1992, with a 30-percent fall in fares on the Stockholm-Malmo route and a 15-percent increase in passenger numbers. The domestic Swedish monopoly of SAS and Linejflyg was broken by domestic competitors such as Transwede, Malmo Aviation and City Air Scandinavia. Early in 1992, SAS bought 50 percent of Linjeflyg for US$ 50.2 million. Norway's domestic market is shared between SAS and Braathens. As SAS has high labor costs, the liberalization of the Copenhagen-Stockholm-Oslo routes in 1993 will put pressure on it from both domestic and Scandinavian rivals and other lower cost EC airlines. Swissair, Finnair, Austrian Airlines and Icelandair are also high cost producers who face increasing competition after 1993.

7. European Charter Airlines

Charter airlines in Europe developed in a less rigid regulatory regime because of the wish of some countries to develop their tourism sector. Charter airlines have traditionally charged fares of about one-third of scheduled airlines and have served mainly the Mediterranean basin. In 1986, 18.8 million people flew from Britain to Spain, Portugal, Italy and Greece. The charter share was 78 percent, ranging from 52 percent on the Italian routes to 90 percent between Britain and Spain. The market success of charter airlines is based on high load factors, high productivity, and aircraft utilization. Doganis (1992) notes that the charter airline Monarch "got more than twice as many flying hours out of its Boeing 757s than British Airways did" (p. 182).

There are also large savings in ticketing, sales and promotion costs. Rather than operate expensive retailing offices and travel agents, charter airlines sell to tour operators. The Civil Aviation Authority data for 1988 show ticketing sales and promotion costs per passenger of £28.33 for British Airways, £6.09 for British Midland and 18 pence for the charter airline Monarch.

Charter airlines fill 85 percent of their seats as compared to only 65 percent for scheduled. Charter airlines have 15 to 25 percent more seats than scheduled airlines operating the same aircraft. Charter airlines also generate higher duty free sales per passenger than scheduled airlines.

The *cascade studies* examined cost differences between scheduled and charter airlines. Table 12 shows the steps in a cascade study. Table 13 shows the cascade analysis for British Airways and a UK charter airline in 1975-76. The studies deduct the various

TABLE 12

Basic Steps in a Cascade Study

	Step	Description
1.	Sales Commission:	These costs are not relevant to the charter service and are thus deducted.
2.	Tourist Class:	A first class service does not exist on charter flights and the effects are eliminated.
3.	Seating Density:	Allowance is made for the different seating pitch in scheduled and charter flights.
4.	Load Factor:	Account is taken of the effect of increasing the passenger load factor from 55% for scheduled services to 85%, which is typical for charter operations.
5.	Peak-Trough Ratio:	Charter airlines have a larger seasonal variation in passenger numbers and allowance is made for their resulting higher costs.
6.	Utilization:	Charter services are assumed to be able to achieve 25% higher utilization of both crew and aircraft than scheduled airlines and appropriate adjustments are made.
7.	Standards:	Account is taken of the costs attributable to the higher standard of service provided by the scheduled airline.
8.	Not Applicable:	Adjustment of those costs and revenues that occur for scheduled services but not for charter ones. These relate to two main areas: sales, reservations and advertising costs, and cargo revenue and bar profit.

Source: European Commission, Scheduled Passenger Air Fares in the EEC (1981), pp. 42-47.

components of the scheduled air fare from the cost differences between the scheduled and charter airlines. Table 13 shows that by adjusting down the services of the scheduled airlines they could produce a charter-type product at a cost broadly comparable to the actual cost of charter airlines.

The scheduled airlines have used the cascade studies to support the case that there are no significant efficiency differences between scheduled and charter airlines which cannot be explained by differences in the two types of product, i.e., scheduled and charter flights. Other interpretations of the cascade studies have raised issues such as why the scheduled airlines have not produced the charter product given the greater profitability of charter than scheduled airlines. The claimed extra costs of scheduled services may also be due to the lack of price competition among providers of the services. Sales, reservations and marketing costs may be high because of non-price competition. Unbundling the items in

TABLE 13

British Airways Cascade Analysis[a]

Cascade Steps	Route A	Route B	Route C
Total Scheduled Cost per Passenger	100	100	100
1. Deduct Commission	92	92	91
2. Tourist Class	86	84	87
3. Seating Density	77	80	83
4. Load Factor	56	59	60
5. Peak-Trough Ratio	60	62	63
6. Utilization	57	60	61
7. Standards	51	51	53
8. Not Applicable	36	37	39
Derived Charter	36	37	39
Actual Charter	34-37	32	35

Note: [a]The table indicates the reductions in cost in each step of moving from the cost of scheduled to charter aviation.

Source: European Commission, Scheduled Passenger Air Fares in the EEC (1981), pp. 42-47.

the cascade study and selling them separately would test the market to see if passengers wish to trade the purported benefits of scheduled aviation in the cascade study in return for lower fares.

7.1 Charter Airlines in a Deregulated Market

The existence in Europe of a large charter airline sector operating in a high cost environment but charging fares only a third of the scheduled airlines is an important source of potential contestability. The competitive impact of the charter airlines is reduced, however, by their lack of experience of scheduled aviation on the major routes in Northern Europe, where the potential gains from competition are greatest. The charter airlines would have to develop marketing networks to match those of the scheduled airlines. They require access to slots at hub airports.

While the regulatory distinction between scheduled and charter airlines has been blurred by the introduction of group inclusive fares on scheduled services and "seat only" fares on charter services, in general, the movement of charter airlines into scheduled aviation has not been a success. World Airways failed in the US in 1986; Air Europe and Dan Air failed in 1990 and in 1992. Britannia discontinued its limited scheduled services in 1990 in order to concentrate on its extensive charter network. While the scheduled and charter airlines appear unlikely to compete directly on the main scheduled routes, the extent of the competition between them depends on the development of pro-contestability policies by European regulatory authorities after deregulation.

8. Eastern Europe

The major airlines in Eastern European are Aeroflot International (Russia), Balkan Bulgarian (Bulgaria), CSA (Czechoslovakia), Malev (Hungary), LOT (Poland) and Tarom (Romania). Eastern European airlines in general have a significant opportunity for growth because of their cost advantage over Western European airlines, due to markedly lower wage costs. Eastern European airline salaries average US$ 4,000 as compared to $53,000 for employees of Western European airlines. The former would save $268 million a year over a Western counterpart assuming a common work force of 5,000 (Airline Business, June 1992, p. 71).

However, there are also significant problems facing Eastern European airlines. These consist mainly of (1) a lack of hard currency and/or a Western partner; (2) ageing fleets, as many of their aircraft were made in the former USSR; (3) a need to upgrade services in the air and on the ground, including airport terminals; and (4) low airline staff productivity when compared to the West. To illustrate the opportunities and problems facing Eastern European airlines, the airlines operating in the former USSR and Hungary are contrasting case studies. Of the 10,000 jet aircraft in service worldwide in 1988, almost 2,000 were Soviet built and used for domestic flights within the former Soviet Union. Aeroflot had a monopoly on all air traffic operations within the former USSR and had over 400,000 employees. It handled almost 125 million passengers in 1988 (EIU, 1990, p. 109). Table 14 shows details of Aeroflot operations in 1988, and Table 15 shows the traffic output and fleet data for seven East European airlines in 1988.

Aeroflot's monopoly has been broken up with almost 70 registered airlines in its place, all of them laying claim to former Aeroflot assets. Among these are Air Russia, Russian International Airlines and Golden Stars. However, there still remains a quasi-monopoly with over 40 of these new airlines owned by official Russian structures such as the Ministry of Transport. In addition, not all of the newly independent airlines have their own aircraft (Airline Business, May 1992, p. 28).

TABLE 14

Aeroflot Operations, 1989

	International	Domestic	Total
Passengers (million)	4.3	127.3	131.6
Revenue Pass.-Km. (billion)	16.6	211.1	227.7
Available Seat-Km. (billion)	23.0	237.8	260.8
Passenger Load Factor (%)	72.0	88.8	87.3
Freight tons (000)	68.0	3,162.0	3,230.0
Available Ton-Km. (billion)	2.7	30.7	33.4
Revenue Ton-Km. (billion)	1.9	21.8	23.7

Foreign partners are needed by airlines in the former Soviet Union to provide capital, services and marketing experience. In addition, demand is expected to rise by around 20 million a year for domestic and international passenger services (Airline Business, January 1991, p. 44). The shortage of hard currency is further exacerbated by the fact that ruble-paying citizens travelling abroad and connecting with foreign carrier services must be paid for by Aeroflot in hard currency.

Provisional figures filed with IATA in 1989 show that Aeroflot made net profits of US$19.4m on revenues of $1,884m on international services only. However, in order to build up revenues from foreign services, the airlines must improve their image among Westerners in terms of quality of service.

Most of the former regional Aeroflot divisions have little hard currency to invest in their operations. Because of this, they are hampered in attempting to secure foreign investment and it is likely that some of these independents will fold. In addition, poor management and lack of infrastructure have made these carriers unattractive investments.

TABLE 15

East European Airlines, 1988

Country	Airline	Pass.-km (Mn)	Employees (No.)	Jet Aircraft (No.)
Bulgaria	Balkan	2,279	3,954	48
Czechoslovakia	CSA	2,242	5,675	32
East Germany	Interflug[a]	1.6	7,500	32
Hungary	Malev	1,178	4,595	22
Poland	LOT	2,701	6,067	29
Romania	Tarom	1,669	3,250	32
USSR	Aeroflot	213,192	400,000	1,910

Note: [a]1.6 million passengers.

Source: Economist Intelligence Unit, European Liberalization and World Air Transport (May, 1990).

In contrast to Aeroflot, the Hungarian airline Malev is proving to be an attractive investment for Western airlines. It has been in profit since 1988 and is now less dependant on Eastern European revenues, having restructured its network to tap into the more profitable markets within the EC. Malev's situation is helped by Hungary's relative economic development. In addition, Budapest is a convenient geographical regional hub. At the end of 1992, the airline had proposals from five potential partners. KLM wished to buy a 30- percent stake in the airline. Malev planned to sell 19 percent of its equity directly to private investors on the Stock Exchange, with Government and employees holding the remaining 51 percent. A partner would help Malev expand into long haul flight operations (to New York and Seoul) and, in addition, enable it to get support from the European Bank for Regional Development. CSA had developed a similar link with Air France in early 1992 with assistance from the European Bank for Reconstruction and Development.

Because the Eastern European market collapsed and Malev had to focus on Western markets, traffic declined, with Revenue-Passenger-Kilometers (RPKs) falling from 1.63 billion to 1.23 billion between 1990 and 1991. In addition, passenger numbers dropped to 1.04 million from 1.47 million (Airline Business, May 1992, p. 57). However, a five-fold increase in local currency fares and a rise in hard currency revenues saw sales increase from $211.5 million to $289.4 million. Pre-tax profits rose from $21.7 million to $26.5 million in 1991. Part of Malev's success can be put down to the fact that Western aircraft make up 46 percent of its capacity. It has also made advances in terms of its services. It introduced business class on intra-European flights and extended its frequent flyer program to include foreign passengers. Malev has increased the Western European share of its capacity from 66 percent in 1989 to 91 percent in 1992.

CSA, LOT and Balkan Bulgarian are adopting a three-pronged development approach similar to that of Malev. This involves (1) seeking a partner, (2) developing an Eastern European hub, and (3) expansion of long haul services. However, some analysts have pointed to declining yields in Western Europe as one potential difficulty with this strategy (Airline Business, May 1992, p. 59). Another problem, referred to earlier, is that of the need to replace older aircraft within these fleets. FitzGerald estimated that Eastern European countries (excluding the former Soviet Union) would require at least 300-450 Western aircraft during this decade (EIU, p. 167). However, early currency convertibility has helped carriers to restructure their fleets. This makes these airlines more attractive propositions for foreign investors.

9. Liberalization of European and World Aviation

Europe has the highest scheduled air fares in the world and a tradition of non-competing high cost national airlines. While the EC has taken steps to liberalize market access, price competition and capacity competition the gains have been minimal apart from markets such as UK-Netherlands and UK-Ireland. Europe's low cost charter airlines are likely to confine their operations to holiday sun destinations.

New airlines in Europe face an array of obstacles to market entry such as control of hub airports by incumbent airlines, predatory pricing, state aid to national airlines, control of CRS by incumbents, and frequent flyer programs which favor large airlines. In addition, several potential independent competing airlines, such as UTA, Air Inter, Transavia, Air Europe, British Caledonian, Dan Air, TEA and German Wings, have left the market either through takeover or liquidation. The loss of these potential competitors has concentrated aviation around the national carrier in most European countries. National airlines have not yet competed with one another. If such competition were to occur, the loss of the independent airlines would be a less serious obstacle to contestability.

The application of EC liberalization policies to the EFTA states after 1993 is unlikely to produce major changes. The EC and EFTA states have traditionally had close aviation links. The EFTA airlines have had high costs but liberalization in Sweden may have some restraining effect.

Eastern European airlines presently have a substantial labor cost advantage over Western Europe. Liberalization of the total European market would present significant market opportunities for Eastern European airlines to become exporters of air transport with low fares based on low labor costs. The cost advantage would face erosion over time as Eastern Europe's airline staff sought wages and conditions now enjoyed in Western Europe. The cost advantage would also face erosion by EC policies of labor market harmonization such as is mentioned in the Social Chapter of the Maastricht Treaty.

The inclusion of services such as aviation, telecommunications, shipping, banking and insurance in future GATT rounds has been proposed by the United States, whose economy is dominated by the service sector. Aviation has traditionally been treated as a special case in international trade but the sector's argument that it differs from other international trade enjoys declining support. Widening the scope of international trade negotiations to include services such as aviation increases the potential gains from trade liberalization. Whereas in sectoral negotiations the potential loser or high cost producer seeks some compensating gains within that sector, trade negotiations across several sectors allow for compensation elsewhere in the economy in sectors where the country has a comparative advantage.

Europe's high cost aviation sector is unlikely to change as a result of EC and EFTA liberalizations. The impact of new low cost airlines and charter airlines is likely to be diluted by the structural and strategic obstacles to contestability. While a potential source of competition exists in Eastern Europe, this may also be reduced by factors such as general economic difficulties there. There are fears that a "fortress Europe" policy might emerge to defend Europe's high cost airlines from outside competition.

The main sources of such competition are North American and Asia-Pacific airlines. The latter enjoy a substantial cost advantage over European airlines and a reputation in many cases for high service standards. Their home market is the fastest growth area in world aviation and will exceed Europe by 2000. The overall efficiency of European aviation would be increased by competition from North American and Asia-Pacific airlines. A potential free trade area in aviation could combine both the European market and the North American Free Trade Area of the United States, Canada and Mexico. This would allow North American airlines to develop their limited fifth freedom services within Europe on a fully competitive basis. It would allow European airlines the market access to routes within North America which they have frequently sought. However, Europe's greatest cost disadvantage in aviation is with the Asia-Pacific airlines.

Global airlines are likely to replace airlines identified with one country. Transnational corporations have achieved dominance in many sectors of the world economy but historically there have been few in aviation. The exceptions were SAS, which is jointly owned by Norway, Sweden and Denmark, and Air Afrique, which is owned by 10 African states.

The adoption of policies of deregulation and privatization in the late 1970s and 1980s brought acceptance of foreign ownership of airlines. For example, SAS acquired 24 percent of Airlines of Britain, which includes British Midland. KLM acquired 14.9 percent of Air UK which feeds it Amsterdam hub from many points in Britain.

The movement towards a multilateral rather than bilateral regulatory system for aviation has also weakened the identification of airlines with individual countries. In late 1992, British Airways acquired 35 percent of Quantas in its privatization by the Australian government. It also unsuccessfully sought a 44 percent stake in US Air. The maximum permitted share of foreign ownership of US airlines has increased from 24 to 49 percent in 1992. BA also had stakes in Air Russia, Deutsche BA and TAT (France).

In addition to acquiring a stake in overseas airlines, global alliances have been formed by agreements between airlines. For example, SAS formed an alliance with Continental, Thai International, All Nikon, Canadian, LAN Chile. Lufthansa, Air France and Iberia also have an alliance, and Air France acquired a stake in Sabena. Delta has an alliance with Swissair and Singapore Airlines and KLM has an alliance with Northwest.

10. Conclusion

Europe's high cost airlines have enjoyed protection from competition for many decades. However, market liberalization and the change to multilateral rather than bilateral aviation agreements are increasing market pressures on the protected airlines. In addition, the privatization of airlines has paved the way for globalization, when airlines will no longer be identified with a single country. The advantages of the global airline lie in marketing and the ability to survive setbacks in particular markets.

However, there are still many barriers to contestability remaining in European aviation. The most serious of these are the control of airport slots at Europe's major airports and the use of geographical price discrimination against new market entrants. Barriers to new entrants in European aviation should be a focus for EC competition policy. New market entry is important because Europe's national airlines have traditionally not been willing to compete with other national airlines.

In the evolving regulatory framework towards free trade, the EC market will be among the first to be liberalized. The potential efficiency gains are large given the high fares charged and the economic rents earned by producers under protectionist policies. The addition of the EFTA countries to this area of free trade is unlikely to have significant price implications because the EFTA airlines also have high costs. Europe's charter airlines have achieved major cost savings over scheduled airlines but appear likely to concentrate on their traditional inclusive tour market. Eastern European airlines have major potential labor cost savings over those in Western Europe. A full free trade area in aviation throughout Europe offers Eastern Europe airlines important market opportunities in the short and medium term until their costs approach those in Western Europe. A free trade area in aviation between all of Europe and the North American Free Trade Area of the USA, Canada and Mexico would achieve the long-sought goal of

European airlines operating within North America. It would also protect consumers from a fortress Europe policy. In a global free trade market in aviation, the market leaders are likely to be the Asia-Pacific airlines, which at present have significant cost and standard of service advantages over European airlines. There will be strong market pressures on the airlines in a Unified Europe to meet the service and price standards of the Asia-Pacific region airlines.

In facing competitive pressures, European airlines will not be able to rely on government intervention to the degree enjoyed in the past. The most profitable large European airlines, such as British Airways, are likely to become global airlines. Smaller national airline, accustomed to protection and state subsidy, are likely to be absorbed by larger airlines in a liberalized market. Independent airlines will seek market niches where they can survive in the presence of large multinational airlines. In an aviation world of liberalization, privatization, and globalization, many of the instruments and targets of market regulators will be subject to changes even more revolutionary than those facing the airlines.

References

Association of European Airlines, 1984, *Comparison of Air Transport in Europe and the USA*, AEA, Brussels.

Bailey, E.E. and Williams, J., 1988, Sources of Rent in the Deregulated Airline Industry, *Journal of Law and Economics*, 31, 173-202.

Barrett, S., 1987, *Flying High: Airline Prices and European Regulation*, Avebury, Aldershot.

Barrett, S., 1990, Deregulating European Aviation - A Case Study, *Transportation*, 16, 311-327.

Barrett, S., 1992, Barriers to Contestability in the Deregulated European Aviation Market, *Transportation Research* A, 26A, 2, 159-165.

Borenstein, S., 1988, *The Competitive Advantage of a Dominant Airline*, Discussion Paper No. 280, Institute of Public Policy Studies, University of Michigan, Ann Arbor.

Borenstein, S., 1992, The Evolution of U.S. Airline Competition, *Journal of Economic Perspectives*, 6(2), 45-3.

Buchanan, J., 1980, Rent Seeking and Profit Seeking, in *Toward a Theory of the Rent Seeking Society*, Texas A & M University Press.

Civil Aviation Administration, 1983, *A Comparison between European and United States Air Fares*, Paper No. 83006, London.

Demsetz, H., 1968, Why Regulate Utilities?, *Journal of Law and Economics*, 11, 55-65.

Doganis, R., 1992, *Flying Off Course*, Routledge, London.

European Community, 1989, *Report on the First Year (1988) of the Implementation of the Aviation Policy Approved in December 1987*, COM(89) 476.

ECAC, 1981, *Report of the Task Force on Competition in Intra-European Air Services (The Compass Report)*, ECAC, Paris.

Economist Intelligence Unit, 1990, *European Liberalization and World Air Transport*, Wheatcroft, S. and Lipman, G., London.

Graham, A., 1992, Airports in the United States, in Doganis, R. (ed.), *The Airport Business*, Routledge, London.

Humphreys, B., 1991, Frequent Flyer Programs, *Avmark Aviation Economist*, 8(6), 12-15.

Kahn, A., 1988, Surprises of Airline Deregulation, *American Economic Review*, 78, 316-322.

Levine, M., 1987, Airline Competition in Deregulated Markets: Theory, Firm Strategy and Public Policy, Yale Journal of Regulation, 4, 394-494.

Monopolies and Mergers Commission, 1985, *The British Airports Authority*, Cmnd.9644, London.

OECD, 1988, *Deregulation and Airline Competition*, OECD, Paris.

OECD, 1992, Forum for the Future, *New Policy Approaches to International Air Transport*, OECD, Paris.

Pelkmans, J., 1991, The Internal EC Market for Air Transport, in Banister, D. and Button, K. (eds.), *Transport in a Free Market Economy*, Macmillan, London.

Pryke, R., 1991, American Deregulation and European Liberalization, in Banister, D. and Button, K. (eds.), *Transport in a Free Market Economy*, Macmillan, London.

Saunders, D., 1985, The Antitrust Implications of Computer Reservation Systems, *Journal of Air Law and Commerce*, 51, 157-196.

Sorensen, F., 1991, The Changing Aviation Scene in Europe, in Banister, D. and Button, K., *Transport in a Free Market Economy*, Macmillan, London.

Windle, R., 1991, The World's Airlines, A Cost and Productivity Comparison, *Journal of Transport Economics and Policy*, 25(1), 31-50.

TRANSPORT IN A UNIFIED EUROPE. Policies and Challenges.
D. Banister and J. Berechman (Editors)

Chapter Six

WATERWAYS AS AN ALTERNATIVE MODE

Maria Giaoutzi
Peter Nijkamp

1. Introduction

The European countries are increasingly showing signs of an integrated economy, in which trade barriers are gradually removed and spatial interactions are increasing (Bonnafous, 1989; Simons, 1990; Violland, 1988). The full exploitation of a nation's competitive advantage in such an open international economic system has long been recognized as an important key force for maximizing national economic growth. At this critical stage in the history of Europe, the potential and importance of network infrastructure for the development and integration of the European economy is increasingly apparent.

In this context it is noteworthy that Andersson and Strömquist (1989) claimed that each new stage in the history of Europe was accompanied by a so-called "logistic revolution". They distinguish four such revolutions:

* The *End of the Middle Ages*, when new banking and trade systems emerged together with the development of new transport systems (e.g., the Hanseatic League);

* The *Golden Age*, when new navigation techniques and trade agreements allowed a rapid expansion of the European economy;

* The *Industrial Revolution*, when new industrial mechanics had a decisive impact on transport systems (railways, steamships, cars); and

* The *Informatics Revolution*, when the new information and telecommunication technologies exerted a drastic influence on the development of modern logistic systems.

Thus, from the history of Europe it is evident that there is a close link between economic development and infrastructure (Nijkamp, 1988; Rietveld, 1990). The main question to be dealt with in this chapter is whether the potential of an infrastructure is fully exploited in Europe, in particular as far as waterways is concerned. Current discussion focuses much attention on bottlenecks and congestion in networks, but it may be more relevant to pay attention to the opportunities offered by (adjustments in) network infrastructure (including waterway infrastructure).

This chapter deals with the existence of important barriers (missing links and missing networks) in European waterway infrastructure. First, a brief sketch of some general megatrends in European transport and communication infrastructure will be given, followed by an overview of important transport policy issues. The evaluation of the European network infrastructure will be based on five critical success factors comprised in the so-called "pentagon model": hardware, software, orgware, finware and ecoware. Analysis of these five factors is relevant for both infrastructure in general and for waterways in particular.

Based on the pentagon model, we will explore the assumption that waterways offer an important but underutilized potential for regional and national development in Europe. This potential is at present hampered by many bottlenecks, although -- in view of recent socio-economic and political developments in Europe (the completion of the internal market, the reunification of Germany, the opening of some East European markets, the potential of both Mediterranean and Nordic countries) -- the awareness is growing that there is much scope for sophisticated waterway transport, involving both inland waterways and coastal transport in Europe.

Therefore, the chapter will also discuss bottlenecks in waterway transport, followed by an outline of new policy strategies which might improve the current position of this potentially important part of Europe's infrastructure.

This chapter is organized as follows. First, a brief sketch of current megatrends in European transport and communications is given, so as to provide a background for identifying trends and bottlenecks in European waterways infrastructure. After a discussion of five critical success factors in waterway transport, the potential of this mode and desired policy strategies are spelled out.

The general conclusions from these considerations are straightforward: infrastructure -- including European inland waterways -- is a prerequisite for further economic development and integration of the European network economy. Quality is apparently of more strategic relevance than quantity nowadays; therefore, infrastructure and transport systems planning ought to take pre-specified performance and service quality levels as a strategic point of departure. This holds not only for waterways but for all types of infrastructure.

2. Some European Megatrends

The field of transport, communications and mobility is in full motion. International commodity transport -- in terms of both volume and value -- is increasing, international passenger transport is rapidly rising, and international telecommunication is also increasingly gaining importance. From an international (i.e., cross-European) perspective, the following megatrends, which also have an impact on European waterways, can be observed *inter alia* at the European level:

* Despite many institutional frictions, there is an increasing tendency towards an integrated and open European market, which by 1993 will become the largest trade block in the world. This trade block will increasingly include EFTA countries as well. Consequently, there will be a need for compatibility and standardization in all modes of transport.

* At a European level, many initiatives are being taken to improve and expand the current infrastructure (e.g., the Channel Tunnel, the extension of the French TGV, the construction of the Trans-European Motorway, the design of an advanced European telecommunications system) so that all European countries will be linked to each other via a common and accessible network. European waterways may well contribute to the European network economy, including the links to East Europe.

* Internationally, the heartland of Europe is shifting towards both the east and the south, which has enormous economic and social implications for transport and mobility all over Europe. Furthermore, many different kinds of border problems

still have to be solved in Europe's unification policy. The linkage to the Black Sea from Western Europe is a first sign of the integrating potential of inland waterways in Europe.

* International spatial interactions in the form of physical movements of persons or commodities are increasingly influenced by recent developments in communication and information technologies (including telematics).

* The area of commodity transport is going through a rapid transition phase, especially due to the emergence of modern logistic systems. For both national and European freight transport, this development has far-reaching consequences, not only in efficiency but also in terms of social consequences.

Clearly, the above-mentioned examples of transport megatrends are by no means exhaustive, but they do suggest that the 1990s will require new policy strategies in which a meaningful blend has to be found between allocative efficiency, distributional equity and environmental spillovers (and other externalities) for both the private and the public sector. Such strategies are especially important in the highly dynamic urban and regional setting of European countries marked by structural changes in technology, socio-economic conditions, lifestyles, socio-demographic patterns and scarce (natural and financial) resources (for an interesting overview see Masser et al., 1992). Coping with barriers in order to generate competitive behavior in all modes will become a major challenge.

Transport and communications systems are thus never static but always in a state of flux. In general, transport modes -- like any other commodity category -- exhibit a product life cycle marked by phases of takeoff, adoption, market penetration, large scale use, saturation and declining market shares. Transport modes will thus tend to show a history beginning with a period of low volume, high cost adoption, followed by further expansion and improvement, and ending with general acceptance and widespread use. Clearly, in a way parallel to transport technologies, transport management styles will also exhibit similar life cycle phenomena. Technical change may intervene here by providing new hardware to facilitate better control or enhance the quality of information which is available to management.

Dynamics in transport systems may take various forms: shifts in size and market shares, inter-modal substitution or complementary transport, emergence of new transport modes, and qualitative upgrading of existing modes (rapid trains). Grübler and Nakicenovic (1991) have made an interesting historical overview of the evolution of many transport systems from the viewpoint of a life cycle approach. Based on a logistic growth hypothesis related to various technologies, they sketch the expected time trajectory of various transport modes. Clearly, such projections have to be interpreted with great caution. The lost share of waterways in these analyses is mainly concerned with passenger transport and not with freight transport. Nevertheless, such projections clarify the dynamics and structural changes in various transport modes. They also show that efficiency and a market orientation will be necessary to survive. Inert policy strategies will, by definition, lead to elimination of less appropriate modes, irrespective of the adoption of new transport and communication technologies.

Even if no new technologies become available in the near future, drastic changes in the flows of persons, goods and information might still emerge, notably for two reasons. In the first place, we increasingly see a shift in emphasis from isolated transport modes towards an integrated systems technology. This implies a more efficient use and management of all (sometimes competing) transport infrastructures, i.e., combined transport via roll-on-roll-off (RoRo) techniques. Next, it is noteworthy that an open European market will supposedly generate a high degree of international freight transport, commuting and telecommunications.

Clearly, in the long run, completely different transport systems may emerge to replace current ones as the prevailing modes (train, bus, private car) seem to be in the final phase of their life cycle. The current revolutionary changes in the field of superconduction may induce a new generation of rapid, environment-friendly and energy-saving transportation vehicles. An example is the plan to build new subterranean vacuum tunnels for commodity transport in Europe (Nijkamp, 1990).

It is clear that the production of technological trends is fraught with many uncertainties. Experiences shows that R&D and investments in the private sector will be oriented towards areas with relatively long term financial benefits. Thus, it is likely that new transport policies emphasizing efficient management and control, small environmental impacts, and a high degree of polyvalence may become the winners in the competition for new transport modes. Furthermore, the behavioral responses of individuals, households and firms deserve closer analysis as, so far, these factors have turned out to be rather unpredictable. Finally, it should be noted here that the evolution of transport systems is not only supply-driven (i.e., technologically determined) but also critically influenced by the market and by political interventions. European waterways offer glaring examples of this situation. Since the present paper will mainly focus on barriers and missing networks in waterway transport, in the next section we will describe some trends in this sector.

3. Qualitative Trends in Coastal Transport and Inland Waterways in Europe

Changes in the international division of labor are concomitant with a new pattern of international trade flows, especially by sea and waterways. Existing natural barriers impede the development of a common European strategy for the latter mode, while strong competition between harbors within the European community has recently prodded development of the inland waterways network. These also have implications for coastal short sea and deep sea transport. We will here discuss some trends in inland waterways, coastal transport, and port traffic, followed by some general observations.

The main trends in this field are diverse but indicate that many new developments may be expected. Consistent numerical information across European countries is not available; therefore, we will only sketch qualitative developments in various fields.

Inland waterways:

* Efforts towards unified rules for taxation, standards for infrastructure development, type of ships, cargo, dams, bridges, berths, draft of the rivers, speed etc., in all parts of the network (international standardization);

* Increased use of inland waterways and adjacent land as places for conservation of the European ecosystems (e.g., in the Netherlands);

* Integration of the network which will heavily affect transport time and its related cost through synergy and efficiency (e.g., via telematics);

* Segmented local efforts for infrastructure development accompanied by efforts towards a global/unified legal, economic and financial framework;
* Standardized systems for facilities in transit areas in all parts of the network (e.g., common carriage facilities);

* Increasing awareness of ecological problems resulting from the lack of environmental policy integration in the European waterway system; and

* Integration and cooperation between countries (e.g., the Rhine countries).

Coastal transport:

* A tendency towards removing all types of cabotage in order to increase efficiency; and

* A decline of fleets in the Mediterranean because of overcapacity.

Port traffic:

* Reduced oil imports, a trend developing since 1979;

* Increased imports of steam and household coal, and greater traffic in cereals and other bulk vegetable products. The last few years have been marked by the fairly widespread growth in bulk solids, although ore traffic (except in Rotterdam and on the Rhine waterway) has slackened or even disappeared;

* A strong upsurge in mixed cargo traffic, although the rise in exports from Europe levelled off after 1979 owing to the recession associated with the second oil crisis. Mixed cargo traffic is increasingly containerized, while general cargo shipping on board conventional vessels is decreasing;

* Small ports have increased their total trade to a far greater extent than the large ones, due to a combination of factors, such as modernization of port facilities and port linked overland transport infrastructures, and the development of the hinterland's industrial potential; and

* Geographically, ports in the Channel-North Sea and Mediterranean-Adriatic areas have developed more vigorously than those in the Atlantic-Irish Sea and Baltic areas. These trends can be seen from the overall traffic figures, although available statistics, broken down by freight categories do not enable specific geographical features to be pinpointed, except for the pronounced increase in container traffic in the ports of Southern Europe, which are making up for lost time.

General trends:

* All shipping categories are undergoing a considerable increase;

* Ship size and specialization are also changing drastically:

  - Increase in size (tankers, bulk, ore, dry cargo, general cargo),

  - The benefits from economies of scale offered by high carrying capacity are reduced by rising fuel costs,

  - Size and specialization of ships used have been influenced by the geographical features of shipping zones;

* Transhipment and cargo handling techniques to reduce turnaround time are being sought in both ship design, and loading and unloading, handling, and storage operations;

* Port activities and employment are also showing signs of drastic change:

  - Cargo handling is changing radically, leading to lower employment, but higher job status,

  - A number of traditional port activities, particularly ship operation and transport in the broad sense, are in comparative decline, owing to industrial monopolization as much as to rationalization. It is therefore partly a shift of activities to other sectors,

  - Keen competition among ports to attract trading and international transport companies. Key location factors are probably the creation of a suitable business climate and the development of maritime transport along new lines.

The previous trend observations have shown that transport by waterways is showing an extremely dynamic development trajectory. The waterway as a significant transport mode will face much competition and hence only increase in efficiency through a removal of barriers which will make this mode viable. This raises the question of the critical success factors for this mode.

Having now presented the main trends, in Section 4 we will propose an analytic framework for identifying barriers and missing networks, based on the so-called "pentagon prism".

4. The Pentagon Prism

Waterways are part of the European network economy. Networks generally refer to all physical infrastructure configurations related to transport and communications interactions. They are based on technical equipment, information processing and control, organization and management; the quality of services of networks has to be judged on the basis of their financial, socio-economic and environmental performance.

Networks consist of nodes and links. But transport and communication networks are multi-modal and multi-functional, and they extend across national borders. For this reason, a map of a physical infrastructure network does not reveal very much, even though it may draw attention to missing links. The map does not tell the story of what happens on the links and nodes. The problems that are met when trying to analyze the capacity and performance of these networks very often relate to the non-physical sphere. For this reason, a broader view on missing networks is taken in this paper. The notion of "missing networks" thus refers to the absence of strategic layers or components of Europe's transport and communication infrastructure, be they material or non-material in nature (Maggi et al., 1992).

In the past, the problems created by the reduced efficiency of infrastructure, caused by missing links or missing networks, have been viewed as pure infrastructure bottlenecks with only two dimensions: viz., "hardware" (physical infrastructure) and "finware" (funding). To view the foreseen level of spatial interaction in an open Europe, a more comprehensive way of looking at networks is necessary. In this paper, five basic dimensions of transport and communications networks are considered, all of which have their specific relevance for the theme of missing networks:

* *Hardware* (physical infrastructure)
* *Software* (logistics and informatics)
* *Orgware* (institutional and organizational setting)
* *Finware* (financial arrangements and funding)
* *Ecoware* (environmental impacts)

These five dimensions form a "pentagon of concern": a multi-layer view which is a pre-condition for the identification of barriers and missing networks (see Figure 1).

The above considerations also hold for European waterways. Without sufficient hardware (e.g., technologically advanced sluices), European waterways will not become viable. Automatic customs procedures (software) are also a *sine qua non*. Improved international coordination and standardization (orgware) is likewise a necessary condition for an efficient European waterway system. Despite the Mannheim Treaty, financing new developments is a major bottleneck for international transport via waterways, as user charges are prohibited on the Rhine (a finware problem). Finally, it is generally taken for granted that waterway transport is relatively environmentally friendly (ecoware). The above observations will be dealt with in more detail in the next section.

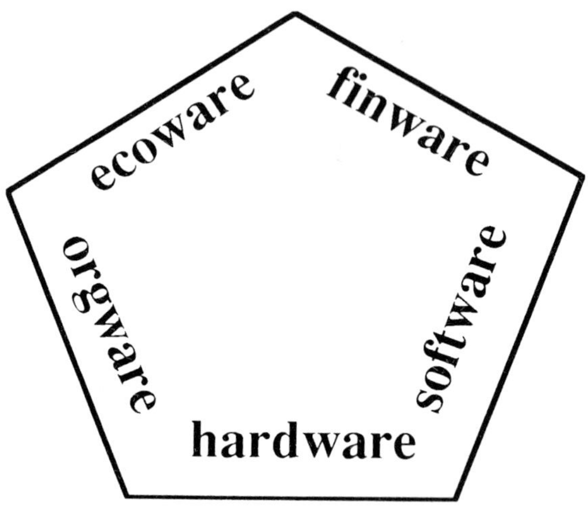

FIGURE 1 The Pentagon Prism

5. Barriers and Missing Networks in European Waterways Infrastructure

Following the pentagon prism presented above, we will present now a systematic listing of bottlenecks in Europe's waterways, based on extensive literature surveys on European waterways.

Hardware:

* Overcapacity and growing inefficiency, because of too slow a substitution of outdated, smaller, ships by modern, larger ones;

* Lack of standardization of dimensions of vessels and containers;

* Lack of demand-oriented capacity of ports, waterways and sluices;

* Unsatisfactory geo-nautical conditions (limitations in beam and draught, because of the varying channel depths and existing curves);

* Lack of sophisticated navigation systems (reducing weather and day-time dependency); and

* Lack of direct, multi-modal links between sea ports and hinterlands.

Software:

* Unsatisfactory statistical information on trade flows; and

* Lack of information in general and especially EDI-systems (market conditions; multi-modal).

Orgware:

* The absence of a competitive market structure (current freight exchanges) and high barriers to entry (ban on cabotage, transit restraints, national regulations); and

* The absence or insufficiency of government policy to induce efficiency in transport (e.g., by means of breaking up premiums).

Finware:

* Very low returns on investments in ships because of large over-capacity, providing a strong disincentive to investments;

* Lack of breaking up premiums to lower the level of obsolete capacity;

* Lack of investment in modernization of the existing fleet;

* Lack of support for the purchase of modern equipment or multi-modal solutions; and

* Lack of subvention of new building activities.

Ecoware:

* Lack of a European viewpoint and planning system regarding the environmental deterioration caused by transportation;

* Lack of standard rules regarding the transport of hazardous materials; and

* Lack of European-wide incentives to the development and use of environment-friendly transport systems.

The use of the pentagon prism as an analytical tool suggests the existence of many bottlenecks -- and sometimes even missing networks -- in European waterways infrastructure. This holds not only for inland waterways, but for coastal transport as well. Some elements of the latter will be discussed in Section 6.

6. The Potential of Coastal Transport

Coastal transport in Europe (especially in the Mediterranean) has gone through a difficult stage in the past decade (MARIN, 1985). Competition is high, although cabotage causes many inefficiencies. The modernization of the fleet is not a matter of technology but of market conditions, coastal transport policy, and improvement of waterways infrastructure (e.g., ports, linkage to other modes). Some figures on the development of the European fleet by flag and type during the period 1980-1984 can be found in Tables 1 and 2 (Giaoutzi, 1990; MARIN, 1985).

These tables have to be interpreted with great care. First, the number of ships sailing under a national flag has shown drastic changes which are different for each country. Next, the cabotage regulations which are linked to the previous phenomenon are different in European countries. This means that the tables are indicative only for the change in the fleet size in general. Nevertheless, the overall trend is a declining one.

It becomes apparent that the largest reduction in European fleets in terms of deadweight (dwt) took place for the size category larger than 1,600 grt and particularly for multi- and shelter-deckers. This fleet category decreased from 13.55 to 10.95 million tons during 1980-1984, a reduction of 19 percent. The fleet below 1,600 grt declined from 6.29 to 5.6 million dwt, a reduction of 11 percent. These figures are inclusive of the RoRo and

TABLE 1

The European Fleet by Flag and Type per Thousand DWT, 1984

	101-1,600 grt[a]		1,601-6,000 grt[a]		101-6,000 grt[a]	
Countries	Single Deck	Multi-Deck	Single Deck	Multi-Deck	RoRo and Cont[b,c]	Total
West Germany	227	992	131	342	263	1,955
Netherlands	326	307	40	314	38	1,025
UK	242	76	55	46	130	549
Denmark	75	338	5	95	64	577
Norway	143	239	67	26	74	549
Spain	190	170	353	276	219	1,208
Other West European[d]	183	206	135	209	517	1,250
Total N & Atl Europe	1,386	2,328	786	1,308	1,305	7,113
Italy	172	158	95	102	123	650
Greece	297	145	417	808	63	1,730
Cyprus	121	254	404	379	65	1,223
Total South Europe	590	557	916	1,289	251	3,603
East Europe[e]	274	55	3,446	1,790	266	5,831
Total Europe	2,250	2,940	5,148	4,387	1,822	16,547

Notes: [a]Multi- and shelter-deck; [b]Excluding RoRo passenger ferries; [c]With regard to the specialized container vessels, it should be noted that many of the smaller modern vessels, not identified by their container capabilities, are in fact "con-bulkers"; [d]Belgium France, Portugal, Sweden, Finland, Ireland and Iceland; [e]USSR, Poland and East Germany.

TABLE 2

The European Fleet by Flag and Type per Thousand DWT, 1980

	101-1,600 grt[a]		1,601-6,000 grt[a]		101-6,000 grt[a]
Countries	Single Deck	Multi-Deck[b]	Single Deck	Multi-Deck[b]	Total
West Germany	308	946	72	504	1,830
Netherlands	338	328	19	113	798
UK	462	162	231	345	1,200
Denmark	118	383	41	139	681
Norway	176	258	141	170	745
Spain	210	202	421	320	1,153
Other West European[c]	187	328	166	687	1,368
Total N & Atl Europe	1,799	2,607	1,091	2,278	7,775
Italy	181	202	97	260	740
Greece	443	225	1,083	2,440	4,091
Cyprus	164	264	253	699	1,380
Total South Europe	788	691	1,433	3,399	6,311
East Europe[d]	329	79	3,179	2,173	5,759
Total Europe	2,916	3,377	5,702	7,850	19,845

Notes: [a]RoRo and container tonnage included, except RoRo passenger ferries; [b]Multi- and shelter-deck; [c]Belgium, France, Portugal, Sweden, Finland, Ireland and Iceland; [d]USSR, Poland and East Germany.

container fleet. In 1984, the size of the RoRo and container fleet above 1,600 grt was 1,416,000 dwt, while under 1,600 grt it was 406,000 dwt. When the number of vessels is considered, the percentage reduction in the smaller size bracket is much larger, caused by the withdrawal of the 499 grt coasters. Between 1980 and 1984, the total European fleet decreased by 16.6 percent in terms of deadweight and by 17.7 percent in terms of number of vessels.

Nevertheless, international agencies (EC, ECMT) claim that the market position of coastal transport is by no means a lost case: its future potential depends to a large extent on network connectivity (i.e., links with complementary infrastructure). The large volumes of goods transported from Northern Europe to Southern Europe by road indicate that there is a market for large scale north-south commodity transport systems, and coastal transport (being oriented north-south in Europe) could in principle claim a much higher market share than it does nowadays. There are however, many barriers to overcome, and these will be discussed in the next section.

7. General Lessons for Infrastructure Policy

From the above observations on waterway infrastructure in Europe, we can derive some general lessons for European infrastructure policy. One of the common problems in transportation is the lack of standardization, both in a uni-modal (e.g., exchange of locomotives in trans-national rail transport) as well as in a multi-modal context (e.g., exchange of containers). The need to arrive at a long term transport and environmental policy aims calls attention to changing cargo and vehicle standards, the efficiency and costs of transport, and the costs of new investments and sunk costs; the potential for combined transportation is not helped by different standards. This means that standard dimensions for cargo should serve the transportation needs of all modes. Lack of standardization is not simply a technical question, it is primarily an institutional problem. National standards in a number of transport modes are in fact used to protect national vehicle manufacturers and transporters from external competition. This holds for all modes in European transport.

With respect to policy actions, ERT (1989) has suggested a series of items for a policy agenda regarding bottlenecks, inefficiencies and ineffective planning processes in the transport sector in general. Most of them are also relevant for European waterways.

Bottlenecks:

* Decentralization of political power in the last 15 years has resulted in increasing the number of stages and levels of the decision making process on transport issues. The transfer of power to local levels is a response to calls for greater regional autonomy. This also means that European waterway transport could become more deregulated in order to comply with market contestability.

* Bureaucratic claims to exclusive competence play an important role at the national level in decision making. Conflicts abound between finance ministers, transport ministers and administrators. A larger private sector involvement in European waterways also seems logical.

* Lack of coherence in the decision making process for transport infrastructure planning growing out of the conflict between long term transport policy planning and short term (annual) budget decisions. The ultimate result is at best a process which tends to focus on short or medium term planning. This situation is much to the detriment of European waterways, as they are often regarded as an outdated transport mode.

Inefficiencies in the Decision Making Process:

* Complexity has increased as special interest groups (environmental groups, local residents, and others affected by infrastructure projects) have become a permanent factor to be reckoned with in the decision making process. Lack of space in most European countries contributes to making the planning of new or additional infrastructure projects much more complex than in the past. Divergent interests contribute to reinforcing opposition to a global approach. Since waterways are relatively environment-friendly, they could strengthen their position from this perspective.

* There is an insufficient participation of the private sector in the decision making process for transport infrastructure, leading to a failure to mobilize the considerable resources this sector can bring to bear on many of the problems already cited.

* Many converging factors (budget constraints, economic uncertainty, inefficient and complex decision making structures, limits to the growth of transport infrastructures) have lengthened the decision making process in all European countries to some 10 to 12 years for major infrastructure projects. The Rhine-Main-Danube Canal even took many decades before completion. This suggests the desirability of a European Waterways Authority.

Ineffective Planning Processes:

* The lack of a "systems" approach for identifying long term needs and alternative solutions is a serious deficiency at both the national and European levels. Such a concept combines a broad view of European infrastructure problems and priorities, and the realistic, knowledgeable input that comes from being close to the problem. Such an approach could give considerable vitality to the planning

process and improve its effectiveness. Standardization is most probably of paramount importance for European waterways.

* The lack of a European-level body to facilitate planning and decision making inhibits the development of an integrated European transport infrastructure approach. A new institution should serve as a facilitator for the transport infrastructure development process at the European level rather than a replacement for national governments.

References

Andersson, A.E. and Strömquist, U., 1989, The Emerging C-Society, in Batten, D.F. and Thord, R., (eds.), *Transportation for the Future*, Springer, Berlin.

Bonnafous, A., 1989, What Will be the European Traffic Transportation in 1992? -The Influence of the European Community Single Market Consolidation, *IATSS Research*, 13(2), 64-68.

European Round Table of Industrialists, 1989, *Need for Renewing Transport Infrastructure in Europe*, ERTI, Brussels.

Giaoutzi, M., 1990, *Missing Networks in Europe: Shipping*, Dept. of Geography, National Technical University, Athens.

Grübler, A. and Nakicenovic, N., 1991, *Evolution of Transport Systems*, Research Report RR-91-8, IIASA, Luxenbourg.

Maggi, R., Masser, I., and Nijkamp, P., Missing Networks in European Transport and Communications, *Transport Reviews*, 12(4), 311-321.

Masser, I., Svidén, O., and Wegener, M., 1992, *The Geography of Europe's Future*, Belhaven Press, London.

MARIN, 1985, *European Coastal Fleets*, Maritime Research Institute Netherlands, Rotterdam.

Nijkamp, P., 1988, Infrastructure and Regional Development, *Empirical Economics*, 76-89.

Nijkamp, P., 1990, Europe in Motion, in *Proceedings of the Conference Transport: Europe on the Move*, Delft Transport Foundation, Delft, 1-13.

Rietveld, P., 1990, Employment Effects of Changes in Transport Infrastructure, *Papers of the Regional Science Association*, 66, 14-30.

Simons, J.G.W., 1990, *De Europese Vervoersintegratie: Nieuwste Ontwikkeling Eind 1989*, Amsterdam.

Violland, M., 1988, The Lessons to be Drawn for European Transport Policy from the Experience Acquired in the Process of Regulatory Reform, W.8052m, Paper Presented at the Congress on Road Transport Deregulation, Experience, Evaluation, Research, OECD/INRETS, November 2-4, Paris.

TRANSPORT IN A UNIFIED EUROPE. Policies and Challenges.
D. Banister and J. Berechman (Editors)

Chapter Seven

FREIGHT TRANSPORT

Kenneth Button

1. Introduction

The role of freight transport in economic development is a disputed one. One line of argument gives it a significant priority, seeing high quality transport as a necessary, but not sufficient, condition for growth. The "unbalanced growth school" takes a somewhat different line. It argues that social overhead capital, such as good freight transport provision, can lead to growth but, equally, in other circumstances, "directly productive activities" are more important; transport then simply follows to prevent bottlenecks in the economic growth process. Another school argues that empirical evidence suggests that only minimal levels of freight transport are required for economic expansion and that, therefore, transport supply simply adapts to the economic demands placed upon it. Whatever the truth, it seems that the debate is far from over. In political terms, there is a belief that good freight transport *is* an important component to the growth and prosperity of the pan-European economy.

The importance that the political community attaches to providing an adequate freight transport infrastructure and an appropriate operational environment for freight services provision can be seen in the actions of the European Community (EC) and, more widely, in the priorities set by the European Bank for Reconstruction and Development in its dealings with the post-communist states of Central and Eastern Europe. In terms of freight transport operations, the Common Transport Policy was one of only two major common policies contained in the founding Treaty of Rome.

This chapter sets out the existing pattern of freight transport within Europe. While there is a natural focus on trends within the EC, its size and importance making this almost inevitable, the coverage extends beyond them. It also looks at the factors currently influencing this pattern and the nature of various barriers which stand in the way of much freer freight movement. These are not just physical barriers imposed by nature and limitations of investment resources but also institutional constraints. To complement this, some discussion of the actions which have been taking place in recent years to circumvent the worst effects of these barriers is included. Finally, some comment is provided as to possible problems which are likely to arise in the transport of freight into the next century.

2. The Nature of the Activity

Freight transport within Europe and between Europe and the rest of the World is frequently a multi-modal activity with many freight activities involving various combinations of collection, truck haul and distribution elements. The cost structure of the sector, however, is such that consolidation and transhipment activities tend to be minimized, especially when commodities are of high value, involving high inventory costs, or where their physical nature makes handling difficult. These characteristics lead logistic management to seek transport strategies which minimis modal or vehicle changes and which afford the maximum flexibility in their operations. While there have been very important developments in the technologies deployed by railways and waterways, the role of road freight transport tends to dominate in many Western European countries, where users have a choice, and is very rapidly rising in importance in Eastern Europe's post-communist nations, where centralized direction of resources in the past has favored fixed-track modes (Button, 1993b). The relative importance of pipelines has also grown considerably with oil fulfilling an increasingly important role as an energy source (see Figure 1).

Some general indications of the current pattern of freight transport within European states can be gleaned from Tables 1A/B and 2A/B. A number of points become apparent. First, road transport in terms of tons moved, the main freight mode in all countries for which data is presented, losses some of its dominance when length of haul is incorporated. This is in part due to the advantages, in terms of reliability and cost, enjoyed by rail over longer distances where the importance of transhipment in the overall cost function is relatively less. It also, reflects, however, regulatory regimes which tend to favor rail for longer distances for reasons of social cost in many European countries.

The longer term perspective is that the demands for freight transport are likely to continue to grow in Europe. Quantification of these trends is never easy and nothing original is attempted here. What does seem to be agreed to by all analysts, though, is that

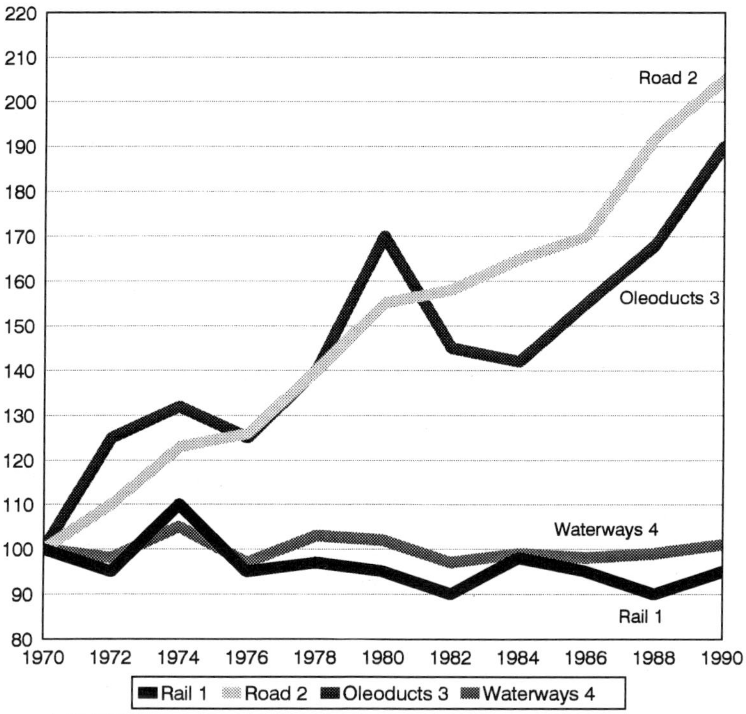

1. All ECMT countries
2. 15 countries: D, A, B, DK, E, SF, F, I, L, NL, UK, S, CH, TR, YU.
3. 12 countries: D, A, B, E, F, I, N, NL, UK, CH, TR, YU.
4. 11 countries: D, A, B, SF, F, I, L, NL, UK, CH, YU.

FIGURE 1 Index of Growth in European Freight Traffic, 1970-1990, by Ton-kilometers (1970 = 100).

Source: European Round Table of Industrialists (1991).

TABLE 1A

Freight Transport in Europe by National Vehicles on National Territory per Million Tons, 1980 and 1990

	Road[a]		Rail[b]	
Country	1980	1990	1980	1990
UK	1,340	1,686	154.0	126.9
Belgium	337	350[e]	71.0	68.5
Denmark	188	194	6.0	8.0
Germany[c]	2,496	2,889	318.0	304.1
Germany[d]	730	550[e]	311.7	335.0[e]
France	1,517	1,457	209.0	150.4
Greece	...	140[e]	4.0	3.7
Ireland	103	84	4.0	3.3
Italy	...	...	56.0	60.0[e]
Luxembourg	17	14[e]	17.0	17.6
Netherlands	358	393	22.0	18.4
Portugal	...	252	4.0	6.7
Spain	...	1,450[e]	45.0	37.0[e]
Austria	...	165[e]	52.0	62.6
Czechoslovakia	1,235	1,260[e]	285.9	254.0
Finland	340	460	29.4	34.5
Hungary	584	500[e]	129.2	89.0[e]
Norway	210	300[e]	11.5	8.0
Sweden	382	340[e]	57.0	57.6
Switzerland	292	340[e]	46.0	51.8
Yugoslavia	...	370[e,f]	85.0	77.4

Notes: [a]In vehicles about a size threshold which (for EC countries) may not exceed 3.5 tons net or 6 tons gross vehicle weight; [b]Carried by national and foreign vehicles; [c]Area of the former Federal Republic of Germany; [d]Area of the former German Democratic Republic; [e]Estimated from previous year; [f]For hire and reward only.

Source: GB Department of Transport (1992).

TABLE 1B

Freight Transport in Europe by National Vehicles on National Territory per Million Tons, 1980 and 1990

	Inland Waterways[a]		Sea-Going		Inland Pipeline	
Country	1980	1990	1980	1990	1980	1990
UK	11.0	6.0	103.0	110.0	52.0	53.9
Belgium	100.9	100.0	...	...	37.0	21.9
Denmark	0.0	0.0	7.1	11.2[d]	...	6.0[d]
Germany[b]	235.8	231.6	5.1	3.0[d]	76.0	72.6
Germany[c]	16.3	20.0[d]	...	...	41.6	38.0[d]
France	92.2	66.1	15.5	11.1[d]	106.7	78.0[d]
Greece	0.0	0.0	16.9	21.0[d]	...	...
Ireland	...	...	1.2	0.6[d]	...	...
Italy	3.1	0.9[d]	52.9	62.0[d]	86.5	62.0[d]
Luxembourg	10.5	10.9	0.0	0.0	...	...
Netherlands	269.3	287.4	...	...	44.0	41.2
Portugal	...	...	1.5	...	...	...
Spain	...	...	42.0	40.0[d]	10.0	19.0[d]
Austria	7.6[f]	8.1[f]	0.0	0.0	35.7	35.1
Czechoslovakia	10.0[f]	13.0[d,f]	0.0	0.0	19.0	16.5
Finland	0.9	1.8	8.7	8.0[e]	...	...
Hungary	3.5[f]	2.8[f]	0.0	0.0	15.6	15.3
Norway	0.0	0.0	62.9	78.0[d]	21.6	14.7[d]
Sweden	0.0	0.0	17.9	14.2[d]	...	...
Switzerland	15.8	14.5[d]	0.0	0.0	12.7	12.5
Yugoslavia	34.1	26.1	2.8	2.0[d]	2.0[e]	10.1

Notes: [a]Carried by national and foreign vehicles; [b]Area of the former Federal Republic of Germany; [c]Area of the former German Democratic Republic; [d]Estimated from previous year; [d]Estimated from previous year; [e]For hire and reward only; [f]By national craft on national or foreign waterways.

Source: GB Department of Transport (1992).

TABLE 2A

Freight Transport in Europe by National Vehicles on National Territory per Billion Ton-Kilometers, 1980 and 1990

	Road[a]		Rail[b]	
Country	1980	1990	1980	1990
UK	90.8	133.0	17.6	14.1
Belgium	18.3	32.0[e]	8.0	8.5
Denmark	7.8	8.0[e]	1.6	1.7
Germany[c]	103.0	13.0	63.8	74.8
Germany[d]	21.0	17.0[e]	56.4	58.0[e]
France	103.9	112.0[e]	66.4	53.2
Greece	...	12.5[e]	0.8	0.7
Ireland	4.5	5.5[e]	0.6	0.6
Italy	119.6	165.0[e]	18.4	22.0[e]
Luxembourg	0.3	0.2[e]	0.7	0.7
Netherlands	17.7	22.1	3.5	3.1
Portugal	11.8	16.2	1.0	1.6
Spain	98.9[b]	145.0[e]	11.2	12.0
Austria	7.9	8.0	11.0	12.7
Czechoslovakia	21.3	24.0[e]	72.6	64.3
Finland	18.4	26.3	8.3	8.4
Hungary	11.4	14.0[e]	24.4	16.8
Norway	5.3	8.5[e]	2.3	2.0
Sweden	21.4	23.0[e]	16.7	19.4
Switzerland	5.9	7.4[e]	7.4	8.9
Yugoslavia	19.0	25.0[e,f]	25.0	23.2

Notes: [a]In vehicles about a size threshold which (for EC countries) may not exceed 3.5 tons net or 6 tons gross vehicle weight; [b]Carried by national and foreign vehicles; [c]Area of the former Federal Republic of Germany; [d]Area of the former German Democratic Republic; [e]Estimated from previous year; [f]For hire and reward only.

Source: GB Department of Transport (1992).

TABLE 2B

Freight Transport in Europe by National Vehicles on National Territory per Billion Ton-Kilometers, 1980 and 1990

	Inland Waterways[a]		Sea-Going		Inland Pipeline	
	1980	1990	1980	1990	1980	1990
UK	0.4	0.2	52.8	54.3	9.4	4.7
Belgium	5.9	5.5	...	1.0	1.8	...
Denmark	0.0	0.0	1.6	2.5[d]	...	1.8
Germany[b]	51.4	54.8	0.4	0.6[d]	14.3	11.7
Germany[c]	2.2	2.3	...	...	5.0	4.3[d]
France	12.2	7.6	...	...	34.7	31.0[d]
Greece	0.0	0.0	...	...	...	...
Ireland	...	...	...	...	...	...
Italy	0.2	0.1[d]	31.1	35.0[d]	11.3	10.0[d]
Luxembourg	0.3	0.3	0.0	0.0	...	...
Netherlands	22.4	35.7	...	...	5.0	4.9
Portugal	...	...	...	...	...	...
Spain	...	...	31.1	30.0[d]	3.0	4.5[d]
Austria	1.6[f]	1.7[f]	0.0	0.0	7.1	6.4
Czechoslovakia	3.4[f]	5.0[d,f]	0.0	0.0	9.8	9.0[d]
Finland	0.2	0.4[d]	3.4	2.7[d]	...	...
Hungary	1.9[f]	1.9[f]	0.0	0.0	3.0	2.9
Norway	0.0	0.0	9.8	13.0[d]	7.6	10.8
Sweden	0.0	0.0	10.3	8.5[d]	...	...
Switzerland	0.1	0.1	0.0	0.0	1.1	1.2
Yugoslavia	7.6	7.3	...	...	2.2	3.5

Notes: [a]Carried by national and foreign vehicles; [b]Area of the former Federal Republic of Germany; [c]Area of the former German Democratic Republic; [d]Estimated from previous year; [e]For hire and reward only; [f]By national craft on national or foreign waterways.

Source: GB Department of Transport (1992).

whatever the short term effects of recession on the demand for freight transport in the early 1990s, the long term trend is for growth, especially regarding the international movement of goods (Gwilliam and Allport, 1982).

The key factors likely to influence at least the medium term future of European freight transport all suggest increasing demand for services. The continued development of the EC, coupled with the almost certain increase in its size and closer ties with other blocs (e.g., EFTA), provide the basis for more international trade and, with it, more international goods movement. Equally, these ties would seem to offer, through economies of scale, scope and specialization, the basis of more rapid growth *per se* which has, following historical precedents, almost always led to more domestic freight transport (Cecchini *et al.*, 1988). The changes which are taking place in the former communist countries will add to this international dimension as new markets open up and new sources of supply become available. The problems with forecasting here would seem to pertain much less to the direction of change than to which links will become important in new trading arrangements and at what speed they will develop. Some effort has been made to predict the probable long term freight transport corridors, based upon population size and links in the transport network (see Figure 2), but the timing and phasing of events crucially depends on the responses of the various economies to the new market environment in which they find themselves.

One can also anticipate that growth in demand for freight transport will favor certain modes rather than others. Changes in the nature of goods to be carried is particularly relevant in this context. In terms of characteristics, manufacturers are increasing the products moved; there is also growth in intra-industry trade. This, in turn, has led to the growth of just-in-time production management with all that entails in terms of additional transport services and emphasis on reliability. While just-in-time has grown in significance, its use is still relatively small compared with Japan (where about 70 percent of firms employ it) and the U.S. (about 40 percent of firms). While exact figures are hard to come by, the available data suggests that in Europe, only about 10 to 15 percent of firms employ just-in-time methods. The wider adoption of more careful inventory management will itself lead to more transport but, equally, just-in-time methods will also have other implications as it often requires new manufacturing hardware. This could well lead to changes in the location of production, and hence freight transport patterns, as well as increases in the aggregate demand for transport services. As Drucker (1990) says, with just-in-time, "...the plant no longer functions as a step-by-step process that begins at the receiving end dock and ends when finished goods move into the shipping room. Instead, the plant must be redesigned from the end backwards as an integrated flow".

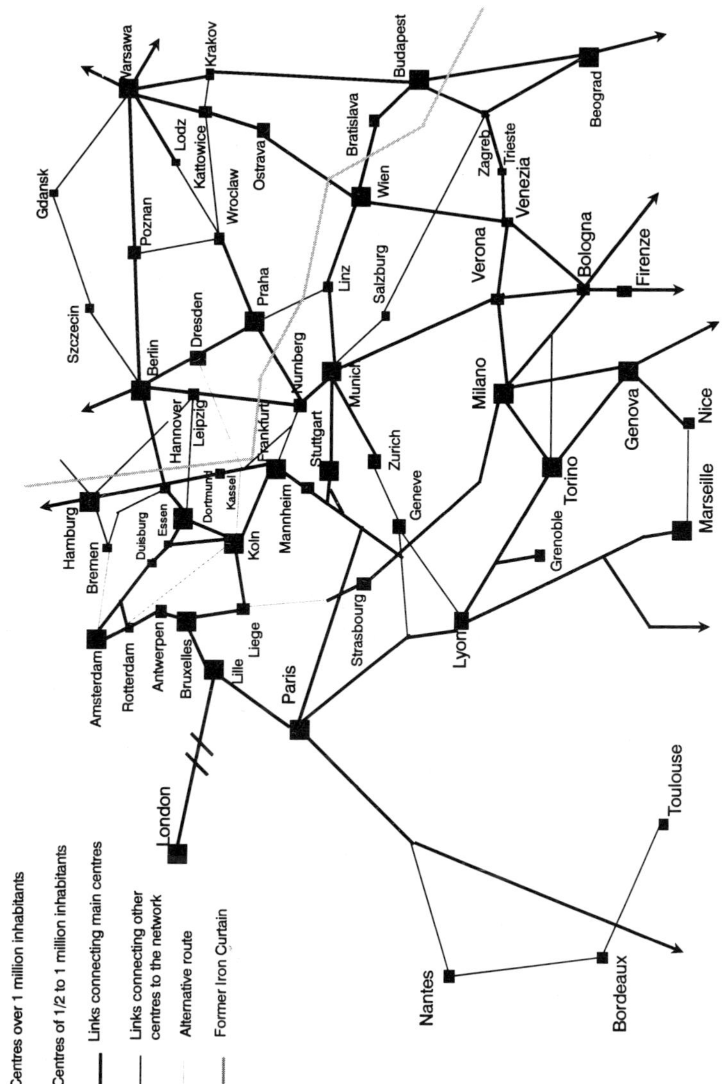

FIGURE 2 Major European Transport Nodes and Links

Source: De Waele (1991).

A final important trend which will have a bearing on the way European freight transport develops is the emphasis placed on environmental and other external costs. Transport in general is not environmentally friendly. It inflicts local costs on communities (noise, local atmospheric pollution, accidents, etc.), imposes trans-boundary costs (acid rain gases, water pollution) and contributes to global problems (greenhouse gases, emissions damaging to the upper ozone layer: Button, 1993a). Freight transport especially contributes to these problems. The rising concern about the sustainability of prevailing environmental trends is leading to a long term effort to internalize, in a variety of ways, the environmental damage associated with various economic activities. This will inevitably have implications for both the speed at which freight transport grows and the transport modes which will be used.

3. Barriers to Development

There exist a diverse range of barriers which have, to varying degrees, impeded the development of a fully efficient freight transport sector in Europe. At one level, there is the problem that freight transport policies are not only formulated by a large number of national governments but also by different established power blocs -- such as the EC, BENELUX, and the European Free Trade Area (EFTA). At another level, there are the natural problems of geographical variations and the implications of wide variations in the transport infrastructure available. To help put a little more flesh on these bones, it is helpful to divide the main barriers along the following lines.

3.1 Geographical and Political Barriers

What constitutes a natural transport market and, therefore, an appropriate area in which to develop a strategic freight transport policy, is a difficult question. Interestingly, it is one which has received rather scant attention. However, it was suggested some years ago (Thomson, 1976) that a common transport policy can only be applied to a relatively self-contained area in which there are many movements among its main parts but few between it and the external world. An ideal freight transport network, under this criterion, would exist if most of its parts are of importance to most of the countries in the market area but are of no major significance to other, outside countries. Adopting this definition, the ideal European transport network would be bounded by the Mediterranean, the Atlantic, the Arctic and the now much less rigid constraint of the "Iron Curtain".

Following the above definition, the membership of EFTA and, more importantly, the EC, for example, do not represent natural transport markets. To keep discussion within bounds, we restrict our focus to the EC.

First, a number of key regions are not members of the EC -- for example, Switzerland, Austria and the states which formerly constituted Yugoslavia -- which means that many routes ideally suited for development within a strategic EC freight transport network are outside the EC's sphere of influence. Key arteries linking Italy to the rest of the EC involve routes through Switzerland and Austria, while Greece is isolated by the necessity of transversing Bosnia, Serbia, Croatia, and other Balkan States. A further problem is that since the first enlargement of the Communities in 1973, several members (i.e., the UK and Ireland) are physically separated from the Core of the EC by water.

Beside the obvious physical problems that exist, the rather artificial nature of the EC's freight transport market means that the Communities' policy initiatives tend to overlap with initiatives of other agencies. Numerous examples of this exist and only a few are cited. For example: the European Conference of Ministers of Transport which, among other things, concerns itself with questions of haulage licensing; the Economic Commission for Europe of the United Nations concerns itself with technical and administrative matters; the Environmental Directorate of the Organization for Economic Cooperation and Development has an interest in transport's impact on the natural environment; Eurocontrol coordinates and administers aspects of air navigation and traffic control; and the European Civil Aviation Conference concerns itself with coordination of aviation activities. All these organizations have memberships which differ from that of the EC. This has not, in practice, proved to be a serious problem but it does offer the opportunity to pass thorny questions from one organization to another rather than to stimulate a concerted effort towards their resolution.

3.2 Philosophical Factors

Attitudes and approaches to transport priorities differ among European states. While each has slightly different ideas and views, there are two broad types of philosophy with regard to transport policy.

First, there is what is sometimes called the "Anglo-Saxon" philosophy. This is essentially a commercial (or quasi-commercial) approach concerned with maximizing the internal efficiency of the transport system. The emphasis is normally on the role of market mechanisms although, in recognition of potential market distortions (e.g., monopoly power and externalities), some minimal government involvement is usually deemed necessary. Governments pursuing this line tend to regard transport as a service for which the primary objective of policy is simply to meet demand at the lowest possible cost.

In contrast, the "Continental" or "European" philosophy treats transport as an instrument in a wider, social framework and focuses on the role transport can play in achieving larger, usually distributional objectives; the French, for instance, talk of the *droit de transport* (the right of transport). Transport is seen as an integral part of the social infrastructure, affecting the distribution of population and employment and shaping the social life of the community, underpinning its administration and defence, and influencing its health and environment. As such, pure efficiency within the transport sector may be sacrificed. Relatively high levels of government intervention are usual with sectors left to market mechanisms when it is felt this is the best way of attaining specified transport-related objectives.

The difficulty is that within groupings such as the EC, there is a division between members as to the appropriateness of the two philosophies. Generally, the majority of the original six members (the Netherlands, and to a more limited extent Belgium, being something of exceptions) subscribed to the social view of transport if not to the details of implementing a policy based upon it. The subsequent expansion of the Community, particularly the joining of the UK, has led to greater emphasis on commercial considerations and on internal efficiency within transport industries. Because, in general, countries adopting the social philosophy tend to favor greater expenditures on infrastructure, there is inevitable discord between their attitude and those of other members as to the desirability of expanding direct Community expenditure on it. This results in quite noticeable differences in national expenditures on roads, railways, etc. (European Conference of Ministers of Transport, 1988).

The differing philosophies are also reflected in the national institutional arrangements which European countries have adopted to develop their freight transport policies. In terms of transport infrastructure, countries such as France, Switzerland, and Germany, in particular, take a much longer term view of the role of transport in economic development and political integration. This is reflected both in the time horizon aspect of their technical approaches to such things as investment appraisal and the degree to which "master planning" enters into the process. Belgium, in comparison, has a transport philosophy more akin to the Anglo-Saxon tradition and planning is clearly much less pronounced.

Perhaps a point of general interest emerging from studies of policy, however, is the relative lack of internal integration of national transport which seems to exist within Europe (Round Table of European Industrialists, 1987). In some ways this may be seen as posing a problem for developing a continent-wide freight transport policy but it may equally be seen as offering some political opportunities given the relative lack of formalized systems (each with its own vested interest) at the national level.

3.3 Legacy Effects

For a variety of geographical, historical and political reasons, the nature of transport systems within Europe varies considerably among countries. Trans-border routes tend to be particularly poorly served. The existing infrastructure is, almost by definition, a legacy of the past. For instance, the various enlargements of the EC have not only brought in members which have interests in particular modes of transport previously of little concern to the original members (e.g., the UK and Greece with shipping), but they have also affected the actual structure, as well as the scale, of the transport infrastructure which exists. The opening up of Eastern Europe poses problems as its transport system is both qualitatively and quantitatively different from that in most western countries.

Concentrating on the EC, as a broad generalization, the Core area has a substantial and well-established transport infrastructure. While high quality road transport infrastructure exists, there is also a well-established series of rail networks. Contrasting with this, the peripheral areas rely rather more heavily upon road freight transport (see Tables 1a/b and 2a/b), although the quality of their road systems is itself not high.

Overlapping this is the existence of extensive inland water transport systems in the central area. These provide a major component of freight transport, especially of bulk commodities, conducted in Germany, the Netherlands, and France. The emergence of the Eastern Bloc countries highlights further differences, with the very heavy reliance of most Eastern European countries on rail freight transport, given their relatively underdeveloped road networks. The traditional importance of coastal shipping also means that several European states have a legacy of extensive port and dock investments.

The importance of rail freight transport in central EC countries is, in part, a function of their historical development and the nature of national resource endowments. Industrialization took place before the widespread adoption of the internal combustion engine and was based on heavy industry for which rail transport normally enjoys a natural comparative advantage. Further, the geographical distribution of population and markets served by these countries is such that rail transport provides a more economic mode of transport here than it does in many peripheral states. In particular, concentrations of population and economic activity have tended to encourage traffic flows along a north-south/south-north axis concentrated along the Rhine. Generally, because of the relatively high capital costs but low distance-related operating costs of railways, they are competitive with roads in the carriage of freight on routes over a threshold of 240 kilometers (Johnson and Garnett, 1971). This is in line with the lengths of haul found between the major centers on such routes (but considerably greater than those found in peripheral countries such as the UK).

Given these conditions, it is not surprising that over the years, the Core EC area countries have favored transport infrastructure development in connection with rail and water-borne modes while the peripheral states, whose traditional trade patterns have been somewhat more complex, have favored more flexible modes. The difficulty now is that although the infrastructure exists, it has been largely written down. It has a long outstanding life in technical terms, but does not necessarily offer the modal balance required to meet the EC's growth objectives nor may it have the flexibility to meet all of the short term requirements of an expanded European economic zone.

3.4 Institutional barriers

Markets exist within a constitutional context. An important observation regarding the EC was made by Despicht (1969) some twenty years ago, when he argued that, "Community institutions themselves were inadequate to the task of making policies for long established, technical but politically sensitive activities". There are, in fact, several reasons why the institutional arrangements of the EC are not conducive to the development of a Community- wide infrastructure investment program in transport.

Lack of complete Community control over funding is a major consideration. Member states still control the majority of funds deployed for transport infrastructure development. The notion that one can develop a program of investments which would result in the establishment of a network of routes of Community importance faces the problem of convincing members to allocate national resources for projects which may only benefit through freight traffic, in transit between other member states or between a third party state and a member. Essentially, members are naturally jealous of their own powers to determine priorities in national investment budgets and their preferences reflect a strong national self-interest.

Linked to this, the scale of public sector expenditure on transport infrastructure is sufficiently large so that adjustments to programs and rescheduling of activities form a major element of national demand management policy. As long as states within the EC remain only loosely tied, it is unlikely that their separate economic cycles will move in unison and, *ipso facto*, it is unlikely that national attitudes towards transport infrastructure expenditures will converge. Consequently, given the number of national economies concerned, this makes it especially difficult to coordinate long term investment plans.

While national control over the majority of monies is important, there are also problems with the way actual decisions are arrived at within the Community. The Directorate for Transport, for example, has no powers of its own but must obtain agreement from member states to implement its proposals. This only normally comes after lengthy debates by the Council of Ministers. The final outcome is often influenced not just by transport considerations but by the "logrolling" which inevitably goes on within any essentially "political" committee. Modified transport proposals are accepted by opponents in exchange for agreements on measures relating to other sectors where they have a positive interest.

Finally, while the EC may develop policies towards transport infrastructure, it is generally the responsibility of national governments to administer them. As Gwilliam (1980) has pointed out, this seems likely to encourage a Member State which reluctantly embraces a policy to operate it in exactly the same spirit.

3.5 The Changing Political Map of Europe

The very rapid developments in Eastern Europe over the past three years have added a very particular dimension to the constraints confronting policy makers in Europe. At one level, there will be an inevitable increase of trade between East and West as the economies of the former move forward. But in addition to this, a certain amount of trade diversion will occur as each state seeks to develop its own comparative advantage. This will put pressure on the existing transport systems in Europe and more investment will inevitably be needed. But, in addition to this, the enlargement of the market area of Europe in such a sudden way and with, at this time, relatively unclear long term consequences, adds to the basic uncertainty involved in defining medium term developments (Button, 1993b).

In very broad terms, the transport systems of Eastern European countries tend to differ in two major respects from their Western counterparts. The basic infrastructure is different and the method of management is different. The eastern European states are heavily reliant upon rail for freight transport but their systems tend to be old and the efficiency of operations is highly questionable. There is also the difficulty that, after decades of separation, the investments which have taken place are not in sympathy with a more integrated pan-European economic system.

In terms of management, the transport systems of most Eastern European countries are much more labor-intensive than those found in Western Europe. The management of transport systems by command-and-control instruments which, to varying degrees, has typified the approach in Eastern European economies is particularly disadvantageous in a modern industrialized society where many movements are of non-bulk commodities, irregular in nature, and heavily dependent on service quality to achieve consumer satisfaction. Flexibility is essential and local responsiveness normally desirable, but these are the very features missing in a centrally planned transport system.

4. Policy Responses

Changes in European freight transport are gradually taking place as transport industries react to the new environment and challenges that confront them. In many ways, it is remarkable how inventive and flexible freight transport suppliers are. The long term outcome is almost certainly going to be an evolutionary change in the nature of European freight transport. We can consider the types of impacts which have been observed, together with the direction in which they seem to be going, under a number of separate headings. However, it should be remembered that many of the threads are closely entwined and any division, while serving expositional needs, inevitably introduces a degree of simplification into the discussion. Further, the headings are set out in no particular order in terms of the importance of their subject matter.

4.1 International Coordination

The apparent consensus amongst forecasters is that, in relative terms, international freight transport within Western Europe will grow more rapidly than national transport in the next 20 years. This does, however, contain the implicit assumption that there will be greater coordination of transport policies. If one simply looks back at the history of the Common

Transport Policy of the EC, this may seem to be a rather optimistic assumption. Agreeing on common objectives, let alone policies for achieving them, has proved extremely difficult for the institutions involved; the attitude has continually been one of states both protecting their own freight transport supply industries and using transport policy as an instrument of national industrial advancement.

Within the European Community, the liberalization of freight transport market and the creation of arrangements to improve the quality of transport infrastructure provision, both within the geographical boundaries of the Community and with respect to facilities in countries which Community traffic transits, have been elements of recent initiatives. As a result of this, the position regarding freight transport has changed considerably when contrasted to the lack of progress made over the first fifteen years or so of the Community. Indeed, the frustration felt by the Commission in the early 1970s can be seen in a Communication sent to the Council of Ministers:

> The neglect of Community action in the realm of transport, as well as the failure to fulfil the obligations imposed by the Treaty on the Community institutions, also impairs the development of the general policy of the Community (Commission of the European Communities, 1971).

These changes have come about because of two significant developments. First, the agitation and concern expressed by the Commission and others in the 1970s and early 1980s has led to progress in the creation of the Common Transport Policy. Second, on a somewhat narrower front, the agreement to move to a Single European Market by 1993 forced policy changes in those areas specifically related to this aspect of Community activity (Button, 1992a; Crowley, 1993).

In the document which set the scene for the creation of the Single European Market, the *Cockfield Report* (Commission of the European Communities, 1985a), a number of specific transport issues were raised. With regard to international transport of goods by road between member states, the key points included the need to phase out the quantitative restrictions (quotas) and to establish the conditions under which non-resident carriers could operate transport services in another member state (cabotage). With respect to the international transport of goods by inland waterway, there was a need for the freedom to provide services where this was not yet the case and, where necessary, to establish conditions under which non-resident carriers could operate inland navigation services in another member state. Regarding sea transport, freedom to provide services between member states was necessary. The Council of Minister, in accepting the broad thrust of the *Cockfield Report,* drew up a list of four principles to guide the liberalization of transport markets (Commission of the European Communities, 1985b). These were quality of treatment within and between different forms of transport; freedom of competition; free choice of uses and coordination of infrastructure; and the need to develop policies with respect to the environment based on the polluter-pays principle.

The actual pace of change has been somewhat slower than the *Cockfield Report* advocated. Cabotage in road haulage is being slowly phased in but only with controls insisted upon by Germany and France. The number of EC licenses is being increased and holders may provide services throughout the Community provided they conform with national laws and rules. However, governments can limit operations if foreign carriers are found to have a significant share of any geographical market within their borders. There has been some movement towards freer maritime markets (Brooks and Button, 1992) but total cabotage has been limited in some markets, such as the Greek islands, to protect national flags; the changes are to be phased in over a period extending to 2004. Passenger aviation is to be freed in stages with complete cabotage by 1997, which is of importance to air cargo as much of it is carried in the bellies of commercial passenger planes or in "combi" aircraft.

On the broader front, partly stimulated by the creation of the Single European Market, new initiatives have emerged with respect to some of the other elements of the Common Transport Policy, especially regarding infrastructure construction and the removal of transport bottlenecks with the EC (Button, 1990). There is a growing commitment to provide new infrastructure and to coordinate national policies in this sphere. This was made clear in 1989:

> Benefitting from the positive effects from the completion of the internal market implies ensuring the interconnection and interoperability of existing infrastructure networks. Creating the conditions in which from its conception any new infrastructure incorporates the European dimension must enable the avoidance of the creation of new missing links and respond to the wishes of business and minimis their costs. It is, in fact, more costly to interconnect after the event than to ensure an integrated connection from the start. This also requires a reorientation function to ensure an integrated connection from the start.

> ....that infrastructures are currently conceived and developed principally at national level and that, consequently, gives rise to problems of compatibility and interoperability which effect their efficiency (Commission of the European Communities, 1989).

As indicated, changes are now taking place not only as the EC becomes a Single Market but also as Eastern and Central Europe begin to appreciate the need to integrate their markets with those in the West. To overcome some of the bottlenecks which already exist in the freight transport system, and others which are going to develop as patterns of trade change, European infrastructure investment and transport regulatory policy must inevitably become transnational in its orientation. There are, however, going to be limits to the extent to which fully effective integration occurs.

It is now appreciated that there is a danger when attempting international coordination of transport to seek some utopian "blue print" of what the ultimate networks should look like. Experience from the past, and especially regarding the early years of the Common Transport Policy, suggest that this approach to integration is both difficult to carry out (mainly because of the diverse views of the states involved as to the form these networks should take) and, in any case, given the lengthy construction periods involved, it is improbable that the outcome will in any way conform to final notions of the ideal system.

To be successful, integration must be strategic in its orientation and flexible in its implementation. What we are increasingly likely to witness in the foreseeable future in Europe is progress towards the development of such an approach rather than its full implementation. It is also, in a sense, likely to be reactive in its ethos. There is already agreement that key bottlenecks in the existing infrastructure should be removed, agreement on some aspects of controlling environmental degradation, agreements on some standards, and formalized mechanisms for the interchange of information.

4.2 Modally Integrated Transport

Integrated transport systems of various kinds have been discussed for many years in Europe but policy making has continued to be dominated by modal demarcations. However, this situation is changing and is likely to continue to do so in the future. The pressures of increasingly congested infrastructure and concern with environmental protection on one hand, coupled with the needs of modern industry and the increased size of the potential European market on the other, are leading to rather more careful thought as to where scarce marginal resources should be allocated. The implicit tradeoffs involved mean that, inevitably, the issue of modal integration becomes important. The development of efficient electronic data interchange (EDI) technology also means that one of the main problems with supplying high quality integrated transport services has been overcome.

In the past, efforts at encouraging the use of such integrated systems as "piggy-back" and "kangaroo" trains have tended to rely on subsidies and manipulation of licensing arrangements. For example, within the EC, countries such as Germany have traditionally given extra bilateral road haulage permits allowing other members' haulers additional movements in the country if a designated number of trips were made on the combined transport facilities. Integration has also tended to be thought of in terms of technical possibilities and to be viewed as a matter of national concern. The difficulties are those of cost and technical standardization. In countries such as Switzerland, geographical and environmental factors provide both commercial and social incentives to adopt combined transport which fosters the use of rail as a key component. The large amounts of transit traffic add to this logic. In other cases, the nature of modern production and distribution suggests that other notions of integration are of more importance. These notions are being developed within the transport industry rather than policy makers trying to impose them from outside.

The need for high quality and reliable service, associated with just-in-time procedures, coupled with the demonstrable economies of scope and density associated with hub-and-spoke operations, is increasingly leading to more consolidation and transhipment. EDI systems now enable rapid discovery of problems in the system and facilitate detailed tracking of goods and vehicles. Increasingly, modal integration is developing via the market rather than through government interventions. We already see this happening with the very rapid growth of express parcel services in Europe (e.g., TNT, DHL, UPS); a new sector relatively free of restrictions. These companies operate integrated long distance road and air services and local distribution and collection via hub-and-spoke structures. Other recent developments include shipping lines, such as the Royal Nedlloyd Group, buying into port container facilities and road haulage companies.

Not all of the current impetus for intermodalism is demand-driven, some of it is coming from new developments on the operations side. One can also point to important trends in infrastructure investment. The Channel Tunnel, while for rail use only, has necessitated the development of new lorry/rail loading techniques to cater for through road freight traffic.

The position of the established intermodal carriers has been reactive to this situation. For example, the Belgium Joint Declaration, signed in 1990 by organizations (especially rail-based ones) involved with international European intermodal transport, has produced an agreement on a common strategy covering the design, operation and active marketing of intermodal transport. While such coordinated strategies have not produced much success in the past, the new market situation in Europe coupled with the emergence of new, mainly private sector players, may well prove more stimulating for those involved in these initiatives in the future. The prospects for combined transport in Eastern Europe are somewhat less clear. At present, little freight is even containerized: for example, in the German Democratic Republic (GDR) prior to reunification, only about 1.5 percent of traffic by volume went by container. Consequently, there is scope for investment and expansion but, at the same time it is not clear, whether the necessary framework for efficient decision making exists. There may well be a tendency to put excessive resources into outmoded technology.

4.3 Fiscal Reforms

One thing seems fairly clear: the overall costs borne by users of transport within Europe are going to increase in the short and medium term. This is quite simply because, in the past, transport has not covered its full costs and has enjoyed pricing structures which have not led to its efficient use. The circumstances allowing this are now changing.

Transport is an economic activity but has, in the past, tended to be treated rather differently than many other economic activities. This is one reason why the transport networks of Western Europe are experiencing increased congestion and why those of Eastern Europe are substandard. In the former case, prices paid for using transport infrastructure bear little resemblance to economic prices. Setting aside issues of environmental costs, the methods of charging for road, port and air transport infrastructure seldom bear any relation to the opportunity costs involved. In particular, users are simply not aware of the congestion that individual trips impose on others. The problem in Eastern and Central Europe has been that transport has not been treated as a "productive activity" and resources have been allocated so as to avoid duplication irrespective of potential demand, as such traffic and investment have been directed by administration rather than by market requirements.

The pressures of increased transport are mounting in Western Europe and the old ideas of building more infrastructure are being seen as having limited value for reducing the problem. Technical improvements, while helpful, are also not a long term solution. More rational pricing of transport in Europe is increasingly being seen as the way forward. At one level, there is obviously something of what, in the UK, is called the TINA ("There is No Alternative") syndrome at work. But additionally, there is mounting recognition that appropriate economic pricing has the advantage not only of making more efficient use of existing infrastructure but also in giving clearer guidance as to where expansions in the system will generate the greatest benefits. It more closely links transport use to investment (i.e., "earmarking") priorities and, in helping to reduce the external, environmental costs associated with excessive congestion, it generates social benefits.

The need to generate revenues for new infrastructure has also brought about innovative schemes which directly relate the costs of construction to those who use the new facilities. Toll rings in Bergen, Trondheim, and Oslo for financing local road and other transport projects are examples. Plans for additional tolled, and sometimes private, motorways and trunk roads in the UK and several other European countries are also illustrations of the ways in which additional revenue can be generated.

The question of environmental costs must be added to these purely transport considerations. The mounting awareness of the environmental damage caused by transport, particularly road transport, is creating political pressure for remedial actions. Some of these will inevitably come about through the introduction of regulations and standards, or the tightening and more stringent enforcement of existing laws. These actions will not be costless in narrow economic terms and, despite their accompanying stimulus for greater efficiency, will lead to rate, fare and other price increases for the transport user. Again, the gap between payments and resource costs will be closer.

More transparently, there is mounting evidence that the exploitation of the physical controls available has very nearly reached its effective limit and that direct fiscal measures (e.g., pollution charges, tradeable emission permits, and differential taxation) are now required. It can also be argued, partly because of their flexibility and revenue-raising potential, that they are more effective tools. The wider use of these policy instruments to restrict environmental degradation would bear directly on the perceived costs of transport.

Neither the congestion nor the fiscal concerns on the part of macroeconomic policy makers are likely to diminish over the next decade, and the question of environmental quality is not going to disappear. Consequently, one must anticipate an increased emphasis on more soundly based policies regarding the funding and charging for the use of transport infrastructure. There is already evidence of considerable thought being given to the fiscal aspects of transport provision and operation in Europe, and seen at all administrative levels. Over the next decade, rather more of these concerns will be translated into actions than in the past.

4.4 Infrastructure Provision

There are at present major inconsistencies in the ways that the different modes of transport are treated within Europe. There is a clear separation of infrastructure ownership and control in aviation, shipping and road transport but, with limited exceptions such as Sweden, rail operations and infrastructure come under unitary authorities in all European countries. The logic of having unitary authorities for railways stems from managerial notions of coordination coupled with technical arguments regarding the problems of separating operations from infrastructure. In particular, it is claimed that unlike air, road, and sea transport, there is only limited scope for overtaking on a railway. This poses problems for timetabling and rescheduling in the event of late running or accidents if anything other than a fully integrated management system is adopted.

Recently, however, concern over the efficiency of regulated monopoly railway undertakings, especially regarding the ways subsidies are used, have raised questions concerning the desirability of separating the responsibility for operating services from the responsibility for infrastructure (i.e., track, signalling, and stations) management. This concern dovetails into problems of revenue generation for the maintenance and improvement of rail infrastructure.

While monopoly control of infrastructure, with associated problems of potential inefficiency, remain under this type of regime, it has been argued that competition for use of this infrastructure by operating companies, both private and public, would help to enhance the performance of the overall rail system. Essentially, a track authority would sell, possibly through a bidding process, "space" on its track to operating companies. Further, if there was a European-wide authority responsible for the internationally important infrastructure, it could assist in coordinating investment programs and help ensure greater compatibility of technical standards.

This division of responsibilities is one option which has been adopted, albeit in a limited form, in Sweden and is under serious review in the UK. At the international level, separation has also been suggested as a policy for improving international rail systems, i.e., "Any railway undertaking....shall be granted access on equitable conditions to national railway infrastructure in the country of its establishment" (Commission of the European Communities, 1986).

In terms of new transport infrastructure, the key question will be that of ensuring efficiency in the expenditure of resources. Technically, the faster one can provide a transport service, the smaller the physical amount infrastructure which is required. The difficulty with the vast majority of Europe's transport infrastructures is that they are multipurpose and tend to reduce overall traffic speeds. This has implications for the capacity required. There are exceptions, such as the TGV in France, but roads and railways in Europe carry both passenger and freight transport. They also often cater to local and long distance traffics. Specialization of infrastructure, therefore, has considerable merit and there are also good reasons, in the case of railways, to focus investment on the major arteries.

Further, while some of the ongoing investments and modernization represent genuine coordination within a multinational framework, such as the EC, other events are also of importance. There are, for example, an increasing number of bilateral agreements, or actions by small groups of nations, to pursue investment policies in which those involved have a common interest. Additionally, the independent, self-interested actions of some countries in developing their own infrastructure have significant implications for the larger European transport network. This is particularly true of the "Core Area" countries which both form a substantial traffic-generating base and attract freight traffic destined for/or originating from elsewhere, and also handle considerable volumes of through-traffic. In this context, for instance, the actions of such countries as France and Germany add to the overall EC transport infrastructure.

4.5 Privatization

Over the past decade there has been increased privatization of transport in Europe (Button, 1992c). This has involved some selling off, either in their entirety or in part by means of equity issues, of formerly nationally owned assets. More often, it has involved supplementing the nationally owned assets by additional private sector provision. While the main impact has been in the passenger sector, where public ownership has been more common, opening up formerly state monopoly markets for freight transport services to private sector suppliers has also taken place.

Much of the impetus for this has been generated by the need for more rapid expansions of infrastructure than national governments, for macroeconomic reasons, were prepared to finance from public funds. Additionally, some of it has come about because of concerns over the efficiency with which public enterprises are operated. The major problem is that of developing, in the absence of market criteria, an effective set of criteria to enable management to judge their performance against the general policy objectives before them. Ideological considerations have also played their role.

From a predictive perspective, it seems inevitable that private sector involvement in both the provision of transport infrastructure and in freight transport operations will increase. The reasons promoting recent trends are likely to strengthen rather than diminish in the future. Certainly it is difficult to see any reversal.

First, even if effective restraint measures stem the increased use of transport in Europe, there are still bottlenecks which require investment and the maintenance of existing infrastructure is likely to pose increasing financial burdens. In particular, Eastern Europe requires its transport infrastructure to be modernized and its quality upgraded. It seems unlikely, to put it rather weakly, that this can all be funded from public monies. Indeed, the European Bank for Reconstruction and Development, which devotes a considerable part of its investment funds to transport in Eastern Europe, still sees many of the necessary resources being drawn from the private sector.

Second, while there are national differences in attitude, the general trend in Europe is towards greater involvement of the private sector in supplying goods and services. The developments in the post-communist countries means that this trend will, on an overall European basis, inevitably continue into the foreseeable future. Linked closely with this, the issue of efficiency, although not totally dominant, has become increasingly more important and there seems no reason why this trend will be reversed.

Third, as Europe becomes more economically (and possibly politically) integrated, national transport policies will have to be incorporated into wider international policies. National ownership and operation of transport has, whatever the initial intention, the inherent danger that national governments will attempt to manipulate it to their own economic ends. This has been one of the traditional stumbling blocks in the creation of an EC Common Transport Policy. Although not strictly related to privatization, the efforts of the EC Commission to separate railway infrastructure from national ownership and to put more resources into the Commission-controlled element of the EC Transport Infrastructure Fund are early indications that this problem is appreciated at the EC level.

Taking this one step further, the transfer of elements of transport supply from national or Commission ownership to the private sector reduces political involvement further and could well prove to be more attractive to many Members.

5. The Challenges Ahead

The anticipated long term growth within Europe as the economic integration of markets takes place will inevitably bring about changes in both the scale and nature of the demands placed on the freight transport industries. This will raise a number of important challenges before the freight industry and those responsible for the policies which control it. Some of these inevitably relate to what has gone before but others are somewhat different in nature.

One factor which has been increasingly appreciated in recent years is that while new infrastructure is needed and the upgrading and improved maintenance of what we have is essential, the demand for more capacity will outstrip the supply. There is need for considerably improved management of the system if freight transport is to grow at anything like the rate suggested in unconstrained circumstances. Part of this growth must be associated with the infrastructure itself. The introduction of more logical road-user charging systems would seem to be an essential component of such a policy to ensure that the scarce space available is allocated effectively and that modal choices are made on the basis of comparable marginal infrastructure cost allocations. The challenge comes in introducing such a regime in a market where road users in particular have been familiar with non-hypothecation of license fees and fuel taxation revenues.

An associated challenge is the introduction of the modern telematics which ensure that freight transport routings and collection/deliveries are optimized. The removal of the more stringent quantity control measures which govern freight transport both within many European states and between states provides the opportunity for reducing empty running and improving routing. There is a private financial incentive to maximize these gains by employing telematics, but this only materializes once provision of the necessary infrastructure, possibly by the state, is carried out. This is the second challenge, to ensure suitable public infrastructure is available.

The growth of freer trade within a pan-European context is inevitably going to require some form of policy integration (Button, 1992b). The institutions and agencies which have grown up in a rather *ad hoc* manner since the 1940s have provided some degree of coordination in policy making during the past half century, but none have the breadth of remit, geographical coverage or implementative power necessary to develop the types of policy required to cope with the demands of European freight transport in the 21st century. The challenge is to find a means of replacing the current plethora of bodies with one genuinely pan-European institution to oversee the strategic development of the Continent's freight transport system.

Concern about the environmental costs of transport, although muted in the early 1990s at a time of economic recession, is unlikely to abate in the longer term. This will lead to mounting pressures to at least contain the problem and, probably, reduce it. In the case of global matters such as emissions leading to undesirable green house effects or damage to the upper ozone layer, the impacts will be international in their orientation and Europe will be a part of a much broader policy making framework. Other matters will require greater cooperation between the states of Europe. The challenge will be to meet the pressing need to sustain the quality of the environment while at the same time ensuring that freight transport's role in meeting narrower economic aspirations is optimized.

6. Conclusions

The past 20 years have witnessed remarkable changes in the way freight transport operates in Europe. It has become more efficient both as new cost saving technologies have been introduced and as increased reliance on market forces has brought it closer to customer needs. However, the demand for freight services continues to grow. The challenges of the future are those of meeting these demands where it is cost-effective to do so in circumstances of constraints on infrastructure capacity and mounting concern over environmental damage. This chapter has made no direct effort to suggest detailed ways of reconciling these problems, other than to suggest that the wider adoption of basic economic principles would be helpful. Its purpose has been to highlight the problems and issues and to present their underlying causes.

References

Brooks, M. and Button, K.J., 1992, Shipping Within the Framework of a Single European Market, *Transport Reviews*, 12, 237-252.

Button, K.J., 1984, *Road Haulage Licensing and EC Transport Policy*, Gower, Aldershot.

Button, K.J., 1990, Infrastructure Plans for Europe, in Gillund, J. and Tornqvist, G. (eds.), *European Networks*, Umea: CERUM, Umea.

Button, K.J., 1992a, The Liberalization of Transport Services, in Swann, D. (ed.), *The Single European Market and Beyond: A Study of the Wider Implications of the Single European Act*, Routledge, London.

Button, K.J., 1992b, *Europäische Verkehrspolitik-Wege in die Zukunft*, Bartelsmann Foundation, Gütersloh.

Button, K.J., 1992c, Privatization in the Transport Sector: Some of the Key Issues, *Economisch en Sociaal Tijdshrift*, 45, 29-48.

Button, K.J., 1993a, *Transport, the Environment and Economic Policy*, Edward Elgar Press, Aldershot.

Button, K.J., 1993b, East-West Transport: the Problems, Potential and Possible Policies, in Banister, D. and Berechman, J. (eds.), *Transport in a Unified Europe*, Elsevier, Amsterdam.

Cecchini,P., Catinat, M. and Jacquemin, A., 1988, *The European Challenge 1992: The Benefits of a Single Market*, Wildwood, Aldershot.

Commission of the European Communities, 1971, *Communication from the Commission to the Council Concerning the Community Organization of the Market for Transport*, Sec(71) 3190 Final, EEC, Brussels.

Commission of the European Communities, 1985a, *Completing the Internal Market*, COM(85)310 Final, EEC, Brussels.

Commission of the European Communities, 1985b, Towards a Common Transport Policy, *Bulletin of the European Communities*, 11, OOPEC, Luxembourg.

Commission of the European Communities, 1986, *Report: Towards a European High-speed Rail Network*, COM(86)341 Final, EC, Brussels.

Commission of the European Communities, 1989, *Council Resolution on Trans-European Networks,* EC, Brussels.

Crowley, J.A., 1993, Inland Transport in the European Community Following 1992, *Antitrust Bulletin*, 36.

De Waele, A., 1991, Consequences of East-West Relations, in European Conference of Ministers of Transport, *Prospects for East-West European Transport*, ECMT, Paris.

DeSpicht, N., 1969, *The Transport Policies of the European Communities*, European Series No. 12, PEP, London.

Drucker, P., 1990, The Emerging Theory of Manufacturing, *Harvard Business Review*, 68, 97-102.

European Conference of Ministers of Transport, 1988, *Statistical Trends in Transport 1965-85*, Paris: ECMT.

European Round Table of Industrialists, 1987, *Need for Renewing Transport Infrastructure in Europe -- Proposals for Improving the Decision-making Process*, ERTI, Brussels.

European Round Table of Industrialists, 1991, *Missing Networks: A European Challenge*, ERTI, Brussels.

Gwilliam, K.M., 1980, Realism and the Common Transport Policy of the EEC, in Palak, J.B. and van der Kamp, J.B. (eds.), *Changes in the Field of Transport Studies*, Martinus Nijhoff, The Hague.

Gwilliam, K.M. and Allport, R.J., 1982, A Medium Term Transport Research Strategy for the EEC: Part 1, *Transport Reviews*, 2, 305-16.

Johnson, K.M. and Garnett, H.C., 1971, *The Economics of Containerization*, Allen and Unwin, London.

Organization for Economic Cooperation and Development, 1991, *The State of the Environment*, OECD, Paris.

Thomson, J.M., 1976, Towards a European Transport Strategy, in Lee, R. and Ogden, P.E. (eds.), *Economy and Society in the EEC*, Saxon House, Farnborough.

United Nations Economic Commission for Europe, 1987, Consumption Patterns in the ECE Region: Long Term Trends and Policy Issues, *Economic Bulletin for Europe*, 39, 425-82.

Part Two

POLICY ISSUES AND CHALLENGES IN EUROPE

TRANSPORT IN A UNIFIED EUROPE. Policies and Challenges.
D. Banister and J. Berechman (Editors)
1993 Elsevier Science Publishers B.V.

Chapter Eight

MISSING TRANSPORT NETWORKS: A POLICY PERSPECTIVE

Gerold Hauser
Rico Maggi

1. Introduction

This chapter deals with missing transport and communication networks in Europe. Missing networks are defined as deficiencies in the transport system, not only in infrastructure but also, and probably more eminently, in the organization of the transport market, the logistic strategies, and the software needed to implement them. In addition, funding problems and environmental externalities are equally important. These five issues and their political relevance for Europe have been studied in a research project under the auspices of the European Round Table of Industrialists (ERTI, 1990; Maggi et al., 1992; Nijkamp et al., 1990). The conclusion reached was that the efficiency of European transport networks can be significantly increased by interpreting the above five network aspects as a pentagon of concerns for policy guidance.

However, there are some apprehensions in Europe that improving the efficiency of networks will increase the transport volume and, in turn, lead to higher environmental externalities. Therefore, it is sometimes argued that it is better to leave the missing networks problem unsolved. In terms of welfare economics, this argument is not necessarily valid. To demonstrate this, the present study offers a theoretical analysis of the welfare implications of doing away with missing networks. When evaluating the welfare effects of such a policy, it is vital not only to consider externalities but also internal benefits of transport. Therefore, the aim of this paper is to consider the effect of missing transport networks in Europe on internalities as well as environmental externalities, and to discuss the welfare implications of policies increasing network efficiency.

Missing transport networks in Europe relate to missing infrastructure links, inefficient market organization, insufficient software to steer traffic flows, lack of funding, and environmental problems. These lead to an inefficient network in terms of congestion, unreliability of transport services, detours and less-than-truckload traffic, transmodal coordination problems, etc. In the next section, we discuss the kind of environmental effects that are of special relevance to missing networks. Section 3 discusses the welfare effects of an efficient transport network policy on the basis of a formal model.

In general, missing networks unduly increase congestion and provoke detours. Hence one might conclude that low cost investments for overcoming these deficiencies would increase social welfare. But problems arise from the fact that a reduction of detours does not necessarily reduce traffic in terms of ton-kilometers and may, therefore, cause excessive external disadvantages and reduce social welfare. In addition, it may be that external effects are more obvious to households than are the internal benefits -- a fact that may cause difficulties on the policy level. In Section 4 we will spell out some possible policy measures and discuss the problems of their implementation on the European level.

2. Transport, Missing Networks and the Environment

In this section, we will not repeat the arguments that can be made about the environmental effects of transport in general. Rather, we shall attempt to illuminate the specific relationship of missing networks with the environment.

The most cited aspect of missing networks are missing infrastructure links. Their major impact is on congestion in the network. This is most obvious in the case of road transport. Where missing links exist in the road network, there will normally be bottlenecks leading to congestion. This will usually also bring about an increase in air pollution and noise emissions. Sometimes the argument is made that these bottlenecks are a substitute for traffic regulation by means of pricing and that the high congestion price reduces traffic and hence the environmental effects of transport. While one can no more than speculate about the net environmental effect, it is clear that congestion is an inefficient pricing system. Although overall traffic may be reduced, pollution in the congested areas is most certainly increased. Environmental policy here becomes spatial distribution policy. We shall come back to this point in Section 4.

Most missing network problems do not simply arise from specific non-existent links but from missing networks as a whole. All the deficiencies in software, market organization or funding mechanisms reduce the efficiency of the European transport network as well. Does this reduced efficiency increase environmental externalities and, if so, by which pollutants? We will discuss this with reference to Table 1, which gives an overview on environmental effects of transport.

As was demonstrated by Nijkamp et al. (1990), in the case of freight transport, important missing network problems are related to rail traffic and combined road/rail transport. Rail-specific missing networks tend to increase the competitiveness of road haulage and thus its market share, which is already relatively important due to the locally very dense road network of Europe. With reference to Table 1, this implies that transport is potentially shifted from a lower emission to a higher emission mode. This holds primarily for air pollution and, to a lesser extent, for noise, solid waste and water pollution, and risks of accidents. A missing network problem with similar implications is the lack of a pricing system internalizing the external costs of road traffic in general, i.e., including private and public car traffic. This shortcoming implies a subsidy to road users and helps raise the modal share and, therefore, the environmental effects of road traffic.

Missing networks will, in addition, give rise to detours. The most striking example is the "hole" created in the European road network by the 28-ton limit on trucks in Switzerland. In 1988, trans-Alpine freight traffic amounted to 60 million tons. As can be seen from Table 2, the split of this volume among countries and modes is biased. For a majority of origins and destinations, the shortest path across the Alps would lead through Switzerland. However, only a total of 13.64 million tons in freight crossed through Switzerland, and merely 1.51 million out of a total of 33.06 million tons of road traffic took this route. On the other hand, almost half of the goods transported by rail used the "direct" link.

Not only regulatory differences but also congestion in areas where the problem of missing networks is acute can lead to detours. Detours lengthen the distances travelled between given pairs of origins and destinations, aggravating pollution on the one hand and redistirbuting it in space on the other.

A further consequence of missing networks is the under-utilization of truck capacity. Empty space on trucks which is not traded on a European scale by means of electronic include

TABLE 1

Selected Environmental Effects of Principal Transport Modes

	Marine and Inland Water Transport	Rail Transport	Road Transport	Air Transport
Air			Air pollution (CO, HC, NO_x, particulates and fuel additives such as lead) Global Pollution (CO_2, CFC)	Air pollution
Water Resources	Modification of water systems during port construction and canal cutting and dredging		Pollution of surface water and ground water by surface run-off; modification of waters systems by road building	Modification of water tables, river courses and field drainage in airport construction
Land Resources	Land taken for infrastructures; dereliction of obsolete port facilities and canals	Land taken for rights of way and terminals; dereliction of obsolete facilities	Land taken for infrastructures; extraction of road building materials	Land taken for infra-structures; dereliction of obsolete facilities
Solid Waste	Vessels and craft withdrawn from service	Abandoned lines, equipment and rolling stock	Abandoned spoil tips and rubble from road works; road vehicles withdrawn from service; waste oil	Aircraft withdrawn from service

Continued

TABLE 1 (Continued)

Selected Environmental Effects of Principal Transport Modes

	Marine and Inland Water Transport	Rail Transport	Road Transport	Air Transport
Noise		Noise and vibration around terminals and along railway lines	Noise and vibration from cars, motorcycles and lorries in cities and along main roads	Noise around airports
Risk of Accidents	Bulk transport of fuels and hazardous substances	Derailment or collision of freight carrying hazardous substances	Deaths, injuries and property damaged from road accidents; risk of transport of hazardous substances; risk of structural failure in old or worn road facilities	
Other Impacts		Partition or destruction of neighborhoods, farmland and wildlife habitats	Partition or destruction of neighborhoods, farmland and wildlife habitats; congestion	

Source: ECMT (1990).

TABLE 2

Detours of North-South Road Freight Traffic Around Switzerland

Mode	Volume of Freight Traffic[a] on Road and Rail Between Northern Europe and Italy (1988) Through:		
	France	Switzerland	Austria
Road	14.15	1.51	17.40
Rail	9.00	12.13	5.80

Note: [a]In million tons.

Source: LITRA (1991).

markets cause low load factors and increase the number of trucks necessary to transport a given amount of goods. Here, too, pollution increases due to inefficient traffic.

A distinct feature of the missing networks concept as outlined above is the pentagon of concerns (Nijkamp et al., 1990). The idea is that deficiencies of the transport networks in Europe are not caused mainly by a lack of physical road or railway links but by inadequacies on the level of organization, environmental protection, funding and software. Hence policy options do not entail primarily expensive infrastructure investments but relatively low cost improvements in market organization (mainly through deregulation policies), the introduction of pricing schemes, investments in route guidance, and other RTI means. If the efficiency of the transport network can be increased through measures other than construction of new infrastructure links, the environmental effect in terms of land resources and those under the heading of "other impacts" in Table 1 are minimal.

The question remains whether increasing efficiency through improvements in the organization and the software of the transport network lead to an increase or a decrease in pollution. This is a tricky issue. There is some reason to believe that accidents on a less congested network will be lower but more severe. Moreover, reduced congestion will very probably also reduce air pollution. However, the net effects on pollution are difficult to establish. There is ample evidence that transport significantly contributes to noise and

TABLE 3

Selected Data on Transport and the Environment[a]

	North America	OECD Europe	OECD Total
Road Network Length (growth in %)	11	9	9
Motorways (growth in %)	59	143	79
Road Vehicle Stock (growth in %)	67	101	89
Car Ownership (veh./capita)	0.55	0.32	0.35
Road Traffic Volume (growth in %)	68	81	76
Per Capita (1000 veh.-km/capita)	11.92	4.69	7.06
Total Final Energy Consumption by Road Transport			
Gasoline (growth in %)	24	56	34
Gasoline (share of total in %)	83	60	74
Diesel (growth in %)	168	149	162
Diesel (share of total in %)	16	38	25
Noise from Road Traffic: Population exposed to >65dB(A) in millions	19	61	119
Air Pollution: Share of Transport in Total Emissions in %			
- NO_x	47	51	48
- CO	71	81	75
- HC	39	45	40
- SO_x	4	3	3
- Particulates	14	8	13

Notes: [a]All growth data cover the period 1970-1987. Other data refer to 1987 or the most recent year available.

Source: ECMT (1990).

air pollution. Table 3 gives an overview on the development of transport and air pollution in North America and the OECD for the period 1970 to 1987. Just looking at the figures for OECD Europe shows a 143-percent increase of motorways, a 101-percent growth of the vehicle stock and an 81-percent growth of the total road traffic volume. In 1987, transport accounted for 51 percent of NO_x, 81 percent of CO and 45 percent of HC emissions. Due to technological improvements and political efforts in setting tighter standards on pollution, there is some reason to believe (ECMT, 1990, p. 28) that emissions per vehicle-kilometer have globally decreased since 1970. But on the whole, emissions did not significantly decrease in any country because the stock of motor vehicles in use grew enormously over the period considered (see Table 3).

Thus, past development indicates that a considerable global trend of growth in motor traffic and mobility is well possible without further significant increases in pollution. It is against this background that we want to trace the welfare effects of improving the efficiency of the European transport networks. We shall not speculate about the net effects in terms of pollution. Rather, shall we turn to an economic appraisal of environmental effects to be expected when missing networks in Europe are tackled. Evaluation will typically be based on welfare economic evaluations of internal and external transport effects. This is undertaken in the next section, where the focus is specifically on road freight transport.

3. Missing Networks and Externalities

As was shown above missing networks generally aggravate congestion and make detours necessary. It is worthwhile pointing out again that in our context, detours are not mainly a consequence of missing infrastructure links but rather an outcome of different national transport networks regulations, deficiencies in the operation of these networks, and the like. This argument is developed in the framework of the traditional model of external costs and road transport. Using familiar diagrams, we intend to uncover the internal as well as external welfare implications in terms of net willingness to pay when the problem of missing networks is attenuated. A complication arises with respect to the analysis of detour reduction by the fact that freight transport services are measured in ton-kilometers, i.e., as the product of transported tons per distance travelled. Linking origins and destinations more directly tends to shorten distances covered on the one hand but, on the other, reduces supply prices at the destinations and, therefore, is conducive to lengthening transport distances. It is worth pointing out that this dual effect, at least in principle, is absent from a reduction of the generalized tariff (e.g., by means of a change in fuel prices) leaving link distances untouched. Two questions emerge: (1) which of the two effects will dominate and determine the direction in which transport demand in terms of ton-kilometers will change, and (2) how can this dual effect be integrated into the usual simple transport market model?

The elements of the following transport model derive from the model of spatial markets along a line. To explicitly incorporate detours as a distinct feature of missing networks into the model, a distinction is made between the effective and the direct distance from source to destination. For practical purposes, the direct distance can be identified with air distance. It is assumed that consumers are distributed with constant density along a line market in equally spaced clusters (i.e., towns). The distance x from a representative firm i to a town j is measured along the direct route. Assuming that detours have to be made due to missing networks the effective transport distance y of the goods supplied by the firm i to town j is longer: this is captured in the coefficient s, which is, on average, assumed constant within the road network and not smaller than 1. Therefore, $y = s \cdot x$, ($1 < s$). Further, for simplicity we presume the load factor to be 1 ton per vehicle.

By assumption, consumers' demand is one ton per head as long as the cif price does not exceed their reservation price P, which is considered constant. Given the fob price P, the market boundary R is a function of s and t, generalized transport cost per ton-kilometer:

$$P + t \cdot x \cdot s = \Pi \quad \therefore \quad x = \frac{\Pi - P}{t \cdot s} = R(t,s) \tag{1}$$

Consumers located beyond R kilometers air distance away from the firm prefer to forego purchase from the particular firm. Of course, the market spreads out to the right as well as to the left, but for our purpose it suffices to consider only one side. The relationship between the variables mentioned is illustrated in Figure 1. In the north-east quadrant, the market boundary is determined in terms of effective transport distances. Starting from the firm's location at 0, the cif price increases with effective kilometers traversed and reaches the consumer's reservation price P above point M. In the south-east quadrant, this boundary translates into R air distance kilometers via the detour coefficient s. An exogenous decrease of the generalized transport tariff t extends the market boundary in effective as well as air distance. In contrast, a reduction of the detour coefficient s, e.g., by improving transport conditions along more direct routes, leaves M untouched and yet extends the market boundary R. In other words, reducing s amounts to physically increasing the productivity of road transport: more consumers can be reached by the firm in question with a given number of ton-kilometers.

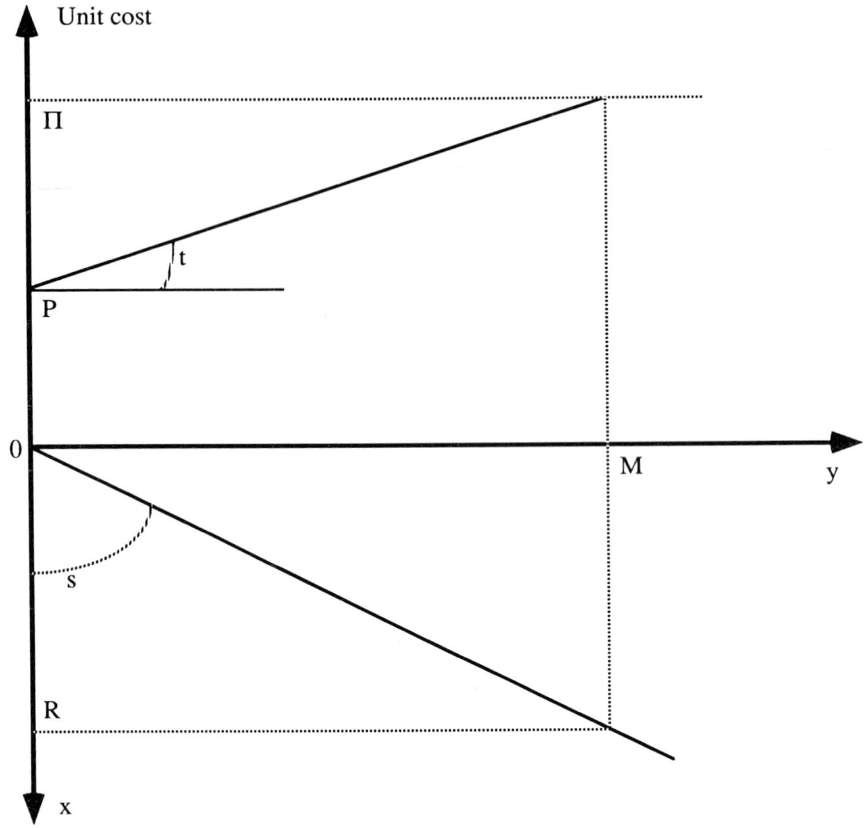

FIGURE 1 A Simple Model of a Spatial Transport Market

In order to determine the effect of t and s on the demand for road transport services, it is necessary to introduce total consumers' demand T for the good transported, i.e., the bulk of transported tons. T is arrived at by aggregating individual demand along the market, starting from the firm's location. Having assumed that consumers are located in clusters along the market line gives rise to a steplike summation function and, in consequence, entails unnecessary computational difficulties. To simplify matters we approximate total demand by means of the following integral, where h is the average and constant density of consumers along x:

$$T = \int_0^R h \cdot dx = h \cdot R(t,s) \tag{2}$$

Equation (2), in connection with (1), implies that with respect to the transport volume T, the detour coefficient s and the generalized tariff t are equivalent. A reduction of t or s by a given percentage will enlarge the market in the same manner and by the same amount. This symmetry does not hold with respect to total demand for transport services measured in ton-kilometers V, which is defined by (3):

$$V = \int_0^R h \cdot x \cdot s \cdot dx = h \cdot s \int_0^R x \cdot dx = \frac{1}{2} h \cdot s \cdot R^2 \tag{3}$$

Here, a decrease of t will act merely via R, inducing extra long haul transports to the edge of the extended market. But a reduction of s, which has the same effect on R as does a reduction of t, will also increase transport productivity in the sense that a given task of good distribution can be achieved with fewer transport services. The productivity effect attenuates the influence acting via R. In this context the question naturally arises as to whether the productivity effect can swamp the market boundary effect, thus leading to an adverse reaction of transport demand measured in ton-kilometers. In the spatial model described above, it turns out that a reduction of s will always increase demand V. Transport demand can be expressed as tons transported (=T) multiplied by average transport distance (=AD). Decreasing s in this model extends the market R, therefore enlarges T, but leaves AD untouched, so that V increases. This result follows from the assumptions of a constant h and P and zero price-elasticity of consumer demand per head for the good in question. Should the density of consumers h taper off quickly enough with air distance from the firm, then average distance AD could drop sufficiently to lower transport demand V. A similar result may emerge if the reservation price P declines sharply enough as we approach the edge of the market, or if we abandon the assumption of constant price-elasticity.

The above argument applies to a representative firm in a given static economic surrounding. Total demand for road transport is arrived at by aggregating individual demand over all firms, taking due account of structural changes induced in the various markets by lowering s. As s is reduced and markets become spatially enlarged, market opportunities and competitive pressure increase, transport costs forfeit importance in comparison to production costs. On the assumption of economies of scale and scope in production, low cost firms will widen their market shares at the disadvantage of high cost firms. In consequence, short haul transports are replaced by long haul traffic, increasing the average transport distances. Although similar results are to be expected from a fall in the generalized tariff t, a reduction in s is distinct from a decrease of t because it exerts its influence on demand via an increase of transport productivity.

To identify the effects of a policy towards eliminating missing networks, the demand for transport services has to be confronted with their costs. In (4) we define total operating costs C as a function of ton-kilometers (V) produced and traffic density d:

$$C = C(V,d) = V \cdot c(d); \qquad d = \frac{V}{K(a,e)} \tag{4}$$

This relation makes average operating costs per ton-kilometer dependent only on d, which is defined as total ton-kilometers produced divided by road network capacity K. K is made a function of total road area a and an efficiency coefficient e. It is assumed that increasing a by infrastructure investment and/or e, e.g., by means of traffic management, enlarges capacity K and reduces average operating costs, given V. This is illustrated in Figure 2. As usual in the context of similar analyses, the average costs can be identified with the private marginal transport costs of road users. They comprise fuel, variable depreciation costs, time in transport, etc.

However, a change in a and/or e may not only diminish average operating costs but also affect the detour coefficient s. The relationship is dependent on the influence of a and e on the structure of traffic flows and is, for this reason, awkward to capture in the highly aggregated model presented above. We restrict ourselves to a verbal description. Insofar as an increase of a or e induces a shortening of effective transport distances between origins and destinations, e.g., by diverting traffic to shorter links, it also becomes relevant for demand by decreasing s. In this case, the change of capacity K is accompanied by a significant structural shift of traffic flows. As a result, the average operating cost curve

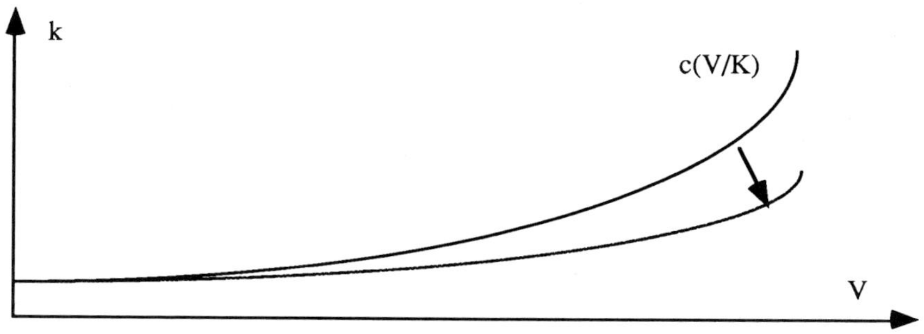

FIGURE 2 Network Efficiency and Average Cost

is lowered and the demand curve moved to the right. These effects are characteristic for policy measures directed towards eliminating "missing links". If the increase of a or e does not entail major structural variation of traffic flows, then only capacity is enlarged but s, i.e., the demand curve, remains untouched. Keeping this relationship between a, e, and s in mind, the model is closed and we can proceed to general conclusions.

Figure 3 summarizes the results so far. At the outset, road market equilibrium is characterized by point E if externalities are not internalized. An increase of a or e which does not significantly change traffic flows lowers the average operating cost curve relevant for transport decisions. As a result, traffic increases along the demand curve to a new equilibrium E', where average operating costs are lower on account of reduced congestion and time costs per transport. As the effective distances between origins and destinations are not or only slightly affected, s remains constant. Increases in a or e which significantly reduce detours may have the same effect on capacity K of the network and on the average operating cost curve as before, but, in addition, they shift the demand curve to the right. The resulting equilibrium now lies in E'', where traffic is definitely greater than in E and E'; average operating costs, however, are higher than in E' but not necessarily lower than in E. Although time costs per ton-kilometer may fall, total time spent in transport can increase.

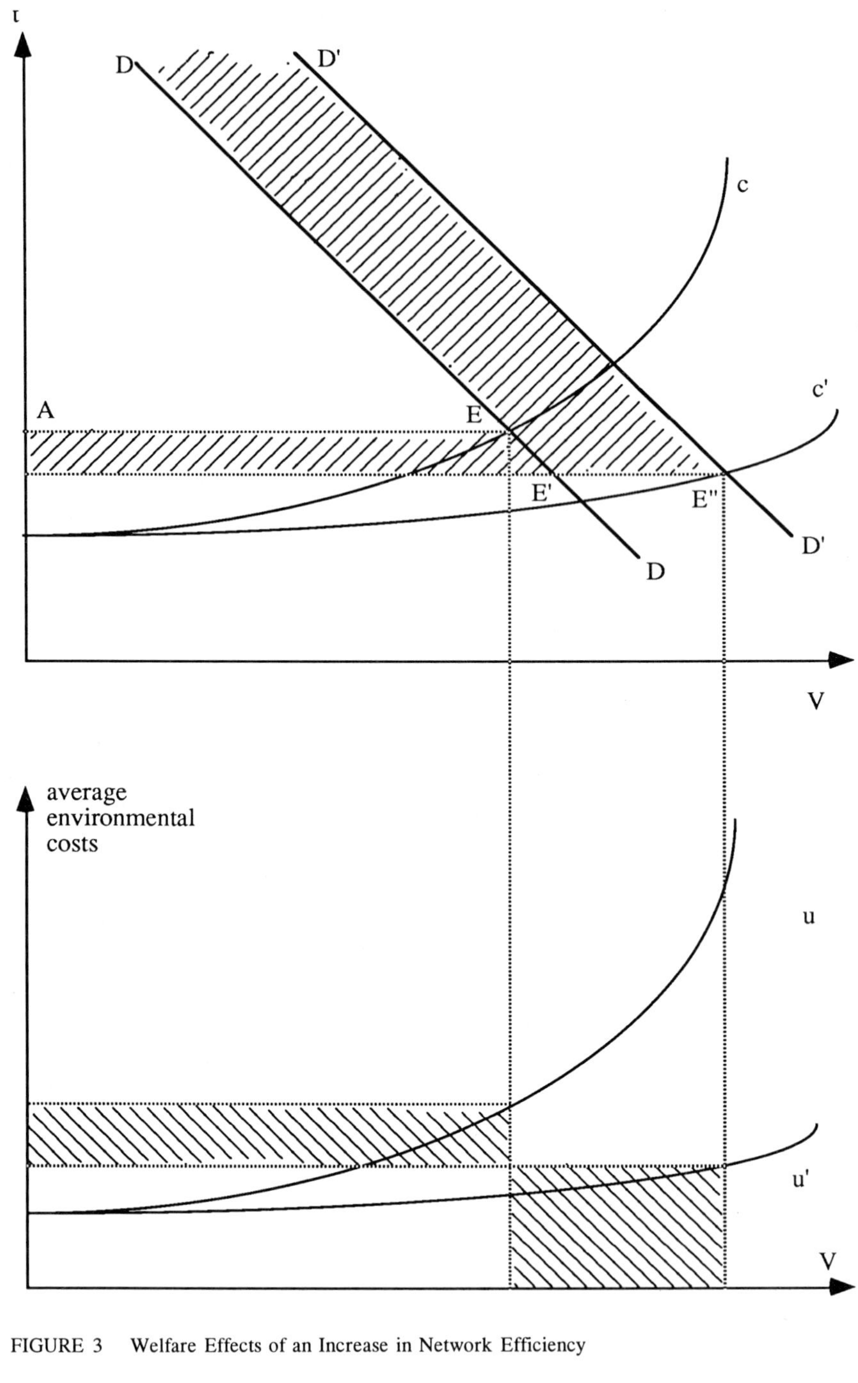

FIGURE 3 Welfare Effects of an Increase in Network Efficiency

Figure 3 essentially characterizes road transport equilibria under the alternative conditions specified above. It can also serve as a basis for estimating the welfare effects of road transport. The DD curve incorporates long term demand, i.e., demand for transport services on the condition of all-round competitive markets driving prices to average costs, thereby reducing profit margins to zero. If we neglect external environmental costs from the beginning, the current welfare gain induced by the road network of existing capacity can be measured by the amount by which the willingness to pay surpasses total road transport costs. As the average operating cost curve merely includes user's variable costs, this gain corresponds to the area below DD and above AE diminished by fixed road costs. By enlarging road capacity, a reduction of s or an increase of e will, on the one hand, flatten the average operating cost curve and slightly shift it downwards, and on the other hand, move the demand curve to the right to D'D'. As a result, welfare is increased by the amount corresponding to the shaded area minus extra fixed capacity costs caused by the introduction of the policy measures. If these latter costs are considered unimportant -- as might be expected for various measures realized -- the welfare gain is approximately equal to the area indicated.

As yet, external environmental costs have not been considered. They are examined separately in the lower panel of Figure 3. The u curve reflects average external environmental costs, which are assumed proportional to time costs per ton-kilometer and, in particular, to congestion. It is assumed that a capacity increase will, therefore, lower the c as well as the u function. This supposition is by no means justified in all cases. A reduction of detours may, in some instances, shorten distances and save transport time but increase environmental costs by guiding traffic through more densely populated areas. On other occasions, it may lower time costs and attenuate environmental costs. The relationship between the two types of costs heavily depends not only on the particular circumstances in question but also on the economic alternatives open to the agents affected for evading damages incurred by transport. Without additional information, it seems reasonable to presuppose proportionality, in which case a reduction in detours will vary total environmental costs in proportion to total transport time. The latter in, turn, is determined by the time-elasticity of demand, the strength by which existing detours hamper long term demand, and the elasticity of average operating costs. If total time costs increase in the model, so will total environmental costs.

Without introducing estimates of the various parameters and evaluations (e.g., the price of transport time, of pollution, of fuel to the economy) no definite conclusions as to the change of total environmental costs can be drawn. Three points should, however, be noticed.

* Overcoming missing networks may increase external environmental costs but also increase transport productivity and generate internal benefits. Welfare considerations demand that the two effects be considered. Short of evaluating pollution, prohibitively high judgment on appropriate policy measures only from the point of view of the environment is not vindicated.

* Technical advances in the development of environmentally "cleaner" vehicles lower average pollution costs. In consequence, the positive effects of overcoming missing networks come to the fore as time goes by.

* Benefits from overcoming missing networks do not necessarily accrue to those population groups who bear the burden of extra environmental damage, i.e., implementation of appropriate policy measures involves more or less significant redistribution of real income. It is to this aspect that we now turn our attention.

4. Options and Obstacles for a European Policy

From the arguments made above, it emerges that solving the missing networks problem can have a positive effect on welfare even if externalities are not internalized. This effect is produced by a policy of improving the efficiency of the existing networks rather than building new roads and links. Some elements of such a policy related to freight transport are now presented (for more detail see Maggi et al., 1992; Nijkamp et al., 1990).

A solution for many of the current problems in European freight transport might be the realization of a multi-layer network which combines road and rail transport. The first layer would consist of a combined transport network, where the nodes would be large European freight terminals near the major European agglomerations; links would be established by block trains running according to a timetable. This network would be based on a standardized container technology. The terminals would be equipped with advanced transhipment technology. A second layer would have to be installed, based on what might be called soft technologies, in combined transport. The nodes of this network would be the existing freight stations in Europe. These stations could be used for combined transport due to the use of transhipment techniques which allow drivers to change their loads (piggy-back transport, roadrailers, kettle lift containers). The links would consist of piggy back trains. This network links smaller centers all over Europe. Points for change between the two modes would be dictated only by logistic and market reasons, not by network restrictions.

This two-layer system requires an advanced logistic system. A future integrated European Electronic Data Interchange (EDI) system for combined transport, which deals with the movement of freight on road and rail at the same time, is urgently needed. Logistic centers placed at large terminals should provide services on a commercial basis to any hauler who wants to operate combined transport. Important measures for reestablishing rail freight transport as an important, distinct market force, then, would be the reorganization of European rail companies in terms of the concept of common carriage and the establishment of a network of normal and combined freight transport following an inter-modal rather than inter-nation logic.

The potential of rail freight and combined transport on road and rail in the near future should not be overestimated, however. Therefore, other solutions have to be found for road haulage. One possibility might be a satellite-based network of mobile telecommunication in the European truck fleet. The equipment of vehicles with onboard computers and communication systems would make it possible to exchange information on position and load, leading to realtime revisions of route assignments. The installation of such a system (consisting of sensors on the mobile units and data processors and user interfaces in mobile units as well as at headquarters) would considerably reduce the movement of empty trucks, increase the efficiency of road transport, and thus enormously increase the capacity of the existing network. As Beroggi and Wallace (1991) show, realtime control of freight movements is possible via satellite tracking systems. In the U.S., two systems are already in operation, namely GPS (Department of Defense) and GEOSTAR. An equivalent to the latter for Europe (LOCSTAR) is planned. The installation of such a communication system, consisting of sensors on the mobile units and data processors and user interfaces in mobile units as well as headquarters, could greatly improve the efficiency of the total road transport system, including empty truck space trading.

Organization also presents a problem. One reason for the number of empty vehicles which adds to the congestion of the European road network is the structure of the transport sector and the organization of transport and logistics by large firms. In many cases, the warehouses of different retailers are located next to each other, at a motorway intersection. Large numbers of half-empty vehicles roll in the same direction, with similar destinations, to and from these clusters. Some measure of coordination between the logistic departments of firms could certainly contribute to a reduction of road congestion problems and reduce costs. Empty truck space could, in principle, be traded through an agency. Proposals exist, e.g., in Switzerland, to introduce such an institution with an electronic data base. According to some recent estimates, a quarter to one half of the estimated 45 percent of empty trucks on the Swiss network in 1989 could be taken off the road with such a measure. Market organization obviously also relates to regulation. The current deregulation of the road haulage sector in Europe will also increase the efficiency. In our context, the possibility of cabotage would greatly reduce the amount of less-than-truckload traffic.

The implementation of the above proposals would help to attenuate the problem of missing networks in freight transport. But only a definite European-wide economic interest in the realization of these solutions will increase the chance of their implementation. We have demonstrated that there might be important positive welfare effects from solving the missing networks problem. We will now discuss how the distribution of these effects in space and among groups reduces the chances of such policy measures being implemented.

Increasing the efficiency of the European road network will produce positive internal benefits for the households and firms who express a demand for transported goods. These are located in the centers (or clusters) of population along the route. But to the extent that traffic is concentrated on some main links, as are some alpine valleys, the population along these links is more strongly affected by the external effects in terms of pollution than by the positive internal effects. This creates regional resistance against improving the efficiency of the road network in many regions. The unequal distribution of costs and benefits in space will hamper the implementation of the measures. This especially holds in situations where local or national political processes are more effective than European ones. The forces in favor of the policy must address their demand to the less effective European level while the opposition can fall back on well-developed national or regional policy processes.

A second resistance factor relates to the way in which households perceive the policy impacts. The benefits of improved road network efficiency are internal benefits to the consumers of the transported goods. On the one hand, the effects in terms of variety and prices of products are not easily discernible and are not necessarily identified as being the outcome of improved transport conditions. On the other hand, environmental problems, which have a multitude of sources, are identified by households as being produced mainly by the transport sector and, more specifically, by cars. In many European countries, this has led to an ardent demand for an effective environmental policy which reduces road traffic. In this context, increased efficiency of the European freight transport system is seen by households primarily as producing bigger environmental problems. Hence, households will object to a European solution to the missing networks problem. Again, this opposition has a spatial aspect because the environmental interests of households are well-organized on a regional and national level, while there is no pressure group for the interests of households as consumers on a European level. Moreover, households, who normally add to pollution through their own mobility behavior, can use this policy to blame outsiders for the pollution. Not only can blame be put on freight transport in general, but on "foreign" freight transport in particular, intensifying regional or national interest in protection.

If we consider the industrial sector, it can be said that its interest lies generally in an improvement of the performance of the transport sector on a European level. Their concern is for the "costs of non-Europe" (Cecchini, 1989) associated with among others, the problem of missing networks. Although the heavy regulation on road haulage in many countries will soon be abolished, and important plans for a rapid train system and combined transport have been put forward (CEC, 1989), there remain important obstacles which are related to national borders. What does this imply for the solution of the problems of missing networks in Europe?

Basically, the industry has a clear interest in an increase in efficiency because they expect to gain higher profits. However, this interest is straightforward only in the case of competitive firms which can expect to survive in a European market and thus reap the fruits of improved efficiency. A clear indicator is provided by reports of the European Round Table of Industrialists (ERTI, 1987). Firms which are not competitive will be more interested in national protection than in an improved European transport network as the latter would expose them to stronger competition. Hence, the competitive industries will demand improvement of network efficiency and express it on a European level, while non-competitive sectors will join households in their demand for national protection.

Given the structural weakness of European political institutions and the tradition of national regulations, there is some reason to believe that national restrictions on freight transport have greater chances of realization than do European measures for improved efficiency of the transport networks. Hence, the lever for change would be deregulation of the transport sector on the national level because this would essentially force all players in the game to compete on the European market as well as, in consequence, to address their policy demand on this level.

5. Conclusions

This paper began from the assertion that missing networks on a European scale can be identified in all transport and communication modes. It was argued that networks have at least five different aspects which have to be considered in the framework of a European policy. These dimensions are hardware, software, market organization, funding problems and externalities. We have concentrated on low cost efficiency-improving measures on the software and organizational levels rather than on the construction of new infrastructure links.

We have discussed the impacts of such a policy from the point of view of welfare. It was shown that on the one hand, the reductions of network deficiencies will lower time and environmental costs on present transport links but, on the other hand, they tend to extend market areas of competitively strong firms and to increase the demand for transport services in the long run. Therefore, apart from the negative environmental impacts through increased traffic, important internal benefits are generated as well. These have to be balanced against each other. The net effect cannot be evaluated without empirical investigation.

Policy strategies to solve the missing networks problem were shown to exist on the organizational and software level. Problems were identified regarding the implementation of such measures on a European level. Only competitive industries have a straightforward interest in increasing the efficiency of transport networks throughout Europe. Local interest groups, who lose more from pollution than they gain in terms of internal benefits, will join forces with non-competitive firms and households who can better identify environmental externalities than internal benefits stemming from improved transport networks. Together they will ask for reinforcement of national protectionist transport policy measures that will inhibit solutions to the problem of missing networks in Europe. It is concluded that only a national deregulation policy will create the preconditions for a European transport policy.

References

Beroggi, G.E.G. and Wallace, W.A., 1991, Real-time Control of the Transportation of Hazardous Materials, *URISA Proceedings*.

Cecchini, P., et al., 1989, *The European Challenge 1992, The Benefits of the Single Market,* Gower, Aldershot.

Commission for the European Communities (CEC), 1989, *Council Resolution on the Trans-European Networks,* Com(89) 643, EC, Brussels.

European Conference of Ministers of Transport (ECMT), 1990, *Transport Policy and the Environment,* OECD, Paris.

European Round Table of Industrialists (ERTI), 1987, *Keeping Europe Mobile. A Report on Advanced Transport Systems, Prepared for ERTI,* Stockholm.

European Round Table of Industrialists (ERTI), 1990, *Missing Networks. A European Challenge*, ERTI, Brussels.

LITRA, 1991, *Der oeffentliche Verkehr 1991*. Informationsdienst fuer den oeffentlichen Verkehr, Bern.

Maggi, R., 1992, Swiss Transport Policy for Europe? Federalism and the Dominance of Local Issues, *Transportation Research A*, 26A, 2, 193-198.

Maggi, R., Nijkamp, P. and Masser, I., 1992, Missing Networks in European Transport and Communication, *Transport Reviews,* 12, 311-321.

Nijkamp, P., Maggi, R., Masser, I. and Vleugel, J., 1990, *Missing Networks in Europe*, ERTI, Brussels.

TRANSPORT IN A UNIFIED EUROPE. Policies and Challenges.
D. Banister and J. Berechman (Editors)

Chapter Nine

THE LINKS BETWEEN MOBILITY AND ENVIRONMENTAL SUSTAINABILITY

Vlasta Dugonjic
Veli Himanen
Peter Nijkamp
Juraj Padjen

1. Introduction

The role of transport in our modern societies is hybrid in nature. Transport has created many socio-economic benefits; all societies rely heavily on transport services for their economic functioning. However, transport has also given rise to numerous and severe problems in many places. The unconstrained transport growth in Western Europe appears to have reached a point beyond which any increase in traffic is counter-productive (i.e., a situation of negative marginal benefits).

Natural resources most affected by transport are energy, air, land, and water which are, in a wider sense, also connected with human life and health, flora, fauna, and the aesthetic quality of the human environment. Priority of these problems vary according to whether global, national, regional or municipal considerations are used.

In densely populated parts of Western Europe, traffic has in many places reached the available capacity of the transport system, resulting in heavy congestion. And all over Europe, road traffic has exposed cities -- and significant parts of whole nations -- to continuing noise and pollution impacts, not to speak of the everyday risk of traffic accidents. Furthermore, in the European core areas, transport also competes with other activities in terms of claims on the available land area.

Despite the increasing popularity of just-in-time (JIT) systems and related concepts (e.g., materials requirement planning -- MRP), the actual practice of both freight and passenger transport is disappointing and often frustrating. Severe traffic congestion is a phemonenon at the urban or metropolitan level (e.g., Athens, Rome, Paris). Unacceptable delays are common in medium and long distance transport during peak hours, unsatisfactory levels of service are found on European railway systems (and public transport in general), unreliable airline connections result from limited airport capacity, and slow technical and institutional renewal of air traffic control have all contributed to the difficult situation within the European transport sector. And there is no clear perspective for a drastic improvement in this situation.

Since many transport problems can be interpreted as a symptom of both failing market mechanisms and failing government policy, these problems can hardly be solved within the transport sector alone. Confronted with a clear inconsistency between demand for more mobility and negative effects of traffic, Europe is faced with the need for stronger governmental actions in order to ensure a balanced relationship between demand and supply. When we regard the volume of cross-border traffic, the international nature of the car industry, the national trade interests and the global aspects of air and water pollution, it is obvious that actions of the national governments are bound to remain insufficient. Actions at the European and global level are needed.

In the next section (Section 2) a sketch of the evolution of transport problems is presented, followed by a review of general megatrends (Section 3) as well as a discussion about trends in transport policy (Section 4). Future prospects of European transport policy are then examined with the aid of a scenario analysis (Section 5).

2. The Evolution of Transport Problems

Transport problems can be subdivided into three categories: traditional, modern, and post-modern. Traditional transport problems refer to the everyday question for individuals: how to get from one place to another? A feature of the 1990s is the emergence of large scale (national and international) transport networks with huge volumes of circulating vehicles, which have enabled unforeseen mobility (Bovy et al., 1992). The resulting environmental problems and high accident rates form a key issue in modern transport problems. The post-modern transport problem is typical of densely populated societies with congested networks and without much room for further expansion (Banister, 1989). In this situation, selective use of infrastructure seems necessary, involving difficult distributional conflicts among user categories. In the following section, the phenomenon of the modern transport problem, which is in sharp conflict with environmental sustainability, will be elaborated further.

2.1 Congestion, Accidents, and Land Use

Congestion is an obvious phenomenon in all heavily used transport systems. In Europe, congestion is especially felt on the main roads of core areas as well as in all European metropolitan areas and at many international airports. The intensity of this problem depends on the time of day and location, on the transport network, and on the type and mode of transport. Many peripheral regions and some less densely populated parts of Central Europe are still relatively free of congestion and resulting damage (Group Transport 2000 Plus, 1990). Traffic congestion in the core areas of Western Europe is related mainly to the high density of population and economic activities. In addition, there is also a traditionally heavy north-south traffic flow which crosses the core areas through a limited number of corridors. Also, more recently, a rapid development of east-west traffic flows has been apparent (Gérardin and Viégas, 1992). According to some authors, the available transport capacity is no longer sufficient to keep the traffic flowing during the peak periods. At the same time, building of new infrastructure has to face increasing difficulties related to competition for available space, the high price of land, and increasing consciousness of environmental questions (ERTI, 1989). The situation has already led to severe problems in the Greater Tokyo area in Japan.

One extremely important but often neglected aspect of the social costs of surface transport has to be added: about 50,000 people are killed every year, and some 1,500,000 further are injured on European roads (Group Transport 2000 Plus, 1990). According to Masser et al. (1992), in the former Federal Republic of Germany (FRG), more than half a million people have died in road accidents since 1950. The same authors allege that through safer cars and better roads, traffic deaths per 100,000 population have more than halved between 1970 and 1985 (from 32.0 to 13.1), but this still means 8,000 fatal accidents per year.

In this respect, remarkable differences exist between European countries: from 22 people per 100,000 population per year killed in traffic in Portugal to 10 people in the Netherlands (see Table 1). The situation in former socialist countries is even worse.

TABLE 1

Road Transport Fatalities Per Year and Per 100,000 Inhabitants, 1989

Country	Number of Persons Killed per Year	Number Killed per 100,000 Inhabitants
Austria	1 402	18.4
Belgium	1 993	20.1
Denmark	670	13.1
Finland	734	14.8
France	10 528	18.7
Germany, Fed.Rep.	7 995	12.9
Greece	1 699	17.0
Ireland	460	13.1
Italy	6 410	11.2
Luxemburg	67	16.8
Netherlands	1 456	9.8
Norway	381	9.0
Portugal	2 375	22.7
Spain	7 188	18.5
Sweden	904	10.6
Switzerland	925	13.9
United Kingdom	5 554	9.7
EC + EFTA	50 741	14.8

Source: ECE, Statistics of Road Traffic Accidents in Europe, 1991.

In Lithuania, 30 people per 100,000 population were killed in road traffic in 1991. In all the Baltic countries, road deaths have increased by 60 percent since the mid-1980s (Segercrantz, 1992).

Finally, there is the issue of land use by the transport sector. In the former Federal Republic of Germany (FRG), the entire transport infrastructure took a fraction of its total area, about 5 percent (approximately 1.2 million hectares). In agglomerations like the Rhein-Ruhr area, the share of transport infrastructure is more than 10 percent of the area, and in some cities even considerably more, especially if we include parking space and other transport provisions. In the time period from 1968 to 1988, the area needed for roads in the former FRG increased by about 35 percent due to an extension of the road network and widening of existing roads (Blum and Rothengatter, 1989). A similar situation can also be found in the Benelux countries, England and some parts of France. If the increase in road traffic with accompanying road construction continues in Europe, we may face the American situation (Renner, 1989), where at least one-third of an average city's land is devoted to roads, parking lots, and other forms of traffic infrastructure.

2.2 Energy Consumption, Air Pollution, and Noise

The transport sector constitutes one of the major consumers of energy in Western Europe and its share is growing in relative and absolute terms. In the European Community (EC) the transport sector accounts for some 20 to 25 percent of total final energy consumption (with a correspondingly high share of carbon dioxide (CO_2) emissions) and 40 to 50 percent of oil consumption. More than 95 percent of the energy used in the transport sector originates from oil while less than 5 percent is in the form of electricity (ECE, 1990).

Road transport is the highest energy consumer. Inland waterways and air transport also depend exclusively on oil. In contrast, most of the European railways carry out the bulk of their operations by electric traction, making the railways the only motorized mode of transport which is less dependent on the supply of oil-based fuels.

After the energy crisis of the 1970s, total energy consumption per capita has slightly decreased. However, the energy savings in road transport due to more energy-efficient and smaller cars have now been largely eradicated by the increasing tendency to use larger cars and to make more and longer trips (Masser et al., 1992).

Because cars run almost exclusively on oil-based fuels, road transport is very sensitive to changes in the price and availability of oil. Moreover, as Renner (1989) has rightly pointed out, a transport system centered on the private passenger car can impose tremendous costs on society, whether in the form of escalating fuel import bills or huge expenditures of capital and resources to tap domestic fuel sources. In the longer run, it should also be remembered that oil wells will sooner or later dry up and alternative energy sources are far from being ready for commercial use. Despite possible technical progress, the penetration of renewable forms of energy into the transport sector is likely to be extremely slow (Group Transport 2000 Plus, 1990).

Transport -- cars, trucks, vans, and buses in particular -- cause exhaust fumes and other wastes that have a negative influence on the quality of air, water, and soil. In the countries belonging to the Organization for Economic Cooperation and Development (OECD), the transport sector contributes about 90 percent of carbon monoxide (CO), 40 percent of hydrocarbons (HC), and about 50 percent of nitrogen oxides (NOx) emissions (Linster, 1990).

It is plausible that the synergetic effects of air pollution are perhaps most significant (Renner, 1989). The best known and most pervasive of these effects is photochemical smog, which causes health disturbance, restricts visibility, erodes buildings and monuments, reduces crop yields, and is at least partly responsible for the massive forest damage afflicting Central Europe.

The installation of catalytic convertors in passenger cars and vans with petrol engines appears to be very effective. According to a recent survey (Mäkelä et al., 1990), exhaust emissions per kilometer from new private cars using gasoline in 2010 will be 30 percent (CO), 10 percent (HC), and 18 percent (NO_x) of the corresponding levels of emissions in city streets in 1989. On highways, the corresponding figures will be approximately 25, 50 and 6 percent. The above figures refer to petrol engines. An effective technical solution for lorries and buses with diesel engines is still being developed.

Traffic increases, cold startups, use of diesel engines and inevitable maintenance problems will however, affect the possible gains in emission reductions. In the USA, where catalytic convertors have been in use as of the late 1970s, the emissions of HC and CO from transport in 1987 were still around 60 percent of the emissions observed in 1975, and only a very minor reduction in the NO_x emissions could be observed (Linster, 1990).

Road transport noise is another widespread phenomenon. More than 50 percent of the population of OECD European countries are exposed to noise levels of more than 55 dB(A) (Linster, 1990). According to a 1986 survey, in the former FRG, 65 percent of the respondents felt affected by road traffic noise, 25 percent of them severely (Blum and Rothengatter, 1989).

The evolution of transport problems in Europe is tightly connected to European socio-economic development, changes in global ecology, and directions in European transport policy. These matters will be further discussed in the next sections.

3. A Review of Megatrends

3.1 From the Industrial to the Post-industrial Age

According to Bruckmann (1987), the economic history of man can be subdivided into three ages: the pre-industrial, the industrial, and the post-industrial age. We are now living at the turning point between the last two. What is most interesting is that Bruckmann supposes that the whole framework of our social evolution is changing. During the history of mankind, there has always been scarcity but no limits in growth. Now we have become affluent but the limits in further growth are obvious. The affluence is of course only related to the developed nations. Scarcity still prevails in developing nations as well as in former socialist countries in Europe. All are, however, equal in facing the limits in growth. King and Schneider (1991) are waiting for a new era, as witnessed in the title of their new report to the Club of Rome, "The First Global Revolution".

The characterization of human activities up to a level where we can speak of an industrial age is a very rough one. Industrial production of artifacts is actually only a continuation of pre-historic handicraft. The difference is mainly in scale and the technology used. The major point is the affluence starting with industrial development, which has changed and expanded all human activities.

The importance of agriculture has not diminished during the industrial age. We are still totally dependent on it for our food. In the post-industrial age we will remain dependent on agriculture for food and on industry for artifacts. What is actually changing is the number of people directly working in production. Because of rationalization and automation, the quantity of workers needed per produced item is steadily and structurally diminishing. This implies that more and more people can be engaged in other human activities.

Sarkar (1967) has developed a theory that world ages change according to the dominant "Weltanschauung", which is based on archetypes. The relevant archetypes are soldiers, intellectuals, capitalists, and workers. The last ones have never had power, but the three previous groups of people have become -- one after the other -- dominant in the past. A change from one period to another may in the long run be beneficial because after a good start, all epochs are likely to exhibit a tendency toward destruction. In developed countries, various people believe that we are now probably living in the final stage of the capitalist dominance and that new ideas are about to arise. There are several signs of a new society of law and order, in which the policy on prevailing global problems (e.g., how to obtain environmental sustainability) may be concentrated in the hands of international organizations, such as the United Nations or the EC. In any case, internationalization of political power seems to be an inevitable trend, and this will have far-reaching implications for the transport sector.

3.2 Human Activities and Nature

The global nature of many human activities (including transport) also has many implications for the environment. Human life is dependent on an uninterrupted functioning of natural ecosystems. Sun, soil, water, air, plants, and animals form the basis for all human activities. We are using energy and raw materials from our natural environment and, after their use in production and consumption processes, return them as waste and heat back to the natural system.

With increasing affluence and increasing population, the human influence on nature has greatly expanded. Natural ecosystems do not always immediately react to distorting human activities as, because of their resilience, they can continue to function for a long time by means of stabilizing feedback; but they cannot resist structural and intensive environmental disruption (Knoflacher and Himanen, 1991; Stutz, 1986). According to Stigliani et al. (1989), the environmental hazards caused by human activities in Europe are accumulating in such a manner that many profound changes in production and consumption systems are needed.

It should be noticed that the European transport sector is only a fraction of the global system responsible for worldwide environmental problems. Its share is however, not negligible. According to King and Schneider (1991), there are at present four predominant cases of macro pollution at a global scale: (1) diffusion of toxic substances in the environment; (2) the acidification of lakes and the destruction of forests; (3) depletion of the ozone layer; (4) greenhouse effect. The major impacts of transport are connected to the second and the fourth. In view of all these severe problems, it is important to map out the present prevailing trends in European economies (with particular emphasis on the transport sector).

3.3 European Trends

The field of transport, communications and mobility is in full motion. International commodity transport (in terms of both volume and value) is increasing, international passenger transport is rapidly rising, and international telecommunication is increasingly gaining importance. From an international (i.e., cross-European) perspective, the following megatrends at the European level can, *inter alia*, be observed:

* Despite many institutional frictions, there is an increasing tendency towards an integrated and open European market, which by 1993 will become the largest trade block in the world. This trade block will increasingly also include EFTA countries.

* On the European level, many initiatives are being taken to improve and expand the current international infrastructure (e.g., the Channel Tunnel, the extension of French TGV, the construction of the Trans-European Motorway, and the design of an advanced European telecommunications system), so that all European countries will be linked to each other via a common and accessible network.

* Internationally, the heartland of Europe is shifting towards both the east and the south, which has enormous economic and social implications for transport and mobility all over Europe. Furthermore, many different kinds of border problems still have to be solved in Europe's unification policy.

* Many countries have officially adopted a "basic right" principle towards peripheral or less accessible areas, which means that a certain level of accessibility is ensured on the basis of this equity paradigm. However, in the case of severe budget stress, such principles tend to be easily neglected, particularly when it is accompanied by privatization of (parts of) the infrastructure networks for public transport services, telecommunications, etc. This may lead to severe imbalances and serious equity problems at the European level.

* The European trend toward more deregulation and decentralization may seduce policy makers into questioning whether there is a case for planning at all. More particularly, the seemingly higher efficiency gains of a market-oriented planning system need to be traded off against the social welfare gains of public interventions (Section 4.1).

* International spatial interactions in the form of physical movements of persons or commodities are increasingly influenced by recent developments in the field of communication and information technologies (including telematics).

* The area of commodity transport is going through a rapid transition phase, especially due to the emergence of modern logistic systems. For both national and European freight transport, this development has far-reaching consequences, not only in efficiency terms but also in terms of social consequences.

* The conflicts between economic efficiency, social equity ("access"), and environmental sustainability goals become increasingly sharper in the transport sector.

Clearly, the above-mentioned examples of megatrends in transport are by no means exhaustive, but they do suggest that the 1990s will require new ways of analyzing policy in which a meaningful blend has to be found between allocative efficiency, distributional equity, and environmental spillovers (and other externalities) in a highly dynamic urban and regional setting of European countries marked by structural changes in technology, socio-economic conditions, scarcity of (natural and financial) resources, lifestyles, and socio-demographic patterns.

In the spatial design of European transport networks and transport activities, there are tendencies for both decentralization and centralization. Decentralization policies are based upon the expectation that disparities between central and peripheral countries may be reduced. According to this policy, the European Parliament has established the European Regional Development Fund having extensive powers to redirect economic activities from the core agglomeration to the peripheral areas (Masser et al., 1992). Opponents of this policy allege that it has been only partly successful. It has somewhat helped to reduce regional disparities within Europe but it has also constrained global competitiveness in the world market.

Centralization of economic and transport activities is based on the locational advantages of the core European regions, such as the supply of high skilled labor, the industrial heritage, and good access to international transport and communication networks. These will guarantee the growth of high tech manufacturing and information-based service industries. Consequently, current transport policies are likely to reinforce rather than counteract today's centralization tendencies.

4. Trends in European Transport Policy

4.1 A Shift in Transport Planning Orientation

The context and substance of transport planning has drastically changed in the past decade. Until recently, transport planning has been strongly dominated by engineering views on network use and expansion. Social science-oriented views have begun to enter the discussion of transport behavior and infrastructure only in recent years, as transport policy in Europe increasingly faces a dilemma between economic-technological potential and environmental-social constraints. Transport infrastructure is a critical factor for successful internationalization of our economies whereas, at the same time, further network expansion is incompatible with the need for a high quality of life. Therefore, transport policy does not only require engineering solutions but it also has to be implemented on the basis of concern for our societies (Nijkamp et al., 1990).

An important background factor is that "Euromobility" has become a widespread phenomenon in all European countries, at all geographical scales ranging from local to international (see Table 2). This mobility drift is clearly not technology-driven, but has arisen as a result of far-reaching changes in our ways of living, thinking and working. Our welfare societies are generating a complex array of contact patterns (material and immaterial) which require physical interaction on an unprecedented scale. Nevertheless, the daily travel time per person has hardly increased; this "law of conservation of travel time" essentially means that the average travel speed -- and hence distance -- has increased. Apparently, there is an intrinsic resistance against unlimited travel time, so that the need for quality improvement of transport networks has come to the fore (Nijkamp and Priemus, 1992).

In addition, awareness of the limits to growth in mobility has also dramatically increased. Environmental and safety considerations have become major factors in the social acceptance of our mobile society. Thus, new transport solutions and technologies will have to be implemented within increasingly narrower limits imposed by our society. The range of such solutions is even further limited by the simultaneous behaviour of all actors in the transport sector generating congestion effects (Kreutzberger et al., 1992).

TABLE 2

Number of Cars, Average Annual Car-Kilometers and Total Car-Kilometers in the Netherlands, 1970-1989

Year	Number of Cars (1000)	Annual Car Kilometers	Total Car Kilometers (10^6)
1970	2 405	14 890	35 810
1971	2 637	14 980	39 510
1972	2 833	14 390	40 760
1973	3 005	14 300	42 960
1974	3 134	13 850	43 400
1975	3 289	14 430	47 450
1976	3 444	14 530	50 050
1977	3 636	14 380	52 290
1978	3 811	15 010	57 190
1979	4 052	14 360	58 190
1980	4 240	13 880	58 850
1981	4 314	13 570	58 520
1982	4 350	13 860	60 260
1983	4 438	14 220	63 110
1984	4 519	14 460	65 340
1985	4 600	14 120	64 950
1986	4 462	14 680	68 140
1987	4 755	14 980	71 230
1988	4 921	15 350	75 530
1989	5 086	15 190	77 260

Source: Blaas et al. (1992).

The "undesirable" outcome of a highly mobile society is -- almost paradoxically -- the result of rational and plausible actions of a great many individuals. Social science research has convincingly demonstrated that the neglect of social costs in individual decision making must, by necessity, lead to a macro outcome that is far from optimal. This explains the worsening quality of life conditions in European major cities.

Thus, it seems as though quick and effective actions to cope with the negative externalities of the transport sector are absolutely necessary. On the other hand, many people in our society are not convinced that such actions should necessarily be a responsibility of governments, as they see a clear conflict between goals, measures and social acceptance of policies in the transport sector. Therefore, it is necessary to pay more explicit attention to the role of governments in the transport sector.

4.2 The Role of Governments

Under certain conditions, conventional welfare economics teaches us that government interventions may be at odds with a Pareto-efficient allocation of goods and production factors. However, in every country with a market system, the government usually intervenes. In addition, the degree of government intervention in various segments of the market economy is increasing in some countries, while in other segments it is decreasing. Two questions in particular then arise. Why does the government attempt to intervene in the autonomous mechanism of the free market? And will government interventions lead to an improvement in the performance of the system in all cases (and if so, to what extent)?

Traditionally, there are two reasons why governments intervene in the market, namely, correction of market failures and considerations of ethics or justice. Both motives will be discussed here.

Correction of Market Failures: In reality, a market economy does not always result in a Pareto-efficient allocation. This is only the case if it meets a whole set of conditions. In practice, these conditions are not at all or only partially realized. Then we observe so-called market failures so that the price system cannot guarantee a Pareto-efficient allocation of resources. Therefore, correcting market failures can be a reason for government intervention. Therefore, the aim of government measures should be to correct the deviations from the optimal allocation of production factors in such way that perfect competition will be reached. That is, the role of the government can be to stimulate the theoretically pure situation of perfect competition.

Some Causes of Market Failures: Imperfect competition, imperfect information, and absence of markets. Such situations are fairly common in the transport sector. For instance, imperfect competition may emerge when the production of transport services infrastructure requires indivisible and/or large scale investments. In such cases, a public monopoly is an obvious solution. A situation of imperfect (usually asymmetric) information may be another reason for government intervention, for instance, in cases of transport of dangerous goods when the real information is only available to the transporter. Minimum risk regulations are the obvious solution, which means that less dangerous goods are transported at too high costs. Finally, absence of markets is a well-known reason for government intervention, especially in cases of externalities and public goods. Environmental damage from transport (as an unpriced cost category) is a good example of external effects leading to government concern, with the aim of restoring a Pareto optimality (via eco-taxes, subsidies, or regulations). Public goods situations may also lead to governmental intervention, for instance, a motorway based on a toll system.

Norms of Ethics and Justice: A second reason for government intervention in the economy occurs if, in accordance with ethical or political beliefs of society or governments, outcomes of the market economy are regarded as inequitable or unacceptable. One may think of the great socio-economic inequality to which the market system may lead. An obvious case is discounted fares for children or the elderly in public transport. In addition, the government may hold the view that the consumer is inclined to underestimate the structural importance of some goods and services (merit goods). That is why consumption is at times made compulsory (e.g., compulsory car insurance) or consumption goods are provided free of charge or at a reduced price (e.g., school milk). It may also occur that the consumption of some goods will be decreased for everyone's interest (demerit goods). This occurs, for instance, by imposing high taxes (e.g., gasoline taxes) or by forbiding consumption (e.g., high travel speed).

However, it is gradually recognized that government intervention does not always lead to an improvement. It may happen that government intervention itself is not free from imperfections with regard to the increase and/or distribution of welfare. These are then called government or non-market failures (Barde and Button, 1991). One kind of non-market failure may result from an imperfect insight into the real demand for public services (e.g., parking space). Second, imperfections may occur in the case of non-optimal production of public services. Third, non-market failures can result from an insufficient recognition of the (positive and negative) effects of policy that occur in the longer run. It may occur that, among other things, a service in terms of quantity is too low (in case of positive effects) or too large (in case of negative effects). Furthermore, government intervention may result in unintended, but in reality possible, (re)distributions of income, knowledge and power, which create conditions for new kinds of inequality and discrimination. Finally, government intervention is often accompanied by bureaucracy, complicated and convoluted legislation and regulation which, among other things, result in an increase of social costs for government and firms.

In reality, many government interventions cannot be explained by the existence of market failures or by a desire for a more equal distribution of income and wealth; government interventions sometimes cause more misallocation of economic resources than they correct; and intervention is often accompanied by considerable transaction costs for industry, consumers and/or the government itself.

Nevertheless, there may be a case for government intervention in the transport sector. First, lack of socio-economic equity is so clearly mirrored in the mobility patterns of society that norms of justice (e.g., access to services) may induce governments to play an active role in providing transport services to less favoured groups (e.g., children, the elderly) or regions. A second argument plays a more important role in the context of our paper: the problems of unsustainable development are not exclusively, but at least significantly, caused by our modes of travelling and our mobility behaviour. Since the long run effects of current mobility patterns exceed the decision or choice horizons of individual trip makers, a strict intervention from the side of the government -- in its role as "trustee" of new generations -- seems to be warranted. Thus, the prevention of long run (often irreversible) external effects may be seen as a major justification of government policy at the interface of transport and environment.

4.3 National Policies in the International Context

Europe is a continent with a variety of administrative and policy making bodies; this has far-reaching consequences for environmental policies in relation to transport. Transport in Europe has traditionally developed primarily according to national objectives and priorities; this has resulted in considerable divergence between one country and another. As a result, the European transport system is an assembly of unique national transport systems, rather than a coherent continent-wide system (ERTI, 1992).

The characteristics of transport modes differ greatly from country to country, particularly between Eastern and Western countries. Almost every country has constructed railways and roads largely by applying their own specific technical criteria. Thus, railways still suffer from divergence in infrastructure, electrification, voltages, and signalling systems. In European road transport, fundamental problems concern the standardization of vehicle dimensions and the national restrictions on the free movement of transport vehicles. European inland waterways diverge significantly, particularly with regard to maximum air and water draught of vessels authorized to use them (European Parliament, 1991; Giaoutzi and Nijkamp, 1992).

The respective roles of public authorities and private operators also vary significantly between East and West in Europe. As to public authorities, the share of responsibility between local, regional and central authorities differs as well. In the former socialist countries, those distinctions had little meaning in the past, as all transport operators were a part of the public authority. In Western countries, the situation is more complex and the allocation of responsibilities differs from country to country. In general, railways are run by a public body and road transport services by private operators. In inland waterway transport, the private sector's share is quite important.

The ongoing transition from planned to market economies in the former socialist countries is opening the way for the development of private transport. The transition from centrally planned management to market economies in the transport sector can be achieved only gradually. The inevitable increase in road traffic will place an enormous burden on the already inadequate infrastructure of those countries. During the complex transition period, institutional reforms rank high on the agendas of international development agencies as part of their technical assistance programs.

Conditions of access to the market in road and inland waterway transport have been and continue to be very different in each country. In rail transport, the fact that each railway organization -- with a few exceptions -- is the only main operator on its lines represents a severe commercial handicap for international transport.

Interfaces between national transport systems (e.g., border crossings) play a principal role in international transport. Inefficient functioning of customs services may hamper the fluidity of traffic. Border formalities have been the cause of important delays in international traffic, both passenger and freight, particularly between East and West. Much progress has been made in facilitating border crossings but much still remains to be done, especially for rail transport in Europe and for all modes at the borders of former socialist countries.

There have been bilateral agreements between neighbouring countries, multilateral agreements within groupings of countries such as the EC, and cooperation with the aid of various international organizations such as the European Conference of Ministers of Transport (ECMT), the former CMEA or COMECON and the United Nations Economic Commission for Europe (UN/ECE). However, all these activities have been either limited in geographical scope or could not proceed beyond a certain degree of cooperation as a result of the former division of Europe into two blocks.

The ECE has elaborated a set of new agreements on integrated European infrastructure networks for each transport mode: rail, road, inland waterways, and combined transport[1]. Work is underway at present on similar guidelines for the integrated high speed rail network. These agreements and guidelines are being extended to include the former socialist countries. Similar work has been carried out by the Commmission of the European Communities (CEC). The CEC has stressed that in the future, its infrastructure policy would concentrate on covering all modes, including the intermodal dimension, in order to take account of all major flows of passengers and goods. It would favour the introduction of new technologies, better passenger safety and improved environmental protection. Its policy would also be established in concert with non-EC countries (ECE, 1991).

In order to assess at an early planning stage the possible harmful transboundary environmental impacts of proposed transport infrastructure, an ECE Convention on Environmental Impact Assessment in a Transboundary Context has recently been adopted. With regard to transboundary pollution control, a Convention on Long Range Transboundary Air Pollution has been adopted by the ECE countries and is widely adhered to by industry, including the transport industry. In conclusion, some progress on environmental policy in relation to transport may be expected in Europe, but the path towards sustainable development is still covered with many obstacles.

5. Transport Scenarios

In view of the future uncertainties, it seems plausible to develop some relevant scenarios. Here, the relationship between transport policy and environmental sustainability is analysed in two steps. First, some examples of scenarios made for various purposes are presented and the possible impacts of the scenarios are assessed. Second, the demands imposed by environmental sustainability on the transport sector are described and compared with the impacts of the proposed scenarios.

5.1 Examples of European Transport Scenarios

The four scenarios presented here were developed for different purposes and by various authors in the past few years:

1. ECMT's scenarios examine five options in economic and transport development (ECMT, 1987, p. 118):

* Continuation of the present infrastructure policy with three possible long term reactions: (1) continuation of the present level of investment and increasing the number of bottlenecks, (2) better use of existing infrastructure, and (3) changes in production location due to transport capacity shortages;

* Increase of infrastructure capacity, mainly in road transport and moderately in railways, in order to cope with transport demand; the most evident consequences of this option are the needs for additional financing for new infrastructure and the emergence of serious environmental problems;

* Diversion of traffic to different routes with the aim of alleviating bottlenecked corridors and making use of free capacity of the same carrier, with probably very limited practical effects, but also at minimal costs;

* Diversion of traffic to other carriers with more free capacity by encouraging measures such as highly competitive pricing or different levels of service. The effects of these measures are also likely to be limited;

* Diversion of traffic to other carriers by coercive measures which can include the limitation of admitted transport distances, the type of goods, and the period of transport. This option brings about immediate changes in modal split, but its net effect is not likely to reach maximum expectations.

Confronted with the advantages and disadvantages of these particular options, the author of the above scenarios suggests the combination of several above-mentioned measures.

2. Focusing attention primarily on ecological aspects of transport policy in Europe, a group of authors has distinguished the following four "ideal types" of scenarios (Himanen et al., 1992, p. 152):

* A. Status quo scenario as a simple trend extrapolation of current events;

* B. Rigorous traffic restraint with more rigorous application of present and some new protection measures;

* C. Redistribution of transport demand by mode, time and space; and

* D. Reduction of transport demand by better land use planning.

The authors noticed that scenario (C) was a necessary complement to scenario (B). Scenarios (B) and (D) aim at the same goal, the first with stringent restrictions and the latter by long term development. The authors estimated environmental impacts in Western Europe obtainable through scenario (B) to be as follows:

* Energy consumption (and CO_2 emissions) would decrease by 10 percent and NO_x emissions by 85 percent compared to the situation of late 1980s, or

* Energy consumption (and CO_2 emissions) would increase by 10 percent and NO_x emissions would decrease by 80 percent compared to the situation of late 1980s.

The differences between the two outcomes were triggered by two different forecasts in scenario (A), which formed the starting point for measures of scenario (B). In the first car traffic was supposed to increase by 40 percent and in the second, it would increase by 70 percent before implementing measures according to scenario (B).

3. Masser et al. (1992) designed long term scenarios of transport and communications in Europe based on explicit assumptions. Three component scenarios representing different policy directions were developed for each field:

* The *Growth Scenario* shows the most likely development of transport and communications in Europe if all policies emphasize economic growth as the primary objective and if state intervention would be as little as possible;

* The *Equity Scenario* shows the impacts of policies that primarily try to reduce inequalities in society in terms of both social and spatial disparities; and

* The *Environmental Scenario* emphasizes quality of life and environmental aspects and hence assumes restrained use of technology and some control of economic activity.

Since growth, equity and environment are three partially conflicting paradigms, the authors of this work find a combination of these scenarios the "most preferred" one.

4. When considering various policy dilemmas the EC is faced with, the Group Transport 2000 Plus (1990, p. 28) mentions three possible options, of which they recommend the third scenario:

* The continuation of present policies, which could result in many negative effects;

* The intensification of infrastructure investment in order to alleviate the congestion problems, which could also increase negative effects; and

* The new short, medium and long term policy guidelines that assume a total change in transport mode preferences.

In none of the above cases are the authors recommending the continuation of current policies. Neither do they seem to believe that building more roads will provide a permanent solution. All are searching for a new solution by combining various measures. This is also the way that the CEC is formulating its policy statement on transport (CEC, 1992). Quantitative information is unfortunately rare; only in one study are the actual impacts quantified. In the following subsection, these figures will be compared with the demands we are facing from environmental sustainability.

5.2 A Comparison with Environmental Sustainability

Clearly, the precise implications of measures stimulating or improving environmental sustainability are difficult to assess, especially because the effects of transport cannot easily be separated from effects emerging from other segments of our mass consumption society. In the so-called Brundtland Report by the World Commission on Environment and Development (1987), where sustainability was discussed, no clear goals for reducing the environmental effects of the transport system are given. King and Schneider (1991), in a report by the Council of the Club of Rome, propose a carbon dioxide reduction of 30 per cent by the year 2005 for the industrialized countries. It should be noted here that atmospheric concentrations of greenhouse gases adjust slowly to changes in emissions. The longer emissions continue at high rates, the larger the eventual reduction would have to be. According to Döös (1991), an immediate reduction of over 60 percent of net emissions of long-lived gases (carbon dioxide, CFCs, and nitrogen oxides) from human activities would stabilize concentrations at today's levels.

International agreement for limiting the emissions of carbon dioxide was approved in Rio de Janeiro in June 1992. According to this agreement, the industrialized countries ought to limit the emissions of carbon dioxide to the 1990 level and the developing countries ought to reduce the growth of their emissions. The obvious problems inherent in limiting carbon dioxide emissions are related to mass consumption in developed countries and to the rapid population increase in many developing countries. The mass consumption system is in many ways closely connected with the massive use of fossil fuels. The need for economic development in developing countries will call for even more consumption of fossil fuels.

European nations have agreed to lower emissions of sulphur and nitrogen oxides, but according to Döös (1991), these commitments are far from sufficient to stabilize the harmful effects of acid rain in Europe. The agreed reduction was 30 percent. According to Kauppi et al. (1990), a 90-percent decrease (compared to the year 1987) of annual sulphur and nitrogen deposits would be needed in order to stop acidification of forest soil in southern Finland. In order to meet the less stringent requirement that forest acidification be allowed to the extent that forests are not in danger, a 75-percent decrease of deposits would be sufficient. Similar figures are also given for Sweden by Eriksson and Hesselborn (1990). Other gases responsible for the acidification problem are mainly produced outside the transport sector, for instance, sulphur dioxide in energy production and ammonia in agriculture.

Refering to the above figures, it can be stated that there is a gap between international agreements obtained by government decisions and the need for environmental sustainability advocated by scientists. According to the government agreement, it is sufficient if carbon dioxide emissions stay at the level of the year 1990, whereas scientists are asking for a reduction of 30 percent (King and Schneider, 1992) or 60 percent (Döös, 1991). For nitrogen oxides emissions, the same holds true: the government agreement asks for a reduction of 30 percent, but scientists (Kauppi et al., 1990) are seeking a reduction of 75 or 90 percent.

The international target for carbon dioxide emissions, i.e., keeping the emissions at the 1990 level, seems to be obtainable through transport policies regarding car traffic (see Section 5.1). As car traffic forms the major element in surface transport and also provides the fastest growing sector, it is probable that the target can be reached in all surface transport modes. The government agreement in Europe to decrease nitrogen oxides emissions by 30 percent seems easy to reach, at least in car traffic, with the aid of catalytic convertors. With the aid of proposed stringent regulations for diesel vehicles, it may be possible to obtain the target in all surface transport activities.

However, in Europe, it does not seem not possible to obtain the 30- or 60-percent reduction of carbon dioxide emissions proposed by scientists. This holds true even though the measures included in the scenarios studied are very stringent compared to the present situation. It seems possible to reduce nitrogen dioxide emissions by more than 75 percent for European car traffic, needed for forest preservation. However, the possible reduction falls somewhat short of the 90 percent which would stop acidification. Some caution is necessary here, even with the reduction of 75 percent, because practical results from the U.S. are much more modest (see Section 2.2).

6. Conclusion

In light of the above considerations, it is obvious that current transport policies are not adequate. There is a pressing need for rigorous implementation and enforcement of the legislation and measures adopted at all levels, including the European level, and some consensus does exist about the direction needed.

International agreements about the reductions of emissions are very modest; th reductions obtained through transport policy up today are even more modest. Futu transport policies, according to the above scenarios, can obtain the targets stated in thos agreements by using stringent measures. However, prospects for securing more far-reaching targets are rather uncertain. This poses some unanswered questions: is there a lack of knowledge and understanding when confronting complex global questions and/or is it possible to turn mass consumption societies towards the path of environmental sustainability?

When considering the nature of the governmental actions presented in Section 4.2, the possibilities of reaching environmental sustainability seem to be very distant. At this point, transport policy does not stand alone. The same question is posed to the whole of Western society, including all production and consumption sectors. What does it really mean when we say we are moving from an industrial to a post-industrial age? Is "the first global revolution" the only way to reach environmental sustainability? Such questions provoke much concern among transport policy makers in Europe.

In contrast to the trend towards deregulation in transport, environmental policy is critically dependent on regulations and interventions on both the supply and demand sides. In particular, technical restrictions, such as limitations on emission levels for motorcars or perhaps a selective prohibition of the use of certain transport modes, are likely to be imposed. Recently, a plea for a carless city has even been made. Transport policy makers in most European countries find themselves in extremely complicated situations. A large number of interest groups, ranging from multinational companies to local environmentalists, are urging action, often in quite different directions. On the one hand, it has become obvious that the environment poses its limits on the volume, character and pace of the extension of the transport infrastructure. On the other hand, many business firms in Western Europe are concerned about their competitiveness in a global context due to an inadequate infrastructure.

It should be noted that economic models are clear: the user and the polluter should pay the full costs of travel, including all externalities. However, there are many problems with the implementation of such concepts as public acceptability is low, and international agreement is difficult to achieve. For instance, any such implementation would have to be fiscally neutral, otherwise the policy would be inflationary and could lead to increased unemployment.

Environmental costs imposed by the transport sector are high and rising, despite extensive legislation at the European and national levels. Clear policy directions need to be given to the transport industry so that production processes can be cleaned up, and more environmentally benign transport modes can be encouraged. The private sector contribution would complement that of the public sector in giving priority to public transport and cycling within cities, and in encouraging energy-efficient urban forms. In general, one may claim that the private sector has an important role to play in supplementing the public sector investment in transport and communications infrastructure.

Notes

1. European Agreement on Main International Railway Lines (AGC), of 31 May 1985 (ECE/TRANS/63); European Agreement on Main International Traffic Arteries (AGR), of 15 November 1975 (E/TRANS/16, Corr. 1 and Amend. 1); European Agreement on Important International Combined Transport Lines and Related Installations (AGTC), of 1 February 1991 (ECE/TRANS/88).

References

Banister, D., 1989, The Final Gridlock, *Built Environment*, 15(3/4), 163-165.

Barde, J.Ph. and Button, K.E. (eds.), 1991, *Transport Policy and the Environment: Six Case Studies*, Earthscan, London.

Blaas, E.W., Vleugel, J.M., Louw, E. and Rooijers, T., 1992, *Autobezit, Auto ebruik en Rijgedrag*, Delftse Universitaire Pres, Delft.

Blum, R.U. and Rothengatter, W., 1989, Intervention Failures in Transport Policy and their Consequences for the Environment - A Case Study for West Germany, Paper Prepared for the OECD, Environment Directorate, Paris.

Bovy, P.H.L., Orfeuil, J.P. and Salomon, I., 1992, A Billion Trips A Day, Mobility Patterns of The Europeans, NECTAR International Symposium, ESF, Strasbourg and Royal Netherlands Academy of Arts and Sciences, Amsterdam, March 18-21.

Bruckmann, G., 1987, Will There be a Fifth Kondratief?, in Vasko, T. (ed.), *The Long-wave Debate*, Springer Verlag, New York.

Commission of the European Communities (CEC), 1992, *The Future Development of the Common Transport Policy; A Global Approach to the Construction of a Community Framework for Sustainable Mobility*, ECE, Brussels.

Döös, B. R., 1991, Environmental Issues Requiring International Action, IIASA, RR-91-16, Luxembourg.

Economic Commission for Europe (ECE), 1990, *Europe's Railway of the '90s, A White Paper*, United Nations, New York.

Economic Commission for Europe (ECE), 1991, *The Transport Infrastructure Policy in the European Economic Community*, Document TRANS/SEM, 8/R.19, 23 February 1991, Seminar on the Analysis of Traffic Flows Within Transport Corridors in Europe, June 4-6, Volos.

Eriksson, G. and Hesselborn, P.O., 1990, *A Transportation System Adapted to the Environment*, TFB Report 1990:15, TFB, Stockholm.

European Conference of Ministers of Transport (ECMT), 1987, *Activity of the Conference, Resolutions of the Council of Ministers of Transport; Reports Approved in 1986*, OECD Publication, Paris.

European Parliament, CEC, and UN/ECE, 1991, *Prague Declaration on All European Transport Policy*, October 31, 1991, Pan-European Transport Conference, October 29-31, Prague.

European Round Table of Industrialists 1989, *Need for Renewing Transport Infrastructure in Europe*, ERTI, Brussels.

European Round Table of Industrialists, 1992, *Getting Together*, ERTI, Brussels.

Gérardin, B. and Viégas, J., 1992, European Infrastructure and Networks Current Policies and Trends, Paper Presented at the NECTAR International Symposium, ESF Strasbourg and Royal Netherlands Academy of Arts and Sciences, March 18-21, Amsterdam.

Giaoutzi, M. and Nijkamp, P., 1992, *European Waterways; Forgotten Component of European Infrastructure*, Research Memorandum, Dept. of Economics, Free University, Amsterdam.

Group Transport 2000 Plus, 1990, Transport in a Fast Changing Europe, Brussels.

Himanen, V., Nijkamp, P. and Padjen, J., 1992, Environmental Quality and Transport Policy in Europe, *Transportation Research A*, 26A(2), 147-157.

Kauppi, P., Anttila, P. and Kenttämies, K. (eds.), 1990, *Acidification in Finland*, Springer Verlag, Berlin.

King, A. and Schneider, B., 1991, *The First Global Revolution*, A Report by the Council of The Club of Rome, Simon & Schuster, London.

Knoflacher, H. and Himanen, V., 1991, *Transport Policy Between Economy and Ecology*, Research Notes 1221, Technical Research Centre of Finland, Espoo.

Kreutzburger, E., Nijkamp, P. and Vleugel, J., 1992, Maximum Capacity of Infrastructure, Paper Presented at the WCTR Conference, July 1992, Lyon.

Linster, M., 1990, Background Facts and Figures, Transport Policy and the Environment, *ECMT Ministerial Session*, ECMT, Paris, 9-45.

Masser I., Svidén, O. and Wegener, M., 1992, *The Geography of Europe's Future*, Belhaven, London.

Mäkelä, K., Kanner, H., Himanen, V., Laurikko, J., Salusjärvi, H. and Anila, M., 1990, *Tieliikenteen pakokaasupäästöt, ennustava tietojärjestelmä, LIISA II (Road Traffic Exhaust Emissions in Finland, 1989 and Forecasts)*, Research Report 826, Technical Research (ERTI), Centre of Finland, Espoo.

Nijkamp, P. and Priemus, H., 1992, Cities and Capacity of European Infra-structure Networks, ECMT Conference, May 1992, Lisbon.

Nijkamp, P., Reichman, S. and Wegener, M. (eds.), 1990, *Euromobile: Transport, Communications and Mobility in Europe*, Gower, Aldershot.

Renner, M., 1989, *Rethinking Transportation*, Transport, No. 25/1989, Commission Library, Brussels.

Sarkar, P. R., 1967) *Human Society*, Part 2, Proutist Universal, Washington D.C.

Segercrantz, W., 1992, *Road Traffic Safety in Estonia, Latvia and Lithuania*, Contractor Report, Road, Traffic and Geotechnical Laboratory, Espoo.

Stigliani, W.M., Brouwer, F.M., Munn, R.E., Shaw, R.W. and Antonovsky, M., 1989, *Future Environments for Europe: Some Implications of Alternative Development Paths*, RR-89-5, IIASA, Luxembourg.

Stutz, F.P., 1986, Environmental Impacts, in Hanson, S. (ed.), *The Geography of Urban Transportation*, Guilford, New York.

World Commission on Environment and Development, 1987, *Our Common Future*, (Brundtland Report), Oxford University Press, Oxford.

TRANSPORT IN A UNIFIED EUROPE. Policies and Challenges.
D. Banister and J. Berechman (Editors)

Chapter Ten

REGIONAL TRANSPORT INFRASTRUCTURE POLICIES

Jörgen Kristiansen

1. Introduction

1.1 Background

The internal market and the European Community (EC) policy developing continent-wide networks are in progress. The geographical scope of these networks includes Western, Central and Eastern Europe, as well as the external links to the North Atlantic, North Africa, the Middle East and the SNG/CIS countries (Commonwealth of Independent States). The integrated European market is already being established in the form of a common European trade area including the present EC countries and the European Free Trade Association (EFTA) countries. The market is also expected to be joined by the Baltic countries, Eastern European countries and some SNG/CIS countries. At the same time, the peripheral regions in Europe are facing the increasing problems of developing viable industrial and commercial structures. These problems are accentuated by the prevailing trends of business and logistic developments at the continental level. Their need is urgent with regard to the formulation of regional strategies and the related transport infrastructure policies.

1.2 Methodology and Content

This chapter considers the potentials for peripheral regions to develop adequate transport solutions within the framework of overall European development. It consists of two sections. In the first, a brief description is provided of the prevailing trends of continental development, including the geographical scope as well as socio-economic and technological development characteristics. The case of the Scandinavian Link corridor versus the Nordic Link corridor is presented in order to highlight the variety of regional transport infrastructure problems and to identify transport policy issues of importance for peripheral areas, with a specific emphasis on maritime regions.

In the second section, a short presentation is provided of the industrial and logistic transition which the European continent is experiencing. The regional impact of transport infrastructure is discussed using the cases of the Öresund subregion within the Scandinavian Link corridor and the Skagerrak/Kattegat subregion within the Nordic Link corridor. Some of the major infrastructure issues in relation to regional development are identified. On this basis, a new and comprehensive concept of transport infrastructure is introduced as a planning tool. Specific recommendations and suggestions are put forward, concerning ferry routes and terminals as essential parts of the transport infrastructure in maritime regions. The main problems, findings, and recommendations are summarized at the conclusion of the chapter. The term *"intermodal"* transport indicates combined transport along a route consisting of a chain of at least two different modes, for example, road-ferry-rail, road-rail, or TGV-air. The term *"multimodal"* corridors indicates that goods or passengers are able to choose from among alternative modes serving the same route or corridor.

2. Policy Options for Maritime Regions

It is envisaged that the socio-economic and commercial developments in Western and Central Europe are presently in a structural transition phase. The process is being accelerated by the geographical extension of the integrated market to the Scandinavian countries, Central, and Eastern Europe. During the same period, a long term expansion of continent-wide transport and communication networks will be implemented. Within this framework, the peripheral regions of the European continent will need to formulate a coordinated strategy for industrial and infrastructure development. Hitherto, the emphasis of EC and national infrastructure policies has been placed on the improvement of overland transport links between capitals and national centers. This policy approach implies the construction of large civil engineering projects and a strong general focus on physical infrastructure. Regional policy interests have to identify new types of infrastructure as an alternative to accepting a role as marginalized areas in the continental economy. This applies to maritime regions in particular, where short sea transport is a prerequisite for a coherent trade pattern.

The following description first provides a brief presentation of the prevailing trends of development, including the geographical extension of the integrated European market as well as other socio-economic and technological development characteristics. A short description is given of the increasing focus on new regional concepts, both in terms of geography and institutional/political changes. The purpose of this introductory description is to pinpoint the megatrends of specific interest in transport policy formulation at the regional level. As several peripheral areas of the European continent can be characterized as maritime regions, it is argued that these peripheral regions should include ferry links as important elements of the transport network. Finally, the case of Scandinavian Link versus Nordic Link is presented in order to identify similarities and differences between these two specific schemes and to provide a basis for the discussion about the regional impact of transport infrastructure of the final section of the chapter.

2.1 The Megatrends of Development

The general conditions framing regional development can be described by the new political and socio-economic relations, technological and commercial development, and specific developments within the transport sector.

The *political and socio-economic* megatrends are mainly characterized by the expansion of the EC internal market, the transition of the Eastern European and the SNG countries economies into market economies, and the new emerging political structures. A higher degree of uncertainty is connected to the future regional maneuverability within the political framework of the widening of the EC, and within the national constitutions.

The *technological and commercial* development trends relate to:

* The "technical-organizational revolution" stimulated by telematics and informatics,

* The industrial requirements of the regional and continental logistic structures in terms of the efforts to promote a logistic transition, and, finally,

* The future global role of transnational companies versus the potential of developing viable commercial structures at the regional level.

The increasing role of environmental policy issues should also be stated. Already, in the near future, they are expected to make a significant impact on macro-economic and commercial structures.

Within the *transport sector*, some specific development characteristics can be identified. These are:

* Deregulation and harmonization of the market for transport services;

* The integrated application of information technology, such as informatics and telematics, both for individual transport services and for transport flows and traffic management at the macro level;

* Construction of European-wide transport infrastructure schemes, e.g., the Channel Tunnel and the high speed rail network; and

* The growing environmental requirements for the transport sector, leading to the concept of "sustainable mobility" (Commission for the European Commission, 1992).

These development aspects of the transport sector will be described in more detail in the following discussion on regional transport strategies.

2.1.1 Peripheral Regions in Focus

Discussions on the future role of regions have intensified during recent years. Especially, the establishment of the EC internal market, the development toward an EC Union, and the newly established multi-party democracies in Central and Eastern Europe have called for new regional perspectives. One example is the *Baltic Sea Region*, which includes all the countries around "Mare Balticum". This regional concept is expected to be revitalized and play an important future role within the new political and economic framework. The common European trade area may expand in the future and engulf all the countries around the Baltic Sea (Nordic Council, 1992).

Due to the geographical shape of the European Continent in general -- and the EC area in particular -- the peripheral regions and offshore islands contribute a considerable share to the overall continental economy. This importance of the peripheral regions will probably increase when the geographical scope of the integrated European market is expanded. Furthermore, several peripheral areas of Europe can be characterized as maritime regions, where short sea transport is a significant part of the overall transport structure.

In relation to the transport sector, two main issues of the EC integration policy can be identified as being of specific interest, namely, the development of trans-European networks and the principles of coherence and regionalization. The aim of the European-wide infrastructure networks is to effectively connect the peripheries to the continental market. The focus on regionalization aims at developing industrial and commercial networks at the regional level but, at the same time, interregional relations will be enhanced. Thus, there is a growing awareness of the regional development issues. At the same time, weighty reasons exist for an increasing environmental concern in relation to the practical implementation of transport policies, both at the regional and continental level. However, these considerations call for a strengthened and integrated transport infrastructure policy, from a regional viewpoint as well.

2.2 Maritime Regions and Short Sea Routes

As stated above, a number of regions in the geographical periphery of Europe can be characterized as typical maritime regions. In Northern and Western Europe, these maritime regions include the Baltic, the Skagerrak/Kattegat, the North Sea, the Irish Sea and the English Channel. The Adriatic Sea and a number of Mediterranean subregions (e.g. the Greek Archipelago) can also be identified as maritime regions. Accordingly, ferry links may be of importance to several peripheral areas, and of interest for both regional and continental transport policy formulation. Following analysis of this issue, the "sustainable mobility" concept will be briefly discussed in relation to the peripheral maritime areas vis-à-vis the core area of the European continent.

2.2.1 Strategic Ferry Routes

The North European maritime regions are shown in Figure 1.

For these areas, adequate regional networks can only be developed by considering ferry links and other short sea transport routes. A number of the short sea route corridors indicated on Figure 1 are providing for, at present, a considerable share of total goods

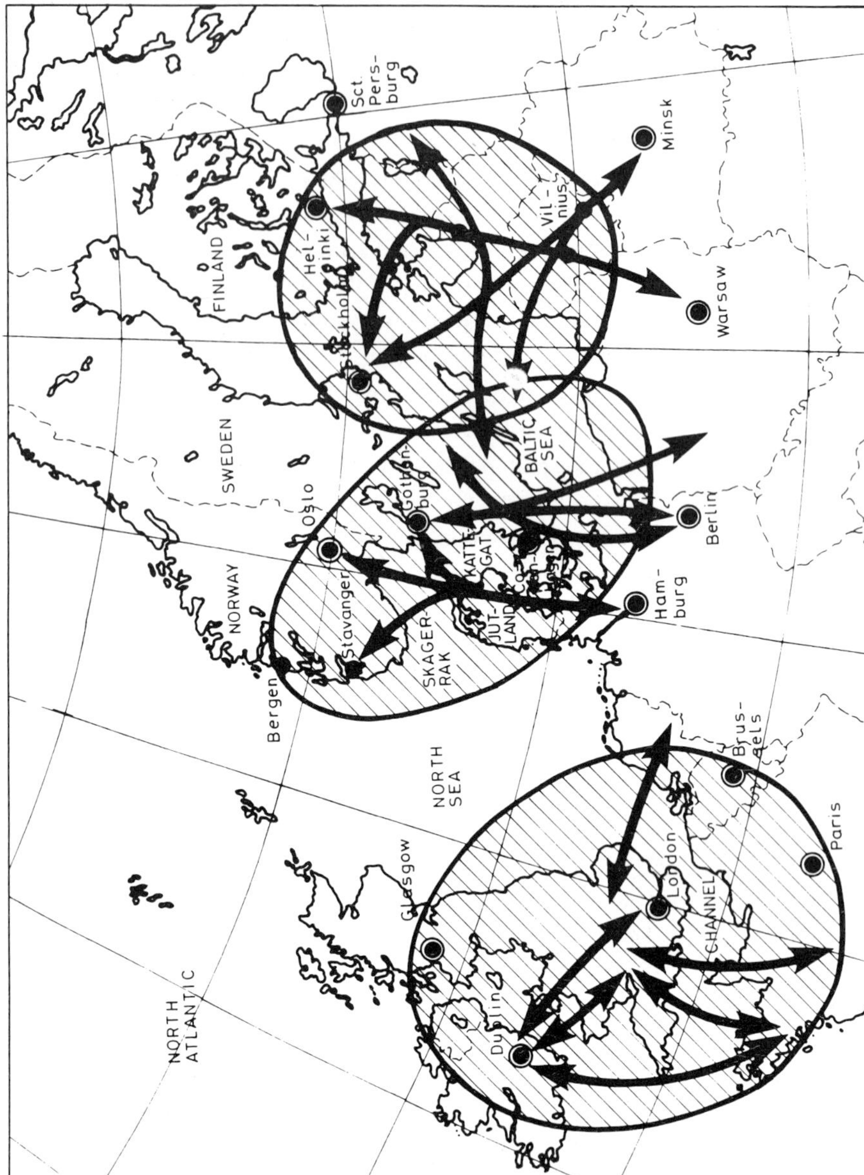

FIGURE 1 Maritime Regions and Short Sea Route Corridors in Northern Europe

flows, including the transit flows and the flows between the countries within the indicated regions. The future function of short sea links should also be seen in the light of the increasing role which water-borne transport systems, including maritime transport and inland waterways, are expected to play. The aim is to reduce the traffic flows on the trunk networks of roads and rail, which currently are causing both congestion problems and environmental problems in the central parts of the continent. In combination with land-based transport modes, the ferry routes can enhance the performance of intermodal transport networks, including road and rail transport, for both freight and passenger transport. Some of the ferry routes will probably develop into key links in order to effectively connect the peripheral maritime regions to the continental network. Thus, these links should be identified as being of current or potential interest to the EC transport corridors.

The importance of the strategic ferry routes will be accentuated if the EC internal market is extended to include Sweden, Finland, the Baltic countries and Norway. At that stage, the Baltic Sea and the Skagerrak/Kattegat will become "inland oceans" in the common European Economic Area. Several short sea routes, across the Skagerrak and the Kattegat, connect Norway and Sweden with the Continent via Jutland in Denmark. Apart from that, Skagerrak and the North Sea are to be considered as a main gateway to the North Atlantic countries: the Orkney, Shetland and Faroe Islands, Iceland, Greenland and Canada. The direct ferry routes across the Baltic between Southern Sweden and Germany will also remain as important transport links in the future.

2.2.2 Sustainable Mobility

The *core areas* of Western Europe are already facing severe congestion problems in the central parts of the transport networks, specifically on the motorways. These problems are increased by the general tendency of traffic volumes, which are growing very fast. The congestion problems cannot be solved solely by the efforts to increase the capacities of the motorways, the terminals, and the railways. Basically, there are structural problems to be solved, not only in relation to the transport systems but also related to commercial localization structures and distribution patterns. Some of the potential means are comprehensive intermodal transport networks and multimodal transport corridors, including road, rail, and water-borne transport.

The *peripheral areas* are facing the particular problem of not having established efficient transport links to the continental market and to other regional markets in order to meet just-in-time requirements. Due to long distances and relatively modest traffic flow volumes, an expansion of the motorway network and the high speed railway network to all parts of the continental periphery would lead to extremely expensive infrastructure investments in comparison with the macro-economic rates of return. Also, in several cases, topographical conditions make it unrealistic to expand the overland transport network. At the same time, the development of intermodal transport solutions and the comprehensive application of telematics may stimulate a further development of adequate logistic solutions at the regional level. These solutions do not necessarily require excessive financial resources in order to implement expensive and large civil engineering projects.

The core areas are burdened with overwhelming logistic problems due to an excessively high level of mobility compared to the capacity of the type of transport networks which will be economically realistic to sustain. In contrast, the logistic problems of the periphery arise due to a low level of mobility in relation to the lack of access to the core area networks and markets. However, the peripheral regions do not suffer from any basic congestion problems within the transport network. This fact, in the long term, may provide the regional economies with competitive advantages.

2.3 The Transport Corridors

Hitherto, the policy of developing trans-European transport networks has focused on connecting the capitals of the peripheral countries to the continental centers by means of fixed links. This policy implies that some strategic ferry links run the risk of being placed in a subsidiary position in relation to fixed links such as the Channel Tunnel (to be completed in 1993-1994) and the Fehmarn Belt crossing (expected to be completed after 2000). Thus, the case of the Scandinavian Link versus the Nordic Link will be introduced in the following subsection in order to highlight the options of short sea ferry routes with regard to the overall transport infrastructure network.

The transport links between the countries of the Scandinavian peninsula and the continental part of Western Europe, via Hamburg, consist of two main corridors. These are shown in Figure 2. One of these corridors is the "Scandinavian Link", crossing the island of Zealand in Denmark and continuing through Western Sweden along the Kattegat coast to Gothenburg in Sweden and to Oslo in Norway. The other corridor is the "Nordic Link", passing through Jutland, and with ferry connections across the Skagerrak and the Kattegat to Southern Norway and to Gothenburg in Western Sweden (see Figure 3). Both corridors have a branch connection to Stockholm.

2.3.1 The Scandinavian Link

The *Scandinavian Link Scheme* is a plan for a transport corridor connecting Oslo, Gothenburg, and Stockholm with Malmö, Copenhagen and Hamburg by means of a coherent high speed route, encompassing a four-lane motorway and a dual-track railway. The Scandinavian Link was identified by the European Round Table of Industrialists as one of the "missing link" projects, considered as necessary in order to renew and extend the continental transport infrastructure of Western Europe (ERTI, 1984, 1989). The plan includes the construction of fixed links across the Öresund (or the "Sound", a narrow strait between the Copenhagen metropolitan area and the Malmö urban area in Southern Sweden) and the Fehmarn Belt (between Denmark and Germany). A fixed link across the Öresund is expected to be completed by the year 2000, and will probably be followed by the construction of a fixed link across the Fehmarn Belt a few years later (Scandinavian Link, 1988). The Öresund Link project is a Danish-Swedish joint venture; the Fehmarn Belt Link project will be a joint venture between Denmark and Germany. Both Links have a total length of approximately 19 kilometers; the construction costs are expected to be toll-funded, at price levels approximately the same as the present ferry rates.

The existing transport chains within the Scandinavian Link corridor include several ferry routes across the Öresund and across the Fehmarn Belt/Baltic Sea. The ferry routes across the Baltic Sea, directly between Southern Sweden and Germany, should also be considered as a part of the Scandinavian Link transport corridor. Some of the ferry routes will still be of importance for the total transport network, even after the two fixed links have been completed. The total annual volume of ferry freight crossing the EC border between Sweden/Norway and Denmark/Germany in the Scandinavian Link corridor was approximately 6.0 million tons by road and 3.0 million tons by rail in 1989-1990. These volumes include the ferry routes across the Öresund and the direct routes between Southern Sweden (Skaane) and Germany across the Baltic Sea (see Figure 3), excluding the rail ferry route between Trelleborg and Sassnitz. This route carried 5.0 million tons of freight, part of which may also be considered as potential freight for the Scandinavian Link corridor. However, a considerable share of rail ferry goods consist of bulk items which are not suitable to transport in containers and trailers.

2.3.2 The Nordic Link

The *Nordic Link Scheme* comprises a transport corridor from Hamburg, passing through the Danish peninsula of Jutland. This corridor will be connected to Southern Norway and

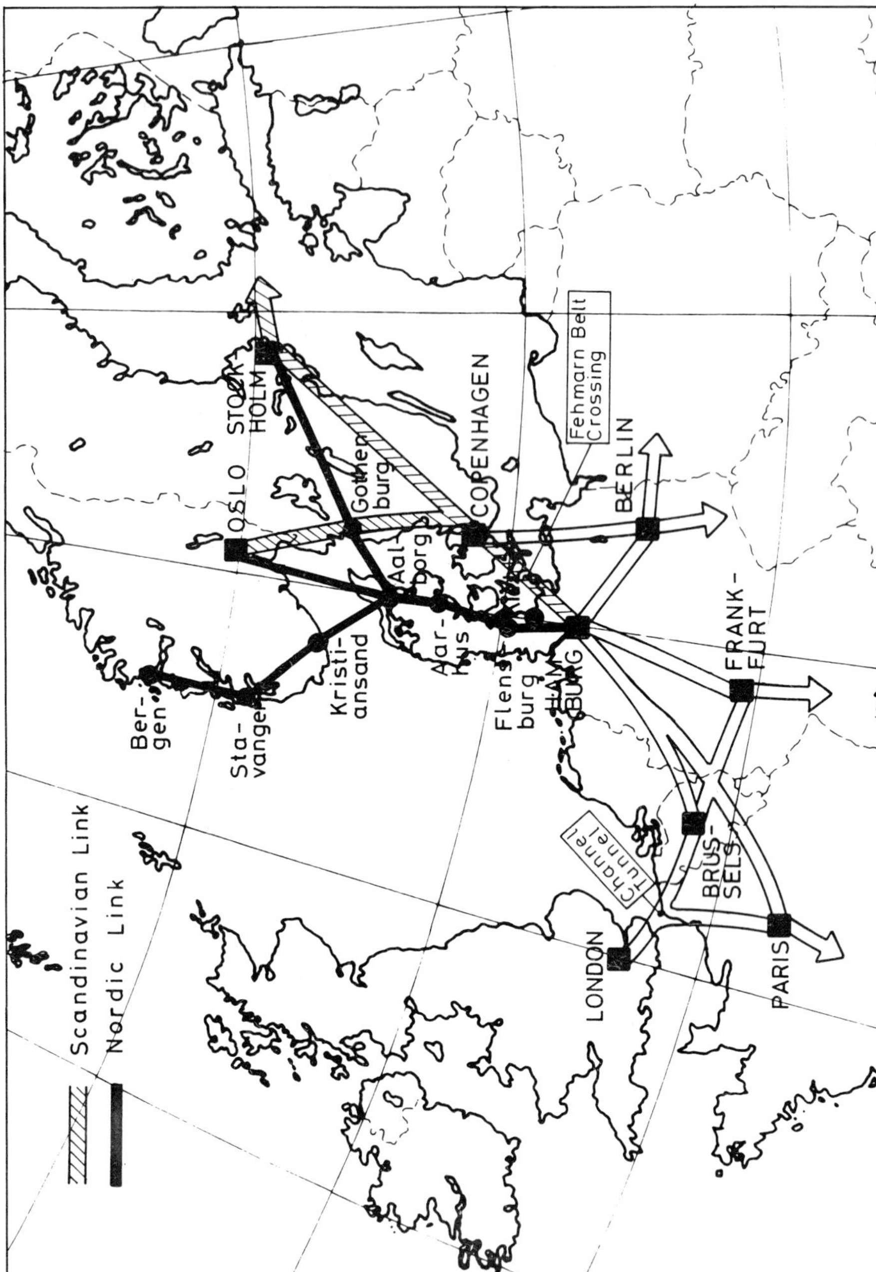

FIGURE 2 The Scandinavian Link and The Nordic Link in a Continental Setting

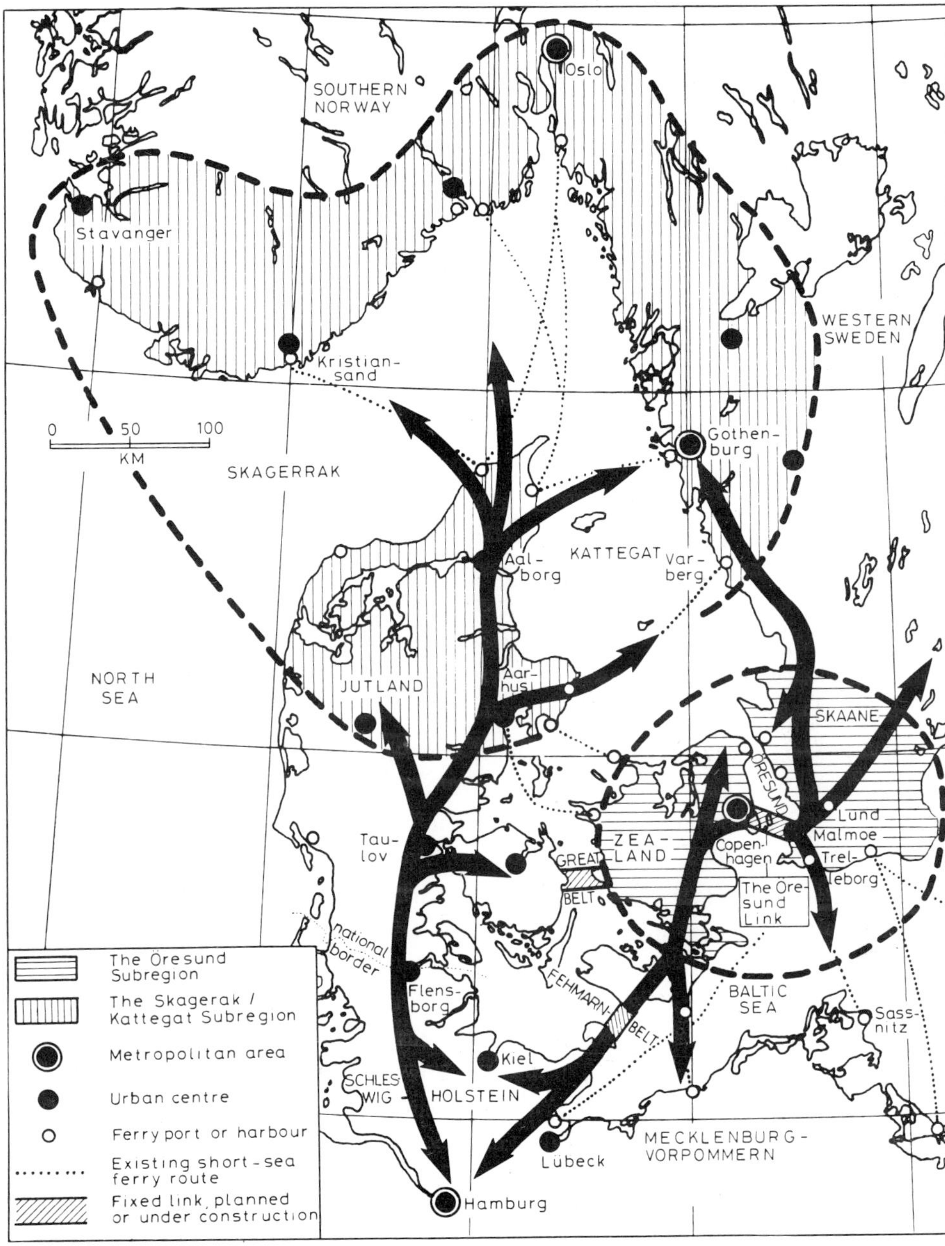

FIGURE 3 The Scandinavian Link and the Nordic Link in a Regional Setting

to Gothenburg in Sweden by ferry links. The section between Hamburg and North Jutland includes a four-lane motorway which will be completed by the end of 1994, and an upgraded dual-track railway. Logistic centers, equipped with transmodal facilities and information systems, are already established in Taulov and in North Jutland, approximately 250 kilometers and 450 kilometers north of Hamburg, respectively. At present, the ferry links include three or four ferry ports in Northern Jutland, four ferry ports in Southern Norway, the harbor of Gothenburg, and the ferry port of Varberg on the West coast of Sweden. The ferry routes in the Nordic Link corridor have lengths of 90 to 180 kilometers, and future fixed links across the Skagerrak/Kattegat are not considered as feasible.

The ferry routes of the Nordic Link corridor all cross the external EC border along the Skagerrak/Kattegat, between Norway/Sweden and Northern Jutland. In 1989-1990, the annual freight volumes served by these international ferry routes accounted for approximately 3.0 million tons, all carried by lorry/road to and from the ferry ports. Only a negligible part of the ferry freight was provided by rail transport. About one-third of the ferry freight volumes were transit flows between the Scandinavian Peninsula and the Continent, while two-thirds were regional flows to and from Western Denmark and the northern part of Schleswig-Holstein.

2.3.3 The Scandinavian Link versus the Nordic Link

At present, the two corridors offer similar conditions in terms of travel time and transport costs per unit load. When the two fixed links in the Scandinavian Link corridor have been completed, this corridor will gain a relatively more favorable competitive position in relation to the time consumption of transit flows. However, the Nordic Link corridor will still have the potential of offering competitive services for goods transport in terms of costs and attractive timetables. The indicated figures of ferry freight volumes, along the two corridors, may not seem impressive compared to the quantities of goods being provided by traditional bulk carriers. However, most of the ferry freight consist of commodities with very high value/weight ratios -- an average of 2 to 3 ECU per kilogram. The bulk flows often have value/weight ratios of less than 1 to 10 percent of these figures. Thus, the ferry freight flows provided by the ferry routes between Norway/Sweden and Denmark/Germany represent a considerably higher total trade value than the bulk flows by ship.

The Nordic Link corridor and the Scandinavian Link corridor are both competitive and complementary routes for freight transport flows. Apparently, the Nordic Link corridor is of importance for the continental transport networks, as far as road haulage is concerned. The main reason why goods transport by rail appears in significant quantities only along the Scandinavian Link corridor is that, at present, no coherent and competitive rail services are offered within the Nordic Link corridor. Furthermore, a relatively higher share of the freight flows crossing the Öresund and the Fehmarn Belt is in transit through Denmark, in comparison with the ferry freight flows across the Skagerrak/Kattegat. From a *continental policy viewpoint*, it seems more favorable to rely on two transport corridors instead of one single route between Scandinavia and the Continent, both from security reasons and in order to obtain a more efficient utilization of total transport systems capacities. From a *regional development viewpoint*, both corridors have economic and industrial potentials. These two alternative corridors, between Gothenburg and Hamburg, cover similar population potentials, i.e., approximately 4.5 to 5.0 million inhabitants in either corridor, not including the urban areas of Gothenburg and Hamburg. In terms of the need for transport infrastructure investment, the Nordic Link corridor is not expensive in comparison with the Scandinavian Link, which includes two large infrastructure projects representing construction costs of a total amount estimated at approximately 8 billion ECUs.

3. Transport Infrastructure and Ferry Links

Current continental development may leave the peripheral regions as marginalized areas due to the tendency towards economic concentration in core areas and along specific corridors, such as the Scandinavian Link. However, another trend is subregional integration, due to the expansion of the integrated market and the emergence of new industrial networks at the regional level. A key issue for the peripheral and maritime regions is how to identify some adequate transport infrastructure measures in order to pursue a successful regional development strategy. Another essential question is how to strike the balance between deregulation and infrastructure regulation.

This section starts with a brief discussion of the current logistic transition at the continental scale and with regional implications. Next, the regional impact of transport infrastructure is discussed and illustrated by the cases of the Öresund subregion within the Scandinavian Link corridor and the Skagerrak/Kattegat subregion within the Nordic Link corridor. On that background, a comprehensive concept of transport infrastructure is elaborated in order to analyze the specific transport policy issues at the regional level within the two transport corridors, which were described in the first section. The role of transport infrastructure vis-à-vis market-regulated services are also discussed. In relation to ferry routes and terminals, some specific functional requirements of transport infrastructure are identified and some guidelines are formulated concerning the choice of systems technology for the regional transport networks.

3.1 The Logistic Transition

Industrial structure is departing from the specialized and large scale manufacturing organized in hierarchical structures. Instead, developments are leading towards flexible production processes which are organized in networks. Future manufacturing systems will also be able to provide a broader variety of commodities in order to respond more quickly to changed market conditions. Thus, the aims of the companies are to induce the transformation from large scale manufacturing to a network organization of production (Andersson et al., 1988; Kearney, Inc., 1992). At the same time, the goal of the EC in the course of the 1990s is to complete the integration of the greater part of Western and Central Europe into a single market, without borders or institutional and legislative obstacles. In other words, conditions are being established to provide for the free movement of capital, commodities and labor. A single European market was already formally established by the end of 1992. It encompasses the EC countries, partly joined by the EFTA countries, which forms the European Economic Area.

At present, Western Europe is assumed to be facing a logistic transition. A period which is characterized by a high degree of structural instability where a comprehensive and long term extension of new networks will be constructed. This is a transition stage from one logistic era to another (Andersson et al., 1988). Hence, a slow but steady improvement of the logistic networks will bring about a significant change in the conditions of the production and distribution of commodities and services. This will require a total transformation of the economic structures, involving the occurrence of similar changes in the social, cultural and political relations at the societal level. The commercial and industrial decision makers expect the future transport infrastructure in Western and Central Europe to play an important role. Efforts are focused on a change of both institutional and technological conditions in order to extend and improve the transport infrastructure of the continent and its offshore islands (ERTI, 1989).

Within this framework of development, the *continental goal* is to integrate Western and Central Europe, not only into a common economic and commercial system, but also into a superior industrial system. The introduction of micro-electronic techniques has altered the technological preconditions which facilitate a further extension of the logistic structures and transport networks. These changes have appeared in the form of efficient systems of telematics and informatics. By the end of the 1990s, the institutional and technical barriers will possibly also have been removed, and the way will be open for an efficient utilization of the continental transport infrastructure (Kristiansen, 1990).

At the *regional level*, companies demand efficient access to interregional transport and communication services. This will be required in order to facilitate the implementation of just-in-time solutions. Both the regional and the continental network organization of production will result in growing trading activities, and more frequent transport services for smaller consignments will prevail (Andersson et al., 1988). The value/weight ratios are generally expected to increase drastically due to combined commercial and environmental requirements. Today, the value of the products is significantly influencing the choice of transport system, namely, the modal choice. This indicates a further increase, in market shares, for road transport and air transport, as long as intermodal transport systems -- including rail transport and ferry routes -- are not able to offer functionally and economically competitive solutions. However, within the maritime regions, just-in-time requirements will give preference to short sea ferry routes offering high frequencies at the expense of traditional maritime freight services.

The general development is expected to be served by continent-wide types of mutually integrated networks, encompassing financial, communications, and logistic networks. Scientific analyses of alternative development options encompassing the economic and social dimension should also include an ecological dimension. However, EC policy formulation is still in an initial phase of identifying measures needed to provide a continent-wide infrastructure for environmental protection.

3.2 Subregional Integration

Within a broader geographical scope, there is a need to identify *"subregions"* which will be able to develop a certain degree of functional and economic identity and autonomy. These subregions, or micro-regions, are often found, geographically, as border regions or transborder regions (Kristiansen, 1992). The two Scandinavian transport corridors also encompass subregions of this type, i.e., the Öresund Region and the Skagerrak/Kattegat Region (see Figure 3).

3.2.1 The Öresund Region and the Fixed Link

The Copenhagen metropolitan area in Denmark and the Malmö-Lund area in Southern Sweden are physically separated by the Sound (Öresund), and institutionally separated by a national border. Hitherto, there has only been a limited socio-economic interaction between the two metropolitan areas, in terms of commuting and the exchange of commercial and scientific services. A fixed link, in the form of a railway and a motorway, is planned to be constructed across the Öresund and to start operation in 2000. This will also establish Copenhagen Airport as a common international terminal for the entire Öresund subregion. The fixed transport link (the Öresund Link) will connect two closely localized, but hitherto strongly separated, regional economies which have a total population of approximately 2.5 million. In combination with the EFTA member state, Sweden, joining the integrated European market, along with the EC member state, Denmark, the infrastructure improvements will be able to initiate a process of socio-economic integration between the two economic centers. As an alternative to a fixed link, the infrastructure extensions could also be achieved by introducing a comprehensive ferry service system, as an improvement to the presently inadequate ferry routes.

At present, the traffic between the Copenhagen area in Denmark and the Malmö-Lund area in Sweden is served by a number of ferry routes across the Öresund. A larger portion of passengers and freight on these routes will be transferred to the fixed link. Additionally, a considerable part of the freight transport along the direct ferry routes across the Baltic Sea between Southern Sweden (Skaane) and Germany may possibly shift to the fixed Öresund Link, especially when the fixed link across the Fehmarn Belt has been completed around 2005. The total construction costs of the Öresund Link are estimated to be approximately 3-4 billion ECUs, and the project will be user-funded by tolls. The presumption is that both passengers and goods will pay fares at the same level of costs as the tickets or fares for the present ferry services until the loans have been repaid. However, this issue is open to political decisions in favor of a lower level of toll payments.

If, and when, Sweden joins the European Economic Area, the institutional barrier along the Öresund will also start to crumble. The combined effect of penetrating the institutional and physical barriers, in the medium and long term, may turn the Öresund Subregion into a single labor and service market. This process of integration will imply significant changes of the commercial structure and localization pattern, on both sides of the national border along the Öresund. These changes will be further stimulated by the current development within the field of information technology, and will be accentuated by the general changes in industrial and commercial macro-structures.

3.2.2 The Skagerrak/Kattegat Region and the Ferry Links

As indicated in Figure 3, the areas around Skagerrak and Kattegat may also be identified as an economic subregion. This subregion consists of Southern Norway, Western Sweden, and Northern Jutland in Denmark. Approximately 4 million people live in these areas, adjacent to the shores of the Kattegat and Skagerrak. The areas are separated not only physically by seas, but also institutionally by the national borders between Norway, Denmark and Sweden. The Skagerrak/Kattegat transborder region includes a number of urban centers, ranging from the large cities, or metropolitan areas of Gothenburg and Oslo, to smaller or medium-sized urban centers, especially along the Norwegian coast and in Jutland. At present, a number of ferry routes across the Skagerrak/Kattegat provide services for both passengers (including private cars) and freight. A significant increase in transport flows demand a higher capacity at the ferry terminals, but this will only require limited amounts of public infrastructure investments in comparison with the construction of fixed links.

Some main problems of these ferry services are outlined in the following from an overall logistic point of view. There are a limited number of private ferry operators providing the international routes across the Skagerrak/Kattegat. These companies are forced to make efforts in order to strengthen their monopoly position in each specific ferry port. Thus, the private ferry operators are often permitted by the port authorities to invest in their own berths, terminals, buildings, etc., for the exclusive use of the ferry company in question. If a competitive situation was prevailing, these facilities would be considered as common physical infrastructure for competing operators. However, it is common for a potential competitor to get permission from the port authorities of a neighboring local authority to establish a new parallel route which may not have a solid commercial basis. Such an "exceptional" ferry route may only be in operation for a short period, but it would still be able to undermine the economic basis for the more stable trunk route (Jacobsen, 1992). Accordingly, the dominating ferry operators also make efforts to obtain control over potentially competing routes. These conditions are the source of the development of an unstable and scattered route structure, with low and fluctuating frequencies and, at the same time, conducive to the extension of the monopoly position of a few economically strong operators.

Another essential problem is that the main source of income for the ferry operators on the international routes between Denmark/Germany and Norway/Sweden originate from tax-free sales on board and the "shopping tourism" stimulated mainly by the lower price and tax levels in the EC country, Denmark, compared to Sweden and Norway. These income sources will probably evaporate, or diminish, before year 2000. These jumbo ferries also imply low frequencies on the routes. Thus, the present concept of expensively equipped jumbo ferries will not be economically viable under the new conditions.

Therefore, a number of coordinated regional policy initiatives are needed in order to develop an optimal structure of ferry terminals, routes, frequencies, and price policy (Jacobsen, 1992). Investments in physical infrastructure should be concentrated in the ports of a few strategic ferry links, with adequate connections to the trunk networks of roads and rail. The software transport infrastructure should provide the "rules of the game" to enhance concentration of the goods flows along the strategic links and ensure that a competitive situation prevails in the ferry ports/terminals in order to obtain high frequencies, adequate service levels, and attractive timetables. An additional prerequisite for the market to be competitive is that ferry port facilities should not be controlled by individual operators but should function as infrastructure, providing access for competing operators on equal terms. This institutional requirement is similar to those of access to airport hubs. In exceptional cases, where the traffic volumes are relatively limited, introduction of concessions may be considered as the most adequate overall solution.

In the Skagerrak/Kattegat area, the short sea ferry routes will still be crucial elements in the transport infrastructure, in combination with the promotion of intermodal goods transport systems which include road, rail, and maritime transport. The regional connection to the Nordic Link transit corridor is expected to provide efficient links to the Nordic countries and to the Western part of the European continent. In the medium and long term, this may strengthen regional trade relations and commercial networks across the Skagerrak and Kattegat, especially if the European Economic Area, within the near future, expands to include all the three Scandinavian countries. In the present situation, the national borders act as barriers for trade and socio-economic relations, within an area of similar socio-cultural and ethnic characteristics.

3.3 A Comprehensive Transport Infrastructure Concept

It is common knowledge that the presence of transport infrastructure in a particular region does not automatically enhance economic development in that area. The provision and improvement of regional transport infrastructure has to be adapted to, and integrated in, a comprehensive regional development strategy which includes other infrastructure services as well as the pursuit of socio-economic and industrial objectives.

There is a need to elaborate and clarify the concept of transport infrastructure, because no general consensus has yet been reached regarding what should be understood by the term "infrastructure". Thus, a new and comprehensive concept of transport infrastructure is briefly outlined in the following.

A primary distinction is often made between economic infrastructure and social infrastructure. In this chapter, the focus is on economic infrastructure, which is synonymous with the common conditions of production. Accordingly, transport infrastructure encompasses the common measures and conditions required in order to provide for the physical flows of goods and passengers for commercial purposes. More specifically, the transport infrastructure includes a number of both technological and institutional transport conditions. Furthermore, the technological conditions include hardware as well as software components. In most cases, it will be adequate to define the transport infrastructure at a continental, regional, or local level.

The common institutional conditions as well as the common technological conditions regarding, respectively, the physical flows and the flows of information, should be encompassed by a comprehensive concept of infrastructure. This means including the transport as well as the communication infrastructure. The common financial network may also be considered as a specific type of infrastructure. Thus, the function of the economic transport infrastructure is to provide common conditions of production and services. These conditions can be distinguished by dividing them into technological hardware conditions, technological software conditions, and institutional conditions. Considered as a total entity, the infrastructure and the logistic processes constitute a *logistic network*.

The *technological hardware conditions* are synonymous with transport infrastructure in the traditional sense of the concept. Thus, the category encompasses the common material or physical transport structures. For example, it includes highways, railways, ports, terminals, and related transport equipment and operation systems which serve as the prerequisites for individual transport activities and logistic processes. The *technological software conditions*, or immaterial infrastructure, comprise the common structures of organization (the "orgware") and the common information systems within the transport sector. Included in this category are the common services of scientific knowledge and information, which are offered with non-profit conditions to the actors within the transport sector. The *institutional conditions* are synonymous with the common "rules of the game" for the transport sector. Thus, they constitute the comprehensive framework of legislation and statutory instruments for the regulation of transport services and for traffic management and control. Also included are the public institutions and administrative systems which facilitate the planning, construction, operation and maintenance of the common transport structures.

3.3.1 Critical or "Missing" Links

In specific stages of an industrial and regional development (e.g., during the current logistic transition), the transport infrastructure will be able to play the role as a decisive factor for shaping the localization pattern of socio-economic activities and trade relations. Furthermore, an adequate transport infrastructure will act as a basic precondition for further industrial and commercial development, particularly if the transition phase of structural changes prevails.

We consider here two or more geographical areas or subregions, which were previously separated by physical and institutional barriers, often in combination with national borders. If those barriers are removed, or penetrated, by means of an extended transport infrastructure network, some significant economic and technological integration benefits may be achieved. This is especially the case if the improvement of transport infrastructure takes place in combination with an economic penetration of the institutional barriers; for example, when the EC integrated market is being extended across national borders. In this case, the strength of the joint regional economies will probably exceed the sum of economic potentials of the previously separated regions. In this way, the establishment of critical or "missing" links between two or more economically viable regions will create a structural and qualitative improvement of the logistic network. Thus, the impact on regional development may be significant and wide-ranging even in connection with relatively modest investments in the physical transport infrastructure.

3.3.2 Infrastructure and the Market

The functional performance of infrastructure derives from the transport policy decisions. These decisions concern two, mutually overlapping issues. One of these issues is the need for competition and deregulation versus the need for coordination. *Competition* should enhance the sound commercial conditions of the transport operators, including the monitoring of private investments and individual transport services. *Coordination* should aim at providing an adequate overall transport structure, as well as ensuring socio-economically efficient utilization of the transport system as a whole. The other issue is the identification of the functions which are to be publicly provided (i.e., infrastructure) or market-regulated. It is of paramount importance to make a distinction between those parts of the transport system which play the role as infrastructure and those transport activities and services which are regulated by the economic conditions of the market.

The aim of the transport infrastructure is to provide the common conditions for individual transport activities to be performed. Thus, infrastructure has to be viewed as those particular elements of the transport structure which are subject to public regulation and collective precepts. The individual transport activities and deregulated services, for their part, are mainly influenced by the relations between commercial and operative conditions, by the supply of transport service, and by the economic demand in terms of purchasing power. However, the conditions are seldom as simple and clear-cut as described above. Often, the transport companies hold a monopoly position, thus hampering an adequate functional division between infrastructure services and market-regulated services. Furthermore, the question of exactly where the line between infrastructure and market should be drawn in the specific cases is a political issue.

3.4 Ferry Links as Infrastructure Elements

The implementation of the Scandinavian Link Scheme will result in an uninterrupted road and rail link along the entire route between Oslo/Gothenburg and Hamburg. However, as far as the Nordic Link Scheme is concerned, a basic organizational precondition is the implementation of a more complex network of intermodal transport chains and multimodal transport services along the corridor. Thus, a basic physical prerequisite for the Nordic Link corridor is the presence of efficiently functioning ferry links between Northern Jutland and Norway/Sweden. The ferry routes, which connect Southern Sweden directly to the Continent via Germany, could also be considered as elements of the Scandinavian Link Scheme, due to their complementary and competitive function in relation to the future fixed link across the Fehmarn Belt. The Channel Tunnel, vis-à-vis the ferry links across the Irish Sea and the English Channel, has similarities to Scandinavian Link versus Nordic Link. Despite the presence of fixed crossings within these maritime regions, some of the ferry routes will develop into key links between the peripheral areas and the continental transport networks. These ferry links will not be fulfilling primarily local, regional, or bi-national transport functions, but will serve as strategic elements in the continent-wide transport infrastructure.

The importance of the strategic ferry links will possibly increase in the near future because there is a need to integrate and connect the peripheral networks to the continental trade and transport networks, as well as to alleviate the growing capacity problems along the central transport corridors. The need to spread the advanced technological development geographically, and thus mobilize the industrial potential of the whole community, will also support the focus on ferry services.

3.4.1 Infrastructure Functions

The infrastructure requirements of the ferry terminals and ferry routes originate from their function as elements of the continental logistic network and from their importance to regional accessibility and mobility. Accordingly, the main functions of the strategic ferry links are to serve as:

* Alternative links contributing to the overall capacity of the network and thus reducing the severe congestion problems which occur in the core areas; and

* Key links for the multimodal transport corridors which serve the peripheral regions and offshore islands.

In relation to the transport infrastructure functions of strategic ferry links, it will be necessary to assess the specific regional requirements of the transport infrastructure network and to identify an adequate separation between infrastructure services and market-regulated services. These issues, together with the technology aspects, will be discussed in the following subsection. The discussion should form a basis for the formulation of adequate transport policy strategies which can be applied for the peripheral regions.

3.4.2 Ferry Links as an Issue of EC Infrastructure Policy

Ferry transport differs significantly from conventional maritime transport with regard to the functional and organizational requirements, as well as the institutional aspects and transport policy issues. Most of the ferry routes are interconnecting links between overland transport networks located on both sides of a sound, a strait or a sea. From a modal point of view, ferry transport is maritime transport. However, from a systems viewpoint, the strategic ferry routes and terminals should be considered as integrated links of combined freight transport systems, mainly operating overland. The strategic ferry links function as elements of the intermodal routes and multimodal corridors. The freight ferry services provide for efficient interconnections and complementarity between road, rail and maritime transport. Thus, in logistic terms, they are required to operate as competitors with road transport haulage.

This lack of a conceptual clarification regarding *the infrastructure role of ferry links in intermodal transport* may be the main reason why ferry services have not been recognized so far as parts of the continental transport networks, either at the national or the EC levels. A supplementary reason could be that several ferry routes serve mainly local or regional traffic. Apparently, a great number of local ferry routes are of no major importance to the pan-European transport systems. However, there remain a number of international ferry routes which, in fact, serve as essential parts of the continent-wide transport networks. Some of the current problems of these routes are stated below.

Most of the present ferries operating on the international routes are of the jumbo type, and are combined carriers of passengers, private cars, commercial vehicles and trailers. However, the preference of the ferry operators is for passenger transport and tax-free sales earnings. The income from the freight rates covers only a fraction of the total turnover. These prevailing business conditions have created the present situation, where the jumbo concept dominates the ferry service market. Accordingly, the introduction of logistically oriented ferry services -- in terms of high frequencies of departures and flexible freight booking systems -- is not economically attractive for the operators. The development has gone steadily in the direction of larger ferries and lower frequencies. Furthermore, the time schedules are not always coordinated to a satisfactory degree with the connecting overland goods transport services (Jacobsen, 1992). Thus, there is a need to formulate a coherent set of transport infrastructure policies and guidelines in order to obtain equally competitive market conditions for ferry services within the whole continent as well as to attain balanced competition among the various modes of transport.

3.5 Functional Requirements of the Regional Networks

It is necessary to identify the technical, operational, organizational, and legislative requirements for ferry terminals and routes. This applies, specifically, to the strategic ferry links recognized as part of both the European-wide and regional transport infrastructure. Specific needs and requirements depend on regional development strategies and related transport policies, if such are formulated. For the market to establish and provide adequate ferry services, according to the logistic demands, it is not necessary to view ferry routes as infrastructure -- except for the basic port facilities and the connecting road sections. However, it is not likely that this situation prevails in many cases.

3.5.1 Ferry Routes and Terminals as Infrastructure

The infrastructure functions of ferry ports and routes are gounded in global logistic considerations (i.e., coherence of the continental logistic network) and regional development interests (i.e., regional connectivity and inter-regional accessibility to the continental network). Our discussion of ferry link infrastructure requirements will focus on the following topics:

* Coordination of ferry design, schedules, and overland connections to both road and rail networks;
* Enhancement of intermodal transport solutions;
* Improvement of commercially related transport services for passengers;
* Relatively low and competitive fares for freight transport; and
* Overall and long term logistic network considerations in terms of adequate and stable service levels.

Traditionally, the infrastructure role of specific transport structures (the strategic ferry links) have been viewed by some politicians as conflicting with the ideological goal of overall deregulation. In the case of ferry routes, there actually is a necessity to identify some specific rules of "the game". In other words, an institutional infrastructure is needed -- not to act as a straitjacket for individual transport services -- but in order to secure an element of competition and to avoid a total monopolistic situation in order to provide an adequate service level for the overall networks.

3.5.2 The Choice of Systems Technology

The function of the regional system of transport in relation to the ferry links depends on the *ferry route structure and functional innovations* of new ferry concepts, the *technical innovations* of new ferry design concepts and standards, and the *ferry terminal functions*. The systems technology includes the function as transport infrastructure, the logistic and functional requirements of freight ferry services, the legislative framework for ferry services, terminal operations, organization, management and financial solutions and, finally the application of integrated telematics.

Specific attention should be drawn to the ferry ports as crucial nodes of the network. The ferry ports provide terminal functions, i.e., they are intermodal transfer points and centers of intermodal connections where transfers between rail-ferry or road-ferry, and vice versa, occur. This circumstance provides potential for introducing flexible types of automatized ("intelligent") freight ferries and rapid transhipment techniques. Some of the most favorably localized ferry terminals/ports will have the potential for development as integrated centers for rail, road, and water-borne transport.

3.5.3 General Considerations

Multimodal and intermodal transport solutions, in combination with a relatively diffuse feeder and distributor pattern, will require specific coordinating efforts. In this regard, there is a need to further clarify the concept of "transport infrastructure" in order to make it an operational planning tool. This indicates inclusion of both technological and institutional conditions, as described previously.

Traffic flows should be concentrated to the degree which enables introduction of efficient technology and adequate frequencies. The peripheral regions will have to establish a network of standardized logistic centers, or terminals, localized in conjunction with major transport flows and nodes, thus connecting the regional logistic flows with the continental network. The functional requirements related to ferry links which permit them to perform as integrated elements of regional transport networks, are also described above. Due to specific topographic and other geographic conditions, regional transport policies should include some of the ferry links as essential elements of the transport infrastructure. This technological approach may be adopted by several maritime regions, such as in the Mediterranean areas, across the Skagerrak/Kattegat in the Nordic Link Corridor, across the Baltic Sea between the Nordic countries and Eastern Europe, within the British Isles, and between the British Isles and mainland Europe. In particular, there is a need to consider certain strategic ferry links as important elements of the overall transport infrastructure network. The potential for technological innovations within ferry transport is promising in relation to an integrated application of informatics and telematics, and in connection with the implementation of multimodal transport corridors.

The regional transport networks may also contribute to *environmental sustainability*, or "sustainable mobility", by offering greater flexibility in the choice of technological innovations and solutions. In order to obtain this, the network extensions should include the development of maritime necessary transport networks, viable rail transport services, and intermodal systems, enabling these networks to operate on logistic terms equal to those of road haulage transport.

4. Conclusion

The case of the Scandinavian Link versus the Nordic Link provides evidence that the choice of transport infrastructure and technology may have a crucial impact on the subregional development, within corridors between the Scandinavian periphery and the core of the European continent. In particular, this is the case for transborder regions, where existing national barriers will be penetrated by the integrated market. Maritime regions and subregions have potential for sustainable development both in terms of regional economy and environmental stability, provided that the ferry links be considered as a policy issue for the strategic choice of transport infrastructure solutions. The pattern of goods transport for the peripheral and maritime regions are relative diffuse and scattered. However, for the maritime subregions around the Skagerrak/Kattegat and the Baltic Sea, there are promising options in relation to an integrated application of telematics, ferry transport, new organizational concepts and intermodal solutions.

In this regard, a clear distinction should be made between infrastructure functions and market-regulated services. This is particularly needed in the case of ferry ports and ferry services. In order to support a comprehensive planning methodology, a new transport infrastructure concept is proposed, with greater emphasis on technological software and institutional conditions, compared to the provision of physical infrastructure. Furthermore, some specific guidelines are recommended in order to meet the functional requirements of regional transport networks. A policy approach, similar to the one described in this chapter, is recommended for adoption by several maritime regions around the European continent.

References

Andersson, Å.E. and Strömquist, U., 1988, *K-Samhällets Framtid* (The Future of the C-Society), Prisma, Sweden.

Commission of the European Communities, 1992, *Europe 2000: Outlook for the Development of the Community's Territory*, Directorate General for Regional Policy, Brussels.

Commission of the European Communities, 1992, *The Future Role of the Common Transport Policy, A Global Approach to the Construction of Community Framework for Sustainable Mobility*, The White Paper, CEC, Brussels.

Jacobsen, U. and Kristiansen, J., 1992, Transport Networks for Peripheral Regions, *Transportation Research A*, 26A, 2, 199-210.

Kearney, A.T., Inc., 1992, *Achieving Customer Satisfaction Leadership in Europe,* Management Report No. 37, Chicago.

Kristiansen, J., 1990, *The Transport Infrastructure in Western Europe - Past and Future Development*, Working Paper No. 56, Dept. of Development and Planning, Aalborg University, Denmark.

Kristiansen, J., 1992, *Urban Development and Regional Transport Infrastructure*, Working Paper No. 101, Dept. of Development and Planning, Aalborg University, Denmark.

Nordic Council, 1992, *Cooperation in the Baltic Sea Area,* Nord 1992:24, Stockholm.

European Round Table of Industrialists (ERTI), 1984, *Missing Links: Upgrading Europe's Transborder Ground Transport Infrastructure*. Roundtable Secretariat, Brussels.

European Round Table of Industrialists (ERTI), 1989, *Need for Renewing Transport Infrastructure in Europe*. European Round Table Secretariat, Brussels.

Scandinavian Link, 1988, *Transport 1988-2000, General Report on the Scandinavian Link Project*, Summary, Copenhagen.

TRANSPORT IN A UNIFIED EUROPE. Policies and Challenges.
D. Banister and J. Berechman (Editors)

Chapter Eleven

REGULATORY REFORM IN LOCAL PUBLIC TRANSPORT IN SCANDINAVIA

Bjorn Andersen

1. Introduction

This paper presents an investigation of the objectives of privatization and deregulation and the underlying factors explaining these processes in transport. The specific problem is dealt with in reference to changes in local public transport systems in Europe.

Since 1980, radical changes have taken place in Britain public transport policy. In many other countries, there have been discussions as to what course to follow in this area. The reasons for the discussions are several, but there is one clear explanatory factor found in most of the West European countries: the need for reductions in public budgets. This has resulted in policy discussions in which privatization and deregulation have become options in a process leading to a more effective and more competitive public transport market, one which would, in turn, relieve the public budgets.

Another important factor has been the relevance of ideology to the process of change (i.e., whether there are clear ideological reasons for change). Again, Britain can be used as an example where ideology has played a part in defining objectives such as a reduction in the role of the state and an increase in share ownership by ordinary people, management, and employees through the sale of state assets. Again, the question to be asked is whether there is a general trend towards privatization of public transport in Western Europe or whether this is merely restricted to Britain.

The issue to be explored in this chapter is whether there is any general trend towards deregulation or privatization in Western Europe and whether the reasons for the changes found lie more in the need for reductions in public expenditure and for control of inflation rather than in ideology. Another important reason for the lack of a general trend towards deregulation and privatization can be found in the fact that many governments in Europe tend to consider public transport a social service, not a competitive industry. Public transport is provided as a right for users, or as an important public service on equity and environmental grounds.

However, tendencies towards more competitive elements can still be found, especially in Scandinavia, through the development of intermediate systems such as franchising/tendering. Tendering has been used there as a method for combining market principles with the need for a policy based on social effectiveness. The chapter tries to analyze the reasons for and some of the results of the changes in the Scandinavian countries (Norway, Sweden and Denmark) and the implications for Europe of the Scandinavian experience,

2. Review

Two different approaches have been used to explain the forces behind privatization and deregulation policies. An economic explanation has been argued by Adamson, Jones and Pratt (1991), Banister (1990), Kay and Vickers (1988) and Rickard (1988); a mainly political explanation has been used by Derthick and Quirck (1985).

Adamson, Jones and Pratt (1991), Banister (1990) and Kay and Vickers (1988) all define the privatization and deregulation in the same broad categories of policies:

* Privatization through the transfer of ownership in the public sector by sales of assets. These sales can be of whole undertakings or parts (specific assets), and can be carried out through management/employee buyouts or through sales to the general public.

* Franchising or contracting out of services previously supplied collectively or through publicly owned undertakings/organizations. This category can be seen as both a form of privatization and as deregulation, for example, through competitive tendering systems.

* Liberalization of market entry to allow entry to previously regulated markets.

This paper deals with the second and third categories, primarily on the deregulation side because these are the issues which have generated most discussion in local transport. Outside Britain, very little has happened in terms of transfer of ownership that cannot be explained by franchising policies, particularly with respect to local transport.

Banister (1990) argues that to understand the process towards privatization, it is necessary to understand the reasons behind government ownership and control of transport. His hypothesis states that more important than an individual explanation was the time at which decisions were made. He argues that the pluralist approach of the 1960s and early 1970s became untenable as the number of interests increased along with people's expectations, and that the corporatism of the 1970s arose as a response to recession, inflation and unemployment. But even this approach became impossible as the level of taxation and balance of payments deficits increased, and standards of living were at best only maintained. All these factors resulted in radical alternatives being put forward.

Rickard (1988) has given three main reasons for privatization seen from the government's side. First, there are the supply side benefits of greater efficiency. These benefits could be achieved through the introduction of greater competition, through giving management greater freedom from public sector control, through forcing companies to raise capital in the market, and through making management accountable to shareholders. Second, there is the argument of widening share ownership and thus reduction of the role of the state. Third, there is the need to secure proceeds from sales for the financing of government activities. The ideological arguments found here concern wider share ownership and the reduced role for the state.

Adamson, Jones and Pratt (1991) -- referring to the Beesley and Littlechild (1983) and Kay and Silberstone (1984) -- Kay and Thompson (1986), and Vickers and Yarrow (1988) all define the objectives of privatization and deregulation to be: first, improving the economic efficiency and customer service in part through clarifying the role of the public sector; second, reducing public sector borrowing requirements; and third, promoting wider share ownership. They argue that the primary criteria of privatization is the promotion of economic efficiency.

Derthick and Quirk (1985) take another approach and argue that deregulation cannot be made explicable by reference to mainly economic events. They reject the argument that regulation crumbled because the original public interest rationale for it ceased to conform with economic reality. They question whether it ever did. They argue that there are several problems with this interpretation: first, that the economic rationales advanced in defense of regulation were the real reason for its adoption in that it overlooks the underlying political forces and the fact that economists' rationales as well as economic realities have been subject to change; and, finally, that original rationales and current realities quite commonly diverge without being subject to intellectual scrutiny.

Derthick and Quirk (1985) also dismiss the second theory of economic explanation based on the so-called economic theory of politics (Carron and MacAvoy, 1981; Downs, 1957; MacAvoy, 1979) arguing that deregulation occurred because under changed economic circumstances, regulated industries and economically interested groups actually wanted it. This, in their opinion (1985), exclusively places the emphasis on the pursuit of self interest as a prime motive of political action.

Eads (1982) argues that economic regulation failed because it was incapable of dealing with the rapid structural change which altered the issue the regulatory agencies had to deal with. This in turn resulted in a demand from the regulated industries for deregulation. Derthick and Quirk (1985) dismiss these arguments because there is very little evidence for such action from the regulated industries in the U.S.

Derthick and Quirk's (1985) hypothesis is that the process of deregulation in the U.S. can be explained as a process of political evolution with three stages:

* Economists advocate deregulation as a way of reducing the social costs resulting from unnecessary public utility regulation.

* The political establishment (presidents and leading senators) advocate it as a way of responding to widely shared desires, sentiments and values.

* Deregulation becomes a more or less automatically preferred style of political choice.

Derthick and Quirk (1985) argue that what ultimately made economists' arguments relevant to politics were:

> events that no one could have foreseen: the development of severe inflation, the rise of consumerism, and a vague, but widely diffused dissatisfaction with a government that seemed to grow uncontrollably and irresistibly. Ironically, the economists' arguments became relevant the largely because the profession was so thoroughly at a loss to offer any

> better, more plausible cure for inflation, and not because anyone seriously thought that the inefficiencies created by public utility regulation were a significant cause of the inflationary spiral.

Derthick and Quirk's (1985) views are also supported by Kay and Thompson (1986), who argue that the case for privatization/deregulation is less clear and does not have any sophisticated rationale; rather, as it lacks any clear analysis of purpose or effects, any direction which seems achievable is hence seized for justification. They argue that the outcome is that no objectives are effectively attained and that political goals have dominated, thus subordinating economic efficiency.

The conclusion reached by the Derthick and Quirk (1985) and Banister (1990) are similar, namely, that politicians look for radical alternatives to confront present problems such as inflation and political unrest within the government. The answer has become privatization and deregulation. In Banister (1990), the arguments for change are defined as: first, the overall perceived failure of the public sector and welfare state created after the World War II; and second, the argument that the private provision of services is inherently more efficient as there is a simple performance measure, namely, profitability (see Rickard, 1988).

The hypothesis underlying this study is that the main forces of change found in Europe outside Britain can be explained by the need for reduced public spending and the control of inflation more than by ideological reasons. It is also hypothesized that in local public transport, there is no clear tendency towards deregulation in Europe but that a weak tendency can be found towards limited competition through franchising systems, placed within a framework of a planned and integrated public transport system.

The process of privatization in Britain can be explicated in two phases (Banister, 1990). The first stage is the company state, where nationalized industries are sold together in a process of liberalization of constraints in order to reduce state interference in the market, leaving areas of safety and working conditions as the main areas of public responsibility. The second phase is the dismantling of the government apparatus through a reduction in its role, from pluralist and corporatist roles to a neo-liberalist "dirigiste" role. This may be seen as a learning process where the experience of stage one is used in carrying out stage two. In Britain, there are numerous examples of activities previously carried on in the state sector and transferred to an executive agency status. The signs of such processes are much weaker elsewhere in Europe.

It is also worth noting that local public transport differs very substantially from other transport modes such as road goods transport and airlines, where there seems to be much more scope for deregulation. Much more extensive deregulation has taken place in these two sectors. This may be explained by the knock-on effect of international transport industries which makes it impossible for one country to regulate if other countries surrounding it deregulate, and where we also find strong supranational organizations like the European Community advocating deregulation.

Central to the discussion of deregulation is the question of regulatory and market failure. Kay and Thompson (1991) discuss regulatory failure in the UK transport sector and distinguish between escapable and inescapable failures. Inescapable failures are defined as those which directly follow as a consequence of the economic sector being regulated. Examples here are where a natural monopoly and high sunk costs prevent a competitive solution and where information assymetries arise as a consequence of monopoly. In such cases, regulation will be inevitable. Escapable failures follow from inappropriate methods of regulation which result in the suppression of competitive solutions.

Kay and Thompson (1991) argue that unnecessary suppression of competition has been an important source of regulatory failure. However, they also argue that deregulation makes market failure more likely and define three types of market failure. First, they identify the situation where market outcomes are regarded as unsatisfactory, (e.g., due to externalities or information assymetries); second, there are cases where a competitive solution may be achieved but where incumbents deter market entry; and third, there are cases of natural monopoly and high sunk costs.

In this chapter, it is argued that there is no general tendency towards privatization/deregulation in local public transport in Europe, but that there are tendencies towards more competitive solutions through franchising. Further, the main arguments for privatization/deregulation are financial rather than ideological. Also, there is evidence in Europe to support the Derthick and Quirk (1985) hypothesis that deregulation is evolutionary, moving from a vaguely and loosely defined process to a preferred style of policy choice, and later to a process of policy fashion, but without any really clearly defined aims. There is much support for Kay and Vicker's (1988) hypothesis that the rationale behind deregulation and privatization policies are weak and that politicians in European countries are not prepared to take the consequences of radical alternatives. If we have a situation where doubts can be raised about the contestability of the local public transport market due to barriers to competition and the inherent advantage of the incumbent, and at the same time the political aims focus on social effectiveness rather than efficiency, then a solution of tendering/franchising may be chosen. These issues, relating to competition for the market, will now be discussed with reference to the experience in Scandinavia.

3. Regulatory Regimes in Europe

Hensher (1988) discussed the question of social effectiveness and productive efficiency in public transport, defining social effectiveness to include allocative efficiency and equity questions. This brings us directly to the central issue of the debate between Beesley and Glaister (1985) and Gwilliam et al. (1985) as to whether it is better to acquire the benefits of supply side competition through competitive tendering, while maintaining a planned and coordinated network with identified cross-subsidization, or whether it is better to go for full deregulation, including opening up the market to competitive tendering of socially necessary services.

The NECTAR survey presents the situation in Europe. The primary aim of the survey was to reveal whether there was a clear tendency towards deregulation in local public transport in Europe. In discussions on transport deregulation in Europe, one can easily get the impression that there is such a clear policy on these issues, similar to processes initiated by the European Commission on road goods transport and in the airline sector. The second aim was to show what kinds of tendencies can be found in Europe when there were any clear signs of deregulation. The third aim was to analyze alternatives (such as competitive tendering) to the radical British solution of almost full deregulation. The fact that doubts can be raised about the British model of deregulation does not mean that there is no concern over public transport policies in Europe.

In many countries, questions have been raised concerning the results of suppression of competition, regulatory failures, and especially the increasing levels of subsidy for public transport and the necessity for market innovations. In short, this is the question of public transport efficiency. There is no doubt that the priority given to contain and reduce levels of subsidy and to ease the burden on public budgets in a time of severe restraint has led several countries to a search for alternatives.

Classifying regulatory regimes is not an easy task because there is considerable variation between different countries according to *the historical tradition* and type of *jurisdiction, i.e., the administrative structure*. By this we mean the administration hierarchy, whether there is a federal structure or not, and which level of government has responsibility for public transport. *The structure of the public transport sector*, especially the mix between private and public operators, the type of *transport policy* pursued, and its effect on public transport policy, also influence any classification.

In any attempt to classify regulatory regimes, it is necessary to look into both the wider involvement of the public sector in industry and the entry conditions to the market. For the purpose of analysis, two main categories of systems can be defined: a fully planned system with a high degree of public involvement and a market-oriented system with a low level of public involvement. The fully planned system would often be one with strong public ownership of operations, where the operation, planning, and financing of the public transport system is fully integrated into one body controlled by politicians. On the other hand, a full market system would be one where there is absolutely no public involvement. The market would decides about the public transport system. In practice, policy in most countries lies somewhere in between the two extreme positions.

The *planned system* has some or all of the following features:

* The idea of a coordinated and integrated transport network (including interchange of information) making it necessary to regulate entry/exit conditions in some way;

* Cross-subsidization between profitable and loss-making routes and parts of networks;

* A uniform farepolicy and fare system, and often a fare system which is independent of operator and transport modes.

* Often a public authority responsible for financing and organizing public transport owned by local authorities, where the state has defined the role of the authority through legislation and the quality of service independent, to a certain extent, of demand;

* In many cases, there is public ownership of operating companies or mixed public/private ownership;

* A relatively high degree of operating network subsidy (revenue support is often greater than 40%) and concessionary fares systems.

On the other hand, a *market-oriented system* can be defined by:

* A route system based on market demand;

* No or very little cross-subsidization between routes and other parts of the network;

* Fares set individually for each route or by each company, but with possibilities for cooperation on fares policy on a commercial basis (not implying collusion).

* Little public interference with the operation of public transport except where there is a social need for transport not provided for by the market and defined as worthy of support by the public authorities, or for special groups through concessionary fares system;

* Independent private operators are the main suppliers of public transport;

* A low level of subsidy, often with the use of tendering systems for subsidized networks or routes.

However, the pure systems are seldom found and, as the survey will show, several forms of intermediate systems exist.

Franchising is an intermediate system, operated by a public authority with the aim of supporting a partially planned and integrated public transport system with a uniform fares policy but, at the same time, using a competitive system to allow entry into the market. Competition is *for* the market rather than *in* the market. In essence, this is a planned system trying to take some advantage of competition but avoiding the severest disadvantages of competition.

There are two types of franchising, depending upon who has responsibility for the *revenue* -- whether the operators have full responsibility for both revenue and costs (operating on a net subsidy contract), or only for costs (operating on a cost contract). In the second system, a public body is responsible for the income side; this reduces the risk for the operators. Not surprisingly, systems based on cost contracts seem to be more popular with the franchising authorities.

There are three basic categories of regulatory regimes with respect to conditions of entry and exit:

* *Needs-based systems:* Long term limited monopoly rights with no competition, e.g., Germany;

* *Contract-based arbitration or competitive tendering*, e.g., Norway; and

* *Competitive-based* systems: free entry/exit to the market or competitive tendering, e.g., Britain

Needs-based licenses give the operator a monopoly for a certain route or route area, either formally or in practice, through renewal procedures for an indefinite time period. In contract-based systems, licenses for operators no longer exist but have been substituted by a contract for a fixed period, either by arbitration or competition. The last category is full competition for and in the market, or at least a combination where we have a market system combined with a tendering system for socially necessary routes. In Europe, fully free markets do not exist.

Entry/exist requirements do not define the role of the state or local authorities in public transport (i.e., the public involvement). There is no necessarily clear relationship between entry/exit regulations and the form of public involvement, especially as concerns the level of subsidy, the fares system, and private/public ownership. The entry/exit regimes must be seen as a part of the whole, but in general, the two first are associated with planned systems and the third with a market system.

The question of whether governments consider local public transport a social service or a competitive industry can be illustrated by looking in more detail at some European countries such as Germany, France, Switzerland, Sweden and Norway. These countries can be divided into the three groups of systems, regulated monopolies with a strong public involvement (Germany and Switzerland); franchising with a strong public, involvement (France); and competitive tendering with some public involvement (Sweden and Norway).

If we look at the public transport policies of these countries, we find clear elements of social effectiveness arguments. In the case of Germany, the two most important acts regulating and financing public transport the GVFG (the Community Transport Finance Act) and the PbefG (the Passenger Transport Act) both have clear equity aims. The first Act has the redistributive aim of transferring money from motorists to public transport users through the hypothecation of motor vehicle fuel tax. It is designed so as to redistributes the monies from rural to urban parts of Germany as about half the tax is collected in each of these areas, but 90 percent of the total revenues is used in urban areas.

The PbefG (Passenger Transport Act) has clear objectives of social effectiveness, such as the improvement of safety and services in rural areas. In addition, the Act has clear rules for protection of railways from bus competition -- the so-called "need proofing", in order to advance regional development.

In Switzerland, the system of need proofing and control of entry to the public transport industry is also strong. The major aims advanced through a regulatory regime of this kind can be found in environmental protection and energy saving purposes. Andersen (1993) has given an account of Swiss public transport policy.

In France, we find the same social effectiveness arguments in the main act regulating public transport, LOTI (the Law on Orientation of Internal Transport, 1982). This can be seen from the following quote from the Act (English translation CETUR 1990):

> The state, and local authorities or associations thereof within the limits of their authority will organize the regular transportation of persons. This service will be provided either through administration by a public person in the form of a public industrial and commercial service, or by a company which has signed an agreement of limited duration to that effect with the competent authority. This agreement sets out the general character and conditions for operations and financing of the service. It defines the actions to be undertaken by both of the parties, with the *object of ensuring the effective exercise of the right to transportation, and the promotion of public transport of persons.*

The important assumption here is that the user has a "right to be transported" in the context of the rights of the citizen to means of reaching his place of employment, social-cultural facilities, and leisure facilities. In France, this implies that there is a good quality public transport system at their disposal.

In Scandinavia, there are signs of more competitive solutions, such as tendering in both Norway and Sweden, and these countries have kept the social effectiveness aims in their public transport policies. In Norway, the Transport Act 1976, which regulates public transport, defines its aims to be effective production based on the social costs of transport in its first paragraph. This Act also includes a regional policy of supporting settlements all over the country, environmental aims, and safety in traffic. This paragraph in the program is still retained even after the change of regulatory regime in 1991, which openned up the possibility for competitive tendering.

Sweden has changed its transport policy during the latter part of the 1980s, but again there is no doubt that the social effectiveness aims of the public transport policy are highly relevant. The government‘s submission to the Swedish parliament on "Transport Policy for the 1990s" (Kommunikationsdepartementet, 1988) states that public transport supply ought to be increased due to environmental and congestion reasons and that public transport must be coordinated and made more efficient. It is within this framework that Sweden has embarked upon a substantial program of liberalization of transport policy and the use of competitive tendering both for buses and for railways/tramways.

The above examples clearly show that even though there are signs of more liberal regimes in some countries, there are still clear signs of social effectiveness aims and even "right to transport" views on public transport. Outside Britain, there are no signs of this policy changing. This means that the governments of these European countries pursue other policies or do not believe that the British solution will give the desired results.

Returning to the Beesley-Glaister and Gwilliam-Nash-Mackie debate over market solutions and integrated solutions with which this discussion started, the answer seems to be predominantly political. But judging from the European scene, there does not seem to be much belief in the British solution to bus deregulation and privatization (excluding London).

Button (1989) has attempted to examine the relevance of established theories of regulation in explaining the evolution of UK transport policy. He has claimed that both the public interest theory and the capture theory of regulation do not offer a broad enough explanation. He advocates a broader approach, along the lines of Levine (1981), arguing that policies supporting cross-subsidization will only be accepted if either the efficiency loss is small or the cost of obtaining detailed information on losses is high compared to the perceived efficiency losses. Thus, if efficiency losses from these forms of regulatory policies either increase or knowledge of them becomes widespread, this will generate pressure for reform; thus, there is an incentive for self-correction of the system of its regulation if becomes too expensive. Button also argues that the theory of winning coalitions can be used as an explanation for the policy change in Britain.

As will be seen in the next sections, where the Scandinavian situation is discussed, there is much to be said for Levine's theory concerning the cost of regulation and the effectiveness of using cross-subsidization. This is one of the explanations for the move towards the more liberal regulatory regimes of today. For example, in Norway, there is a clear connection between the awareness of the effects of cross-subsidization and the level of subsidy, as well as the changing coalitions concerned with reforms. This will be dealt with in the next section. Perhaps Germany and Switzerland have to go through the same cycle, starting with strong pressure on public finance and questions of public transport efficiency. There are signs that both these countries are now beginning to ask questions about the costs of their public transport policies, starting with a discussion of the regionalization of responsibility and fixed levels of subsidies instead of balancing of accounts. It can also be concluded that on the Continent, there are no signs of Banister's (1990) company state or even less of his second phase, the dismantling of the government itself.

Tables 1A and 1B give the results of a survey of European local public transport, classifying the different countries according to the main systems planned, franchising and market. The tables include 18 countries. The information is valid for scheduled urban and local/regional transport, but not necessarily for inter-city traffic, where many countries exercise less control and where opportunities for entry/exit are easier or free entry exists. The results are quite clear: local public bus transport in Europe is dominated by planned systems. Of the 18 countries, at least 12 are clearly planned systems, 5 are intermediate systems where some form of competitive element have been introduced, and only one system, the British, is mainly a market system.

Network subsidies are the most common type of subsidy. This suggests that cross-subsidization could occur between routes by time of day and for groups of passengers. In all countries, except for the United Kingdom, public authorities exercise full or extensive control of fares. However, if we look at the revenue/cost ratio, it is more difficult to draw clear conclusions, as in many countries public transport operators cover more than 50 percent of costs by traffic revenue.

Other forms of capital subsidies must also be taken into account. Capital subsidies are found in countries like Denmark (Copenhagen), France, Israel, Italy, Switzerland, and West Germany. The ratio of revenue/cost does not, therefore, give a full account of all forms of subsidy. In addition, some countries have specific subsidies for concessionary fares, and others include compensation in the general revenue support. The conclusion is

TABLE 1A

Survey of Regulatory Systems in Europe

	Entry/Exit Regulations						
	Excl.Rights to Public Operators	Needs-based Licenses	Contracts by Arbitration	Contracts by Tendering	Free Entry	Period of Time for Licenses (Years)	Regulatory Systems
Denmark	x		x	x		5	Planned Franch.
Belgium	x	x					Planned
Finland		x				5	Planned
France	x			x		7	Planned Franch.
Greece	x	x				-	Planned
Ireland		x				-	Planned
Israel		x		x		-	Planned Franch.
Italy	x	x				-	Planned
Netherlands	x	x					Planned
Norway		x	x	x		5 - 10	Planned Franch.
Portugal		x			x		Planned Market
Spain	x			x		8 - 20	Planned
Sweden			x	x		3 - 5	Planned Franch.
Switzerland		x				10 + 3	Planned
Turkey	x	x					Planned
United Kingdom				x	x	3	Market
West Germany		x				8	Planned
Yugoslavia	x					-	Planned

Key: - = Unlimited.

Source: NECTAR questionnaire and specially collected information.

Table 1B

Survey of Regulatory Systems in Europe

	Entry/Exit Regulations				
	Type of Operating Subsidies	Revenue Cost Ratio	Concessionary Fare System	Control of Fares	Regulatory Systems
Denmark	N/R	55 - 56	x	F	Planned Franch.
Belgium	N	30 - 40		F	Planned
Finland	N	57 - 92		F	Planned
France	N	53		F	Planned Franch.
Greece	N	40 - 50		F	Planned
Ireland	N	80 - 95	x	F	Planned
Israel	N	66	x	F	Planned Franch.
Italy	N	24 - 28	x		Planned
Netherlands	N/R	28 - 40		F	Planned
Norway	N/R	55 - 60	x	F	Planned Franch.
Portugal	N/R	67		F	Planned Market
Spain	N	70 - 90		F	Planned
Sweden	N/R	39 - 48	x	F	Planned Franch.
Switzerland	N	54 - 82	x	F	Planned
Turkey	N			F	Planned
United Kingdom	R		x	L/F	Market
West Germany	N	54	x	F	Planned
Yugoslavia	N			F	Planned

Key: Blank = No information; F = Full or extensive control of fares; L = Little or absence of control of fares; N = Network subsidies; R = Route subsidies.

Source: NECTAR questionnaire and specially collected information.

therefore that it is difficult to use the revenue/cost ratio in its own right as a measure of regulatory regime. Switzerland, which in every respect has the characteristics of a planned system, has a high revenue/cost ratio in towns (the average being 78 percent). However, when judging this ratio we must take into account that several items, such as concessionary fare payments, are regarded as ordinary income and not subsidies. They are defined as a public service obligation paid by the authorities. In addition, there are capital subsidies in Switzerland. One cannot therefore get a full picture without taking all these factors into account, and it is very difficult to draw a full picture without going into each system in detail. However, in strongly regulated countries such as Belgium, Italy, Netherlands, and Germany, there is a tendency to have a lower revenue/cost ratio than in the other countries, but again the weaknesses of the data must be borne in mind.

The conclusion from this survey is that there does not seem to be a general trend towards more liberal regulatory regimes in Europe. Only Britain has opted for free market solutions. Of the remaining 17 countries, we find a tendency towards franchising solutions with competitive tendering in the Scandinavian countries (Sweden 1989, Denmark 1989, and Norway 1991). France and Israel also have a partial franchising system, but the public involvement in France is strong, even within the present system. Elsewhere, there is little sign of the introduction of any substantial competition even though it has been discussed, although only in professional circles. In Germany, for instance, a government commission has suggested more liberal regimes in public transport, but there is no sign of any political breakthrough. In addition, it must be remembered that the federal government has little influence on the public transport policy of the states. However, what is evident is the clear tendency towards devolution, with the transfer of responsibility for local transport to local authorities, as in Scandinavia (late-1970s), the UK (1968-1972), France (1982), and Belgium (1989). These countries, (such as Germany and Switzerland) are, in addition, those which have traditionally had local responsibility for public transport.

The British experience has been dealt with in many papers (Banister, Berechman and de Rus Mendoza, 1992; Glaister, 1990). The Scandinavian approach is dealt with in the next section. The most important reason for undertaking this survey is a move in Scandinavia towards more competitive regimes in the form of a combination of planned systems and the use of the market through a franchising system with competitive tendering.

4. The Scandinavian Experience

4.1 Background

In the late 1970s and the early 1980s, the three Scandinavian countries changed their public transport policies and regulatory regimes. The most important change was that in all three countries, responsibility for local public transport was transferred from the state to local government or local government agencies (transport authorities). The reason behind the changes was revitalization of public transport in Sweden and Denmark. In Norway, the main goal was to create greater efficiency in the use of taxpayers money and to reduce the rate of increase in subsidies. In both Sweden and Denmark, the change can be seen as a corporatist approach to local public transport.

Ten years later, it is interesting to note that all three countries again seem to be moving in the same direction, with the opening up of competitive tendering in local public transport. As a result, a deregulation process has been set up that not only influences local public transport, but the transport sector as a whole and as well as other sectors. The questions raised here concern why this policy change has occurred; whether clear similarities can be found between the three countries as regards the reasons for change; and whether these processes can be explained by a Derthick-Quirk (1985) approach or by clear policy goals of reduction of subsidies and public budgets through greater efficiency in public transport.

Returning to Kay and Thompson (1991), it is clear that their arguments concerning deregulation and market failure (due to externalities or information assymetries, market deterrence from the incumbent or natural monopoly and high sunk costs) have validity. Banister, Berechman and de Rus Mendoza (1992) have shown that doubts can be raised over the contestability of the British bus market and that, at best, it can be defined as a market where imperfect competition prevails. This underlines Kay and Vickers' (1988) arguments that the rationale behind deregulation and privatization policies are weak and that politicians in European countries are not prepared to take on the consequences of radical alternatives. These arguments may explain why there are no signs of full deregulation of local public transport outside Britain. Using Derthick and Quirk's (1985) hypothesis of deregulation as an evolution from a vaguely and loosely defined process to a preferred style of policy choice, and eventually to a policy fashion without really clearly defined aims, we can describe the Scandinavian situation as a policy of competition *for* the market rather than *in* the market. This conclusion is also supported by Button's (1989) arguments about changing coalitions influencing the process of regulatory reform.

In Scandinavia, there is a strong coalition of national governments, local governments, and operators of competing transport modes promoting regulatory change. This coaliton has been stronger than the one against change, promoted by operators and labor unions. It can be strongly argued that this change of strength in coalitions would not have been possible without a previous transfer of responsibility for local public transport to local governments combined with the steadily increasing pressure on the budgets of these regional authorities. Thus, from a situation where local governments and bus operators tried to get as much money out of the central government as possible during central responsibility for public transport, the transfer of responsibilities to local government has resulted in changing attitudes.

Despite this combination of factors, there is still a belief in the social effectiveness aspects of public transport. The changed coalition brought about by regionalization of responsibility for public transport, and a more suspicious attitude toward deregulation on the one hand, and the willingness to take radical action on the other, has resulted in the Scandinavian approach toward tendering.

4.2 Norway

The change in public transport policy since 1977/1978, especially in the regulatory and subsidy systems, must be seen against a background of market development, increasing revenue support for public transport in general, and for local public transport in particular. In 1970, the revenue/cost ratio for all public transport was 84 percent, and about the same for local public transport. But by 1980, this had changed to an overall subsidy ratio of 35 percent, to a 30- to 40-percent ratio for local transport, but to about a 50-percent ratio in the Oslo area. This was called a subsidy explosion but, it is worth mentioning that historically, the revenue/cost ratio in Norway was much higher than in Sweden and Denmark, where only 50 percent of total costs were covered by revenue. The development of the bus industry in Norway in the 1980s can be seen in Table 2.

Table 2 shows that there has been a decline of about 20 percent in the number of passengers carried between 1980 and 1990. This amounts to about 65 million passengers. In the same period, the supply in vehicle kilometers increased by 13 percent but, it must be remembered, that some new unsubsidized express buses had been introduced. Thus, there has been an increase in supply despite the fact that demand has decreased by 20 percent. If we look at real fares, they increased by 23 percent from 1980 to 1983, reducing the level of the subsidy. It was also believed that price elasticities were low. This can explain some of the reductions in demand as well as some of the reductions in real revenue support. Since 1983, real fares have remained constant, vehicle kilometers have increased, a further reduction in real revenue support has taken place, and the net result thus means a more effective use of resources.

TABLE 2

Indices of Local/Regional Bus Transport in Norway 1980-1990

Year	Number of Passengers	Real Revenue Support	Real Fares	Vehicle Kms.	Real Costs per Vehicle Km.
1980	100	100	100	100	100
1981	97	102	111	103	99
1982	91	98	118	100	99
1983	88	93	123	103	95
1984	87	91	124	104	93
1985	87	94	123	106	93
1986	89	91	123	109	
1987	87	91	123	112	
1988	83	82	123	113	
1989	82	80	122		
1990[a]	81	81	123		

Note: [a]Budget estimate.

Source: Official statistical data and data from Norwegian Public Transport Association.

Unfortunately, although there are no available data for cost per vehicle-kilometer for the whole period, data for the period up to 1985 indicates efficiency gains of about 10% percent. Based on information from one of the counties, M¢re og Romsdal, where data are available for the whole period, there have been reductions in real costs per vehicle-kilometer of about 20 percent. The main reasons for this reduction can be found in better utilization of labor, lower real fuel prices, and changes in vehicle use (i.e., increased use of smaller vehicles).

The interesting question is how has it been possible to increase the supply with constant real fares and decreasing numbers of passengers, but still reduce real revenue support by about 20 percent? This must mean higher levels of productivity. There is common agreement in Norway that the bus industry is more efficient today than it was 10 years ago. The main reason for this is change of the subsidy system. In Table 3, the changes in policy are explained.

TABLE 3

The Main Changes in Norwegian Public Transport Policy, 1980-1990.

Before 1981	Operators hold licences. The state is responsible for subsidies through balancing of accounts. Large increases in subsidies from 1975 to 1980.
1981	Transfer of responsibility for local public transport to county councils and introduction of fixed amounts of subsidy transfer for each county from the state, that could only be used for transport.
1983	Introduction of fixed subsidy contracts between operators and counties. (Network subsidies). Operator risk based on net subsidy contracts introduced. Licences still kept by the operators. This must be seen as the most important change as it ended balancing of accounts as a subsidy system.
1986	New block grant system with no longer specified public transport subsidies, but a system where counties can use the grant for any purpose. Introduction of standard costing for efficient bus operators in many counties.
1991	Change in regulatory regime with opening up for competitive tendering with contracts up to five years. Tenders for single routes or packages. Removal of licences from operators, substituted by contracts.

There can be little doubt that the changes in the subsidy system, with the introduction of fixed subsidies on a network basis and a greater awareness of efficient operation through standard costing for efficient operators, have resulted in productivity gains. The discussion in Norway the last four to five years has thus concentrated on whether there is room for more productivity gains and if so, how they should be realized.

Analyses carried out in Norway have shown that the ratio of time in traffic/paid time could be 50 percent or less, and that a reasonable aim for efficient operators is at least 70 percent. There is also ample scope for economies through changes in vehicle size and use of more innovative forms of public transport (e.g., taxis in rural areas). It is also obvious that better adaptation of supply to declining levels of demand can be achieved. Another proposed solution for achieving more efficient operation, better adapted to the market, has been competitive tendering for the market. This would, however, necessitate a change in the regulatory regime for bus operations in Norway.

Since 1980, the process of change in Norway has been initiated by the central government. In the beginning, county councils had little understanding of the need for change in as costs were born by the state. The main goal of the process, seen from the government's side, was to reduce the subsidy burden on the public budgets. Another important factor in Norway was the attempt to remove competitive advantages of bus operators who were also conducting goods transport: they had gained through generous subsidies for passenger transport via cross-subsidization between passenger and goods transport. The ideological or purely theoretical arguments for change were strong.

After the transfer of responsibility to county councils, especially after 1986, when the free use of block grants for all types of activities were allowed, the county councils themselves became very interested in trying to make bus operations more efficient. The conclusion is that since 1986, the forces of change can also be found in the counties. Over the last five years, most counties have not considered public transport as a high priority. This has undoubtedly influenced the attitudes of the authorities towards public transport efficiency, which would enable more resources to be allocated to other areas of public expenditure.

The suggestion for the introduction of tendering for the market and a change of regulatory regime came about in 1984, after the publication of the British White Paper "Buses". However, it has taken six years to carry through the change in the Norwegian Parliament. Today, there is agreement among the main political parties about the changes, but some of the operators and union members still strongly oppose it. Despite this, it is seen as a means for creating opportunities for a better public transport system as there do not seen to be any other options for the more effective use of subsidies. The conclusion for Norway must be that fairly large sums have been saved since 1980 through the changes in subsidy policy, but there is still much to be achieved. More competition is the chosen solution.

It is difficult at this stage to give clear estimates of reduction in costs per vehicle-kilometers but, based on the Swedish experience and the actual cost structure, there is no doubt that reductions of 10 to 20 percent can be achieved in unit costs. In addition, there are obvious efficiency gains to be made through better adaptation of supply to the market, so that the revenue/cost ratio can be improved.

With regard to the reasons behind the process in Norway, it is clearly financial: a reduction of the burden on public budgets. Different governments have also agreed about the changes. Since 1980, there have been two non-socialist and two socialist governments in Norway; and on the whole there has no ideological difference between the two political parties to the change.

In Norway, the actual use of tendering has not yet begun as a result of some complicating factors concerning an agreement on the European Economic Area between the EC and EFTA as to whether the EC directives on public procurement demand the use of competitive tendering for the concession contracts.

However, in Oslo there has been a trial comprising three lines, a rush hour line using large urban buses and two lines using minibuses. The incumbent (the municipal operator) was able to participate in the tender competition on certain conditions, the most important of which was the use of average costs in order to avoid cross-subsidization between tendered and non-tendered parts of the operation. The experience from the incumbent's side was disappointing as they did not win any contracts because most of the other tenders used some form of marginal/avoidable costing. This problem will have to be solved in the future if the incumbent is to participate: without a certain degree of commercial freedom, it will be impossible to compete. However, this requires the definition of a clear commercial policy for the incumbent such as that used for London Buses Ltd., where the firm was given commercial freedom in tendering for services while ensuring that there would be clearly defined returns on investment goals.

Another interesting problem which has to be solved is whether the tendering unit should be a part of the incumbent's administration or transferred to an unit outside the municipal transport authority. This problem has also been discussed in Stockholm, Copenhagen, and London as a way to secure fair competition. The result in Oslo was the creation of a separate unit to deal with tendering. This will be further discussed in the sections on Copenhagen and Stockholm.

4.3 Sweden

In Sweden, the first policy change was introduced in 1978, when responsibility for local public transport was vested in transport authorities owned jointly by the local and county councils. For years, a policy of low fares had been pursued and public transport demand had increased. The reform in Sweden did not change the regulatory regimes on licenses, as they were already held by the operators. This meant that a system was created where the transport authorities were compelled to use local monopolies to supply the planned transport output. The system was based on network subsidies with cost contracts related to the cost structure of each firm. With the licenses held by the operators, there was clearly little scope for improved efficiency and rationalization despite demand changes which had made the previous license boundaries unsuitable. In addition, the operators had no responsibility for income as this role was allocated to the transport authorities. Consequently, operators had no interest in the market. Their main aim was to maximize output in vehicles-trips and vehicle-kilometers as that was the basis of payment.

In the mid-1980s, the discussion of subsidy levels and regulatory reform began in Sweden. Several studies were carried out, resulting in the proposal for the use of competitive tendering, i.e., cost tenders for local transport. The regulatory regime was to be changed as of 1 July 1989. However, there would be a long transition period as the law enacting the change was passed in the Swedish Parliament in 1985. Between 1985 and 1 July 1988, all operators had the opportunity to demand that the transport authorities take over their business and pay full compensation, determined by a special board. A few opted out of bus operation, but this amounted to less than 10 operators of a total of about 1400 enterprises.

Up to 1985, demand for local public transport in Sweden had increased. Between 1978 and 1985, there was an increase of over 40 percent in demand (passenger-kilometers). For bus transport, the increase was even higher.

Since 1985, there has been either stagnation or small decreases, as Table 4 shows, especially in larger urban areas. There is fear that this decline will continue, a view reinforced by the proposal to increase fares by 15 percent as of 1 January 1991. The revenue/cost ratio for all local/regional public transport has also decreased, from 43 percent in 1985 to 39 percent in 1989, due to an increased subsidies in the Stockholm area. For the rest of the country, there has been a slight increase of 1 percent in the revenue/cost ratio to 48 percent. Supply in terms of vehicle-kilometers has also increased over the same period.

The system of competitive tendering began in 1989, and the experience up to now has been positive. Of 24 areas (counties) with transport authorities, the situation in June 1990 was:

* Six counties had tendered all their traffic;

* Another 11 have tendered parts of their local public transport and they are planning for more as their existing contracts with operators expire; and

TABLE 4

Main Indicators of Supply and Demand in Local and Regional Public Transport in Sweden, 1985-1990

	Total Bus, Underground, Tramway and Railway			Bus		
Year	Passengers	Passenger-Kms.	Vehicle-Kms.	Passengers	Passenger-Kms.	Vehicle-Kms.
1985	100	100	100	100	100	100
1986	98	99	100	98	98	99
1987	96	96	102	95	90	102
1988	94	100	105	93	95	105
1989	99	98	105	95	94	104
1990	99	104	107	94	100	106

Source: Data from the Swedish Local Transport Association.

* Of the remaining seven not introducing tendering, three are preparing to use it, including the Greater Stockholm area, where reorganization is being prepared for the publicly owned operator, Storstockholm Lokaltrafik.

The effects of using a competitive tendering system vary, but the average subsidy savings, according to information from the SLTF, (the trade association of the transport authorities) lies between 8 and 15 percent, the average saving being 10 percent.

As regards the structure of the industry and the use of competitive tendering, there have been some interesting developments, especially in 1989, when the Swedish State Railway owned bus operations (SJ and GDG) lost several contracts to private operators, in particular to one large private operator (Linjebuss). The state operators lost contracts for routes requiring 300 buses and the private operator gained contracts for routes requiring 240 buses. Since then, the railways have reorganized their bus operations with clear commercial aims, trading as a joint stock company, with the intention of becoming an operator in the future. However, in other counties, private operators have lost contracts to publicly owned operators.

If we look at the political side of the change in Sweden, it is quite revealing as it was implemented by a socialist government against the protests of non-socialistic parties. The aim of the change in the regulatory regime was clearly a reduction in public spending.

The reason for opposition to the change from the non-socialistic parties was the fear of what was called "double-socialization". This can be explained by the fact that they feared a massive exit from the market as operators were bought out. This would leave the local transport sector in the hands of a few publicly owned transport authorities. In fact, the result has been the opposite, with increased private participation at the expense of publicly owned operators. In the first year, 600 people employed in state-owned bus operators lost their jobs due to the loss of tenders, but most were reemployed by the winning private operators.

According to the Swedish Local Transport Association, the following can be described as the situation (as of April 1992) concerning competitive tendering (see Table 5). This table shows that there are only five counties were no tendering has taken place, one being Stockholm. But during the summer of 1992, Storstockholm Lokaltrafikk published their first tenders for bus traffic and suburban rail/tramways. All of the public transport system in Stockholm will then be based on tendering. The tendering period will start from the autumn of 1993. The bus tender covers 17.5 million vehicle-kilometers while the rail/tramways tender covers three suburban lines of 3.2 million vehicle-kilometers, based on vehicles from the Storstockholm Transport Authority and on an agreement with the infrastructure subsidiary of SL.

Prior to the first tenders going out, Storstockholm Localtrafik was complete reorganized. The incumbent was divided into a planning and tendering authority, responsible for strategic development, marketing and tendering, and nine subsidiaries, including one for bus, one for railways, one for tubes, one for infrastructure, and one for property. This reorganization was necessary in order to enable fair competition and to allow participation of the incumbent's own bus subsidiary.

In Gothenburg, the second largest city in Sweden, the results have recently been published (Summer 1992) of the first tender of urban bus transport, totalling 4.4 million vehicle-kilometers, or about 30 percent of urban transport by bus in the metropolitan area. The two winners are the municipally owned operator and the privately owned Linjebuss, with about 50 percent each. In the future, the rest of the bus operation will be tendered. As a result of the tender, some interesting figures have been published (see Table 6). Table 6 shows that the cost of bus operation in Western Gothenburg has been nearly halved in real terms from 1989 to 1992. This has made possible with a modern bus park and very rigorous environmental standards.

TABLE 5

The Situation of Competitive Tendering in Sweden by Structure of Bus Operations, April 1992

	No. of Normal or Large Buses in Scheduled Traffic		Operators' Share of Traffic by Number of Buses Transport Authority					Share of Traffic Tendered (%)	
Transport Authority Län=County	Total	Urban	Own Ops.	Munic. Ops.	Swebus (Rails)	Linje-buss	Other Ops.	Rural	Urban
AB-län (Stockholm)	1500	500	1500	-	-	-	-	0	0
C-län (Uppsala)	229	162	55	8	114	-	52	1	3
Uppsalabuss	160	160	160	-	-	-	-	-	0
D-län (Søderman.l)	271	90	261	-	-	-	10	0	0
E-län (Østr.gøt.l)	400	167	-	267	65	52	16	100	100
F-län(Jøn.køp.)	292	127	-	90	108	6	88	100	100
G-län (Kronoberg)	112	16	-	-	72	24	16	100	100
H-län(Kalmar)	180	144	-	26	66	41	47	100	100
I-län(Gotland)	34	5	-	-	22	-	12	100	100
K-län (Blekinge)	117	44	-	-	40	58	19	100	100
L-län(Kristi.st)	172	28	-	-	67	58	47	70	100
M-län (Malmøbus)	456	229	-	180	215	39	22	20	0
Helsingb. trafiken	62	62	-	62	-	-	-	-	0
Lunds kom.	37	37	-	-	-	37	-	-	5
N-län(Halland)	146	54	-	45	61	23	17	80	27
O-län (Gotenburg)	107	20	-	20	67	-	20	15	0
GBL & Bohus	410	109	-	5	227	111	67	25	30
GLAB Stadstraf.Gbg	220	220	-	220	-	-	-	-	0
P-län (Älvsborg)	289	119	-	116	127	-	46	25	2

Cont.

TABLE 5 (Continued)

The Situation of Competitive Tendering in Sweden by Structure of Bus Operations, April 1992

	No. of Normal or Large Buses in Scheduled Traffic		Operators' Share of Traffic by Number of Buses Transport Authority					Share of Traffic Tendered (%)	
Transport Authority Län=County	Total	Urban	Own Ops.	Munic. Ops.	Swebus (Rails)	Linje-buss	Other Ops.	Rural	Urban
R-län (Skaraborg)	236	33	-	34	115	-	87	42	68
S-län (Värmland)	253	68	-	60	106	-	87	10	10
T-län (Ørebro)	234	70	200	-	6	-	28	0	0
U-län (Västman.l.)	159	64	153	2	3	-	1	0	0
W-län (Kopparberg, excl. Hedemora)	237	36	73	-	-	65	99	100	100
X-län (Gävleborg)	212	61	-	44	104	-	64	100	25-30
Y-län (Västerm.l.)	299	103	-	153	51	67	28	0	0
Z-län (Jämtland)	186	64	-	79	42	-	65	75	0
AC-län (Väst.bott)	254	73	-	51	75	28	100	20	5
Umeå	56	56	-	56	-	-	-	-	0
Skellefteå (excl.Lycksele)	17	17	17	-	-	-	-	-	0
BD-län (Norrbotten)	232	92	-	22	35	5	170	7	-
Luleå	65	65	65	-	-	-	-	-	0
Piteå (excl.Boden Gälliv, Kalix och Kiruna)	27	27	27	-	-	-	-	-	0
Total:	7,661	3,192	2,511	1,540	1,788	614	1,208		

Source: Svensk Lokaltrafik, 5 Sept. 1992.

TABLE 6

Bus traffic costs in Western Gothenburg (Price level as of January 1992)

Average cost for 1989 all operations	100%
Average cost for 1990 all operations	94%
Average cost for 1991 all operations	86%
Average cost for 1992 all operations	80%
Cost for part tendered 1992 for operations starting in 1993	55%

Source: Svensk Lokaltrafikk, May 1992.

4.4 Denmark

In Denmark, two different acts, one for the Copenhagen area (1977) and one for the rest of the country (1978), placed responsibility for local public transport in the hands of transport authorities owned and financed by local councils. The Copenhagen authority also took responsibility for rail transport operated on its behalf by the Danish State Railways.

Outside Copenhagen, the authorities are responsible for the planning (service and fares) and financing of public transport, but operation is undertaken by contractors, private and public. These contractors had to surrender their licenses, which were replaced by 5-year contracts when the new system came into operation. The contract system was based on a payment model where the authorities had responsibility for income, and operators were paid on the basis of cost contracts. Unit costs were standardized for all Denmark based on the number of buses used and the hours buses were run.

In Copenhagen, the Transport Authority took over all publicly owned operators and, more recently several private operators. In 1989, about 18 percent of all operations in the Copenhagen area was still undertaken by private operators on a contract basis, with a payment system like that in the rest of Denmark but with different unit costs.

The development of public transport in Denmark is different in Copenhagen to the rest of the country. In Copenhagen, the demand for public transport, bus and rail, has decreased by 20 percent between 1981 and 1990. From 1990 to 1991, however, there has been an increase in bus trips of 4 million, about 3 percent. In the rest of Denmark, there was an increase up to 1985, followed by a decrease of 10 percent as budgeted for 1990. The figures are shown in Tables 7 and 8.

TABLE 7

Public Transport Demand and Supply Indicators in Copenhagen, 1981-1991

Year	Total Number of Passengers	Bus Only Passengers	Transport Authority and Contractors Vehicle-Kilometers
1981	100	100	100
1982	101	101	100
1983	94	90	100
1984	85	76	98
1985	88	84	100
1986	85	79	100
1987	84	78	102
1988	83	74	97
1989	79	66	100
1990	78	63	98
1991		65	

Source: Annual Reports, Greater Copenhagen Transport Authority.

TABLE 8

Public Transport Demand and Supply Indicators in Denmark Outside Copenhagen, 1985-90

Year	Passengers	Real Fares	Real Revenue Support	No. of Buses	No. of Bus-Hrs. Per Bus	Contractor Payment Per Run-Hour
1985	100	100	100	100	100	100
1986	98	102	100	101	100	98
1987	98	100	101	101	101	98
1988	95	102	107	100	102	108
1989[a]	94	105	92	100	101	99
1990[a]	90	105	100	95	103	97

Note: [a]Budget estimates.

Source: County Councils Association.

The explanation for the decrease in demand in Copenhagen can be found in the increased use of private cars resulting from increased real income and from changes in the price ratio between public and private transport, in the favor of private transport. The reason for the later response in the rest of Denmark can partly be found in the effects of integration of school transport and other types of transport needs into a good quality system. But the main reason for the decrease is, again, competition from the private car.

Real revenue support increased up to 1988, then decreased sharply between 1988 and 1989; but for 1990, the contracts indicate a further increase. Real fares increased about 5 percent between 1985 and 1990. Outside Copenhagen, there have been small productivity gains, such as those resulting from a 5-percent decrease in the number of buses used by between 1985 and 1990 and a 3-percent decrease in the per hour contract payment.

In the Copenhagen area, the main problem has been the high level of costs of bus operations compared to the rest of the country. If we use data for 1988, the relative average cost per hour operated was 82 outside Copenhagen and 126 within Copenhagen, (i.e., a difference in unit costs of 54 percent where the overall average for all services is 100). The main reason for the difference is a higher wage ratio and better working hours and social payments. In addition, one must of course take account of operating conditions, (i.e., average speeds).

In 1988, the non-socialist coalition government published several bills meant to change the structure of public transport and local government in the Copenhagen area. The most important one for our purposes was a proposal for a revised Public Transport Act for the Copenhagen area, with the clear aim of making public transport more efficient. The measures proposed included a new management structure for the transport authority, the transfer of rail transport back to the state, and the privatization of parts of bus operations through the introduction of tendering, where only private operators could compete, for 30 percent of total bus traffic. The Transport Authority would thus be left with the responsibility for fares policy for the area but with a reduced bus operation.

Although the proposal's aim was to make public transport in the Copenhagen area more effective and thus reduce the burden on public budgets, the process of change was also ideological. The government had declared that increased privatization was one of the measures to be used to reduce public sector involvement and to make room for tax reforms. The socialist opposition in Denmark was very much against the proposal, as was the transport community. In 1989, the proposal secured a majority in Parliament through an agreement with the Progressive Party. Thus, the privatization ratio of bus transport was increased from 18 to 45 percent, (i.e., by 27 percent). This will be carried out in stages through April 1994.

In 1989, the first 20 percent was tendered in two separate tranches. The first tender for five routes in inner Copenhagen amounted to 5 percent of total bus supply. Eleven bids were received, and three groups won, including two new operators. The second tender for a further 15 percent of services secured 21 bids and included 70 routes, all of which were operated by existing private operators. There were large changes in contractors, several of the previous ones losing their contracts. The most interesting change was that a Swedish operator, Linjebuss, won several tenders, covering about 5 percent of total operations in the Copenhagen area after the second tender round.

From 1 April 1992, the third tender round started, resulting in Linjebuss A/S further increasing its share of the operation (in vehicle-hours) from about five percent after second round to 10.4 percent after the third round. In 1992, Linjebuss also bought one of the other private operators covering 3.6 percent of operations, so that it now supplies 14 percent of total vehicle-hours in Copenhagen.

The interesting fact about the third round, consisting of 35 lines in nine different areas of Greater Copenhagen, three of which were in Central Copenhagen, is that one operator, Linjebuss, offered the lowest tenders everywhere. If the competitive tender had been decided on price alone, this operator would no doubt have won all the contracts. However, the Copenhagen Transport Authority had published clear tender rules in advance, and their strategy defined as following:

* Constant competition through four-year renewable and sequential contracts;

* Avoidance of monopoly through more than one operator in every part of the Copenhagen area;

* Tendering in small units, attractive for small operators;

* Tendering according to geographical proximity in order to attract larger operators;

* Effective utilization of resources -- flexibility;

* Competent operators;

* Clearly defined vehicle standards;

* No requirement to take over redundant buses;

* Stipulation to offer employment for redundant transport authority employees;

* Full transparency concerning tenders.

Important in respect to the Linjebuss situation is the avoidance of monopoly. Another interesting element is that the smaller operators had higher tenders than the larger Linjebuss, as we are concerned with cost contracts and not net subsidy contracts. This has not been the case in Britain outside London. Tough (1992) has concluded that in Britain, small operators favor cost contracts and that actual and perceived competition were higher on cost contracts than net subsidy contracts due to more small bidders and reduced risk margins. This seems not to be the case in Copenhagen, where the biggest operator, Linjebuss, with about 180 buses, was also the cheapest. Perhaps the difference can be explained by the fact that the largest operator was not the incumbent but a foreign newcomer. The incumbent municipal operator (HT) was not allowed to participate.

Another important feature of the third tender round in Copenhagen was that the operators had the choice of different length of contracts, the maximum being five years. Of the operators submitting prices for both four- and five-year contracts, there was very little difference in prices (between 0 and 4 percent, the average being 0.5 percent according to HT). This may lead to the conclusion that the operator claims for longer 75 contracts due to investment in buses do not have the importance claimed, or one would have expected bigger differences.

The next round, the fourth, will start in 1994. Of the 35 percent of Copenhagen operations up for tender, 15 percent is new and 20 percent is for the first renewal of 1990 tenders. In the meantime, the discussion on whether the incumbent (HT) should be allowed to participate continues. In 1991, a bill was submitted to Parliament for a 100-percent tender and full competition, including the provision for the Authority's own bus operator to be included. This proposal has to be resubmitted as it was not dealt with in the current parliamentary period. The Transport Authority is preparing for full competition and has divided its operations into two divisions, "A" (planning and tendering), and "B" (the bus operation, which will operate on an arms-length relationship from the "A" division).

As concerns total results of the Copenhagen reorganization, the price per vehicle-hour indicates what has happened (see Table 9).

In 1989, the Danish government published several reports on public transport subsidies, suggesting further reductions outside Copenhagen. No decision has yet been taken to introduce tendering outside Copenhagen, but many transport authorities and operators are now preparing for tendering in the rest of Denmark. However, this cannot be introduced before the present contracts, based on standard costing, expire in 1994. Nevertheless, one of the counties on the West Coast of Jutland already started submitting all school transport for tendering in 1991. The current situation is that tendering will be the favored system as of 1994 because of EC directives for public procurement, which came into effect on 1 January 1993.

TABLE 9

Cost Savings Per Vehicle Hour in 1992 Prices as a Result of Tendering and Efficiency Measures, Copenhagen

	Dkk[a] per Vehicle-Hour
Transport authority own operation (1990)	420
Average price 3 tenders (1990-92)	408
Average price 3rd tender (1992)	383
Linjebuss price 3rd tender (1992)	372
Transport authority own operation (priced agreed for 1992)	410
Transport authority own operation (price for Spring 1992)	399
Goal transport authority own operation (1 Jan. 1993)	380

Note: [a]Danish Kroner

Source: Copenhagen Public Transport Authority (HT), tendering unit.

If we look at the political side of the process, the changes in Denmark have again, mainly, been carried through for financial reasons, but there is also a clear ideological dimension to the process. The introduction of partial deregulation has been much debated, both along strict political and ideological lines as well as part of a more extensive program of privatization.

5. Lessons to be Learned

The last part of the 1980s has seen decline in public transport in the Scandinavian countries. In all three countries, there have been changes of policy, designed mainly to reduce the financial burden to public expenditure through measures aimed at creating a more efficient public transport. The process chosen in Scandinavia has been one of franchising through competitive tendering, having already transferred the responsibility for local public transport to local authorities in the late-1970s. The process has been initiated by the governments and not by operators or local councils. The motivation for change has not been ideological, with some minor exceptions in Denmark, primarily to save money in public budgets.

In all countries there is a reluctance to move towards full deregulation as in Britain. The social effectiveness aspect of public transport is still strong in Scandinavia. The main reason for not introducing a British system has been a strong interest and political will to continue a system of integrated public transport with a uniform fare system for local public transport. The only option available is competitive tendering. In Sweden, the same process is used for local rail/tramways operations, under the control of the local transport authorities.

With respect to the structure of the industry and use of competitive tendering, some clear lessons can be found. In Sweden, there are only two really large private operators, the largest being Linjebuss, with 614 buses in scheduled traffic in 1992. The results of the Swedish tendering process on the structure of the bus industry has been greater concentration, as the smallest operators have lost out in many cases (the average operator in 1988 had 9 buses). There has also been a tendency towards more private operators as many public operators lost tenders in the first year. The conclusion of the Swedish Transport Authorities Association is that we must expect more concentration. Linjebuss is increasing its share of the traffic, as illustrated in the Gothenburg case above.

In Denmark, the structure is different inside and outside Copenhagen. In Copenhagen, there were 1314 buses in 1989, of which 1088 were owned by the Transport Authority and the remaining 226 by private contractors. These companies had an average of about 13 buses. Outside Copenhagen, the average operator size is about five buses per operator. The lessons from Copenhagen show that several new operators can come into the market. The new operators included those previously engaged in non-scheduled passenger transport, goods transport, and one Swedish operator (Linjebuss). There has been no problem with new entrants coming into the market. The tendency in Copenhagen is the same as that in Sweden, namely concentration through larger operators. This tendency would have been even stronger had it not been for the tendering strategy of the Transport Authority.

In Norway, the change has not yet been carried through as only Oslo has carried out a limited tendering process. The structure in the industry is here quite different, with average operator size of about 25 buses; the ten largest operators controlling 25 percent of the total bus fleet. In many areas, especially rural regions, there is only one operator. It will therefore be most interesting to see what happens in Norway.

The subsidy savings in Sweden amounts to about 10 percent on average, but examples of larger savings can be found where tendering has been applied. The results from Copenhagen also show decreases of about 10 percent from 1990 to 1992. This figure has been sustained since the initial round of tenders. If this can be achieved everywhere in Scandinavia, the changes must be claimed to be successful in achieving the main objective of a reduction in public subsidy.

The following main conclusions can be drawn from the Scandinavian experience:

* The introduction of fixed subsidy systems in the form of contracts either by arbitration or competitive tendering has led to subsidy savings. Contracts have been of both the net subsidy and cost types.

* These savings has been produced through increased productivity and more efficient public transport, better adapted to the need of the market.

* Clear policies towards privatization of publicly owned operators can be found particularly in Denmark. In Sweden, this has occurred as a result of loss of tenders by publicly owned operators.

* The process of change has been initiated by central government, mainly as a result of the need for reducing of public spending. After some years of experience, local government has taken the responsibility for public transport.

* There arc no real differences in viewpoint about the measures chosen among political parties in Norway and Sweden, but in Denmark there are clear differences in ideological views.

* There is still a strong desire for integrated and coordinated solutions, with a fairly strong emphasis on the social effectiveness side of public transport.

What can the rest of Europe learn from the Scandinavian experience? There are some clear conclusions:

* The process of change will often take a long time and implies a stepwise process towards regulatory reform.

* It is necessary to have the right coalitions in order to succeed with regulatory reform. It is clear from Scandinavian experience that a first step in a change is to transfer responsibility for public transport to local governments in order to secure their support for change.

* The process of change is almost impossible to bring about unless there is a strain on public budgets.

* The process of tendering is extremely important for the results, especially in order to avoid barriers to competition and the inherent advantages for the incumbent.

* In a situation where there is strong public participation in the operation of public transport, it is very important to have clear strategies on the basis of which public operators may compete.

* The more you define the rules of the tendering process, and the more you define working conditions for labor and the quality of vehicles, the less scope there is for substantial reductions in operating costs.

The question has been raised in Sweden and Denmark, where cost contracts have been used, about the resulting awareness of operators for the revenue side. The conclusion reached is that cost contracts lack the necessary incentives to operators.

6. The Way Ahead

The analysis carried out has shown that mainly two types of arguments can be found for change: the political argument and the economic argument. If we use Britain as an example, the political arguments come from the Treasury. They can be summarized as questions of efficiency, especially whether public undertakings are as efficient as private undertakings, with an underlying assumption that they are not. This has led to the solution of privatization through the sale of state assets.

Economic arguments of course also include the question of efficiency, but on a more limited scale, that is, how to reduce public expenditure to public transport by devising more efficient subsidy systems. It is not necessarily true that the only solution to this question implies privatization in the British form, as the examples from Scandinavia show. In Norway, the ratio of public to private ownership in local bus transport is about 50/50. Without discussion of privatization, the reduced subsidy payments have been the real issue. That has been achieved through change of the subsidy system, creating more opportunities for increased productivity. The changes seen in Scandinavia and some of those seen in other European countries have had this more limited economic rationale rather than the wider political explanations of Britain, although traces of it cannot of course be ruled out.

If this trend continues, the scope for change in Europe will be much more limited, as the discussion here indicates. The most one can expect will be careful changes, particularly in subsidy systems, but also in the discussion of issues such as what level of government shall be responsible for local public transport. This should be seen together with a clearer division between what is defined as the role of management versus that of politicians, because it is here that there is still much to be done to secure efficient operations. The reasons for this can be found in the importance placed upon social effectiveness arguments, supported by the case presented by Gwilliam, Nash and Mackie (1985) rather than that put forward by Beesley and Glaister (1985). This is also supported by Banister, Berechman and de Rus Mendoza's (1992) analysis of the British experience, confirmed by the Kay and Thompson (1991) results on market failure and imperfect market conditions.

However, there are two additional aspects of change that will clearly be of importance in the years to come: first, the role of public transport in an environmental context, and second the importance of the Single European Market, which came into operation from 1st January 1993, the Maastricht Treaty, and the agreement between EC and EFTA concerning the European Economic Space. The impact of the Single European Market and the Maastricht Treaty will influence public transport policies in several ways. First, what will the principle of subsidiarity mean for the question of who has the responsibility for local public transport? Second, if local public transport is defined to be an area national and local government responsibility, what will that mean for realizing the European Community's policy for cohesion within the Community? Third, these questions will also have to be seen against the European Community's policies on environment and transport, as well as in relation to its competition policy in respect of the public procurement of services directive.

The EC green paper *The Impact of Transport on the Environment* (1992) defines a strategy of "sustainable mobility", underlining both the impact of transport on environment and allowing for transport to fulfill its economic and social functions. In the green paper, it is stressed that the interaction of effects of environmental measures should remain compatible with overall objectives while allowing for economic efficiency and commercial viability of transport, the freedom of choice of the user and operator, but at the same time underlining the importance of cohesion, and the possibility of the peripheral regions sharing in the prosperity of the Single Market.

At present, the European Community has no policy for local public transport and, according to the principle of subsidiarity, this ought to be an area left to national and local governments. However, if cohesion and a policy on environment and transport is possible, it is necessary for the Community to have measures that influence public transport at the local level.

In addition, if we take into account the fact that the transport sector has to comply with the competition policy, there is an obvious problem of defining the responsibility of government on the local level on the other hand, and at the national/regional level on the other. The solution to this conflict of interests among the principle of subsidiarity, environmental policies, and competition may be found in a combination of EC responsibility for environmental standards and definition of cost charging measures which take better account of external costs of transport. These can be combined with measures stimulating investment in public transport and clearly defined minimum rules for public procurement of services.

In a proposal from the European Commission (Comm.91/347/Final), public transport network services will be included in the procurement rules for services (Council 90/531/EC). At present there is, however, much discussion as to whether these rules can be applied to services operating on the basis of a license (concession). The result may be that in countries where licenses have been replaced by contracts between a transport authority and the operator (e.g., Denmark and Sweden), the procurement rules have to be used, but in countries where licenses are still used (e.g., Germany), the rules will not apply. The main question is "Who is responsible for passengers, the transport authority or the operator?"

In the future, when there will be no discrimination against nationals and firms from any country within the EC-EFTA area, a stronger emphasis on the role of public transport on environmental grounds will again imply some overall control of public transport. The only way of securing this will be by using tendering in competition for the market. Only in that way it is possible to emphasize the efficiency goals of the European Community, non-discrimination and, at the same time, use public transport to fulfill goals concerning environmental improvement in the transport sector.

Finally, it will only be after the year 2000 that we will find a local public transport system built on policies of social effectiveness rather than pure productive efficiency, and where the European Community has defined some minimum rules of non-discriminatory behavior implying the use of tendering in public transport. The definitions of quality of service, fares and other factors will be left to the national and local authorities according to the principle of subsidiarity.

References

Adamson, M., Jones, W. and Pratt, R., 1991, Competition Issues in Privatization, Lesson for the Railways, in Banister, D. and Button, K.J. (eds.), *Transport in a Free Market Economy*, Macmillan, London.

Andersen, B., 1990, *The Swiss Public Transport System; Regulatory System, Financing and Subsidy System, Fares Policy and Fares System*, MRDH, Molde.

Andersen, B., 1992, Factors Affecting European Privatization and Deregulation Policies in *Local Public Transport: The Evidence from Scandinavia, Transportation Research A*, 26A(2), 179-191.

Andersen, B., 1993, A Survey of the Swiss Public Transport System and Swiss Public Transport Policy, *Transport Reviews* 13(1), 61-89.

Banister, D., 1990, Privatization in Transport: From the Company State to the Contract State, in Simmie, J. and King, R. (eds.) *The State in Action*, Pinter, London.

Banister, D., Berechman, J. and de Rus Mendoza, G., 1992, Competitive Regimes Within the European Bus and Industry, Theory and Practice, *Transportation Research A*, 26A(2), 167-178.

Beesley, M. and Littlechild, S., 1983, Privatization Problems and Piorities, *Lloyds Bank Review*, July 1983; also published in Kay, J., Mayer, C., and Thompson, D. (eds.), *Privatization and Regulation, The UK Experience*, 1986, Clarendon Press, Oxford.

Beesley, M. and Glaister, S., 1985, Deregulating the Bus Industry in Britain -- A Response, *Transport Reviews*, 5(2), 133-142.

Button, K.J., 1989, Economic Theories of Regulation and the Regulation of the United Kingdom's Bus Industry, *The Antitrust Bulletin*, Fall, 489-515.

Button, K.J. and Gillingwater, D., 1986, *Future Transport Policy*, Croom Helm, London.

Button, K.J. and Swann, D. (eds.), 1989, *The Age of Regulatory Reform*, Clarendon Press, Oxford.

Carron, A.S. and MacAvoy, P., 1981, *The Decline of Service in Regulated Industries*, AEI Studies No. 36, American Enterprise Institute for Public Policy Research, Washington, D.C.

CETUR, 1990, *Urban Public Transport in France, The Institutional Approach*, Ministere de l'Equipeement, du Logement, des Transport et de la Mer, Direction des Transport Terrestres, Paris.

Commission of the European Communities, 1990, *The Impact of Transport on the Environment*, Council Directive European Community, Com (91) 347, Final European Community, 1992, European Communission, Brussels.

Department of Transport, 1985, *Problems with Franchising*, Economic Directorate, UK Department of Transport, London.

Derthick, M. and Quirck, P.J., 1985, *The Politics of Deregulation*, Brookings Institution, Washington D.C.

Downs, A., 1957, *An Economic Theory of Democracy*, Harper, New York.

Eads, G.C., 1982, The Reform of Economic Regulation in Telecommunication and Transportation, Paper Presented at the Conference on Impact of Regulatory Reform in Canada and United States.

Finansministeriet, 1989, *Rapport om trafikøkonomi*, Report of Transport Policy, Ministry of Finance, Copenhagen.

Gwilliam, K.M., Nash, C.A. and Mackie, P.J., 1985, Deregulating the Bus Industry -- The Case Against, *Transport Reviews* 5(2), 133-142.

Gwilliam, K.M. and Van de Velde, D.M., 1991, The Potential for Regulatory Change in European Bus Markets, *Journal of Transport Economics and Policy*, 24(30), 333-350.

Hensher, D.A., 1988, Some Thoughts on Competitive Tendering in Local Bus Operations, *Transport Reviews*, 8(4), 363-372.

Kay, J.A. and Silberstone, Z.A., 1984, The New Industrial Policy -- Privatization and Competition, *Midland Bank Review*, Spring, 8-16.

Kay, J.A. and Thompson, D., 1986, Privatization A Policy in Search of a Rationale, *Economic Journal*, 96(1), 18-32.

Kay, J.A. and Thompson, D., 1991, Regulatory Reform in Transport in The United Kingdom, Principles and Application, in Banister, D. and Button, K.J. (eds.), *Transport in a Free Market Economy*, Macmillan, London.

Kay, J.A. and Vickers, J., 1988, The New Industrial Policy - Privatization and Competition, *Economic Policy*, October, 286-351.

Kommunikations-departementet, 1988, *Trafikkpolitikken inför 90-talet*, Regjeringens prop.1987/88:50 och Bilagsdel, (Swedish Ministry of Transport: Transport Policy in the 1990s, Government Submission to Parliament), Swedish Ministry of Transport.

Levine, K.E., 1981, Revisionism Revised? Airline Deregulation and the Public Interest, Law and Contemporary Problems, 44, 179-195.

MacAvoy, P., 1979, *The Regulated Industries and the Economy*, Norton, New York.

Rickard, J., 1988, Privatization in the Transport Sector, in Ramanadham, V.V. (ed.), *Privatization in the UK*, Routledge, London.

Samferdsels-departementet, 1988, *Nye tilskuddsformer i subsidiert transport*, Rapport fra Arbeidsgruppen for kontroll med bruken av transportsubsidier (New Subsidy Systems in Public Transport, Working Group Report), Ministry of Transport and Communications.

Samferdsels-departementet, 1990, *Innstilling fra Transporteffektivitetsutvalget*, (Report of the Transport Efficiency Committee), Ministry of Transport and Communications.

Statens Pris- och Konkurrensverk, 1989, *Svensk Inrikes Transportmarknad, Struktur, Konkurrens och Prissatning, 1988-1989*, (Domestic Transportmarket: Competition, Prices and Structure), Swedish Competition Authority.

Tough, S., 1992, *A Comparison of Minimum - Cost and Minimum Subsidy Public Transport Tendering Methods TSG*, Mimeo, University of Westminster.

Trafikministeriet, 1989, *Subsidiering i trafiksektoren* (Subsidies in Transport), Ministry of Transport, Copenhagen.

Trafikministeriet, 1989, *Lov om Hovedstedsområdets kollektive persontrafik* (The Act of Public Transport in the Capital Region), Ministry of Transport, Copehagen.

Vickers, J. and Yarrow, G., 1988, *Privatization: An Economic Analysis*, MIT Press, Cambridge.

TRANSPORT IN A UNIFIED EUROPE. Policies and Challenges.
D. Banister and J. Berechman (Editors)

Chapter Twelve

EAST-WEST EUROPEAN TRANSPORT: AN OVERVIEW

Kenneth Button

1. Introduction

The changing economic and political circumstances in Eastern Europe -- especially *perestroika* -- are already having implications for transport and longer term impacts are likely to be very considerable. The direct impacts are the strains which are inevitably placed upon elements of the transport infrastructure as newly emerging trade patterns develop between the East and the West; these will inevitably worsen as the volume of trade increases with economic development.

Forty years or more of separation means that linkages between the Comecon countries and the West have seriously deteriorated. Where significant international transport infrastructure investment has been undertaken, it has tended to involve routes linking Eastern European centers. Additionally, the internal transport infrastructure of Eastern European countries is probably inadequate to meet the growing demands which will be placed on it over the next decade and to allow the mobility to which those living in these countries aspire. Further, the emphasis on rail transport -- which is also extremely labor intensive and technologically obsolete in many cases -- means that the flexible and responsive road haulage facilities required to service modern industry are currently seriously lacking. Finally, there is a shortage of good management capable of making the key decisions necessary to carry through major reforms; in general management, tends to be reactive in its approach rather than proactive.

The aim of this paper is to look in some detail at the current state of Eastern European transport and to consider the difficulties which are likely to be encountered over the next decade or so. Speculation is not an objective of the work but some tentative comments will be offered as to ways of circumventing the worst of future transport problems. Given the degree of uncertainty surrounding the pace of change in many post-socialist economies, this is done within a very broad scenario of how change may occur. It is also undertaken very much in terms of the degree to which Eastern European countries can engage in self-help, together with a consideration of the roles Western European states, and in particular the European Communities, can usefully play. While the analysis is concerned with all forms of transport, there is an emphasis on land-based modes, which are those likely to be most affected by ongoing events. It also looks at domestic as well as international transport.

The Gorbachev era initiated a transformation of Eastern Europe. The political and economic changes, *perestroika* foremost, which are taking place in the post-socialist states are inevitably resulting in widespread economic ripple effects throughout the rest of the Continent. There has been a move away from state monopolization of the means of production in much of Eastern Europe, as privatization has been carried through and even within the state sector changes are taking place. Formerly, costs, prices, and interest rates, while often set down on paper, had little relevance in the economic decision making which was geared to the "hard" constraints of resource direction. The current changes may, therefore, be viewed as seeking to harden budget constraints and increase the role of monetary variables in decision making (Funck and Kowalski, 1989).

The changes which are occurring are as pronounced in the transport sector as any other. Indeed, emphasis is being put on improving communications, in the widest sense, between the East and West as a key ingredient in a broader integration processes. The implications involve, however, not just immediate issues of handling changes in international freight flows across the Continent but also longer term matters which extend into issues of reinvestment in the transport infrastructure of most Eastern European countries, the containment of environmental degradation associated with the transport technology employed, the problems of redeploying many hundreds of thousands of currently unproductive workers, and management questions concerning the efficient operations of transport systems.

Further, the changes in the East are taking place at a time when transport policy in Western Europe is itself becoming less interventionist. Not only have many countries liberalized their domestic transport policies as well as bilateral arrangements with other states but, in the wider context of the European Community's (EC) Common Transport Policy, there have been more general movements away from economic regulation (Banister and Button, 1991). Eastern Europe, if it is to successfully liberalize trade, must begin to compete in the larger and less controlled transport framework. Also, domestically, national transport policy makers will need to take cognizance of the inevitable effects which will materialize as travel and communications become freer.

The initial objective of this chapter is to examine the differences in the transport systems of East and West Europe, both in terms of their physical composition and their management, and then to consider the implications of the ongoing political changes in Europe for the future of these systems[1]. While passing references are made regarding most modes of transport, space constraints leads us to focus on land transport. By its nature, such an exercise must also be speculative, especially given first, the uncertainty surrounding larger political developments in Eastern Europe and second, even if there were relative political certainty about the future, there still are difficulties of actually determining the macroeconomic outcomes of the current patterns of change. The derived nature of demand for transport services makes it particularly sensitive to these exogenous forces.

An important caveat must be introduced at a very early stage of the discussion, namely that one must take care not to over generalize about transport in the East and West. There are quite significant differences between transport facilities and policies within the EC and Comecon which in many ways may be more substantive than the differences between the EC as a group and Eastern European countries as a bloc. The differences between the railways of the former German Democratic Republic (GDR) and those of some parts of the EC are, for instance, probably less than those between the rail systems of the Netherlands and Greece[2]. As a consequence of these diversities, as well as space constraints, rather less is said concerning the USSR (in part because of its size and internal differences) and Yugoslavia (in part because of its particular form of self-management) than the other states in that region. But one should also say that these differences extend beyond the physical natures of the national transport systems and relate to priorities and objectives. Decision making in Eastern Europe was, until recently, almost entirely dominated by political criteria rather than the notions of economic efficiency with which we are more familiar with in the West. In consequence, dependent upon the particular political position of the team in power at any one time, the policy of a particular state would change. This creates both variations across countries in terms of their starting positions regarding current reforms and variations in the way in which these reforms are manifesting themselves.

There are, therefore, problems in divining the direction and nature of change in both Eastern Europe and the EC. A number of possible scenarios could be advanced. Here we are less concerned with details but assume that liberalization of markets will continue and that trade between East and West will become freer. It is also explicit in the discussion that this will, over the next decade, albeit at variable speeds and in differing ways, lead to greater economic prosperity for Eastern European economies.

A further caveat relates to the reliability of data. Many Eastern European countries have traditionally been rather sparing with the data that they have released regarding both transport systems and the use made of them. Even where quantitative data are available, consistency is often a problem, especially with regard to qualitative attributes[3]. Further, the lack of convertability of currencies makes it difficult to even determine the international trade of the Council for Mutual Economic Assistance (CMEA, or more popularly, Comecon) nations with outside countries.

Despite these reservations and caveats, it is timely to look at developments in transport in Eastern Europe. At one level -- that of self interest -- there is likely to be a growing market for Western technology and expertise. At a higher level, all parties have a vested interest in efficient transport systems both to lubricate the movement of goods across borders and to ensure maximum efficiency of production within borders.

2. Transport Policy Formulation in Europe

The development of transport policy in Western Europe, especially within the EC, is well-documented in readily available sources and no details are offered here[4]. In broad terms, the EC Common Transport Policy leaves each member state to pursue its own domestic transport strategy within the broader framework of EC antitrust policy, social policy, regional policy, etc. International transport within the EC is gradually being liberalized in line with the move to the Single Market concept, while the EC as a whole is gradually becoming more involved in policy formulation relating to transport between member states and non-members. In particular, the 1980s saw significant changes in the way European transport policy is viewed and in the ways that policies are formulated and implemented. The decision to move towards the "Single Market" for the EC dominated much of this change, especially during the latter part of the decade. But equally are there questions concerning financial arrangements and the degree to which more centralized coordination of investment which still remain largely unresolved[5]. In many ways, therefore, the situation in Western Europe is an evolving one, although the real issues are rather more centered around the exact pace of change and its details rather than the underlying philosophy and fundamentals involved.

In contrast, transport in Eastern Europe has, in general, been heavily regulated and controlled both at the national and international levels. Further, evolutionary changes towards greater liberalization have not been gradually occurring although there have been periods reform (e.g., in the 1970s). The underlying theory of transport policy has been that transport is not a "productive activity" in the material sense; hence planners have aimed at a unified system with a minimum of duplication, which was seen as wasteful. The outcome was that almost any movement required a mix of modes.

At the international level, Comecon has played a central role during the post-Second World War phase to coordinate international transport within Eastern Europe (Tarski, 1981). Comecon essentially had no independent power but relied upon a consensus among the members states. Transport arrangements were, therefore, determined on a bilateral basis very much like those in the EC prior to the 1992 integration. Nevertheless, agencies within Comecon, such as the Permanent Transport Commission did plan integrated transport policies designed to ensure that international transport would be available to meet the objectives of the macroeconomic plans ("perspective production plans") of the different states. This extended to decisions regarding modal supply as well as overall considerations concerning aggregate capacity.

At the national level, the idea that transport is not in itself productive has in many cases led to excessive spread in the transport networks supplied. Essentially, transport was not a major consideration in the planning exercises of the 1950s through to the 1970s, which led to the adoption of dispersed factory systems as part of nationwide industrialization in countries such as Poland (Potrykowski, 1985). In other countries, military factors and efforts at establishing political cohesion dominated over considerations of strict economic efficiency.

However, it would be a mistake to assume that a uniformity in approach has existed. Nationally, Eastern European states have tended to pursue somewhat independent lines. The USSR has what the Soviet literature calls a "unified transport system", in which the state owns all roads, railways, pipelines, etc., so that the system can be planned as a unity. Ideals of eliminating waste and unnecessary competition predominate. Despite this, the USSR has rarely given the highest priority to transport either in terms of resource allocation or development of specific administrative structures to meet its particular needs. Certainly in practice, the method of coordination has major problems. The "branch" method of organization, spreading from the center with, for example, separate branch ministries for rail, roads, shipping, etc., has led to high levels of vertical integration but little horizontal coordination between the modes[6]. It should be pointed out that while some of the blame for the lack of overall coordination can be explained simply in terms of bureaucratic ineptitude (or X-inefficiency, to adopt the jargon of managerial economics), the very inflexibility of the system, which puts pressures on ministries to meet their designated plans, generally leads to high levels of allocative inefficiency.

In many Eastern European countries, state ownership of transport-related capital is the norm. In all countries, the main infrastructure is in state hands, a situation not unlike that in much of Western Europe; however, much of the mobile capital including road haulage is also state-owned. Indeed, the 4,500 trucks in the Bulgarian national transport cooperative (SOMAT) makes it the largest road haulage fleet in Europe. Such state ownership should not always be linked with the strict command approach seen in the USSR. Because of intense competition from low cost suppliers from countries (such as Turkey) in the international markets in which it operates, SOMAT is more akin to firms in the West in its approach to management.

Some countries have been less centralist in their approaches and have allowed some degree of private ownership of transport. This is particularly true in Hungary, following the setting up of a "new economic mechanism" in 1968. This mixed economic approach, however, is not without its own difficulties in countries where market forces are given little sway. In particular, traffic from state enterprises tends to be directed to heavily subsidized state-owned transport, especially to the railways. On the factor input side, obtaining spares, fuel, etc., for private enterprise transport often encounters physical limitations which cannot be circumvented, as in a full market system, by charging higher prices.

3. The Problems

The very rapid developments in Eastern Europe over the past three years have added a particular dimension to the constraints on policy makers in Europe. At one level, there is an inevitable long term increase in trade between East and West as the economies of the former move forward. In addition, a certain amount of trade diversion will occur as each state seeks to develop its own comparative advantage. This will put pressure on the existing transport systems in Europe and more investment will inevitably be needed. But in addition to this, the enlargement of the market area of Europe in such a sudden way and with relatively unclear long term consequences adds to the basic uncertainty involved in defining what any integrated European transport market may look like in a final form.

In very broad terms, the transport systems of Eastern European countries tend to differ in two major respects from their Western counterparts. The basic infrastructure is different and the method of management is different. The many problems created can usefully be reviewed under a number of headings.

3.1 Balance of Trade

In broad terms, the bulk of foreign trade involving Eastern European countries has taken place within the Comecon net, with much less trade taking place with the rest of the world. In 1985, for example, Bulgaria exported about five times as much (in terms of US$) to other Comecon countries as to the rest of the world combined, and imported four times as much. On a similar basis, the ratio was about 3.5:1 for both exports and imports in Czechoslovakia, about 1.5:1 for the USSR, and 2:1 for the GDR. From another perspective, East-West trade accounted for less than 2 percent of the trade of EC countries in the 1980s and less than 13 percent of trade involving Comecon members. Further, the share of manufactures and minerals in exports from Eastern European countries was 50 percent and 30 percent, respectively, compared with 73 percent and 13 percent for worldwide exports.

These features of trade patterns inevitably led to infrastructure being designed to cope with the particular form of internal and Comecon trade, which mainly involves movements of bulk raw materials and semi-finished products, and which bears little relation to world market-determined trade patterns[7]. Forecasts suggest that on the basis of even a relatively conservative scenario, by the early part of the next century this pattern of trading activity will be transformed; with it will come the need for a different form of transport provision (Seidenfus, 1990).

One must add to this that the trade which does exist between the Comecon countries and the EC, in particular, while relatively balanced in financial terms is heavily biased in physical terms in favour of bulk movements from Eastern Europe. According to the United Nations Economic Commission for Europe (ECE), in terms of aggregate tonnage carried by rail, 30 million tons of freight moved from East to West and only 15 million tons moved in the reverse direction in 1987. The comparable figures for road transport are 9.8 million tons and 3 million tons, respectively, as shown by country in Figure 1. These types of imbalance, brought about primarily through lack of appropriate market incentives, result in considerable amounts of empty running coupled with facilities ill-suited to the carriage of manufactured products.

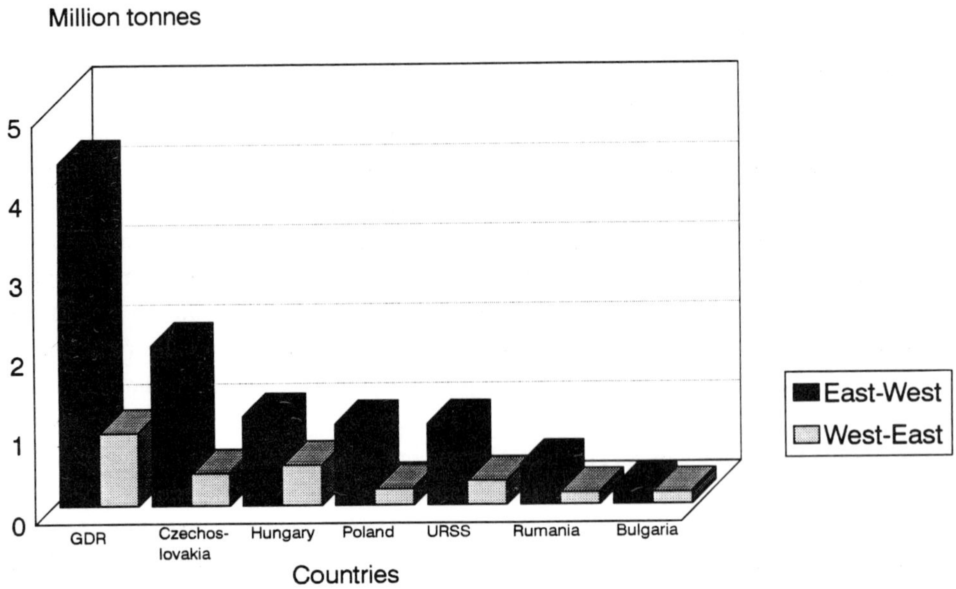

FIGURE 1 Volumes of Traded Goods Transported by Road Between Comecon Countries and the EC, 1986

Within the Comecon block, imbalances in the nature of trade also exist. In particular, the USSR fostered the establishment of a set of freight rates fixed without regard to mode employed or to prime costs, which effectively subsidized the exports of its raw materials to other Eastern European states. Other countries benefitted in that their import costs for raw materials were thus kept down. But they also had to introduce similar pricing structures for their own facilities, which meant that for through-traffic -- e.g., from the USSR through Poland to the GDR -- the transit country often suffered heavy losses. Problems of this kind also extend to the cost side, with differences in rail gauge in Poland and the USSR resulting in vast amounts of resources being expended on building axle-changing and reloading facilities at border points (Alvstam *et al.*, 1985).

3.2 Modal Split

Some indication of the modal split for freight transport in EC and selected Eastern European countries can be seen in Table 1, which provides details of the thousands of ton-kilometers carried in 1988. It is clear that rail is a much more important form of freight transport in Eastern European countries than in the EC. The emphasis on rail freight transport in Eastern Europe also has knock-on effects for other transport activities. The problems of scheduling, for example, mean that most passenger inter-city services in Eastern Europe seldom average 80 kilometers per hour, except in Poland, where a few fast trains per day average about 100 kilometers per hour.

High quality road transport does not offer a substitute both because of the limitations of the available infrastructure and the relatively low level of automobile ownership. Table 2, showing the level of car ownership in these same countries, gives some indication of the potential use made of that mode for passenger transport. Further, whereas private cars in general average about 12,000 kilometers per annum in Western Europe, the figure for Eastern European states is under 10,000.

3.3 Quality of Infrastructure

The Eastern European states are heavily reliant upon rail for freight transport but their systems tend to be old and the efficiency of operations is highly questionable. From Table 1, it is clear that the Eastern European economies have extensive rail networks but equally that, when compared to the EC states, a relatively small percentage of it is double-tracked. Taking another parameter of the need for investment in the Eastern European rail transport system, it is clear that there is a need for more electrification. For example, of 27,284 kilometers of line, 11,669 kilometers (43 percent) are electrified in the states of the pre-1990 FRG, but out of 14,024 kilometers in the old GDR only 3,475 kilometers (25 percent) were electrified and, in Poland, of 26,545 kilometers only 6,296 kilometers (24 percent) are electrified. The rolling stock of the Eastern European railways, especially that required for passenger services, tends to be older than that in the EC and also much more uniform, which makes it difficult to respond to changing economic conditions (Timar, 1990). Further, the facilities for maintaining both track and mobile capital is generally outdated and inadequate. The costs of change are, thus, likely to be high. German reunification alone, for instance, will inevitably mean substantial investments in new rail transport infrastructure[8]. One estimate, made in May 1990 by Dr. Reiner Gohlke, President of the Bundesbahn at a conference of the Community of European Railways, is that some DM100 billion is needed simply to get the old GDR rail system into a comparable condition to the network in the West.

The poor quality of cars is another problem, as is that of the road networks (see Table 2). The high quality road transport systems of most Eastern European countries are comparatively sparse compared to the rest of Europe (Marcel, 1989). This is not only partly a reflection of the relatively weak demand for road use stemming from the low levels of private car ownership in these countries and but it is more closely linked to the ideologies of the decision makers. Resources have tended to be channelled, often in an inefficient manner, into the rail systems.

3.4 The Geography of the Infrastructure

After decades of separation, the investments which have taken place are not in sympathy with a more integrated European economic system. Some of the difficulties can become clear simply by taking the East German situation. Much of the electrified rail network serves a north-south axis rather than an east-west axis, i.e., it serves the needs of the

TABLE 1

Mode Split for Freight Carriage[a] by Thousand Ton-Kilometers, 1988

Country	Road	Rail	Inland Waterways
European Community			
Belgium	26.00	7.00	6.35
Denmark	9.10	1.66	--
France	111.80	52.30	7.33
Germany	151.40	58.50	52.80
Greece	14.00	0.60	--
Ireland	5.00	0.55	--
Italy	169.00	19.60	0.14
Luxemburg	0.40	0.64	0.36
Netherlands	22.10	3.20	33.85
Portugal	9.00	1.56	--
Spain	133.00	12.00	--
United Kingdom	124.80	18.20	2.30
Eastern Europe			
Bulgaria	14.70	17.60	--
Czechoslovakia	13.10	69.40	5.20
GDR	16.40	59.40	2.50
Hungary	13.20	20.20	2.00
Poland	38.80	120.70	1.40
Yugoslavia	20.90	25.40	4.60

Note: [a]Public transport only.

Source: Taken from United Nations, European Conference of Ministers of Transport, International Road Federation and International Union of Railways data sets.

internal GDR market and its politically determined trade links. The same broad picture is also true for the Federal Republic. While there are points where links can be improved in this context, the situation is somewhat worse in other Eastern European countries, where the main investments have linked the economic centers of Bulgaria, Hungary and Poland to the USSR (Turnock, 1989).

The artificiality inherent in much of past industrial location policy in Eastern European also means that in the longer term, as rationalization of production takes place, there will be insufficient capacity on many links in the transport network but excess capacity on other corridors. If one takes the former GDR, for instance, while it has some 14,000 kilometers of railway track, less than 4,000 kilometers would be required to interlink towns of over 100,000 population. The dispersed nature of the railways also means that much of the data cited earlier regarding the quality of the system may well be distorted because there is no indication of the extent to which electrification or double tracking correlates to the use made of particular links in the network.

3.5 Latent Demand

In the past, the economic systems of Eastern Europe heavily relied on physical rationing measures for the allocation of consumer goods (e.g., waiting lists for cars) coupled with a rather ineffectual pricing structure. Liberalization of markets is gradually resulting in increased demands for consumer goods as prices take a more central role in allocating production and consumption. This will inevitably lead to rising levels of car ownership and, indeed, in some areas such as the former GDR, this is already occurring. The important consideration here is that car ownership tends, from both the experiences of Western economies (Tanner, 1983) and less developed countries (Button and Nboh, 1990), to follow a sigmoid growth curve. Consequently, once a certain critical level of ownership is reached, there is a very rapid acceleration in the level of ownership over the following years. Many of the Eastern European countries are near to this critical level of ownership and, under freer market conditions, acceleration seems almost inevitable. The pressures of the existing latent demand released a more market-orientated economic system, and this is likely to be accompanied by additional pressures for car ownership and use as the macroeconomic efficiency of the Eastern European states leads to rising income levels.

TABLE 2

Basic Transport Infrastructure[9] of Selected European Countries, 1988[a.]

Country	Motorways (Kms)	Rail Track[b] (Kms)	Cars per Capita
European Community			
Belgium	1,570	3,554 {74%}	0.364
Denmark	835	2,476 {33%}	0.320
France	5,300	34,365 {45%}	0.400
Germany	8,715	27,278 {50%}	0.472
Greece	90	1,565 {16%}	0.150
Ireland	8	1,944 {27%}	0.208
Italy	6,091	16,015 {35%}	0.430
Luxemburg	75	272 {60%}	0.460
Netherlands	2,060	2,828 {63%}	0.356
Portugal	211	2,850 {15%}	0.210
Spain	2,344	1,2531 {21%}	0.276
United Kingdom	3,100	16,599 {69%}	0.349
Eastern Europe			
Bulgaria	258	4,055 {23%}	0.132
Czechoslovakia	518	12,856 {23%}	--
GDR	1,855	14,024 {30%}	0.225
Hungary	324	7,403 {15%}	0.159
Poland	220	26,545 {34%}	0.119
Yugoslavia	828	9,349 {12%}	0.131

Note: [a]Public transport only; [b]Double-tracked rail.

Source: Taken from United Nations, European Conference of Ministers of Transport, International Road Federation and International Union of Railways Data Sets.

3.6 Management Approach

In terms of productive inputs, the transport systems of most Eastern European countries are much more labor-intensive than those found in Western Europe. For example, while the pre-unification FRG's rail system employed 240,806 people in 1987, the GDR's employed 249,964 and Poland's 360,015. But in terms of performance, the FRG system did over 40 percent more ton-kilometers than the GDR's system, and only 20 percent less than Poland's. In the USSR, which has the world's busiest rail system, nearly four million people are employed on the network. Although, for comparative purposes, it is interesting to note that the US system, which is a 240,000-kilometer network, while admittedly producing only half the tonnage and a quarter of the ton-kilometers, operates with only about 150,000 employees. Part of the problem must be attributed to the lack of power that management has over recruitment and dismissal but, equally, management operates under a confused objective and reward structure which does little to stimulate its efficiency (Ambler *et al.*, 1985). There is thus little to motivate innovation.

The management of transport systems by command and control instruments which, to varying degrees, has typified the approach in Eastern European economies, is particularly disadvantageous in a modern industrialized society where many movements are of non-bulk commodity, irregular in their nature and heavily dependent on service quality to achieve consumer satisfaction. Flexibility is essentially and local responsiveness normally desirable; but these are the very features missing in a centrally planned transport system[10]. It also poses problems at a more micro level, making it difficult to specify targets for management and to identify (and translate into quantitative terms) appropriate performance indicators.

The lack of a profit motive also eliminates both internal measurement of efficiency and criteria upon which facilities may be allocated between users. Furthermore, the heavy subsidies traditionally given to transport in most Eastern European countries adds to this problem. In Poland, for example, where rail transport has been supplied well below cost, enterprises geared to rail transport tend to circumvent legal requirements to employ road transport for short hauls by deliberately using distant suppliers -- the costs of transport in overall production costs being so small, it does not stimulate rational use of resources (Turnock, 1989).

The differing management approaches of the Eastern European nations, coupled with the nature of the ownership of the mobile capital, also leads to potential transitional problems as privatization takes place. Whereas the privatization of transport in Western Europe in the 1980s took place in an economic system and culture where risk management and enterprise were the norm, this is hardly the case for Eastern European states. The skills required are thin on the ground and the mechanisms for transferring assets to private ownership simply do not have a pedigree in systems where banks and financial institutions are not designed to channel private resources into investment activities.

3.7 Environmental Issues

Transport is extremely intrusive on the environment; and there is mounting evidence that the scale of the associated environmental degradation is at least as much due to governmental interventions in markets as to traditional notions of market failure (Barde and Button, 1990). While there are national differences, the environments of Eastern Europe are all heavily polluted and much of the problem must stem from intervention failure. Energy production, raw material extraction, and heavy industry are the major culprits, but transport is also a contributor (Russell, 1990; Turnock, 1989). Data on the exact state of the environment in Eastern Europe, let alone the factors causing its degradation, are sparse but some indications are available. Table 3 gives some calculations regarding Nitrogen Oxide (NO_x), an atmospheric pollutant associated with acid rain. In the West, NO_x emissions are being countered by the fitting of catalytic converters and levels in most countries are stable or falling (Linster, 1990). The vintage and technology of the vehicle park in Eastern Europe also means that the NO_x and similar atmospheric pollution problems are increasing, not abating. Growth in car ownership can only add to these effects.

TABLE 3

Estimates of NO_x Emissions[a]

	All Modes	Road Transport	
Country	1980	1980	Forecast 2000
Bulgaria	89	88	185
Czechoslovakia	91	88	95
GDR	--	81	144
Hungary	100	75	142
Poland	190	185	201
Romania	--	85	105

[a] 10^3 tons per annum.

Source: Laikin et al. (1987).

3.8 Mobility in the West

While there will be development problems in Eastern Europe over the next decade, Western Europe will also be encountering increased transport difficulties, albeit of a somewhat different kind. Traffic growth has been rapid since the 1970s and tended to exceed most official forecasts. In the FRG, for instance, traffic has already reached the 1985 forecasts for the year 2000. But coupled with this, infrastructure investment has tended to slow down and actually fell by 25 percent in the period 1975 to 1984 (Rathery, 1988). The result is that not only are there serious urban congestion problems in most major cities, but that major bottlenecks and "corridors of transport stress" have emerged at points along some of the main Western European communication lines (European Round Table of Industrialists, 1990).

Even without increased movement brought about by an opening of borders to the north, congestion will inevitably grow and traffic from Eastern Europe will add to this, especially at major crossroads. While formulation of scenarios concerning patterns of trade is always enmeshed with problems, it seems almost certain that Hanover, Nuremberg, Vienna and Berlin will become major "junctions" (de Waele, 1991). In most cases, these cities do not possess suitable infrastructure to handle major flows of transit traffic. Berlin's post-war transport infrastructure, for example, was built on the premise of a divided city, while Vienna is in a country already antagonized by high levels of through-traffic and does not itself even have a ring motorway.

4. A Policy Option

The options open to most Eastern European states, assuming that they do not wish to revert back to centralist planning doctrines, are relatively small in number. This is in part because of the time it takes to physically change any major transport system but also the resources available for major restructuring are very scarce. Conditions attached to outside monies, either from government sources via bilateral agreements and through international agencies such as the World Bank, the European Investment Bank, and the Bank for European Reconstruction and Development (BERD), or directly from private sector sources, will also inevitably influence the patterns of change which are possible. Some general points can, however, be made.

One of the big advantages that the post-socialist states enjoy is that they have the opportunity to learn from the past mistakes of Western Europe as well as the pitfalls of their centralist planning history. The experiences of the Comecon countries and the EC suggest that there is a danger in being excessively dogmatic and doctrinaire in drawing up long term transport policies. The demand for transport services is derived from the demands of passengers and freight shippers, which in turn depend upon a multiplicity of economic influences. The traditional Comecon and EC approach to transport policy was to focus heavily on supply side considerations and, even within this framework, to apply static notions of cost and technology. The EC has become more demand-oriented in its thinking in recent years and, inevitably, transport policy makers in post-socialist Eastern European countries will probably follow suit.

The shift towards more demand-driven policy has also coincided with greater reliance on private sector funding for infrastructure together with, in many cases, privatization of the operation of transport systems. This does not mean that the public sector has not had a central role. Indeed, given externalities and property right difficulties, it must retain an overall planning and coordinating function. However, its role has changed. In the context of Eastern Europe, there are good reasons to suggest that outside private sector injections of money are desirable and that privatization of large parts of the existing transport system would also be advantageous. In terms of investment it would mean that resources would be directed at projects offering high commercial returns rather than, as in the past, dissipated across many variable schemes. Perhaps more important is the management of assets, including the privatization of existing ones. There is a danger that in a climate of transition, where current control-and-command systems are breaking down, that present management could both capture new investment and take command of existing transport capital for their personal gain. The reaction of workers to this, in an emergent market economy, is likely to be demands for higher pay. Besides macroeconomic implications for the rate of inflation, this will ultimately reduce the efficiency of transport industries and it will deter further outside investments. Rapid measures to stimulate quite substantial programs of privatization, even if they are far from any theoretical ideal, should act to circumvent this danger.

One should also remember that Eastern European states have the chance to renew their aged infrastructure with modern and appropriate technology. It would be an error to try to bring the 40-year-old technologies of many Eastern European transport systems up to the standards of the 1970s or 1980s. Rather, there is a need to think in terms of the technology and operational systems of the 1990s. Again, this would seem to suggest a central role for the private sector, which tends to be more innovative in its approach but, equally, agencies such as the BERD can be proactive in ensuring that public sector investment are geared to economic development rather than captured by national bureaucrats whose interests are often different.

While it is inevitable that one tends to think in modal terms, and indeed we revert to this below, one of the important opportunities the East enjoys is to improve modal coordination, especially in terms of infrastructure provision. The tendency to think beyond individual modes is only just changing in the West, with high speed rail and motorway systems tying in with airports in hub-and-spoke configurations which allow maximum overall economies of density, scale, and scope to be exploited. Indeed, operators are slowly thinking in these terms, with increasing emphasis on integrated systems for express parcel services and airlines such as Lufthansa extending their interests into rail transport[11].

Turning to specific modes, a number of points can be made.

The Railways: Looking at the geography of the greater Europe, and in particular the distances between the main generators of traffic, i.e., the major centers of population, there are few long distance routes. For instance, it is only 250 kilometers from Vienna to Budapest, just over 450 kilometers between Munich and Prague, and less than 550 kilometers between Warsaw and Berlin[12]. These routes, from the experience of high speed trains in France and Japan, are often seen to be best suited to tracked surface transport.

The rail systems of Eastern Europe are, however, not currently of a standard capable of taking high speed traffic and the incentive to invest may be lacking. There is excess aggregate physical capacity at present on most Eastern European systems and, given the probable change in the nature of East-West trade in the near future and differences in the types of internal traffic which will accompany increased manufacturing output, this excess capacity may well be seen as likely to persist into the next century[13]. Indeed, it has been argued that if the X-inefficiency endemic in most Eastern European rail systems was eliminated, output could be doubled with no expansion of capacity (Rothengatter and Kowalski, 1990). There is a danger that in this type of environment, insufficient investment will be made and that resources will be steered towards maintaining what is there[14]. This danger must be avoided.

User charges must also be more closely related to costs, while the hidden subsidies common to most Eastern European railways need to be made explicit or removed. The introduction of private investment has to be used to stimulate efficiency improvements elsewhere as well as provide monies for investment and modernization[15]. The situation is not so clear with regard to the use of public monies but, hopefully, the national and multi-national agencies involved will make economic pricing a condition of granting loans.

The Road Network: The option of developing the road haulage industries in Eastern Europe as a complement to industrial reform is extremely limited in the short run because of inadequacies in the basic infrastructure. These constraints are qualitative as much as having to do with the extent of the networks. Indeed, the view of the ECE is extremely depressing, i.e., "The present road infrastructure in Central/Eastern European countries has deteriorated such that it is unlikely to be able to cope with increased road traffic volumes" (Lehmacher, 1990). Further, many of the links required to expand East-West traffic are of limited capacity and, in some cases, there are no convenient roads on the Eastern side. But against this constraint must be set the needs of modern industry for flexible transport systems together with a pent-up demand for additional car ownership. Indeed, in terms of the automobile, even if the Eastern European states (excluding the USSR) were to increase the per capita automobile ownership to half the current level in the U.S. or the pre-unified FRG, an extra 11 million vehicles would be seeking road space.

Many Western European countries are currently encountering capacity problems on their road networks, and private investment is seen as one way of injecting funds into the system (e.g., Organization for Economic Cooperation and Development, 1987). Such an approach has obvious attractions for Eastern European economies although some caution would be needed. In particular, while tolled privately financed roads may make users aware of the opportunity costs of their activities, the existing system of free, albeit poor quality public roads may mean that the ultimate use of the entire network is far from optimal. There may thus be a case for going beyond the Western European "club system" of annual licences allowing access to the public road network and to introduce tolls for all major roads irrespective of ownership. Relatively low car ownership levels coupled with predictions of rapid rises in this figure would make it comparatively efficient to initiate such systems at this time, before the problems of mass ownership and the emergence of powerful motoring lobbies of the type found in Western Europe become realities.

Combined Transport: In the past, relatively little use was made of containerization in Eastern Europe, in part because of the nature of the goods carried. This must inevitably change as the economic bases of countries change and as transport is modernized. Other forms of combined transport, such as piggy-back systems, although little used, have recently stirred interest among transport planners who, especially in the context of the doubtful quality of existing road infrastructure, see them as potential means of easing transport problems between the East and West. While there may be some scope for developing such systems, especially if this can be done without incurring very high investment costs, their relatively poor performance in EC countries to date makes it unlikely that they will prove to be a long term solution. Even in the short term, the Eastern European systems are not currently interconnected with those in the West and, in any case, the latter (with the exception of the London-Amsterdam/Brussels-Cologne and Paris-Mannheim-Munich routes) run exclusively north-south, giving little scope for the carriage of Eastern European goods.

5. The Role of the West

Western Europe has a vested interest in ensuring improved transport both between itself and the East and within Eastern Europe itself. Better transport is important to lubricate trade within Poland, Rumania and Hungary as well as an important element in the economic development of these countries. In the special case of Yugoslavia, there is also the incentive to improve transit networks linking Greece with its EC partners[16]. Within Western Europe, the EC put increased emphasis on transport infrastructure development and standardization throughout the 1980s (Button, 1990). However, this should be seen as much in terms of a reaction to increasing problems of bottlenecks in the transport networks and, indeed, to missing networks themselves, as to a proactive program of works designed to stimulate EC economic development.

To ensure that these efforts bear fruit there is a need to coordinate in broad terms the EC policies of the 1990s with those of Eastern Europe. This is most obviously the case with regard to infrastructure provision, and there are already signs that international railway advisory bodies such as the IUR and ECE are thinking in these terms. However, the proposals being produced tend to be rather vague about how Eastern European countries are to generate resources for modernization. The key role of the West in this context must be one of ensuring that scare resources are not wasted. But it should avoid the potential pitfalls of rigid planning, especially in a uni-modal context.

The West is inevitably channelling funds into Eastern Europe. Private sources pose few problems but mechanisms must be found to ensure that institutional funding is not swallowed up in established bureaucracies and that mechanisms exist to encourage technical and managerial innovation. While soft loans may be desirable, a tightening of terms over time may stimulate the necessary care in the use of scarce resources[17]. These resources are also likely to be needed as much to enhance the efficiency of management and to introduced state-of-the-art computerized management systems as to refurbish the hardware of the transport networks. However, there is often a danger in transport that these elements are less attractive to those in the industry and get neglected in policy making.

6. Conclusions

The changes which are taking place in Eastern Europe, albeit at variable paces in different countries and with some backsliding, represent above everything else a movement away from a situation where every issue was viewed primarily as a political (or perhaps a military) problem, to one where economic considerations are often seen to have a dominant role. This means that efficiency considerations are gradually permeating deeply into the decision making process. The long term pattern of change is difficult to forecast, and its implications for Western Europe are far from clear. That transport will need to change both within Eastern Europe and in the West seems unquestioned, the difficulty is to define policies which will, if not optimize the eventual outcome, at least leave the Continent with a transport system capable of meeting the demands of industry and travellers in the next century.

Notes

1 While urban transport problems are often serious in Eastern European countries and the growth of car ownership is adding to local environmental degradation (e.g., through noise generation, etc.) these are given limited attention in the paper. The focus is primarily on inter-urban and international movements. For discussions of the types of urban traffic problems emerging in Eastern European cities and some of the policies being activated to deal with them, see Voigt (1988) and Saitz (1988) on the German Democratic Republic and Roe (1990) and Lesley (1989) on Hungary.

2 As an example of differing situations, while the USSR has a state-owned road haulage fleet which is heavily subsidized and, for the most part seen as part of the defence industry, Hungary has 35,000 private haulers and own-account operators with a total fleet of over 165,000 vehicles.

3 A major problem is a different accountancy convention employed in most Eastern European countries, e.g., for national accounts (with the exception of Poland and Hungary), they use the material product system, which does not include "immaterial outputs", while most other countries use the more comprehensive UN System of National Accounts. At the more micro level, most Eastern European countries have good data on the registration of new vehicles but little idea of scrappage rates, which make estimates of national car parks extremely tentative.

4 The literature on this subject is extensive and the volume of official documentation massive, but a brief, up-to-date review is contained in Button (1991).

5 In early 1991, for instance, an EC commissioned study (Smit-Kroes *et al.*, 1991) stressed the need for increased investment in transport infrastructure, which would run into "billions of ECUs", aimed at discouraging the excessive use of private and commercial vehicles and to increase the use of public transport.

6 Shaw (1985) offers some interesting illustrations of these problems.

7 In particular, the trailing stock employed in Eastern Europe does not met the requirements of Western European railways, especially with regard to the technical specifications consistent with high speed rail passenger and freight operations.

8 However, some limited disinvestment is also likely in areas where subsidized transport has been provided in the FRG to compensate for pre-Second World War markets formerly lost to the East.

9 There inevitably are problems of definition when making comparisons between EC countries and Eastern European states, not the least of which is that infrastructure quality may differ as does the quality of national car parts.

10 For some discussion of an actual case study showing the pros and cons of management in centrally planned economies, see Vlachoutsicos and Lawrence (1990).

11 The actual degree of integration taking place with, for example, the EC is still very limited but, given the levels of congestion which exist coupled with the increased opposition to many major new infrastructure projects, there are pressures to ensure maximum productivity from transport networks.

12 Further, over half the thirty busiest air routes in Western Europe are over distances of less than 375 miles.

13 An interesting perspective on the likely industrial ambitions of Eastern European states is offered by Robinson (1991): "Ironically for countries which used to measures their economic performance exclusively by crude output figures, the effectiveness of their reform policies is now judged by the speed of production decline". In quantitative terms industrial production fell in this region by about 18 percent in the first three quarters of 1990 according to the ECE.

14 Modernisation also implies higher levels of productivity and an inevitable shedding of labor. The political and social problems this can cause have already been experienced in the former GDR, where railway workers staged strikes in late 1990.

15 See, for example, Sumita (1989) on the Japanese situation. He is not convinced these experiences are directly transferable to Western Europe but they may well be to some corridors within a pan-European context.

16 The EC is particularly conscious of this problem and transport investments in Yugoslavia have formed a significant element of its infrastructure budget (Commission of the European Communities, 1986).

17 The use of something akin to the (RPI-X) formula used in the UK to regulate prices charged by newly privatized utilities could be examined in this respect.

References

Ambler, J., Hunter, H. and Westwood, J.N., 1985, Soviet Railways -- Lethargy or Crisis?, in Ambler, J., Shaw, J.B. and Symons, L. (eds.), *Soviet and East European Transport Problems*, Croom Helm, London.

Alvstam, C.G., Berman, Z. and Dawson, A.H., 1985, The Transport Sector in Polish Economic Planning, and Polish-Soviet Traffic Capacity Problems, in Ambler, J., Shaw, J.B. and Symons, L. (eds.), *Soviet and East European Transport Problems*, Croom Helm, London.

Banister, D. and Button, K.J. (eds.), 1991, *Transport in a Free Market Economy*, Macmillan, London.

Barde, J-Ph. and Button, K.J. (eds.), 1990, *Transport Policy and the Environment*, Earthscan, London.

Button, K.J., 1990, Infrastructure Plans for Europe, in Gillund, J. and Tornqvist, G. (eds.), *European Networks*, Umea, CERUM.

Button, K.J., 1991, The Liberalization of Transport Services, in Swann, D. (ed.), *1992 and Beyond*, Routledge, London.

Button, K.J. and Nboh, N., 1990, *Vehicle Ownership and Use Forecasting in Low Income Countries*, Transport and Road Research Laboratory Contractor Report, Crowthorne.

Commission of the European Communities, 1986, *Medium-term Transport Infrastructure Program*, COM (86) 340 Final, EC, Brussels.

De Waele, A.D., 1990, Consequences of Closer East-West Relations, in European Conference of Ministers of Transport, *Development Prospects for European Transport Between East and West*, ECMT, Paris.

European Round Table of Industrialists, 1990, *Missing Networks in Europe*, ERTI, Paris.

Funck, R. and Kowalski, J., 1989, Some Propositions on the Evaluation of East-West Projects, in Knothe, K. et al. (eds.), *Transport Cooperation in East and West*, Technische Universitat Berlin and SNV Studiengesellschaft Nahverkehr mbH, Berlin.

Laikin, R.E., Chadwick, M.J. and Cooke, J.G., 1987, Energy-based Emission Inventories for Modelling Cost-effective SO_2 and NO_X Abatement Strategies in Europe, Paper Presented at the International Workshop on Methodologies for Air Pollution Emission Inventories, Paris.

Lehmacher, H., 1990, The Coordinating of the UN/ECE: Projects and Programs, in *Proceedings of a Seminar on Developing a European Transport Infrastructure Network: The Case of Inland Transport*, Center for European Policy Studies, Brussels.

Lesley, L., 1989, Assessment of an Eastern European City's Public Transport System, *Transportation Research*, 23A, 129-137.

Linster, M., 1990, Background Facts and Figures, in European Conference of Ministers of Transport, *Transport Policy and the Environment*, ECMT, Paris.

Marcel, L., 1989, L'est et L'ouest: Les Transport, *Lloyd Annersois*, December 21.

Organization for Economic Cooperation and Development, 1987, *Toll Financing and Private Sector Involvement in Road Infrastructure Development*, OECD, Paris.

Potrykowski, M., 1985, Some Problems of the Pattern of the Transport Networks of Poland, *Geographia Polonica*, 51, 275-283.

Rathery, A., 1988, Les Investissement dans Les Infrastructures de Transport des Pays de La CEMT au Cours de La Periode 1975-1984, *Renue Transports*, 331, 388-392.

Robinson, A., 1991, From Plan to Market, *Financial Times*, 4 February, 12.

Roe, M., 1990, Transport Planning in Hungary: A Case Study of PECs, *Transport Reviews*, 10, 229-243.

Rothengatter, W. and Kowalski, J., 1990, Prospects for Passenger Transport, in European Conference of Ministers of Transport, *Development Prospects for European Transport Between East and West* , ECMT, Paris.

Russell, J., 1990, *Environmental Issues in Eastern Europe: Setting an Agenda* Royal Institute of International Affairs, London.

Saitz, H.H., 1988, Erfurt City and Traffic: An Example of Transport Policy and Planning in the German Democratic Republic, *Transport Reviews*, 8, 1-18.

Seidenfus, H.St., 1990, Prospects for Railways, in European Conference of Ministers of Transport, *Development Prospects for European Transport Between East and West,* ECMT, Paris.

Shaw, D.J.B., 1985, Branch and Regional Problems in Soviet Transportation, in Ambler, J., Shaw, J.B. and Symons, L. (eds.), *Soviet and East European Transport Problems*, Croom Helm, London.

Smit-Kroes, N. *et al.*, 1991, *Transport in a Fast Changing Europe*, EC, Brussels.

Sumita, S., 1989, *Outline of Privatization and Division of the Japanese National Railways and the Present Situation, in Transport Policy, Management and Technology Towards 2001: Volume 1, The Role of Public Sector in Transport,* Western Periodicals, Ventura.

Tanner, J.C., 1983, International Comparisons of Car Ownership and Use, Report 1072, Transport and Road Research Laboratory.

Tarski, I., 1981, Comecon's Transport Policy: A Socialist View, *International Journal of Transport Economics*, 8, 7-23.

Timar, A., 1990, Prospects for Passenger Transport, in European Conference of Ministers of Transport, *Development Prospects for European Transport Between East and West,* ECMT, Paris.

Turnock, D., 1989, *The Human Geography of Eastern Europe*, Routledge, London.

Vlachoutsicos, C. and Lawrence, P., 1990, What We Don't Know About Soviet Management, *Harvard Business Review*, 68, 50-63.

Voigt, W., 1988, Town Traffic in the German Democratic Republic, *Transport Reviews*, 8, 183-196.

Whitelegg, J., 1988, *Transport Policy in the EEC*, Routledge, London.

TRANSPORT IN A UNIFIED EUROPE. Policies and Challenges.
D. Banister and J. Berechman (Editors)

Chapter Thirteen

TRANSPORT PROBLEMS AT THE JUNCTURE BETWEEN EAST AND WEST

Ulrich Blum
Frank Leibbrand

1. Quantitative and Qualitative Changes

1.1 The Uniqueness of the Problem

The division of Germany into two parts after World War II led to economic and societal development according to completely contradictory values in each half of the nation, resulting in complete alienation and political antagonism between East and West.

In this chapter, we describe the present problems in the German transport sector, especially with respect to the infrastructure in West German border regions near the former Iron Curtain, and that of the whole of East Germany, where a rundown infrastructure has to be reconstructed. We then present a scenario regarding the future development of transport demand. In doing so, we show that a new transport policy is urgently needed as the symptoms of problems (such as increased levels of congestion) were only amplified by unification. Thus, new policy has to be formulated earlier than expected.

The complete lack of a consistent theory on transformation processes from a centrally planned to a market economy, and non-existent or unreliable data, force us to develop a scenario on future transport demand at two levels: (1) we forecast developments in the West and, by identifying pairs of structurally equivalent regions to the East, define the economic position in the new states of Germany; (2) we compute transport demand based on these economic results by adapting a model estimated for West Germany to the whole country.

Our scenario horizon will be the year 2010. We believe that a long term forecast is more reliable than a short term forecast because of the unknown length of the ongoing mental and economic adaptation processes (more precisely, the German Monetary Union, which set an exchange rate of 1:1 for most of the money volume M3 between West and East Germany, the inflexibility of wages, and the opening of the formerly closed East German market led to a reevaluation of the East German Currency by more than 300 percent -- which would have destroyed any economy -- and revealed an enormous productivity gap). In addition, the reforms in the former COMECON countries led to a complete disruption of East German exports, especially in the machine, vehicle and electronics industries, which had benefitted from productivity which was higher than the East German average. Whereas many economists in 1991 believed that "the valley of tears" would pass in 1992/1993, it is still unclear whether the East German economic trough will last for less than another year.

In this sense, the problems of German unity and their repercussions in the transport sector are not only unique in their mix but also in most of their components. As a result, the structure of this chapter is not comparative in terms of the available literature but represents a closed problem structure.

1.2 Infrastructure

Unification and the increasing demand for transport in and through Germany have considerably accelerated the necessity to add infrastructure to the existing networks. In addition, most of the roads and railroad tracks in the East need to be retooled and modernized in terms of quality, communications, and security. The most pressing demand stems from the missing links between the former two parts of Germany and the continuation of links from large East German cities to the east or southeast. For instance, the transit to Prague through Dresden puts an enormous stress on the inter-city road system.

1.3 Reorientation

Whereas the main orientation of the West German transport network was in a north-south direction before unification, an east-west orientation has increasingly emerged, at least in the more central parts of the country. This development is somewhat bizarre as West Germany had to invest considerably in a network that was oriented in an East-West direction after the war in order to adapt it to the emerging North-South orientation of the new Federal Republic. For East Germany, this was also true, but to a lesser extent.

1.4 Trip Distance and Trip Pattern

In the first months after the opening of the border, better shopping opportunities in the West generated an avalanche of visitors to the former border cities of West Germany, sometimes using trains, more often cars. In cities like Hof or the western part of Berlin, this completely crippled the transport system, and sometimes even led to a ban on Trabis (the East German subcompact car with a smoky, polluting two-stroke engine) inner cities.

Trip patterns in a united Germany can be analyzed and forecasts can be made of future developments by using scenario techniques. A careful distinction must be made between those effects emerging from simply applying western structures to the eastern developments and effects emerging from changes in transport behavior, especially trip patterns. The short term effects have to be separated from long term effects, as some of the changes are typical for the transition period and are not likely to prevail permanently. For instance, the high shares of long distance shopping and commuting trips may decline over time.

Most forecasts presently being developed see a steady but small increase in average passenger trip distances, especially in cases of business and leisure trips, as very likely. This is a direct result of the increased size of the country. Table 1 shows that from 1989 to 1990, trip lengths in both parts of Germany grew by about 2 percent, which is twice the rate of the period between 1980 and 1989. These small increases are based in a still ongoing expansion of the settlement structure, especially suburbanization. It will be interesting to see to what extent and when this development will affect the eastern countries.

In addition, unification has changed the existing trip patterns in both the West and the East (especially in the former border areas) for a number of reasons: economic restructuring and adaptation in the East, a new spatial division of labor, and new points of attractiveness. With new opportunities, West Germans have started to discover the East. The regions at the Baltic Sea, the Harz Mountains, the Thuringian Wood and the Erzgebirge in particular, have or will become important attraction points, thus inducing additional leisure and vacation trips. Business trips have also picked up and will grow continuously with the improvement of the economic situation of the new states (i.e., the states formed after unification out of the former GDR) as new economic links develop. In 1989 and 1990, the number and the average length of shopping trips from East to West grew, but this has recently declined as the shopping infrastructure has improved.

Long distance trips to work are also increasing. Citizens of East Germany who live near the old Iron Curtain ("near" sometimes means more than 150 kilometers away) commute to the West for higher wages or more secure jobs. It may take some years until long distance trips for work and education fall again. In West Germany in 1985, before unification, 61 percent of all long distance trips by car were for leisure, 17 percent for business, and 10 percent for work purposes; shopping, education and holidays comprised another 5 percent, 4 percent and 3 percent, respectively. The specific values for East Germany for the same year are not known, but the convergence process is extremely fast, as a recent survey (Spiegel, 1993) for the year 1992 shows.

Small differences exist in the share of certain trip purposes and in the modal shares. For instance, 39 percent of mobility activities in the West are carried out by foot or bicycle against 45 percent in the East, and car use is 50 percent in the West against 41 percent in the East. Most of the differences can be related to a smaller share of leisure trips and a higher share of mass transit in the East. The necessary daily time budgets are 58 minutes in the West against 72 minutes in the East.

In the freight sector, unification has brought a complete restructuring of the modal split in favor of the lorry, together with an invasion of freight shipments from the West to the East to guarantee supply of attractive goods.

1.5 Looking Further East

The problems of Germany with its ill-suited transport networks will further be aggravated by the neighboring Eastern countries. Because they want to save on infrastructure investments in their own countries, cars and trucks (especially from Poland) have increasingly started to use German infrastructure for their transit. Often this means a detour in distance, but not an increase in travel time. It is typical of this kind of development for traffic from northern Poland to the Balkans to use the motorways through Saxony and even further through Bavaria and Austria.

For Germany, this means that providing financial support for a motorway in the Czech Republic (for the route from Dresden via Prague to Vienna) is politically sound as this would directly reduce some of the transit through Germany, especially through Saxony and Bavaria. More generally, transport planning in Western Europe, especially in the EC, must increasingly include at least Poland, the Czech and the Slovak Republics, and Hungary.

This move has already taken place at the level of the UIC (International Railroad Union) for rail, with a proposed European high speed railway network. Concepts for a European system of motorways have also been discussed, but at a lower level of detail.

2. The Role of Passenger Transport and Hysteresis

2.1 Overview on Modes

Before unification, the role of public transport, especially rail, was much more important in the former German Democratic Republic than in the former Federal Republic of Germany. Among the major reasons were a much lower rate of car ownership because of a regulated car supply, combined with a very dense supply of trains which, in most cases, followed the network established before the war. As a consequence, mobility relied to a greater extent on a railway system which was pretty run down and offered little comfort. In sharp contrast, the railway network of West Germany experienced a steady roll back during the 1970s and 1980s in an attempt to make the system commercially profitable (with little success, however), as can clearly be seen from Table 1.

It is worth noting that the availability of cars was not so much a problem of income levels -- at the national scale, in fact, they define production potentials -- but a result of low supply of cars, which resulted in forced savings and queues. With unification and German Monetary Union (GMU), these savings were tranformed into hard currency and partly dedicated to the purchase of cars.

Table 1 reveals several striking factors. Although the income level of East Germany was only about 40 percent of West Germany, the difference in transport behavior is surprising with respect to modal choice, but not so much with respect to trip distance, trip volume, or trip numbers. The smaller average trip distance of 15 kilometers in the East, against 17 kilometers in the West, can mostly be attributed to the smaller size of the country.

TABLE 1

The Role of Road and Rail in Passenger Transport

Year	Pass. Trips	Trips / Inh	Share (%) of Trips Car	Train	Bus[a]	Total Vol.[b]	Pkm / Inh.	Share % of Trips Car	Train	Bus
WG:										
1980	37.2[c]	604	77.7	3.1	18.1	598.6[c]	9,722	78.6	6.8	12.4
1989	39.5[c]	649	81.9	2.9	14.2	687.1[c]	11,264	82.1	6.2	8.9
1990	40.9[c]	660	82.0	2.8	14.1	723.2[c]	11,644	82.1	6.2	8.8
EG:										
1980	7.6[c]	455	45.5	8.0	45.2	108.0[c]	6,433	51.7	20.4	26.0
1989	9.1[c]	553	55.0	6.5	37.7	138.0[c]	8,396	60.8	17.2	21.0
1990	8.6[c]	528	61.1	5.5	32.6	133.0[c]	8,192	67.6	13.5	18.1

Key: WG: West Germany; EG: East Germany; Inh: Inhabitants; Pkm: Person-kilometers.

Notes: [a]Public road transport, mostly buses; [b]Person-kilometers annually; [c]Billions.

Source: Verkehr in Zahlen (1990, 1991).

Among the most important factors driving transport demand is income. If we assume an income elasticity of unity or slightly above (Blum and Gaudry, 1992), the phenomenon can be explained by the fact that its internal purchasing power lies by far above the external economic productivity of the country. It is estimated that East Germany's (external) productivity was about 30 percent of West Germany's (i.e., an East German worker produced 30 percent of the output of his West German counterpart), whereas the value for purchasing power for the average citizen was about 60 percent (in the sense of internal productivity).

Car ownership per 1000 persons in West Germany was 347 cars in 1980, 437 in 1989, and 505 in 1991. The respective values for East Germany are 160, 237, and 355 cars, which means 46 percent, 54 percent, and 70 percent of the West German level. We argue that although the closing of the car ownership gap has accelerated with unification, it was already under way even though the economic performance of East Germany was sluggish in the 1980s.

2.2 Long Distance Transportation in the Year 2010

Although trips by train were very time consuming, a greater proportion of long distance passenger transport had to rely on the railway system for the same reasons as those given above for urban travel. This explains why the number of long distance trips per person in the train mode is higher in 1988 and 2010 in East Germany compared to West Germany (see Table 2). In fact, they are nearly twice as high in the East than in the West in both 1988 and 2010.

TABLE 2

Long Distance Passenger Traffic

Year	Mode	West Germany	East Germany
1985	Road	2.1 bn Trips	n.a.
1988		2.2 bn Trips	0.3 bn Trips
2010		2.8 bn Trips	0.7 bn Trips
1985	Rail	0.14 bn Trips	n.a.
1988		0.25 bn Trips	0.10 bn Trips
2010		0.35 bn Trips	0.15 bn Trips

Source: Blum (1992); Intraplan et al. (1991).

Tables 1 and 2 allow us to compute the number of long distance car trips per person in East Germany in 1988. This level was half of that of West Germany (17 versus 34). This gap will close, with the value rising to about 43 trips per person in 2010. An adaptation of transport behavior of individuals implies an increase in the number of trips using cars of 27 percent in the West and 133.5 percent in the East from 1988 to 2010.

East Germans made more long distance trips by train than West Germans (5.9 versus 3.9 in 1988) and this difference will prevail in 2010 on a higher level. The main reason lies in the fact that the eastern part of Germany will have the highest relative gains in accessibility from the high speed train system which is presently being built.

2.3 Effects of Hysteresis on Modal Choice

With unification, East Germany started to adopt West German traffic behavior patterns much faster than was foreseen by most experts. At present, with an income level comparable to that of West Germany in the early 1960s, they drive like West Germans in the late 1970s. Very shortly after German Monetary Union (GMU), trains and trams emptied and traffic breakdowns became daily events in large cities like Leipzig and Dresden, but also in smaller centers. Some of the major reasons for this reduction in public transport of around 20 percent from 1990 to 1991 are:

* The net migration of about 1 million people from East to West;

* The availability of Western cars which offered far better quality of transport as compared with Eastern cars and existing public transport;

* The breakdown of industry, where output fell by more than 60 percent between 1989 and 1991, accompanied by unemployment and shorter working hours;

* The allocation of employees to public housing. In many cases, inhabitants of one large apartment building worked in the same company. If this company went bankrupt, most of the people became unemployed and some public transport services became obsolete, which in turn resulted in a regionally unbalanced decline.

On the other hand, public transport in West Germany expanded over the same period by nearly 5 percent (see Table 3).

With huge investments in infrastructure and rolling stock, an attempt is being made to reconquer the market shares lost by the railway system, especially to the car. This may be feasible for certain trip purposes, but there remains a question as to whether it will be valid for all activities. The key question is the modal split division, which shows the development of the use of one mode against one or several other modes (in Figure 1: Car against Train) if the difference in attractiveness (in utility terms, U(C) - U(T)) varies.

TABLE 3

Change in Mass Transit, 1990-1991

West Germany			East Germany			Germany		
1990	1991	% Change	1990	1991	% Change	1990	1991	% Change
5.4m	5.7m	+ 4.7	1.9m	1.5m	- 20.0	7.4m	7.2m	- 2.1

Source: Internationales Verkehrswesen, (6/1992).

This path is not linear, and it can well be argued that in addition to captivity and asymmetry, it may exhibit hysteresis, where the development path of the modal share is not independent from the direction of change in attractiveness. This means that the reduction or increase of relative utility is the exogenous factor in the model. In Figure 1, the continuous line describes the average relationship. However, households have a choice

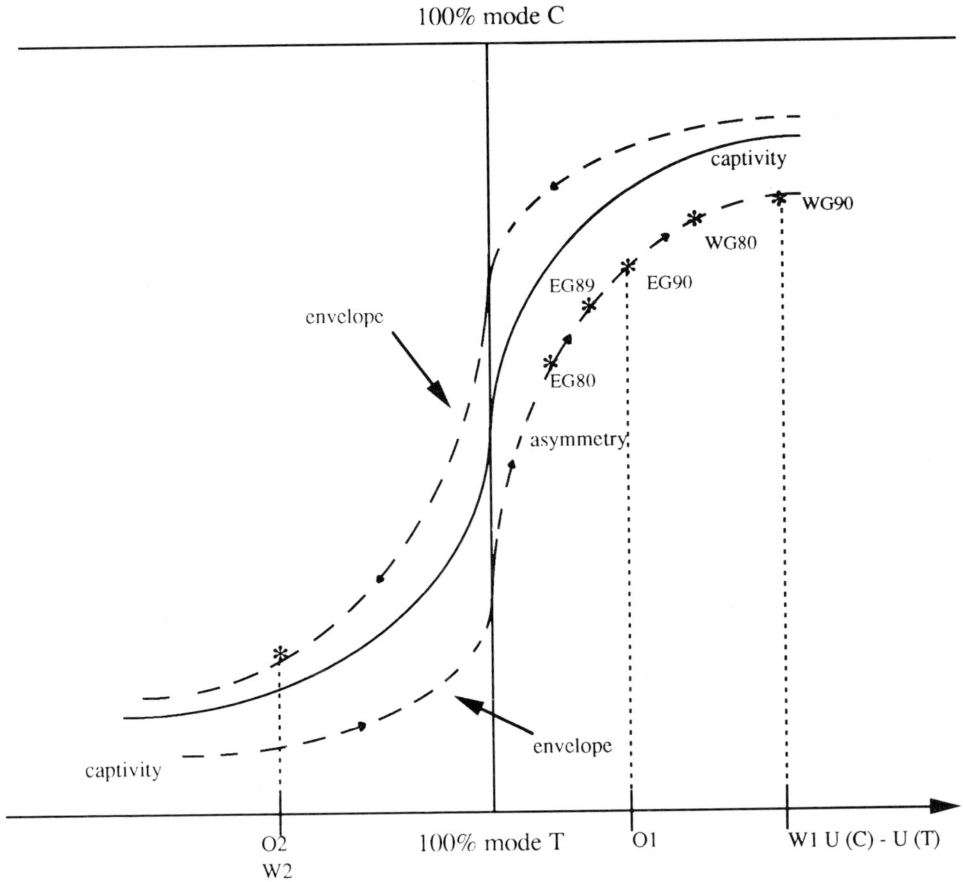

FIGURE 1 Modal Split and Hysteresis

as to how long to use a car and whether to buy or replace it under certain conditions. This implies that, once the decision to purchase a car is made, a new option of public transport only exists if that car needs to be replaced. The age of a car fleet is one of the most important considerations for modal choice. The two broken lines show the envelope of the modal split function, which account for these frictions and transaction costs. Whereas captivity, slope, and symmetry or asymmetry are all *static* elements of the modal split function, hysteresis may be considered as a *dynamic* factor (Figure 1).

We have included some qualitative points for West Germany (WG) and East Germany (EG) for different years. Figure 1 clearly shows that a reduction of the use of car, say to a modal share of 50 percent, is much easier in the East than in the West. In the East, an increase in the relative utility of the train by O1 to O2 is much smaller than that required in the West (W1 to W2). If we refer to a reduction of the same percentage value, say 20 percent, this could be easier to achieve in the East than in the West, where the marginal modal effect with respect to changes in relative utility is smaller than in the East.

3. Freight Transport

3.1 In Search of Autarcy

In their search of autarcy, especially against the "capitalistic" world markets and as of the first oil crisis, East Germany has tried to minimize the import of primary energy resources which had to be paid for in hard currency, namely oil and natural gas. The options for buying large quantities of oil and natural gas in the Soviet Union were limited, as this implied an indirect loss of hard currency for East Germany. As a result, freight shipments by truck over distances above 50 kilometers had to be approved by a district transport authority, which ensured that a preponderance of long distance transport went by rail. As a consequence, the modal share of rail increased in the 1980s (see Table 4).

Because of the industry-oriented structure of the economy, service industries played a small role compared to their roles in market economies at the same level of national revenue. The large share of lignite transport for housing and industry meant that the volume of freight transported per inhabitant in the East exceeded that in the West. In addition, the long term decline in the specific weight per unit value of GNP induced by technological change had not yet emerged in East Germany.

TABLE 4

Internal (National) Freight Transport

	Metric Tons[a]	Tons / Inh	Percent Share: Trucks Long	Percent Share: Trucks Short	Percent Share: Train	Vol. / Tkm[b]	Tkm / Inh	Percent Share: Trucks Long	Percent Share: Trucks Short	Percent Share: Train
WG:										
1980	3,229.0	53.5	9.2	69.9	10.8	255.3	4,147	31.4	17.4	25.5
1989	3,324.0	54.5	12.5	69.2	9.2	288.0	4,721	39.4	16.3	21.6
1990	3,458.8	55.8	12.7	69.7	8.8	300.1	4,840	40.2	16.5	20.6
EG:										
1980	1,099.3	65.7	4.0	62.4	28.3	84.6	5,054	10.1	14.7	66.7
1989	938.5	57.1	2.9	54.7	36.1	82.5	5,020	8.5	12.0	72.7
1990	646.2	39.8	2.8	54.2	36.1	59.1	3,638	10.5	11.5	69.2

Key: WG: West Germany; EG: East Germany; Inh: Inhabitants; Tkm: metric ton-kilometers.

Notes: [a]Millions; [b]Billions.

Source: Verkehr in Zahlen (1990, 1991).

Unification thus led to a severe adaptation shock in East Germany. The new states are simultaneously experiencing a decline in transport volume, in average transport distance, and in the modal share of the train. A considerable part of the reduction in transport volume -- from 5,020 ton-kilometers in 1989 to 3,638 ton-kilometers in 1990 -- may be directly related to the substitution of lignite and coal for natural gas and oil as well as the breakdown of transport-intensive industries. Again, we note that the difference in average transport distance for freight haulage between the two parts of Germany is rather small: 87 kilometers in the West and 88 kilometers in the East for 1989.

3.2 Long Distance Freight Transportation in the Year 2010

It is very difficult to accurately assess the level of freight transport in Germany in the year 2010. Among the major reasons are:

* Transit and foreign origins or destinations play a far more important role in long distance freight transport than in long distance passenger transport -- at present,

about 30 percent against 10 percent. The future development in the division of labor on the European level is very unclear, particularly in the light of the absence of any coherent ecological orientation in the Common Transport Policy. The tendency towards more specialization could be halted or even reversed if "true" transport prices are established.

* It is unclear to what extent the Internal Market will really expand intra-Community trade. This very much depends on the price-setting behavior of firms. The enforcement of "flat" prices could encourage firms to concentrate more on regional or domestic markets, especially in cases of monopolistic competition and hedonistic pricing.

* Finally, the levels of quality and the quantity of infrastructure available for transport inside the Community has not yet been finalized. This, however, will strongly influence the sectoral development, especially the departure from "rust belt" industries in the more developed parts of Europe, will reduce considerably the demand for transport on the railways and internal waterways, and will affect the future modal split.

Most analyses assume that long distance freight transport will increase by about 70 percent with respect to the 1985 base period in the old Federal Republic (Blum, Kessel, Rothengatter et al., 1990). In this chapter, we base our scenario on their findings.

3.3 The Choice between Road and Rail

Because of its industrial structure with its rather large share of "rust belt" industries, the sectoral choice of the railway system for freight shipments was a natural decision for East Germany. More than 60 percent of freight shipments were carried by rail -- twice the share of the West. Unification brought with it a severe sectoral adaptation crisis and nearly led to a collapse of the market. Deutsche Reichsbahn was also handicapped by its outdated rolling stock, which still makes rail transport unattractive.

It is very difficult to forecast the changes that are likely to occur in modal split in the freight sector. If the railway system is to reconquer lost market shares, this will only be possible by redefining the costs of the road so that full social costs are paid, and by increasing additional and supportive political momentum. Furthermore, the future of high speed freight trains is handicapped by environmental concerns, especially with respect to noise pollution in central cities and regions of high density development. Finally, it should be noted that internal navigation also faces a bright future in Germany, not only for dangerous goods but also for the high tech sector, where improved logistics have allowed substantial expansion of transport on the Rhine.

4. Retooling the Network: Bottlenecks and Priorities

4.1 Consequences for the Transport Networks

The main conclusion of our analysis is that the networks that carry the trade and travel between the East and the West within the border corridor of the former Iron Curtain will be heavily congested. New flows will be generated in these areas as a result of the new opportunities that have arisen, and the region will be burdened by additional transit flows. For a considerable period of time, the quality and the quantity of infrastructure will be below average. For instance, none of the routes between the Reichsbahn and the Bundesbahn are presently electrified, even though the main networks of both railway companies run on the same electrical standard.

A numerical example for road use illustrates the problems. Long and short distance transport each account for roughly half of the person-kilometers in Germany. In the border areas, the relationship was 20:80 (=100) due to the closed border. Normality means an increase of long distance traffic, especially through-transit, to 80:80 (=160), an increase of 60 percent. If we expect long distance traffic to increase by about 50 percent and short distance traffic by about 35 percent by the year 2010, then we obtain a split of 120:108 (=228). Thus, traffic volumes will more than double in the border areas as an outgrowth of these structural effects. As a consequence, an infrastructure which was well-adapted to the situation near the Iron Curtain is no longer suited to handle the transport flows after unification given the present regime of transport politics. Thus, it can no longer guarantee the availability of the necessary regional capacities.

4.2 An Example: Northern Bavaria

Northern Bavaria was well-protected by the Iron Curtain from huge transport flows. In the 1980s, it started to benefit from investment programs meant to improve the accessibility of its more peripheral parts. With this objective in mind, motorway A70 between Bayreuth and Schweinfurt, providing a direct east-west link just south of the

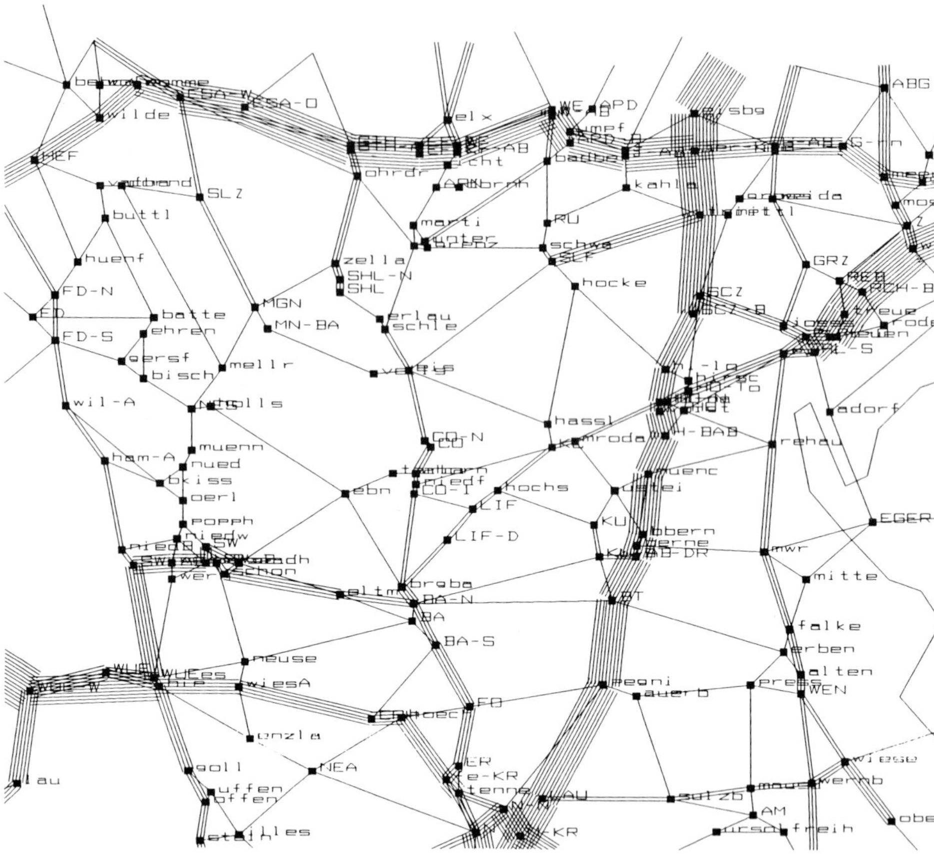

FIGURE 2 Northern Bavaria and Southern Thuringia Without "Reversed Y", Forecast for 2010 .

Key: Each line represents 500 trips per hour.

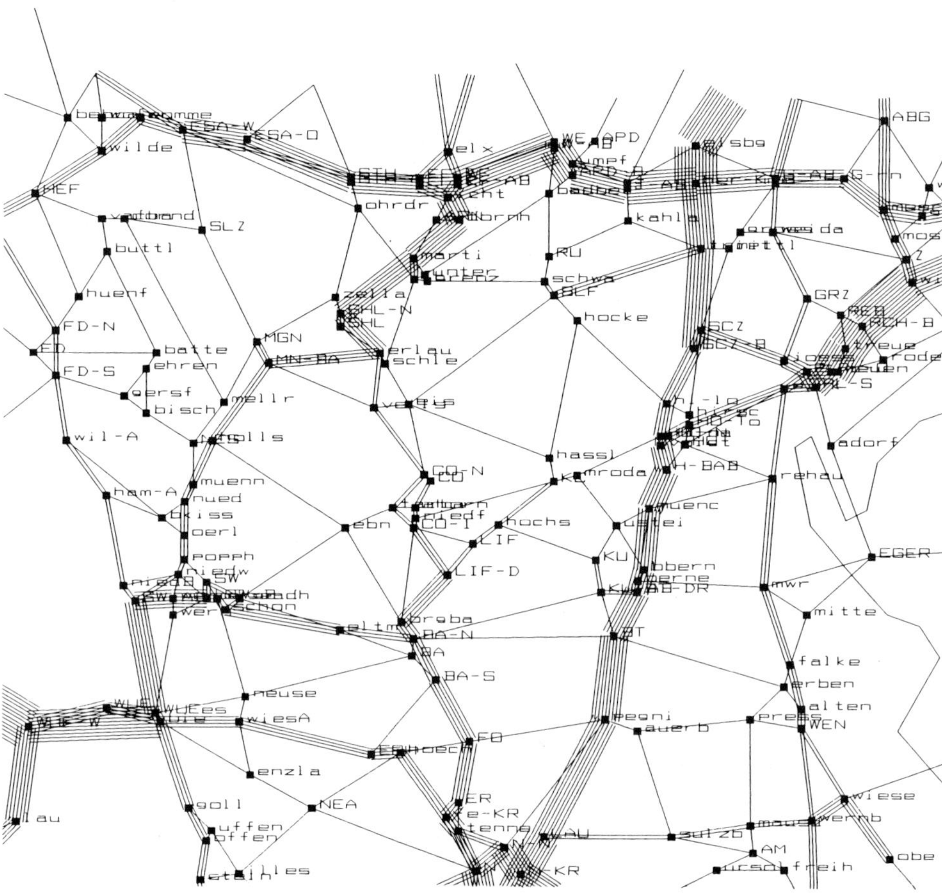

FIGURE 3 Northern Bavaria and Southern Thuringia With "Reversed Y", Forecast for 2010.

Key: Each line represents 500 trips per hour.

border, and motorway A73, linking Bamberg and other cities further north to Nuremberg, were planned. In fact, Bamberg ("BA" in the central lower part of Figure 2) would benefit from the intersection of the A73 with the A70.

When the Iron Curtain came down, parts of these plans had already been realized. One lane of the A70 was completed and the A73 had reached the south of Bamberg. Suddenly, this road, meant to improve regional accessibility to the centers of Germany and reduce the adverse effects of the division of Germany (especially of high transport costs for products produced in northern Bavaria), was flooded with traffic. Among its major causes in the first months were leisure trips for reasons of curiosity, shopping trips (especially to exploit arbitrage in goods markets), and new transit traffic from Poland and the Czech and the Slovak Republics. Later, shopping trips declined, making space for more business trips. Transport volumes on some roads skyrocketed. For instance, on the A9 west of Hof, traffic on the motorway linking Nuremberg with Berlin rose from an average of 6,000 cars per day to 50,000 cars per day. Suddenly, new master plans had to be drawn and the existing infrastructure obtained a new role. This caused considerable dismay to the local population, now suffering from congestion effects which they had never dreamt of before. As a consequence, the completion of these motorways was considerably accelerated and plans were discussed to extend the A73 to Thuringia and Saxony-Anhalt (Bundesminister für Verkehr 1991).

4.3 Forecasts for Long Distance Traffic and Road Use in 2010

Figures 2 and 3 contain forecasts for road use in Northern Bavaria and Southern Thuringia. Figure 2 gives the results of the projections for the 2010. We see the emergence of an important axis from Munich-Nuremberg-Leipzig-Berlin along the A9 motorway, which will be extended to six lanes with hourly volumes of more than 6,000 vehicles. The second axis, the A4, will pass the "Thuringian City Corridor", with more than 8,000 vehicles per hour during daytime. At the left side of the diagram, we indicate motorway A7 between Hamburg and Munich, which will not be heavily congested as it is not well-placed. A product of the German division, its route was planned to be more eastward before the war in order to link industrial areas, and it was not intended to pass through the countryside (at least between Würzburg and Kassel). Heavy congestion on the two-lane highway in the center is clear and this has lead to the suggestion to link Erfurt (ER) in Thuringia to both Bamberg (BA) and Schweinfurt (SW). The Federal Highway Master Plan (see Figure 3) includes an extension of the A73 from Bamberg and of the A81 from Schweinfurt to the north, to join somewhere in the area between Meiningen and

Schleusingen and to continue via Erfurt to Halle. These links will reduce flows on the eastern (A9) and the western parallels (A7), but will also considerably improve accessibility in the area of the ridge of the Thuringian Wood.

Without these links, many of the cities would be flooded with transit traffic, especially along highway B4 (Erfurt-Coburg-Bamberg), and living conditions would become unbearable unless restrictions to traffic were imposed. This would be very difficult to implement in Germany.

5. Conclusions

5.1 General Arguments in Favor of the Railway System

German Unification has accelerated the political insight that more long distance passenger rail service is needed in order to reduce the diseconomies of increased congestion in the road system. The potential of the train becomes especially great once high speed services are introduced, as demand can be nearly doubled. The same holds for freight, where complementarities which favor long distance hauls during the night would considerably increase their competitive advantage over road.

Both arguments necessitate the building of new rail capacities, which are presently being studied and planned. Furthermore, public transport will become increasingly important, particularly for commuters, so that cities can be saved from congestion and certain road capacity can be dedicated to shopping purposes, considered necessary in order to guarantee the economic centrality of city centers.

5.2 Instruments for Increasing Competitiveness of the Railway System

It is often argued that the advantages of accessing areas of high density development through the railway system and building feeder systems at regional and urban levels goes beyond simple efficiency and second-best arguments as many externalities in transport are difficult to quantify at the disaggregate level. However, this does not imply that efforts to adjust pricing to include the social costs should be neglected. Environmental licensing schemes for exhaust fumes and electronic road pricing are both under active consideration for cars and lorries so that "true" social costs can be allocated. The separation of rolling stock from the infrastructure and common carriage could advance this idea.

A strategy to reduce demand for road transport by means of market forces cannot rely on increases of fuel prices only, as the reaction of transport demand is very small (an elasticity of about -0.3). Any strategy should bear in mind that most of the transport infrastructure is sunk costs and that once it is put into place it should be used optimally. We suggest a combination of pricing and licensing schemes. Licenses, including a right to pollute, would be distributed and sold to individuals. The freely distributed part cannot be sold so that adverse effects in the social system and the regional settlement structure are not produced. The other part could be traded. This scheme would partly reduce congestion through the efficiency of engines. Inside cities, dedicated lanes, electronic road pricing, and park-and-ride systems could complement this policy.

Our argument implies that for given road transport pricing regimes, strategies for improving the competitiveness of the railway system should not be limited to the setting of prices alone but should also address the complete set of accessible performance factors. It should include other instruments such as exploiting different spatial structures related to individual values of time, which are higher in city areas that in rural areas. Furthermore, improvement in the quality and comfort of transport modes becomes evermore crucial, especially as cars are become increasingly "similar to a living room".

5.3 Performance Factors and Competition between Modes

It should be recognized that trip purposes have different sensitivities with respect to those factors defined as costs or "utilities" (e.g., prices, speed, terminal time, and comfort). These define different markets which can be exploited by well-adapted market strategies. In a recent survey for East Germany (Meinschien, 1993), the most important advantages of the train where noted to be the more relaxed way of travelling (45 percent see this an important motive) and environmental considerations (38 percent). Understandably, speed was not (yet) perceived as a competitive advantage (8 percent).

This, however, may well change in the long run: 70 percent of all persons interviewed consider the train as the most favorable means of travel for long distance domestic trips. Furthermore, a split according to trip purposes shows interesting sensitivities. The absence of stress and the ability to work in a comfortable environment are very important strategic advantages of the train for business travellers. This mix is different from people going on vacation or leisure trips, who may be more sensitive to the luggage problem. For shorter trips (especially in case of work, education and shopping trips), the train system becomes less attractive, particularly if the time span necessary for reaching the station from home or work (or vice versa) is substantial. Included here are considerations of a security factor of additional time for congestion if the car is used to reach the station. Here we recognize how important a systems approach becomes as the attractiveness of one system (the train) very much depends on the other (the feeder function of the car).

References

Blum, U., Kessel, P. and Rothengatter W., 1990, *Szenario zur Verkehrsentwicklung mit der DDR und Osteuropa*, Freiburg, Karlsruhe.

Blum, U. and Gaudry, M., 1992, Ein verbessertes Straßenverkehrsnachfragemodell für die Bundesrepublik Deutschland, *Internationales Verkehrswesen*, 4.

Blum, U. and Leibbrand, F., 1992, Long Distance Traffic in United Germany, Congestion, Collapse and Beyond, *Jahrbuch für Regionalwissenschaft*, forthcoming.

Blum, U., Leibbrand, F., and Gottschalk, M., 1992, *Alternative Trassenführung A73/A81, Gutachten im Auftrag des Landkreises*, Rudolstadt, Thüringen.

Bundesminister für Verkehr, 1991, *Projekte Deutsche Einheit*, Bonn.

German Ministry of Transportation, 1990 and 1991, *Verkehr in Zahlen*, Deutsches Institut für Wrtschaftsforschung, Berlin.

Internationales Verkehrswesen, *Aufwind im Westen, Rückgang im Osten*, 253-rrust 258.

Intraplan, IAVT, 1991, *Personenverkehrsprognose 2010 (Forschungsbericht Nr. 90 300/90 im Auftrag des Bundesministers für Verkehr)*, Heilbronn, München.

Meinschien, Lothar, 1993, *Fernverkehrskonzepte und die Integration des Nahverkehrs*, Dresden.

Spiegel, 1993, *Auto, Verkehr und Umwelt*, Hamburg.

TRANSPORT IN A UNIFIED EUROPE. Policies and Challenges.
D. Banister and J. Berechman (Editors)

Chapter Fourteen

FINANCING TRANSPORT IN EUROPE

Bernard Gerardin

1. Introduction

The implementation of the Single European Market, the creation of the European Economic Area, plus the current political and economical development in Eastern Europe will inevitably result in an increasing flow of goods, services and people within Europe. Therefore, the future transport networks need to be seen in a pan-European and supranational context in order to reap the fruits of a European market integration. But, presently, most of the investment projects in the transport sector are planned and financed at a national level. In spite of the key role of international institutions such as the EIB and the EBRD, a European-based banking and financing structure is lacking.

This situation has not only created large differences in the level of supply, but also poor adaptations between adjacent networks on two sides of the same border. The challenge is to integrate in a coherent, single European transport infrastructure network, many largely independent national transport networks. There is a need for financial innovation to efficiently combine different sources of funding at regional, national and supra-national levels both from the private and public sectors. To attain such a difficult goal, time and dogged efforts will be required. It will also be necessary to improve existing risk analysis methodologies and appraisal methods for transport investment projects. This article will discuss the basic issues in this field and will suggest some methodological and practical recommendations.

2. The Specific Characteristics of the Transport Sector

Compared to industrial projects, transport projects, especially large scale infrastructure investments such as the missing links between the national networks, have distinctive characteristics which usually cause considerable delay to their realization.

Transport infrastructure projects involve specific features:

* Long planning and construction period (2-10 years);

* Lengthy lifespan after construction (from 20 years to over a century);

* Relatively low operating costs.

Therefore, a significant amount of capital is required during the construction period and provides no revenue during a long period. In terms of cash flow, this means a very negative cash flow during the construction phase and the beginning of the operational phase. The project's risk profile varies during the life cycle of the project. If we look at the project "from the cradle to the grave", there are three phases in this cycle, each with its own distinctive characteristics and inherent risks:

Planning Phase:

* Risks of delay in the decision making and planning process due to political, legislative or environmental reasons. The necessity of making a full environmental impact assessment is a strong constraint because it means not only a detailed impact study but also a formal consultation of the public in conformity with the EC directive 85/337.

* The decision making process is more and more complex and associates decision makers at the local, regional, national and more and more frequently at Community level. The crossing of administrative boundaries and the fragmented property rights can complicate the planning exercise and so increase the rates for private investors during that (often long) planning period.

Construction Phase:

* The construction period is considerably longer for transport infrastructure than in conventional industrial projects. This is due to technical and geographical factors.

The consequence is a very negative cash flow, construction cost overruns are very frequent and decrease the overall profitability. Conflicts between promoters and contractors are frequent and therefore the level of risk is very high during this phase.

Operational Phase:

* Owing to the heavy interest payments on loans and the slow growth of demand, cash flow is very flat during a relatively long period after the beginning of the operational phase; this is a really critical period for the success of the project. Refinancing can be useful to adapt loan reimbursements to the evolution of traffic and revenues.

* Changes in interest and inflation rates and foreign exchange parities can complicate the problems and increase the financial risks.

* After this startup period, traffic increases slowly but surely during a long period (10 to 20 years) and cash flows follows the same trend. The service life of projects is very long and profitability is very high after the amortization period. During that period, the level of risk is low compared with previous phases.

So to sum up, it is clear that investments in the transport sector are long term investments. They can be very profitable if the risks are strictly controlled during the planning, the construction and the first period of the operational phase. It is only after a very long period, which may be 20 years or more, that the project does become truly profitable.

3. Private versus Public Financing

Investment in ground transport infrastructure has declined dramatically over the last 15 years in Western Europe. During the same period, traffic has risen by almost a third in terms of both passengers and goods. National budgetary limitations are more and more strict, while the list of priority projects is growing longer. For the EC Member states, the Maastricht Treaty has defined limitations for budget deficits. More generally, a consensus is emerging on stabilizing the pressure of income tax and social security contributions, which is a key element in maintaining competitiveness in a single market. So, for many politicians and decision makers in the public sector, the use of private funding has already gone some way towards solving this problem.

But this solution is feasible and relevant only if private investors and financial institutions can be persuaded to become involved in the financing of transport projects. For this to happen, private investors must be convinced that they will earn a reasonable return on investment and that the project's risk profile is acceptable. The specific characteristics of the transport sector described in the previous chapter are not very attractive for private investors. Problems are linked and mutually reinforcing:

* Long lead and payback times;
* Technical, economic and political risks;
* Gaps between standard duration of loans and transport infrastructure lifespan.

A long construction period with its negative cash flow and the high amount of capital required during this period can prohibit most of the private investors from investing their money in such risky adventures. This explains why the number of purely privately financed projects in the transport sector is rather low, especially at the international level. Very few projects are able to generate a cash flow considered sufficient to ensure, with a safety margin for uncertainties in the debt service, the coverage of operating costs and a fair return on capital. Private financing is not the universal solution, the "panacea" to solve difficulties due to public budget constraints.

Solutions to financing problems are therefore to be found increasingly in mixed financial packages with joint public and private sector involvement. A combination of public and private sector financing is viable only if the role of each party is clearly defined. The resulting division of responsibility requires a clear definition of the roles to be played both by the promoter and the operator. There is no universal solution for success in this type of business -- if we exclude purely public or private solutions, three types of packages have been experimented with:

1. The investment is financed with private capital. The infrastructure is built either totally or partially by a private body. Thereafter, a public body, controlled by national governments and/or local authorities, is responsible for the operation.

2. The promoter is a public body but funding is partially or entirely private. Management is in private hands and the operator is also a private structure.

Guarantees, loans, fiscal advantages or subsidies can be provided by public authorities.

3. Private funds are invested in the project but promotion, project management, risk guarantees and operation are controlled by a public body. Most of the risks are supported by public organizations directly or indirectly.

The first type of solution is not very common. The two other types of package have often been experimented with in the transport sector, especially at the local or regional level. As already mentioned, the key question is the division of responsibility between public and private partners. Private sector investors will insist on maintaining control over their investment to guarantee the efficiency of the management both during the construction and the operational phases. But at the same time, public authorities must control the use of public money.

According to past experience, contributions of public investors in private projects can be helpful in three areas:

* Reducing the long term risk through some form of guarantee;

* Providing a stable contractual environment with a clear set of rules and transparency in the decision process. This can significantly reduce the short and long term risks; and

* Lowering the cost of finance through various instruments: fiscal advantages, monetary policy, guarantees on loans, etc., and improving the regulatory framework for long term finance.

That does mean in all cases a direct contribution of public investors. Indirect actions are often more efficient than a small participation in equity or subsidies. Another type of contribution is, for example, a long term contract protecting investors against unfavorable shifts in price and/or demand for a key intermediary project (e.g., electricity). Private sector investors may require public entities expertise to evaluate and control different aspects of the project both during the planning and the construction phases. Many other possibilities of cooperation between public and private entities can be envisaged. Each case is a specific case and requires an innovative approach to look for synergies. The conclusion being that a strong cooperation between public and private bodies in the respect of the identity and the objectives of each partner seems to be the most appropriate and productive way to finance transport infrastructures.

4. The Role of Community Instruments For Funding

The European Community by combining different instruments can play a key role in supporting the implementation of the European transport networks. But, since 1957, the European Transport Policy has met with major difficulties, some of which are due to technical questions, but mostly related to political reservations. The European Transport Policy is a key element of the European Community Policy, the importance of which was recognized in the Treaty of Rome in 1957 and was pointed out as one of the major priorities from the beginning.

However, in 1985, the European Parliament asked the European Court of Justice to officially recognize the lack of a real European Transport Policy due to the inefficiency of the European Council of Ministers. This situation partly explains the delay in the process of adapting European Infrastructure to changing European demand patterns. Financing issues are, in fact, strongly related to institutional ones. In that difficult and conflicting context, different community infrastructure funding instruments were created. They can be classified into two categories: grants and loans.

Grants: In 1974, the Commission proposed the creation of a specific instrument to support transport infrastructure projects to the Council of Ministers. For the first time, in 1982, 10 million Ecus were included in the Community budget, despite misgivings of some member states. This instrument was relatively inefficient compared with the amount of capital required for transport investments. But, at this stage, the most important thing was its existence.

Then a commitment was approved for a total of 130 million Ecu's for 1988 and 1989 and then of 140 million Ecu's in 1991 and 161 million Ecu's in 1992. These figures can be compared with the total annual amount of investments in the transport sector in Europe: about 50 billion Ecu's.

The projects funded must comply with the following criteria:

* The removal of bottlenecks within the Community, and

* The improvement of major links between member states.

Other categories of Community grant may contribute to transport investment. The European Regional Development Fund (ERDF) created by the Council on March 18, 1975, is the most important of them. From 1975 to 1990, the ERDF financed transport investment for a total amount of 8.8 billion Ecu's. ERDF was renewed in 1979 to improve its efficiency. Funds are focused on less developed regions, and 75 percent of the grants were to finance projects located in four countries: Italy, United Kingdom, Greece and Ireland. So, ERDF appears as a key element of Community policy.

Loans: Since its creation in 1958 under the EC Treaty, the European Investment Bank (EIB) has provided long term co-financing for transport projects. Over the past 30 years, the EIB has lent its support to transforming separate national transport networks into a smoothly interlocking pan-European transport system.

Between 1986 and 1990, the EIB provided support to the tune of over 15 billion Ecus -- 37 percent of its Community-wide funding for projects covering a wide array of transport and communications infrastructure and equipment.

The EIB's contribution is limited to 50 percent of the cost of capital assets. The maturity of loans may run to 20 years since it operates on a non-profit making basis, lending rates clearly reflect the cost, for each currency, of its borrowing with a standard margin of 0.15 percent added to cover operating expenses.

Loans can be arranged at fixed rates, revisable fixed rates, variable rates or variable rates converted into fixed rates. A grace period on repayment of principal may be allowed in line with the project implementation period. The total amount of loans in the transport sector was 1.8 billion Ecu in 1991.

The EIB is, then, already an important source of funds for infrastructure investment. But the Bank operates under statutory constraints which do not allow the assumption of equity stakes or to issue guarantees. Because of this institutional rigidity, the EIB cannot play a more active role in the promotion of investment projects.

Loans are also provided by other institutions such as the European Community for Steel and Coal (CECA), but with similar constraints. From 1988 to 1991, CECA gave a total of 1.1 billion Ecu's in loans for infrastructure projects.

The Maastricht Treaty on European Union, signed in February 1992, formally recognized the importance of trans-European networks. As a result, the Community has a priority task to promote and support the rapid development of transport networks. The responsibility for planning infrastructure will remain with the individual EC countries. The Community will provide guidance and political and financial support to facilitate network integration.

The key concept of "European interest" and the formal endorsement of specific missing links and projects by the Community institutions will provide a strong support and will limit risks related to the planning phase. New financial instruments, including loan guarantees or deferred interest payments will contribute to the implementation of this Community policy. During the Edinburgh summit in December 1992, it was decided to create a "European Investment Fund" managed by the EIB that will provide guarantees for infrastructure projects. This will require a change in the EIB statutes.

In conjunction with these new instruments and other Community funds, the Regional Fund and the Cohesion Fund will support new projects in less developed regions. These measures will then create favorable conditions for private investors and could generate a catalytic effect.

5. Missing Links and Trans-European Networks

In order to promote the inter-connection and inter-operability of the networks it is essential:

* To establish a reference framework, a masterplan, for trans-European networks laying down the objectives and priorities;

* To identify a limited number of projects of Community interest for the EC;

* To focus funding on these key projects in order to solve the problem of interlinking of national networks.

But, presently, international transport within the European Community is still a relatively limited part of the total traffic, both for passenger and freight transport. That is the reason why frontier effects are so evident, especially for railway services. The level and quality of services are very poor due to the lack of demand. That is the reason why these are named "missing links".

If we look at these missing links with traditional project-oriented methods, there is no chance of involving private investors in most of then. Because of the frontier effect and the lack of demand on a short and long term perspective, the internal rate of return and, more generally, the profitability of these missing links is very low. In a short or medium term perspective, the level of traffic remains too low to justify investment.

Thus, it is clear that the European Community must focus its contribution on these missing links. The Council of Ministers has adopted (December 1991) masterplans for trans-European networks, including a list of missing links. For example, 12 missing links have been identified in the case of the high speed rail network.

At the same time, the EC Council of Transport Ministers made a very interesting declaration of principles and adopted a directive on the need to open up rail infrastructures to users other than the national companies and to separate the networks from transport services, at least from an accountability viewpoint.

Feasibility studies for those projects of European interest to analyze both technical, economical, financial and managerial issues will be financed by the Community. The Community could take a lead in creating new financial instruments such as the European Investment Fund, launched in Edinburgh (December 1992). The key issue is to create new specialized operators able to efficiently combine private and public financing. This issue is presently discussed in many working groups, but until now no clear decision has been taken.

6. Prospects

The problems related with financing European infrastructure networks are strongly connected with institutional ones. The European Countries have a key role to play in defining, developing and promoting trans-European networks. The demand for network services in Europe will increase rapidly in the near future. Demand is driven by the need to make up for past under-investment and by the recent implementation of the single market. In a single market community, extensive road, rail, air, and other networks must be planned involving goodwill and ongoing cooperation beyond national frontiers.

Efficient trans-European networks will be a catalyst for the single market. The Treaty of Maastricht implementation will increase the current pressure in this domain.

Estimates of future requirements are 80-90 billion Ecu per annum. This represents about 1.5 percent of output. According to European Community estimates, about 20 percent of required transport infrastructure investment -- that is to say 18 billion Ecu annually -- are for projects of interest for the Community as a whole:

* 10 billion Ecu for motorway links and upgrades,
* 5 billion Ecu for high speed trains,
* 1.5-2 billion Ecu for ports,
* 1 billion Ecu for inland waterways,
* 200-300 million Ecu for multi-modal facilities.

The Community will fund only a limited percentage of these investments directly. Due to subsidiarity, the Community's task will not be to subsidize these projects, but to support efforts both from public (national and regional governments) and private investors. The Community will promote mixed solutions in order to develop synergies between private and public interests. The European Investment Fund in association with EIB loans will be a key tool to make this possible and will act as a catalyst. The creation of this fund specialized in infrastructure investment will issue guarantees and will thus allow private investors to overcome administrative, legal, prudential and more generally financial obstacles. The success of this infrastructure challenge facing Europe is crucial for Europe's future, its prosperity and its quality of life.

References

BEI, 1991, *Communications*, September.

Commission des Communautés Européennes, 1992, Le développement futur de la politique commune des transports -- approche globale pour détermination d'un cadre communautaire garant d'une mobilité durable.

European Bankers Round Table, 1990, *Private Financing of Major Infrastructure Projects*, September.

European Round Table of Industrialists, 1984, *Missing Links -- Upgrading Europe's Transborder Ground Transport Infrastructure*, ERTI, Brussels.

European Round Table of Industrialists, 1991, *Missing Networks -- A European Challenge, Proposals for the Renewal of Europe's Infrastructure*, ERTI, Brussels.

European Round Table of Industrialists, 1992, *Growing Together -- One Infrastructure for Europe*, A Report by the Working Group on Infrastructure, ERTI, Brussels.

Fondation pour l'Etude de Droit et des Usages du Commerce International (FEDUCI), *Financement Privé d'Ouvrages Publics à l'Horizon 1993*, Colloque de Paris, Mars 26-27.

Gerardin, B., 1989, *Private and Public Investment in Transport, Possibilities and Cost*, Rapport Introductif de la Table Ronde N° 81 "Private and Public Investment in Transport" 11-12 Mai 1989, Paris.

Gerardin, B., 1990, Transport Infrastructure -- Networks in Europe -- Deregulation of Transport and European Integration, *European Transport Towards 1992 and Beyond - Developments and Requirements*, European Transport Planning Colloquium, March 29-30.

Gerardin, B., 1990, Missing Networks in Europe, A Case Study: the European Rapid Train Network, in *Missing Networks in Europe*, NECTAR Study Prepared for the Round Table of Industrialists.

Gerardin, B. and Viegas, J. 1990, *European Transport Infrastructure and Networks: Current Policies and Trends*, Communication Présentée à la Conférence NECTAR, Amsterdam, Mars 18-20.

Rathery, A., 1988, Les Investissements dans les Infrastructures de Transport des Pays de la CEMT au cours de la Période 1975-1988, *Transport* 331.

Yates, C.M., 1992, *Survey of Private Finance for Road Infrastructure*, PTRC Summer Annual Meeting, Nomura Research Institute UK, September 14-18.

TRANSPORT IN A UNIFIED EUROPE. Policies and Challenges.
D. Banister and J. Berechman (Editors)

Chapter Fifteen

INVESTING IN TRANSPORT INFRASTRUCTURE

David Banister

1. The Impending Crisis for Transport Infrastructure

The success of cities and regions has always been based on the quality of their infrastructure. This in turn requires a commitment over a long period of time to continued new investment and replacement of existing stock. Infrastructure is the durable capital of the city and a country, and its location is fixed. In the transport sector it includes roads, railways, communications (e.g., air traffic control), and terminals. Often the services which are obtained from the infrastructure have a spatial dimension (e.g., the distribution of the rail network), with the benefit from that service declining as distance from the supply point increases (e.g., stations). Their key characteristics are that many people benefit from a single infrastructure, that they can be used over and over again, that the infrastructure remains when people and businesses move in and out of an area, and that it provides the means for integration and coordination of activities over time and space. The infrastructure forms the arteries of cities and nations, and the communications systems are the nerves. The health and prosperity of cities and nations depends on the quality of these networks.

This chapter takes a Europe-wide view of the transport infrastructure and argues the case for massive increases in investment required to upgrade that infrastructure. It also argues for new institutional and organizational structures (Section 3), for new methods for financing the infrastructure (Section 4), and for a vision of a Europe-wide strategy of transport and planning (Section 5). The premise taken is that investment is required in all forms of transport infrastructure -- for new construction, for the expansion of existing infrastructure, and for the reconstruction of existing infrastructure -- over a substantial period of time. It is realized that this strategy is only part of the picture as better use can be made of the available infrastructure through technology (e.g., route guidance and passenger information systems), through better management of the system, through pricing (see Jones, this volume), and through better local transport services (see Banister et al. and Andersen, this volume).

Much recent discussion has focused on the inadequacy of the existing infrastructure (e.g., Group Transport 2000 Plus, 1990):

> the overcrowding and saturation of new facilities even at the moment of commission, the need for new links, the choice of layouts, gauges, operating methods. But, above all, the people consulted focused on infrastructure costs, and many of them talked in terms of passing those costs directly to the users (p. 11).

The costs of constructing new infrastructure, and maintaining and replacing existing infrastructure are considerable, and the massive investments in the 1950s and 1960s have been followed by stagnation and decline. Since 1975, investment on inland transport has fallen in Western Europe by 20 percent in real terms, and it has halved as a proportion of Gross Domestic Product (GDP) to 0.8 percent. This reduction in infrastructure investment reflected general reductions in public expenditure, the world recession in the 1970s resulting from high oil prices, and the generally lower levels of increase in transport demand. Decisions to delay investment in the transport infrastructure takes time to show an effect and, given the short term time horizons of politicians, any delay in commitments to expensive projects have meant savings in public budgets and lower taxes. Investment decisions were delayed, particularly expensive new links between countries and those which involved tunnelling.

With the economic upturn in the 1980s, there was unprecedented growth in transport demand, but it also became apparent that growth in transport demand had continued throughout the 1970s as well. Investment had not been reduced because of reductions in demand for mobility, but for other macroeconomic reasons such as pressures on public budgets, high interest rates, and industrial recession. Between 1970 and 1990, annual economic growth in the EC was 2.6 percent in real terms. Growth in passenger travel was 3.1 percent per annum and growth in freight traffic was 2.3 percent per annum, with the figure for growth in road traffic higher than those for rail. Since 1980, air travel in the EC has been growing by 6.1 percent per annum. All forms of transport in the EC have continued to grow (see Table 1), with the exception of rail freight. Most pronounced increases are for air, road freight and road passenger travel (see Table 2).

TABLE 1

Evolution of Transport in the Community, 1970-1990

	Transport in Billion Ton-Km or Passenger-Km		Market Share in Ton-Km or Passenger-Km	
	1970	1990	1970	1990
1. Inland				
Freight				
- Road	377	797	55.0	73.9
- Inland Waterways	101	105	14.7	9.7
- Rail	207	176	30.3	16.3
TOTAL	685	1,078	100.0	100.0
Passengers				
- Road (car/bus)	1,604	3,089	87.8	87.9
- Rail	182	231	10.0	6.6
TOTAL	1,786	3,320	100.0	100.0
2. Air[a]				
Freight	-	196	-	-
Passengers	41	-	2.2	5.6
3. Maritime				
Freight	85	100	-	-
Passengers	-	-	-	-

Note: [a]Air figures are estimates of traffic departing and landing inside the EC only.

Source: Commission for the European Communities (1992b).

That growth is expected to continue as the following forecasts show:

* Road and rail freight haulage will increase by 42 percent and 33 percent, respectively, (from 805 billion ton-kilometers to 1139 billion ton-kilometers by 2010).

TABLE 2

Evolution of Road Vehicles and Road Traffic in the Community, 1970-1987

	1970	1987	Yearly Growth in % 1970-1987
Passenger cars in use (thousands)	57,459	116,947	4.3
Goods vehicles in use (thousands)	7,419	12,881	3.3
Vehicle-Km passenger cars (Billions)	760.5	1,399	3.7
Vehicle-Km goods vehicles (Billions)	157.6	275.4	3.3

Source: European Commission (1992b).

* Car ownership will increase (by 2010) by 45 percent (1985, 115 million cars; 2010, 167 million cars), giving EC averages of 503 cars per 1000 inhabitants (the 1990 level was 381 cars per 1000 inhabitants).

* Car travel will rise by 25 percent from 1727 billion kilometers (1990) to 2166 billion kilometers (2010), and air travel will rise by 74 percent.

The bare facts itemized here only relate to the expected growth in travel demand. There are other factors which may also add to that demand:

* Demographic changes are taking place in Europe with the restructuring of households, more part time and female participation, more working from home, with the motorization effect, increased levels of affluence and the grey revolution, which will all lead to increased levels of mobility.

* Technological changes (such as the extensive use of road transport informatics and advanced transport telematics) will again seek to make travel easier, either through management and control systems applied at the network level, or through guidance and information systems purchased by individual drivers.

* Industry in Europe is being restructured with the switch from basic manufacturing industry to a service based economy based on high technology industry. The service sector accounted for 58 percent of the EC GDP in 1985, and by the year 2000 this will have increased to 66 percent. Most of the growth will be centralized at the core of the EC, but other factors suggest that the distribution

of industry will be more complex. There may be a migration of industry to Southern Europe (the Sunbelt), where the quality of life is good and the costs of labor are cheaper.

* New manufacturing processes allow flexible location of industry and distribution centers, and the new telecommunications infrastructure also permits dispersion to accessible locations. However, underlying all these factors is the requirement for a high quality infrastructure which can accommodate the scale of changes itemized here.

Explanations of these transport trends and secular changes are given in Banister and Berechman, and Button (this volume).

The Group Transport 2000 Plus (1990) summarized the situation as follows:

> European transport faces a serious impending crisis. All the indicators point to this occurring when the Single Market is operational and at a time when there will be a massive increase in the movement of goods and services between the European Community and Eastern Europe. In all likelihood the crisis will paralyse the system, and slow down economic progress, provoke serious social tension, increase damage to the environment and destroy the balance in the central and peripheral regions of the continent. The process of building a unified Europe will be setback severely. Airports, rail systems, roads and urban centers have all faced a traffic growth at a rate far outstripping the increase in infrastructural capacity (p. 45).

The cycle of production and consumption within the transport sector has been disrupted. Growth in demand (consumption) is often short term and relates closely to GDP and levels of individual affluence. The trends over the last 20 years in the demand for travel has reflected these factors, with the underlying growth being enhanced or diminished according to the macroeconomic circumstances. The investment (production) cycle is long term and requires a commitment over a period of time. The lead time required from project generation, the construction time, the continuous process of maintenance, and the ultimate replacement of the transport infrastructure requires this continuity of funding. At any stage in the process the continuity can be broken with decisions on investment being delayed. The short term costs are small, but each delayed decision adds to the "impending crisis" identified above by Group Transport 2000 Plus (1990). One possible scenario would be that all infrastructure reaches the end of its useful life at the same time, as decisions on new investments and maintenance continue to be delayed.

2. Examples of Key Infrastructure Problems and Decisions

The quality of the transport infrastructure is generally high, and within the core area there are several international airports, a high density of roads and railway services. But the growth in traffic and congestion frequently disrupts transport systems and generates more bottlenecks (Gerardin and Viegas, 1992). Figure 1 illustrates the key transport problems in Europe. Congestion is now endemic in both urban and air travel. The consequences are well known and include reductions in effective capacity and mobility, increases in energy consumption and emissions of pollutants, and inefficient use of time. The social and economic costs of road congestion have been estimated at £15 billion a year in Great Britain (20 billion Ecu) and 1 billion Guilders for the Netherlands (European Community, 1992b). By the year 2010, with a 70-percent increase in car use, the costs of congestion in the Netherlands could rise to 4 billion Guilder (1.8 billion Ecu).

Figure 2 presents the likely impact of the growth in demand for air travel over the next ten years as more airports reach their frequency capacity. Half of the 46 major European airports will reach their capacity by 1996, and over two-thirds by 2000. Delayed flights have already increased from 13 percent in 1986 to 23 percent in 1989 (European Conference of Ministers of Transport, 1992). With respect to air traffic control, there is no overall system designed to coordinate all services. There are 22 systems operated out of 44 control centers with only limited coordination through Eurocontrol (Maggi et al., 1992). Automated systems are available, but most contact is still verbal with communication being carried out through a multiplicity of languages (see Barrett, this volume). The costs of airline congestion in Europe are now (1988) put at 1.4 billion Ecu (European Community, 1992b).

The difficulties of implementing a common strategy for infrastructure investment in Europe can best be illustrated with respect to the proposals for high speed trains (see Viegas and Blum, this volume). Within Europe, most inter-city passenger travel is in the range 200-1000 kilometers, which makes it ideal for high speed rail operation. There are four types of approach:

* Modernization of existing infrastructure to allow for speeds of 200-250 kilometers/hour, adopted in Great Britain.

* Introduction of the tilting train where the coaches "lean" on curves which allow for speeds up to 250 kilometers/hour, experimented with in Great Britain (the Advanced Passenger Train) and in Italy (Pendolino).

* Construction of a new line to accommodate both passenger and freight trains to allow for speeds of 250-280 kilometers/hour, adopted in Germany (ICE).

* Construction of a new line reserved for passenger trains to allow for speeds of 250-330 kilometers/hour, adopted in France (TGV).

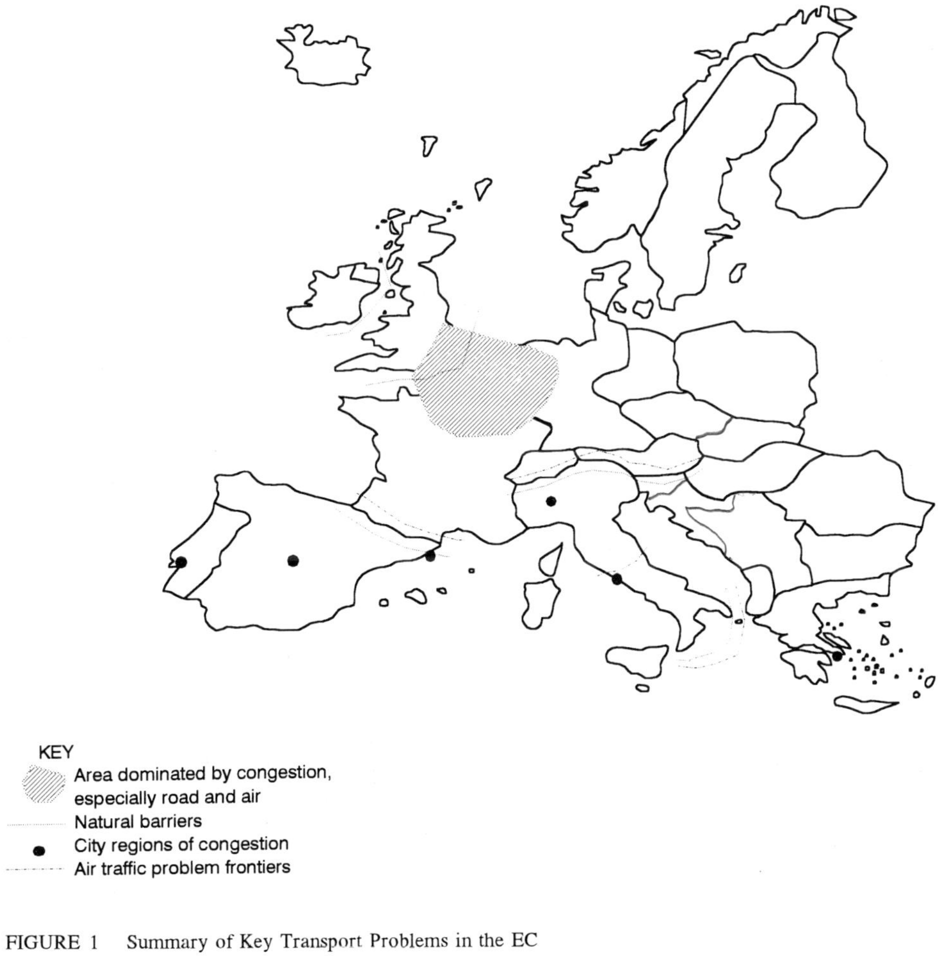

FIGURE 1 Summary of Key Transport Problems in the EC

Source: Group Transport 2000 Plus (1990).

In 1989, the Community of European Railways, which includes the 12 EC countries plus Austria and Switzerland, presented a plan for a European high speed rail network with 30,000 kilometers of high speed track which would cut rail travel times in Europe by half (see Figure 3). The cost of such a network would be considerable (120 billion Ecu), as both infrastructure and rolling stock would be required. Completion of the network could be achieved by 2015, and it would involve 9,000 kilometers of new track, some 15,000 kilometers of upgraded track, and 6,000 kilometers of link track. This European masterplan for railways has been supported by the EC in its directive on the Development of Community Railways (1991).

However, even plans such as these on a European scale raises problems in addition to those of the physical infrastructure and financing. The French TGV runs on tracks built exclusively for fast passenger transport, while the German ICE uses heavier duty track

FIGURE 2 Frequency Limited Airports in Europe

Source: Association of European Airlines (1987).

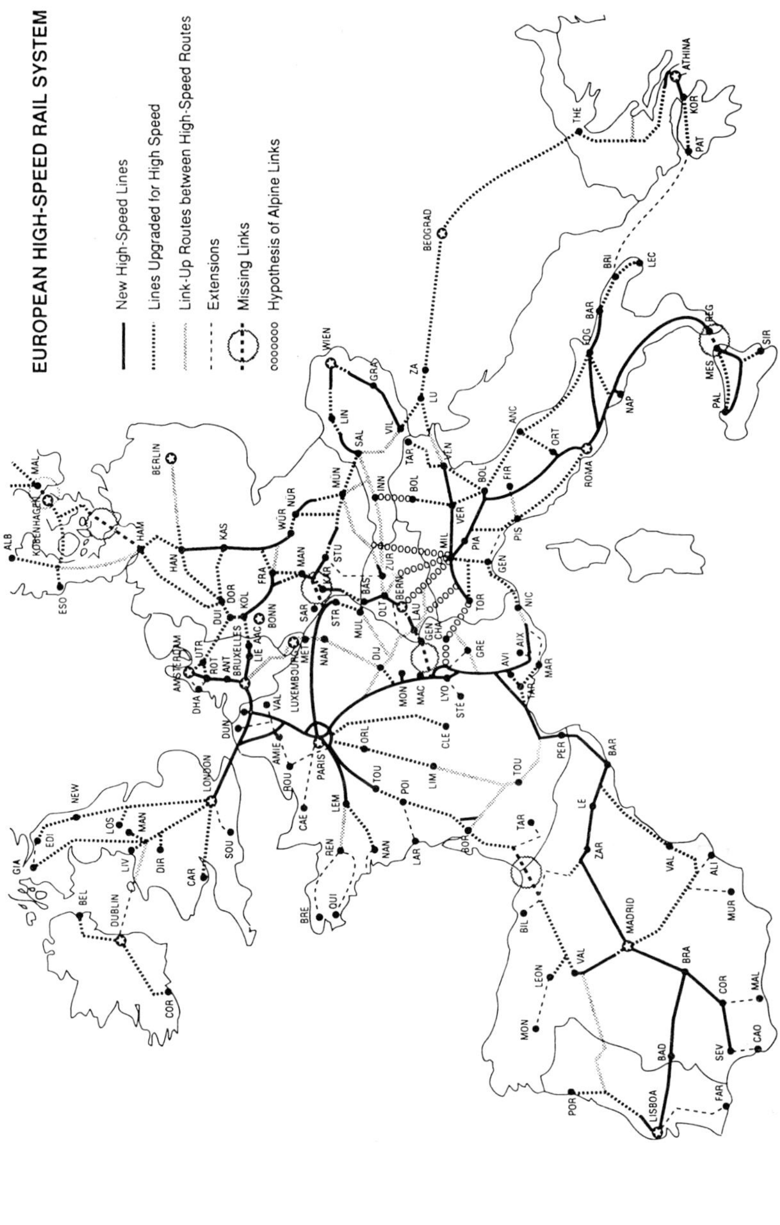

FIGURE 3 The European High Speed Rail Network

suitable for freight and passenger services. An organizational strategy is required to ensure that standards of construction allow through running of services, and such a decision might not come from the national railway companies. Similarly, there are incompatibilities in communications systems (software) between the TGV and ICE networks, and improvements in control technology are required to allow joint running of services at varying speeds. Otherwise, combined operations involving high speed trains (160-200 kilometers/hour average) and TGV/ICE (>200 kilometers/hour average) would reduce the speed and capacity of the network as would combined freight and passenger services on the same track.

The European rail network cannot meet today's requirements. Most dates from over 100 years ago and was not conceived as an international network. National networks have simply been linked up. The proposals for a European high speed rail network go much further than meeting the forecasted growth in travel demand. It offers a means for rail to effectively compete with air, and interchanges on the high speed rail network are likely to develop as the new accessible growth poles. International cooperation is also important in funding such a network, in harmonizing the technology, in joint operations (including rolling stock and ticketing), and in revenue and cost-sharing. The success (or failure) of the high speed rail network will have a symbolic role in unified Europe.

3. The Role of the European Community

Transport was identified in the Treaty of Rome (1957) as one of the areas for development of a common policy. Since then, progress has been slow, with the Single European Act (1986) requiring the removal of physical barriers (at frontiers), reductions in technical barriers, and harmonization of fiscal barriers. In 1985, the European Parliament asked the European Court of Justice to officially recognize the lack of a European Transport Policy and that this failure was due to the inefficiency of the European Council of Ministers (Commission of the European Communities, 1985). In 1986, the Commission put forward proposals for a medium term plan on transport infrastructure (European Parliament, 1991). It described the principal deficiencies of the European transport network; the ways in which the Community could take action to resolve them; the ways in which the Community could declare an interest so that Community action would be possible; and it identified the needs for overall financial investments in infrastructures. The Council of Ministers was reluctant to accept that proposal, and in 1988 the Commission submitted a four year plan extending to 1992 which coincided with the introduction of the Single Market. Again, there was resistance from the Council and the Commission presented more modest proposals which concentrated available resources on a limited number of projects regarded as the most important. This proposal was accepted in November 1990.

Many international initiatives concerning transport have not come from the EC but from the industry itself. For example, the proposal for an international network of high speed trains has come from the Community of European Railways (Section 3 and Viegas and Blum, this volume). The role of the EC has been of secondary importance and restricted to issuing directives such as those on the environment, standards for road freight, cabotage, and reductions in custom's formalities. The Maastricht Agreement (1991) has expanded transport's role to include common rules on international transport and improvements in transport safety.

The EC budget for transport infrastructure investment is limited and any increase in that budget has been resisted by Ministers due to a conflict with national interests and the notions of subsidiarity. Contributions have been made to specific projects, often under the European Regional Development Fund (ERDF) and European cohesion programs. The ERDF has allocated 43 percent of its expenditure (1983-1987) to infrastructure projects of Community interest (Vickerman, 1991). However, only 40 percent of EC territory is eligible for ERDF financing. In Greece, 24 percent of ERDF funding investment is for transport infrastructure, and the corresponding figures for Portugal, Spain, Italy and Ireland are 18, 47, 10, and 39 percent, respectively (European Parliament, 1991). It is only in the air and telecommunications markets that the private sector has been fully involved, and it is here that most of the new investment has taken place (see Table 3). The possibilities for an enhanced role for the private sector, either on its own or through joint ventures with the public sector, have not yet been fully explored for a wider range of infrastructure projects including road and rail (Gerardin, 1989).

The other main agency has been the European Investment Bank (EIB), which co-finances projects (up to a maximum 50-percent contribution) designed to modernize Europe's economy. Between the date of its establishment (December 31, 1982) and 1985, the EIB allocated just over 20 percent of all its financing operations within the Community to transport. More recently (1986-1990), the EIB has further increased its support to over 15 billion Ecus (37 percent of its total budget) for transport and telecommunications infrastructure and equipment (see Table 3). Assessment of projects are based on financial criteria related to the potential profitability of the project (see Gerardin, this volume). The total allocation to transport and telecommunications has increased as follows:

1986	1,945 Million Ecu
1987	1,661 Million Ecu
1988	2,980 Million Ecu
1989	4,001 Million Ecu
1990	4,518 Million Ecu

To enhance European integration, the EIB has given priority to projects which:

* Help to develop regions in difficulties;

* Achieve energy savings or other energy-related investment so to reduce the EC's dependence on oil;

TABLE 3

EIB Financing for Transport and Telecommunications, 1986-1990 (in Million Ecu)

Country	Overland Transport	Air Transport	Shipping	Tele-comms[a]	TOTAL
Belgium	-	6.0	-	-	6.0
Denmark	476.1	241.2	5.6	188.5	991.4
Germany	252.3	30.1	1.2	-	283.5
Greece	208.0	7.4	0.9	-	216.3
Spain	594.7	652.1	40.3	1,203.8	2,490.8
France	2,448.5	45.1	15.8	85.3	2,594.6
Ireland	150.7	144.9	-	135.3	430.9
Italy	1,294.1	414.4	302.0	2,311.5	4,322.0
Luxembourg	-	-	1.6	-	1.6
Netherlands	-	367.3	-	-	376.3
Portugal	639.0	53.6	57.7	176.7	927.0
United Kingdom	640.3	731.0	77.4	44.4	1,892.2
Article 18	-	-	-	660.8	660.8
TOTAL	6,703.7	2,693.1	502.5	5,205.4	15,104.0

Note: [a]Telecomms includes telecommunications and telecommunications satellites; Article 18 projects are located outside the EC (submarine cables, satellites, etc.).

Source: European Investment Bank (1991).

* Assist in European economic integration or towards the achievement of Community objectives such as protection of the environment;

* Modernize and promote sectors with high innovation potential including advanced technology (Abbati, 1986).

EIB loans are generally repayable over 8 to 20 years, and loans can be backed by financial guarantees or by the assets represented in the project itself.

Most recently, the Edinburgh Council (December 1992) recognized the problem by setting up a new European Investment Fund to help fill the *missing links* in European infrastructure and also extended the lending facility of the European Investment Bank. It will now be easier for financial markets to back large infrastructure projects for trans-European networks, including transport, telecommunications and energy. The EIB will contribute 40 percent of the fund's capital of 2 billion Ecus with the remainder coming from the Community (30 percent) and the private and public sectors (30 percent). It is estimated that the Fund could support investment projects worth up to 20 billion Ecus. The crucial assumption here is the expectation that the limited capital in the new Fund will generate this level of borrowing -- a gearing ratio of 10 to 1 is very high. Nevertheless, this is an important step forward in EC thinking as it is the first time that a new financial instrument has been set up in this area. Previously, the Council had confined itself to laying down the objectives of an infrastructure policy and identifying the principal criteria for establishing whether that project is of Community interest. The EIB has recently (1993) approved 14 new infrastructure projects worth a notional 1 billion Ecu, including a Danish rail electrification scheme and an extension to Turin airport. It seems that projects ready to start or already underway have been approved, but a coherent strategy has not emerged. The new European Investment Fund will not be approved before October 1993, and this means that 1994 is the earliest start date for major new infrastructure projects.

However, across the EC there is still no infrastructure policy. The long term loans provided by the EIB support individual projects submitted separately by public and private promoters in each EC country. Although it is recognized that international travel is only a small part of overall travel, some corridors are already at capacity, there are many missing links in the European network, and demand will increase dramatically as a result of the Single Market (see Hauser and Maggi, this volume). Some strategy seems to be essential, particularly when transport policy is set against competition policy, regional development policy and environmental policy within the EC. Congestion in the core area of the EC has resulted from:

* A high density population and a high concentration of economic activities in those regions;

* North-south traffic crosses through this area and it is concentrated in a limited number of congested corridors; and

* Rapid and recent development of east-west flows related to the political and economic changes in central and eastern Europe.

The EC is now proposing a Community strategy based on *sustainable mobility* (Commission of the European Communities, 1992a). A new framework is proposed which sets out strict environmental standards for all modes of transport, for quality standards on pollution, for encouraging environment-friendly modes, and for the promotion of guidelines for infrastructure and the development of urban transport. These guidelines for the development and assessment of Community infrastructure projects would:

> discourage unnecessary transport demand and encourage where appropriate the development of alternatives to road transport, such as railway, inland waterways and combined transport. Guidelines for the conversion and upgrading of relinquished infrastructure, particularly for the purpose of "soft" transport, would be implemented (para. 127).

The common strategy of sustainable mobility should:

> contain the impact of transport on the environment, while allowing transport to continue to fulfil its economic and social functions, particularly in the context of the Single Market, and thus ensure the long term development of transport in the Community. It should also contribute to social and economic cohesion in the Community and to the creation of new opportunities for the peripheral regions (para. 128).

In the EC White Paper on a Common Transport Policy (Commission of the European Communities, 1992b), one of the main themes has been trans-European networks. Incompatibilities between national transport systems have been highlighted, including inadequate interconnections, missing links and bottlenecks, and obstacles to inter-operations. All of these lead to inefficiencies. The EC has had only a limited policy role mainly through the Committee on Transport Infrastructure (set up in 1978), but with thc principal financial contributions coming from the structural funds and instruments which have been mentioned previously:

* ERDF credits (1975-1991) for transport infrastructure of 16 billion Ecu,

* EIB loans (1982-1991) for transport infrastructure of 14 billion Ecu,

* European Coal and Steel Community loans (1987-1991) to TGV track in France and Spain and to canals 1.2 billion Ecu.

The EC now proposes to establish and develop a

> trans-European transport network, within a framework of a system of open and competitive markets, through the promotion of interconnections and inter-operability of national networks and access thereto. It must take particular account of the need to link island, landlocked and peripheral regions with the central regions of the Community (Commission of the European Communities, 1992b, para. 140).

The goal is to improve the integration of the Community transport system and not the improvement of the transport infrastructure in general. It is likely that much of the funding will continue to be allocated to the geographically isolated regions (see Kristiansen, this volume).

On the crucial question of financing, the White Paper (European Commission, 1992b) is pessimistic. The general level of investment in transport infrastructure has been stagnant at about 1 percent of GDP. The volume of investment required for the period 1990-2010 is nearly 1,500 billion Ecu (1.5 percent of GDP: European Commission, 1992b, para. 143). This level is far in excess of the resources available to the EC even if its mandate would permit such intervention. Its role is limited to financing feasibility studies, loan guarantees, and interest rate subsidies. In addition, the EC may have a major dilemma. On the one hand, it sees under-investment in transport infrastructure, but on the other hand it is arguing for sustainable mobility and protection of the environment. It could be argued that these two objectives are incompatible (see Himanen et al., this volume).

The EC policies on infrastructure now extend beyond the 12 Community members, and there is a specific provision for cooperation with third countries. The Prague Declaration adopted by the Pan European Transport Conference in 1991 emphasized the necessity of developing transport networks on a truly European scale and of integrating the greater European transport market. Measures have already been taken with the European Economic Area agreement and transit agreements with Switzerland and Austria. Trade between East and West Europe will increase movements in both directions by more than 50 percent (1990-2000), which in turn will place considerable pressure on the links where little investment has taken place for the past 40 years (European Parliament, 1991; see Blum and Leibbrand, and Button, this volume).

4. Financing the New Investment

The basic political questions concern the amount of infrastructure which should be provided -- whether it should meet unconstrained demand or whether demand should be constrained -- and how it should be financed. Most transport projects are large scale, involve high risk, and have long payback periods. It is only where the private sector has a virtual monopoly position (e.g., in road bridges across estuaries) that real interest has been raised. Transport projects are notorious for their cost overruns, for technical deficiencies in construction and consequent high maintenance costs, and for optimism in their estimates of future demand -- the Channel Tunnel project illustrates all of these problems as does the proposed link between Denmark and Sweden (see Kristiansen, this volume).

In the past, the public sector has been the main contributor, but with the increasing costs of new transport projects and with the desire of governments to reduce public deficits, new sources of capital are required. The most obvious means to raise finance would be to charge tolls on existing motorways. It has been estimated (Keating, 1992) that tolls of 5 pence per mile (similar to current toll levels on French auto routes) on UK motorways would raise about £2 billion per annum; its extension to other roads and urban areas would raise £6 billion per annum. The key argument is whether the tolls are seen as a tax to increase exchequer revenues or a charge which can be reinvested in the transport system (see Jones, this volume).

The private sector is unlikely to invest in major projects unless the conditions are favorable and a reasonable rate of return can be obtained to satisfy their own shareholders. This means that low risk projects would be most desirable:

* To maintain a virtual monopoly position;

* To meet high levels of existing demand and anticipated growth in that demand;

* To ensure a payback over the medium term (about 10 years);

* To have control over the levels of pricing for the new or upgraded infrastructure;

* To have some guarantee from government of the period over which revenues from tolls will accrue to the private sector.

In most cases, one or more of these conditions are not met and as a consequence the private sector has been reluctant about making any firm commitment (see Gerardin, this volume).

It is in partnership between the private and public sectors where most potential lies. The public sector can anticipate the growth in demand which results from the growth in the economy, rising income levels, and from new developments. It can also assist in the land assembly process and in the public inquiry so that time from project inception to completion is minimized. In certain situations, it can also help with the costs of construction of the actual infrastructure, but it is the private sector which will manage and run the facility, including setting the levels of tolls or fares. New private companies could be set up to build and operate the infrastructure, and finance can be raised in a number of ways:

* Through loans from the European Investment Bank and the European Community's European Coal and Steel Community, the Regional Development Funds, and the new European Investment Fund;

* Through transport bonds and other long term investments (such as pension funds) which are extensively used in Japan;

* Through tax incentives to the private sector by making their capital contributions tax deductible;

* Through tolls and road pricing; and

* Through employment taxes (as in Paris and other French cities) or a tax on petrol (as in Germany and the U.S.; see Pucher et al., this volume).

At present there seems to be an impasse between the public and private sectors which must be bridged. Each has an important role to play in the construction, renewal and maintenance of the road, rail and air transport infrastructure. Over the next decade it is likely that new means of financing will be established, yet it should be noted that the public sector cannot withdraw completely. Much of the funding will still remain the responsibility of the public sector, but the role for transport planning must be to facilitate private sector and joint ventures through advice, predictions, land assembly, and accelerated public inquiry procedures. The public sector still has a key role to play:

* Where the market fails and intervention occurs for accessibility, distributional and equity reasons;

* Where there are significant externalities involving the use of non-renewable resources, land acquisition, safety, and environmental concerns;

* Where transport interacts with other sectors, such as the generation effects of new developments and priorities given for regional or local development objectives;

* Where transport has national and international implications, such as promoting a capital city (e.g. London or Paris) as a world city or maintaining high quality international air and rail links.

5. Transport and Infrastructure in Europe in the Year 2000

The European Round Table of Industrialists (1988) has been most vociferous in its criticism of the lack of a strategy on European infrastructure and among the most radical in its proposals. More generally, it seems that there is agreement over the problems and the options for infrastructure investment, and the next stage is to define the means by which priority can be allocated. Gerardin and Viegas (1992) suggest the following:

* Regional policy must be developed to balance the demand for and the supply of transport capacity to accommodate future changes in those patterns. This means that adequate levels of funding have to be guaranteed so that the necessary infrastructure is ready at the time it is needed.

* European institutions have an important role to play in the coordination of regional policies, in the provision of investment, and in the dissemination of information between regions.

* Transport problems and solutions must be dealt with as a multi-modal problem so that the best attributes of each mode can be used. These transport links are particularly important when trans-European networks are being planned.

* Transparency must be ensured between the costs of providing the infrastructure and user charges. Modernization and construction of new networks in Europe require investment on a massive scale. User charges will increase but cannot assume the total burden.

* The private sector has a larger role to play and projects with joint funding will have to balance the internal profitability of the project with the positive or negative external effects.

* The long time scales involved in project development mean increased levels of risk, therefore, joint projects between the public and private sectors require a clear and well-managed planning process.

* The regions represent the decentralized power of Europe and can respond to local requirements; it is important to encourage collaboration between transport and regional development.

The proper role for transport in the process of economic integration in the EC has not been understood and short term national interests have dominated. National transport policies may have reinforced existing barriers to integration (Vickerman, 1991).

In conclusion, five important components of a policy on European infrastructure can be highlighted:

* There needs to be a European strategy for transport and communications infrastructure investment which can be agreed to by all 12 EC countries and followed over a period of time. In the past, transport planning at both the national and international levels has been primarily concerned with the expansion of the physical capacity to meet the inexorable growth in demand. Even in time of recession, it seems that demand continues to rise. Decisions have been taken

on an annual basis as most transport infrastructure is funded from public expenditure, when continuity of both policy and funding over a period of time is required.

* The Group Transport 2000 Plus (1990) has suggested the imposition of a European Infrastructure Fund which would act as an autonomous source for all infrastructure investment with an EC dimension and be related to the number of units of energy consumed. Substantial sums would be raised from the motorist (estimated at 1 billion Ecu per year) and the scheme could be expanded to other European countries on the same basis. Acceptance of the levy would only be gained if the monies raised were used for infrastructure investment and not disappear into other uses. However, such a decision might contradict notions of subsidiarity, and it could be argued that most transport infrastructure investment should be the responsibility of national governments. Both the scale and the international nature of most transport infrastructure investment suggests that decisions need to be placed within an international strategy.

* Solutions are often seen as relating to one mode of transport. Increasingly, multi-modal options must be considered. Here, interchange points in the network which are most accessible will act as growth centers. This has already happened at international airports and at major nodes on the international road and rail networks (e.g., at the Paris Charles de Gaulle Airport and at the Amsterdam Schiphol Airport). Most recently, construction has started on La Cite de l'Europe, a large shopping complex in Calais aimed at users of the new Channel Tunnel. The scheme has allocated 71,000 square meters to a range of retail and leisure activities at a location likely to see a massive growth in traffic as more than 18.5 million people are expected to cross the channel by coach and car after 1995, 13.5 million of them through the tunnel.

* Clear links must be established between a European infrastructure policy and the allocation of costs to users which fully reflect the external costs imposed. However, even here, there may be conflicts between this strategy and the broader requirements of providing infrastructure for social and regional development objectives. There needs to be a balance between these two fundamental European Community policy objectives.

* Transport planning now needs to change emphasis from its primary concern over the quality and quantity of the physical infrastructure to include other factors such

as organizational, financing, technology, and environmental dimensions. Methods are needed to explore the role that information technology can have in increasing capacity; the means by which a continuous flow of private and public funding, together with loans from the European Investment Bank, can be guaranteed over a period of time; the means by which the full costs of travel can be imposed on the user, either through road pricing, or through a levy (e.g., the proposed European Infrastructure Fund; see component 2, above), or through a carbon tax; the appropriate balance between environmental concerns over transport and the considerable benefits that greater mobility and accessibility can bring to society; and the appropriate institutional structure for decision making at the national and international levels. The establishment of the European Investment Fund is a key move in this direction.

The consequences of the growth in transport demand, the lack of investment in the infrastructure, and the absence of a vision for Europe are now being reaped. These factors, together with the changes in demographic and industrial structure and technological innovation have all resulted in new mobility, high energy costs, and environmental degradation. No real attempt has been made to apply consistent rules of competition in transport, the full environmental costs have not been paid by the polluter, transport's role in integration of national and international economies and in assisting regional development has not been realized, and the potential for harmonization between modes has been neglected. The market has not been fully liberalized and adequate, effective and efficient transport is a prerequisite guaranteeing the objectives of the European Community. These problems are currently under discussion in the European Community and they are likely to be considerably increased as the membership of the European Community is widened to include the peripheral nations of Scandinavia and the countries of Central and eastern Europe. It is only when there is a high quality transport infrastructure in the "new Europe" that Europe can be truly called unified.

References

Abbati, C. degli, 1986, Transport and European Integration, *European Perspectives*, Commission of the European Communities, Brussels.

Association of European Airlines, 1987, *Capacity of Aviation Systems in Europe; Scenario on Airport Congestion*, AEA, Brussels.

Commission of the European Communities, 1985, *Official Journal of the European Communities*, C 144, June 13, 1985.

Commission of the European Communities, 1992a, *The Impact of Transport on the Environment: A Community Strategy for Sustainable Development*, Green Paper, DGVII, Brussels.

Commission of the European Communities, 1992b, *The Future Development of the Common Transport Policy*, Com (92) 494, Brussels.

Community of European Railways, 1992, *Railway Cooperation and Services in Europe*, International Union of Railways and Community of European Railways, Paris/Brussels.

European Conference of Ministers of Transport, 1992, *High Speed Rail*, Report of the ECMT Round Table 87, Economic Research Centre, Paris.

European Investment Bank, 1991, *Briefing Series: Communications*, EIB, Luxembourg.

European Parliament, 1991, *Community Policy on Transport Infrastructures, European Parliament*, Research and Development Papers, Series on Regional Policy and Transport 16, EP, Luxembourg.

European Round Table of Industrialists, 1988, *Need for Renewing Transport Infrastructure in Europe, Proposals for Improving the Decision Making Process*, ERTI, Brussels.

European Round Table of Industrialists, 1990, *Missing Networks in Europe. Proposals for the Renewal of Europe's Infrastructure*, ERTI, Brussels.

Gerardin, B., 1989, *Possibilities for, and Costs of, Private and Public Investment in Transport*, European Conference of Ministers of Transport, Round Table 83, ECMT, Paris.

Gerardin, B. and Viegas, J., 1992, European Transport Infrastructure and Networks: Current Policies and Trends, Paper Presented at the NECTAR International Symposium, Amsterdam, March.

Group Transport 2000 Plus, 1990, Transport in a Fast Changing Europe, Paper Commissioned by the Transport Commissioner of the European Commission (Karel van Miert), December.

Keating, G., 1992, Toll Tales on the Highway to Prosperity, *Independent*, December.

Maggi, R., Masser, I. and Nijkamp, P., 1992, Missing Networks in European Transport and Communications, *Transport Reviews*, 12(4), 311-321.

Vickerman, R.W., 1991, Transport Infrastructure in the European Community: New Developments, Regional Implications and Evaluation, in Vickerman, R.W. (ed.), *Infrastructure and Regional Development*, Pion, London.

TRANSPORT IN A UNIFIED EUROPE. Policies and Challenges.
D. Banister and J. Berechman (Editors)

Chapter Sixteen

PASSENGER TRANSPORT IN THE UNITED STATES AND EUROPE: A COMPARATIVE ANALYSIS OF PUBLIC SECTOR INVOLVEMENT

John Pucher
Dimitri Ioannides
Ira Hirschman

1. Introduction

Passenger transport systems in the United States have evolved quite differently from those in Europe, especially in the half century since World War II. Even in the first half of the 20th Century, automobile ownership and use had grown faster in the United States than in Europe, partly due to the lower density of settlements, less-focused travel patterns, and a vast land area with much longer trip distances. However, rapid increases in per capita income after 1945 greatly magnified those differences. Until recently, the standard of living in the United States was much higher than in Europe. A large proportion of Americans have for many decades belonged to the middle class, which in most countries is especially attracted to the advantages of automobile travel. Auto ownership became ever more affordable, and urban land use patterns dramatically decentralized as Americans increasingly moved to single-family houses built at low densities in the suburbs. Unlike Europe, land on the fringes of cities was cheap and seemed in unlimited supply. Likewise, the much longer inter-city travel distances in the United States gave air travel a greater competitive advantage over ground transport modes than it did in Europe. As air travel improved and became less expensive, Americans more quickly shifted to air transport for their long distance travel.

Thus, the preconditions for rapid increases in automobile and air travel were more favorable in the United States than in Europe. Public policies, however, were crucial in facilitating and even accelerating the shift to the automobile and air travel. More generally, public policies in the United States, as in every country, have been important in shaping the transportation system, for both short and long distance travel. Federal, state, and local governments in the United States have pursued different policies than most European governments. Indeed, many of the differences between the two continents in transportation systems can be attributed to such policy differences.

The United States has a history of less social and economic planning than Europe, and that has extended to transport as well. The tradition of minimal interference with private markets has generally meant less public ownership, less government regulation, and less government subsidy. On ideological principle, there has been more respect for the location and travel decisions of individuals and less willingness to sacrifice personal freedom in order to achieve community goals or take into account the social and environmental problems caused by individual actions. Planning in the United States came later, has been weaker, and has generally followed the private market instead of shaping transport and land use developments. As we argue in this chapter, differences between the United States and Europe in the extent and type of government involvement have had important consequences for transportation.

As Europeans ponder the transport implications of an increasingly unified Europe, they might find a review of the American experience useful. In some respects, societal and economic developments in Western European countries seem to lag behind the United States by a few decades. By examining the successes and failures of American transport policy, Europeans may be able to avoid some of the costs of trial-and-error policy making. In some instances, Europeans may find their transport policies clearly superior; in other cases, American policies may be worth adapting for their own use.

The focus of this chapter is on the role of the public sector in American passenger transport, and how it differs from public sector involvement in European countries. We describe recent developments in the United States and compare them to Europe for each of four specific modal groupings: roadways and automobile transport; urban public transport; long distance rail and bus transport; and air transport. We examine government policies in terms of public versus private ownership and operation; public regulation; and financing of operating costs and capital investment through subsidies, user charges, or other private funding. A review of historical trends serves as background to the current situation and emerging developments. Each mode is treated somewhat differently, as the relative importance of the various issues differs among modes. But in every case, the focus is on public sector involvement and its impacts.

2. Overview of American Passenger Transport

Before commencing our detailed discussion of each modal grouping, we first present a brief overview of passenger transport in the United States. Tables 1, 2, and 3 display basic trends from 1980 to 1990 in passenger-miles of travel, modal split, and vehicle-miles of travel.

TABLE 1

Passenger-Miles[a] of Travel in the U.S. by Mode, 1980-1990

Mode	1980	1985	1990
Air transport			
Commercial airlines	204,367	277,836	345,873
General aviation	14,700	13,000	12,300
Total aviation	219,607	290,836	358,173
Highway transport			
Cars and taxis	2,000,872	2,142,960	2,454,899
Small trucks	378,216	484,994	611,543
School buses	41,000	70,000	74,200
Inter-city buses	27,400	23,800	23,000
Motorcycles	11,235	9,995	13,114
Total highway[b]	2,458,723	2,731,749	3,176,756
Long-distance rail (Amtrak)	4,503	4,785	6,041
Urban public transport	39,854	39,581	41,536
Total travel	2,722,687	3,066,951	3,582,509
Travel per capita	12,018	12,889	14,404

Note: [a]Millions of miles; [b]Excludes heavy trucks.

Sources: U.S. Department of Transportation, Research and Special Programs Administration, (June 1992).

As shown in Table 1, the largest absolute increase in passenger-miles of travel was for private motor vehicles. Travel in automobiles and taxis increased by 454 billion passenger-miles; travel in small trucks (including passenger trucks and vans) increased by 234 billion passenger-miles. Air travel also increased greatly: by 142 billion passenger-miles. Indeed, the percentage growth in air travel (70 percent) was considerably greater than the growth in automobile travel (22 percent) and slightly greater than growth in small truck travel (62 percent). By comparison, inter-city bus travel fell by 4.4 billion passenger-miles (16 percent), long distance rail travel increased by 1.5 billion passenger-miles (34 percent), and local public transport travel rose by 1.6 billion passenger-miles (4 percent). Total travel in the United States grew by 33 percent from 1980 to 1990; from 2.7 to 3.6 trillion passenger-miles. Travel per capita increased by 20 percent, from 12,018 miles in 1980 to 14,404 miles in 1990. Thus, the American population has become ever more mobile.

TABLE 2

Modal Split in U.S. Passenger Travel, 1980-1990 (Percentage of Passenger Miles by Mode)

Mode	1980	1985	1990
Air transport			
Commercial airlines	7.5	9.0	9.7
General aviation	0.5	0.4	0.3
Total aviation	8.0	9.4	10.0
Highway transport			
Cars and taxis	73.5	69.8	68.5
Small trucks	13.9	15.8	17.0
School bus	1.5	2.3	2.0
Inter-city bus	1.0	0.7	0.6
Motorcycle	0.4	0.3	0.4
Total highway[a]	90.3	89.0	88.6
Long distance rail (Amtrak)	0.1	0.2	0.2
Urban public transport	1.5	1.3	1.1
Total travel	100.0	100.0	100.0

Note: [a]Excludes heavy trucks.

Source: U.S. Department of Transportation, Research and Special Programs Administration (June 1992).

Private motor vehicle travel (see Table 2) dominates passenger transport in the United States, accounting for over 85 percent of total passenger-miles in both 1980 and 1990. Air travel has become relatively more important, however; its modal split share increased from 8 percent in 1980 to 10 percent in 1990. In contrast, inter-city rail, inter-city bus, and urban public transport together have become relatively less important, accounting for less than 2 percent of total travel in 1990, down from 3 percent in 1980.

Trends in the supply of transport services roughly parallel trends in travel demand (see Table 3). Nevertheless, there are considerable differences by mode. For example, whereas vehicle-miles of air service increased by 57 percent, passenger-miles increased by 70 percent (because of larger planes and higher seat occupancy rates). Vehicle occupancy rates declined for most other modes. The most extreme case was urban public transport, where vehicle-miles of service increased by 43 percent, but passenger-miles of

TABLE 3

Vehicle Miles[a] of Travel in the U.S. by Mode, 1980-1990

	1980	1985	1990
Air transport			
Commercial airlines	2,523	3,046	3,963
General aviation	5,204	4,817	4,831
Total aviation	7,727	7,863	8,794
Highway transport			
Cars and taxis	1,111,596	1,260,565	1,515,370
Small trucks	290,935	373,072	466,827
School bus	3,000	3,400	3,800
Inter-city bus	3,500	3,483	3,936
Motorcycle	10,214	9,086	9,572
Total highway[b]	1,419,245	1,649,606	1,999,505
Long distance rail (Amtrak)	235	251	301
Urban public transport	2,287	2,791	3,274
Total travel	1,429,494	1,660,511	2,011,874

Note: [a]Millions of miles; [b]Excludes heavy trucks.

Sources: U.S. Department of Transportation, Research and Special Programs Administration (June 1992).

use increased by only 4 percent. Auto occupancy rates also declined: vehicle miles grew by 36 percent compared to a 22-percent increase in passenger-miles.

The overall message of Tables 1 through 3 is that total travel in the United States has grown considerably and that the supply of passenger transport services has generally increased even faster than demand. Although air travel became relatively more important over the past decade, the automobile clearly dominates passenger travel. Urban and inter-city public transport modes together account for only about 2 percent of total travel.

3. Automobile Transport

Automobile travel has dominated passenger transport in the United States longer and to a greater extent than in any other country. The auto's percentage of inter-city travel declined from 87 percent to 81 percent between 1970 and 1990 due to increased air travel (U.S. Bureau of the Census, 1992, p. 600), but its percentage of local travel has steadily increased. As shown in Figure 1, the auto's share of urban travel increased from 80 percent in 1969-1970 to 84 percent in 1990-1991. By comparison, the combined modal split share of walking and bicycling declined from 12 percent to 10 percent, and public transport's modal split fell from 5 percent to 3 percent.

Another index of the increasing popularity of the automobile is the continually rising rate of auto ownership in the United States, which has long been the highest in the world. In 1990, for example, the United States had 577 autos per 1,000 population (see Table 4). By comparison, the rates of auto ownership in Western Europe ranged from 160 in Greece to 485 in Western Germany. Likewise, the United States had the most motor vehicles per 1,000 population (746 compared to a European low of 232 in Greece and a high of 569 in Western Germany.)

Corresponding to greater auto and motor vehicle availability, the United States also has the most meters of roadway per capita (25 compared to a European low of 4 in Spain and Greece and a high of 21 in Norway). Clearly, the United States has made a huge investment in its extensive highway and street network, both in urban and rural areas. The automobile is sometimes referred to as private transportation, but its use depends almost completely on roadway infrastructure provided by the public sector. In the United States, roadways have been planned, financed, maintained, and regulated by federal, state, and local governments. Each level of government shares responsibility for the national

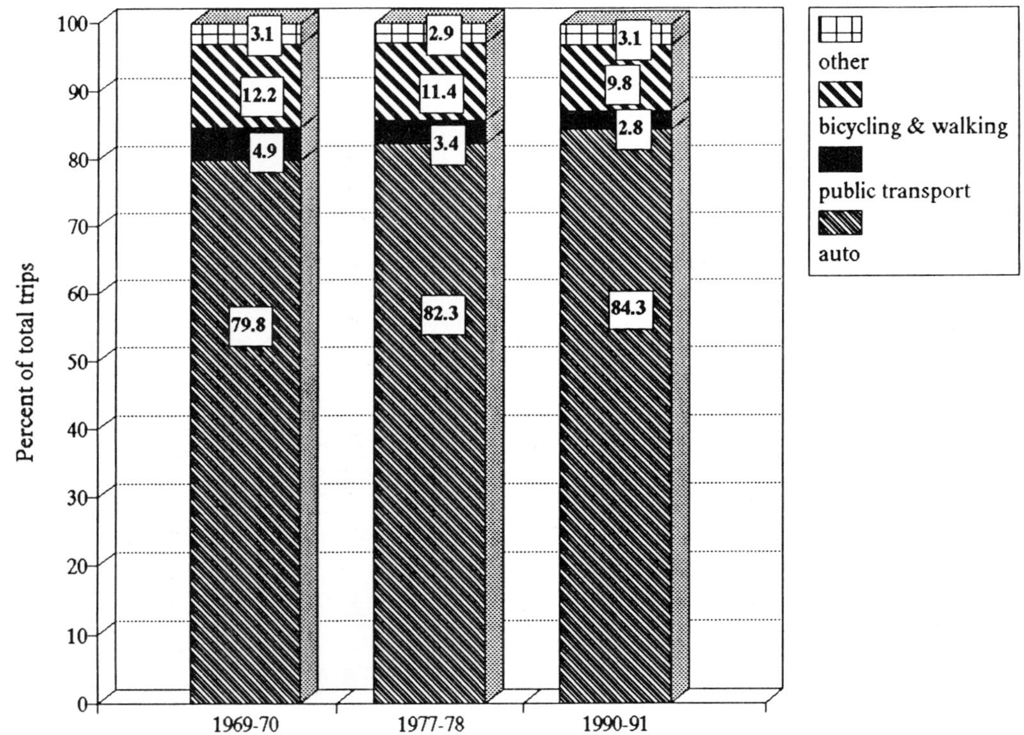

Source: Special tabulations by Pucher of the computer tapes of the 1970, 1978, 1990 Nationwide Personal Transportation Surveys, U.S. Department of Transportation, Federal Highway Administration, Washington, D.C., 1973, 1981, and 1992.

Note: Only local tripmaking within urban areas is included in these figures. Long distance travel and rural travel were explicitly excluded in these special tabulations of the NPTS computer tapes.

FIGURE 1 Trends in Modal Split in U.S. Cities (Percentage of Urban Trips by Mode, All Trip Purposes)

TABLE 4

Motor Vehicle Ownership and Roadway Supply, 1989-1990

	Autos per 1,000 Population	Motor Vehicles per 1,000 Population	Roadway per Capita[a]	Roadway per Motor Vehicle[a]
Austria	380	413	14	34
Belgium	388	429	13	32
Denmark	323	379	14	37
Finland	382	432	15	36
France	415	482	14	29
Germany (West)	485	569	8	16
Greece	160	232	4	--
Ireland	227	272	3	10
Italy	456	499	5	11
Netherlands	368	407	8	20
Norway	381	457	21	45
Portugal	259	341	--	--
Spain	308	375	4	11
Sweden	420	456	16	34
Switzerland	435	474	11	22
United Kingdom	374	420	6	16
USA	577	746	25	34

Notes: [a]Miles.

Sources: International Roadway Federation (1990).

roadway network. Local streets, bridges and tunnels, and traffic law enforcement are the responsibility of city and county governments and regional special districts. State governments are in charge of planning, constructing, maintaining, and operating most of the remaining roadway network; they are also responsible for traffic law enforcement in non-urban areas. The federal government's role is primarily financial, providing funds for main transportation arteries. It also establishes standards for environmental impacts, community participation, and virtually every aspect of roadway design.

3.1 Public Sector Financing

The financial role of the public sector in the United States has been especially important. Government roadway expenditures in 1990 totalled $74,885 million. Of that total, local governments financed 27 percent, state governments 53 percent, and the federal government 20 percent (Federal Highway Administration, 1991, p. 42). Virtually all of the federal contribution was in the form of grants to state governments for highway expenditures. Most of that federal aid as well as the states' own-raised subsidy was directly spent by the states for highway uses, but 13 percent of total highway funding available at the state level was in turn granted to municipal and county governments for their roadway projects.

Roadway user taxes and charges are levied primarily at the federal and state levels for roadway finance. Over 85 percent of the total federal roadway funding is financed through taxes on fuel and motor vehicles (Federal Highway Administration, 1991, p. 42). At the state level, 77 percent of total roadway funding is derived from roadway user taxes. In contrast, at the local government level, only 6 percent of total roadway funding is derived from user taxes. Thus, it is primarily at the local level that roadway users fail to pay the costs of roadways.

Overall, roadway users in the United States pay only 60 percent of the costs of roadway construction, maintenance, administration, and law enforcement through taxes and user charges (see Table 5). The remaining 40 percent (amounting to $30.7 billion in 1990) is subsidized through general government revenues. In contrast, roadway user taxes exceed government roadway expenditures in every European country. The ratio of roadway taxes to expenditures ranges from 5.1 in the Netherlands to 1.3 in Switzerland, but most European countries collect at least twice as much from roadway user taxes as they spend on roadways. Thus, roadway users are heavily subsidized in the United States, whereas in Europe they pay such high roadway use taxes that they contribute significantly to overall government finance.

Total roadway user taxes per motor vehicle are shown in Table 5. Whereas they amounted to only $234 per vehicle in the United States in 1989, they ranged from $786 in Western Germany to $2,323 in Finland. Two important types of roadway user taxes are the gasoline tax and the sales tax on motor vehicles. Figure 2 portrays the much higher level of gasoline prices and taxes in Europe. The gasoline tax per liter there ranges from five to ten times the tax rate in the United States, resulting in gasoline prices that are

TABLE 5

Government Roadway Expenditure and Taxes, 1989-1990

	Roadway Taxes per Motor Vehicle (US$)	New Car Sales Tax[a] (%)	Ratio of Roadway User Taxes to Government Roadway Expenditures
Austria	1,586	52	1.7
Denmark	1,518	105-180	3.0
Finland	2,323	148	2.8
France	1,151	25	--
Germany (West)	786	14	2.1
Greece	--	20-100	--
Ireland	--	10-50	--
Netherlands	1,108	18-27	5.1
Norway	1,145	48-9	--
Portugal	--	20-144	--
Spain	950	33	4.3
Sweden	1,136	19	3.0
Switzerland	1,174	7	1.3
United Kingdom	1,386	2	4.2
USA	234	5-8	0.6

Notes: [a]Sales tax reported here includes sales tax, value added tax, first registration fee, and in certain countries import tax; range of rates due to car size differences.

Sources: World Road Statistics (1990); German Ministry of Transport (1992); U.S. Dept. of Transportation Highways Statistics.

two to four times as high. Most of the difference in gasoline prices between Europe and the U.S. is due to differences in tax rates, not differences in the base price of petroleum. Differences in the sales tax rate on new cars are even more striking. As shown in Table 5, only Switzerland has rates as low as those in the United States (both below 10 percent). Most European countries have sales tax rates somewhere between 25 percent and 40 percent, but the rates go all the way up to 144 percent in Portugal, 148 percent in Finland, and 180 percent in Denmark.

Clearly, government taxation has made auto ownership and use in Europe much more expensive than in the United States. That is partly the result of European Community sensitivity to the social and environmental costs of automobile use and the willingness of national governments to levy roadway user taxes in order to internalize those costs (European Conference of the Ministers of Transport, 1990). In addition, automobile taxation has long been a convenient source of general revenues for European national governments. Unlike the United States, successive increases in roadway user tax rates have been accepted without much political opposition. Perhaps that is because high tax rates were implemented in Europe before auto ownership was widespread. The high cost of auto ownership and use is generally accepted as a fact of life in Europe. In contrast, any attempt to increase gasoline or motor vehicle taxes in the United States is viewed as an attack on the American way of life and is vigorously opposed by the vast majority of voters and by powerful special interest groups such as the auto and oil industries and the American Automobile Association.

Of course, there a number of other important government policies in the United States that have strongly encouraged automobile use and thus accelerated the decline of public transport (Pucher, 1988a, 1990a). For example, the free auto parking provided for over 90 percent of employees in the United States has been treated for many decades as a tax-free fringe benefit for employees and as a tax-deductible expense for firms. That represents an implicit subsidy to auto users variously estimated to range from $12 billion to $50 billion per year. In addition, the federal government has offered mortgage insurance and various tax advantages for homeowners since World War II. In 1988, for example, the federal subsidy to homeowners amounted to $117 billion (Pucher, 1990a). As almost all new single-family housing has been built in the suburbs since 1945, the subsidy to homeownership has also been a subsidy to suburbanization. That, in turn, has been a strong stimulus to auto ownership and use: only the automobile can serve the transportation needs generated by the very low density suburban sprawl that evolved in the United States.

Admittedly, both automobile use and suburban single-family homes have great inherent appeal to American consumers. There can be no question, however, that public policies in the United States not only accommodated those consumer preferences but actually made automobile use and suburban living possible at artificially low prices. Subsidies, tax deductions, roadway construction, suburban infrastructure provision, and the failure to internalize the social and environmental costs of automobile use are all examples of the crucial role the American public sector played in establishing the automobile as the overwhelmingly dominant mode of urban transportation, and the single-family suburban house as the dominant form of residence.

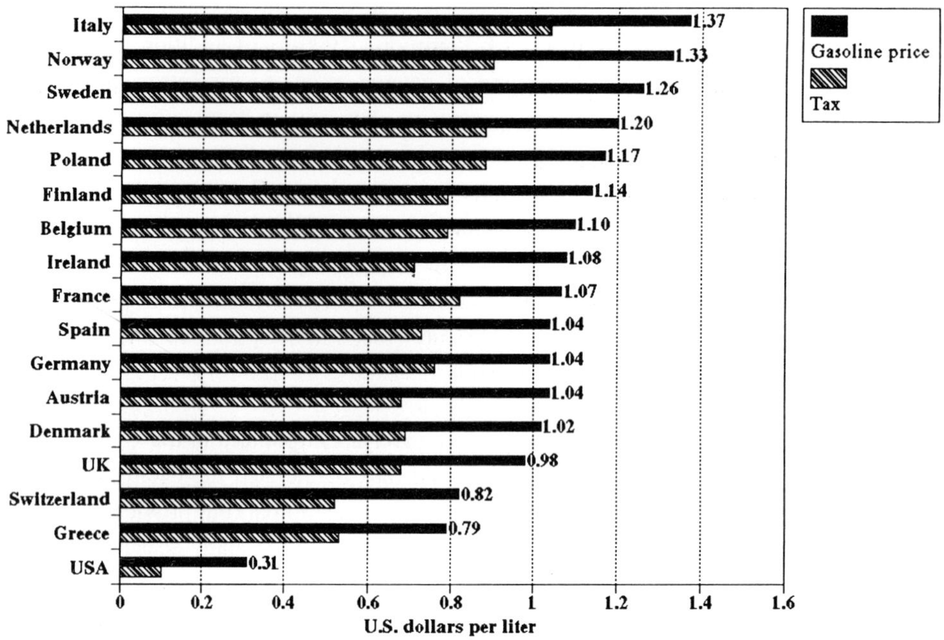

Source: Organization for Economic Cooperation and Development, International Energy Agency, Energy Prices and Taxes, No.3, 1992.

FIGURE 2 Gasoline Prices and Taxes in the U.S. and Europe, 1992 (US$ per Liter)

3.2 Public Regulation

The public sector in the United States has increasingly regulated both roadways and automobiles. Virtually every aspect of the routing, construction, and maintenance of roadways is affected by compulsory government standards. There are extensive guidelines on environmental impacts, community participation, effects on historical and archeological sites, labor wage rates, and safety, as well as detailed requirements for planning and financing.

In addition, motor vehicles themselves have been subjected to ever stricter government regulations. The federal government, in particular, has required manufacturers to meet successively higher minimum standards for pollution control, energy efficiency, and safety. Some states, most notably California, have imposed even stricter requirements. The various standards have raised the purchase price of automobiles but they appear to have produced substantial benefits in reducing pollution, increasing safety, and limiting energy use.

Yet another area of public regulation has directly affected auto user behavior. For many years, state and local governments have established minimum ages for alcohol consumption and maximum levels of alcohol in the blood stream for auto drivers. Likewise, a whole range of traffic regulations, licensing requirements, and driving standards have been aimed at improving safety. Speed limits, turn restrictions, minimum distances between cars, and even the use of lights and horns, for example, have been regulated by state and local governments practically since the advent of auto use in the early 20th Century. Most states also require regular inspections of vehicles for safety and pollution control and, recently, most states have passed laws requiring the use of seat belts by auto drivers and passengers (incidentally, about a decade after the adoption of seat belt use laws in Western Europe).

3.3 Public versus Private Ownership and Operation

Currently, virtually all of the roadway system in the United States is publicly owned, operated, and financed, but it was not always so, and it may not be so in the future. In the 19th Century, over 2,000 private firms built and operated a large number of toll roads, mainly in the eastern part of the country (Klein and Fielding, 1992). Eventually, almost all of them went bankrupt due to inadequate funding, excessive state and local regulations, toll evasion, and premature deterioration of the wooden plank road surfaces used.

In recent years, there has been much interest in expanding the private role in roadway construction, operation, and finance, primarily due to the lack of public funds for infrastructure investment. There are already five private toll road projects underway in California and Virginia, and several more are planned in Florida, Texas, and Colorado. The movement toward privatization has been given ever more impetus from developments in federal laws and regulations that now require maximum possible private participation. In December 1991, the U.S. Congress passed the Intermodal Surface Transportation Efficiency Act (ISTEA), probably the most comprehensive transport legislation in the history of the country. That federal act for the first time allows private firms to own toll facilities (roads, bridges, or tunnels) that have been financed with the help of federal funding (U.S. Department of Transportation, 1992b). The same act also greatly increases the extent to which tolls can be imposed on federally subsidized roadways. That obviously enhances the potential attractiveness of private involvement, although public agencies can also benefit from the increased allowability of toll financing.

In Europe, the only examples of privately operated roadways are the toll roads in France and Italy, but even those are publicly owned. The Kohl Administration in Germany has proposed the privatization of autobahns (by far the most extensive superhighways in Europe) and imposition of annual permit fees. The plan, however, is controversial, and will probably not be implemented soon if at all.

3.4 Dealing with the Problem of Congestion

Several chapters in this book deal at length with the problems of transport congestion and pollution in Europe (Dugonjic et al.; Banister and Berechman; Hauser and Maggi; Jones and Button). As in Europe, the problem of roadway congestion has worsened in the United States over the past two decades. Especially in suburban areas, the supply of roadways has lagged ever further behind increasing travel demand. Both residential and workplace decentralization continue at a rapid pace. By 1990, less than five percent of all jobs in U.S. metropolitan areas were located in the central business districts of cities (U.S. Bureau of the Census, 1992). Most of the increase in travel demand in metropolitan areas has been between suburbs, whereas the commutation trip from the suburb to the city center has become less important. The unfocused pattern of travel within and among suburbs is almost impossible to serve with any sort of public transport, so auto use continues to increase. Moreover, carpooling declined sharply between 1980 and 1990 as an ever higher percentage of auto users drove alone. Thus, each passenger-mile of travel generates more vehicle miles of travel and takes up more roadway space than previously.

At the same time that travel demand was burgeoning, roadway supply stagnated. Community opposition, environmental objections, development moratoria, and funding shortages all contributed to a virtual halt to new highway construction. In addition, many transportation analysts had criticized the massive roadway construction programs of the 1960-1975 period. Not only was new highway construction found to be socially and environmentally harmful, but its short term improvements in capacity were quickly offset by the long term increases in travel demand caused by the extensive suburbanization new roadways stimulated.

The situation today remains difficult. Although the 1991 federal transportation law (ISTEA) provides large increases in federal funding for roadway construction, environmental and community opposition to almost all proposed expansion projects remains intense. It will probably be possible to make a few selective additions to the roadway network, but it is virtually inconceivable that capacity expansion will be the main solution to the congestion problem. Increasingly, academic policy analysts as well as government policy makers seem to be turning to demand management to deal with congestion. Examples of demand management techniques already in use in the United States include priority lanes and parking for high-occupancy vehicles (HOVs); parking supply limitations; selective ramp metering on limited-access highways; flexible work hours (to spread out traffic peaks); discount tolls and parking fees for carpools; and auto-free zones for pedestrians. Such transportation measures are particularly attractive under the present circumstances because they have positive environmental impacts, require only minimal funding, and can be implemented quickly.

Congestion pricing continues to be a popular notion among some transport analysts, especially economists, but in the three decades since it was first proposed, it has made virtually no headway. The 1991 federal transportation act may revive interest, as it provides funding for five experimental congestion pricing projects. Perhaps the experiments will be successful, but it seems inconceivable that Americans would accept congestion pricing for widespread implementation. As a practical matter, it faces insuperable political opposition in the United States. Even small increases in the existing gasoline tax are vigorously attacked by industry lobbyists and consumer groups. Congestion pricing, by comparison, would be viewed as a totally new kind of taxation, an infringement on personal freedom, and an inequitable rationing of mobility. The congestion pricing experiment may yield some interesting data for economic analysis, but it probably will not provide a model that can be widely followed.

3.5 Comparisons with Europe

The biggest difference between the United States and Europe in automotive transport is the much higher cost of owning and operating a motor vehicle in Europe. That higher cost is due to explicit, deliberate policies of high roadway users taxes, partly to internalize the social and environmental costs of auto use, and partly as a convenient source of general government revenues.

In addition, European countries have pursued very different land use and urban development policies. Land use is much more strictly controlled in Europe, either directly through public ownership of land or indirectly through government regulations on the use of private lands. The result is more compact, denser settlement patterns in Europe. Even the newest suburbs in Europe are, on average, four times more densely populated than American suburbs (Newman and Kenworthy, 1992). Laissez faire development policy still dominates in the United States, with only limited consideration given to the wider, long run social and environmental impacts of urban development. Real estate developers and land speculators continue to be the main shapers of American metropolitan areas.

Auto ownership and suburbanization are increasing in virtually all Western European countries, but they remain far behind American levels. That is partly attributable to the much higher cost of auto ownership and use in Europe, the far superior transport alternatives to auto use in Europe (walking, bicycling, public transport), and land use policies that virtually force suburban developments to be relatively dense and compact.

Yet even the much lower levels of auto use in Europe have caused severe problems of congestion, pollution, and safety. (See the chapters by Jones and Hervik and by Himanen, Nijkamp and Padjen in this volume.) The social and environmental problems of auto use are all the more serious in Europe because of higher population densities, less available land, and cities that are far less suited or even adaptable to automobile use. In Europe, it simply is not possible to allow the auto to run wild as it has in the United States. Moreover, there appears to be a consensus among European voters and politicians on the need to control automobile use on account of its negative impacts. That probably ensures the continuation of high taxation of auto ownership and use and strict land use controls. It thus seems inconceivable that Europe will ever see the extremely one sided domination of transportation by the automobile or the endless low density suburban sprawl common in the United States. Europeans need not regret missing out on that uniquely American experience.

4. Urban Public Transport

In the first few decades of the 20th Century, public transport completely dominated urban travel in the United States. Even as late as 1945, public transport accounted for 35 percent of all urban passenger-miles (Altshuler et al., 1979, p. 22). Over the following 30 years, however, public transport went into a free-fall decline from which it is still trying to recover. From 1945 to 1975, public transport ridership plummeted from 22.3 billion to only 7.0 billion trips, a decline of 69 percent (American Public Transit Association, 1985, p.32). Since 1975, ridership has recovered slightly. Exact comparisons of statistics between 1975 and 1991 are impossible because of changes in trip definitions and calculation procedures. Free transfers are now counted as separate trips and included in the total of so-called unlinked trips. Moreover, additional types of public transport are now included, such as cable car, ferry boat, commuter rail, inclined plane, automated guideway, and various demand-responsive systems. Both changes inflate the actual increase in public transport ridership. Thus, the increase of 15 percent reported by the American Public Transit Association exaggerates real ridership growth (American Public Transit Association, 1992, p. 64). A more realistic figure is probably closer to 10 percent, possibly even less. Nevertheless, turning around the long term decline in ridership at all was a considerable accomplishment.

As shown in Figure 3, vehicle-miles of urban automobile use in the United States increased by 114 percent between 1960 and 1975, while public transport ridership fell by 26 percent. From 1975 to 1990, the period of public transport's recovery, auto use increased by 57 percent compared to a real increase of 10 percent or less for public transport. Thus, even in recent years, auto use has continued to grow much faster than public transport. The result is an ever lower modal split share of tripmaking for public transport. As seen previously in Figure 1, public transport's share of urban travel in the United States fell from 5 percent in 1970 to only 3 percent in 1990. For most Americans, public transport has become a totally irrelevant mode of travel which they do not even consider using.

As argued in the previous section on automobile transport, the public sector has played a key role in the evolution of urban transportation in the United States. On the one hand, it heavily favored roadway construction and automobile use through subsidies, artificially low prices, tax advantages, suburban infrastructure investments, and lax land-use controls. It also ignored the auto's many adverse social and environmental impacts. On the other hand, the public sector neglected public transport for many years, most particularly during

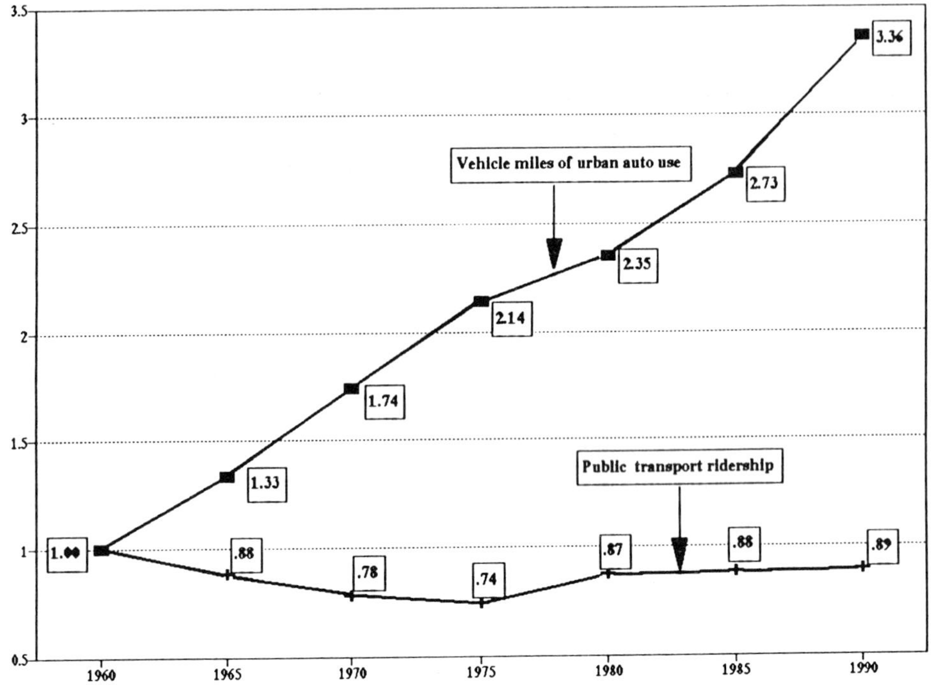

Sources: American Public Transit Association, Transit Fact Book. annual, Washington, D.C., 1970 to 1992; and U.S. Department of Transportation, Federal Highway Administration, Highway Statistics, annual, Washington, D.C., 1960 to 1992.
Note: Usage levels are expressed as a ratio of each year's use to usage in the base year 1960. Vehicle miles of urban automobile travel is the index of auto use. Passenger trips is the index of public transport use.

FIGURE 3 Comparison of Trends in Auto and Public Transportation Use (U.S. Urban Areas, 1960-1990)

those 30 years from 1945 to 1975 when public transport lost over two-thirds of its passengers.

Public sector involvement in public transport can be roughly divided into three periods: a period of neglect up to 1970; a period of skyrocketing government subsidies from about 1970 to 1980; and a period of consolidation and almost constant subsidy levels since then. We deal with each of those three periods in turn.

4.1 Public Sector Neglect

In 1950, only 28 percent of public transport service in the United States was provided by publicly owned and operated firms. That percentage steadily increased over the following years, with systems in the largest cities being the first to turn public. Already by 1970, publicly owned systems accounted for 66 percent of total vehicle miles of service (American Public Transit Association, 1992, p. 33).

Of course, many individual firms had operating losses even in the 1950s and 1960s, but the industry as a whole did not register an operating loss in aggregate until 1968 (Saltzman, 1979). That fact does not reveal the financial problems of the industry in earlier years. Public transport service was for many decades only marginally profitable, having been cross-subsidized by the profits from land speculation, freight transport, and other branches of joint utility firms. As possibilities for land speculation were exhausted and antitrust rulings forced firms to divest themselves of electric and gas utilities, the unprofitability of public transport became ever more apparent. Moreover, the degree of unprofitability increased steadily as the automobile lured away more and more riders. Necessary capital investments were seriously neglected, fares were increased, service was curtailed, ridership fell, and losses grew. The downward spiral of public transport's decline was to last 30 years, and only enormous subsidies were able to stabilize the situation.

During the period prior to 1970, the main government role in the public transport industry was regulatory. Local governments sold monopoly franchises for public transport services to private firms and regulated routes, service frequency, and fares. By the 1950s, systems in a few large cities did receive local government subsidy, but not much. In addition, state governments provided limited funds to prevent discontinuance of commuter rail services to the suburbs. During the 1960s, the federal government gradually developed a subsidy program to support demonstration projects and a few discretionary capital investments. In 1965, the total capital subsidy from all levels of government amounted to only $76 million, and the total operating subsidy was only $14 million (Pucher et al., 1983). By 1970, the total capital subsidy had increased to $200 million, and the total operating subsidy to $318 million. That rapid deterioration in the financial situation of the public transport industry was an ominous foreboding of developments in the following decade.

4.2 Skyrocketing Subsidies and Costs

The decade of the 1970s witnessed phenomenal growth in government financial support for public transport as well as an almost complete shift to public ownership. In addition, public regulation of the public transport industry burgeoned.

Public ownership in the industry increased from 66 percent in 1970 to 90 percent in 1980. By the end of the decade, public transport service was provided almost entirely by publicly owned systems, which in virtually all large cities took the form of metropolitan-wide, regional transportation districts.

As operating losses and investment needs grew, so did government subsidies. The percentage of total operating costs covered by passenger fare revenues fell from 90 percent in 1970 to only 41 percent in 1980 (Pucher et al., 1983). As shown in Table 6, total operating subsidy from all levels of government combined rose from $318 million to $3,705 million. Capital subsidies grew from $200 million to $3,434 million. The combined operating and capital subsidy to public transport increased from $518 million to $7,812 million, a 15-fold increase in only ten years. Even in constant, inflation-adjusted dollars, that represents a ten-fold increase in government subsidy funds for public transport.

As subsidies grew during the 1970s, the federal government bore an ever larger percentage of the financial burden, increasing from 26 percent of the total subsidy in 1970 to 54 percent in 1980 (see Table 6). By contrast, the state and local share fell from 74 percent to 46 percent. During the same period, state and local subsidies to public transport were increasingly financed by taxes earmarked exclusively for public transport support. At the local level, those dedicated taxes usually took the form of percentage surcharges to the sales tax in the entire region served by the public transportation system. In some cities, however, income taxes, employer payroll taxes, property taxes, lottery proceeds, cigarette and alcohol taxes, mortgage recording taxes, and motor vehicle taxes were earmarked for public transport subsidies.

TABLE 6

Government Subsidies[a] to Public Transport in the U.S., by Type of Subsidy and Level of Government, 1970-1992

Operating Subsidies[a]	1970	1975	1980	1985	1990	1991
Federal	0	408	1,094	940	970	945
State	30	549	862	1,105	2,971	3,242
Local	288	944	1,749	3,874	5,327	5,605
Total	318	1,901	3,705	6,919	9,268	9,792
Capital Subsidies[a]						
Federal	133	1,287	2,787	2,510	2,380	2,371
State & Local	67	322	647	996	1,723	1,717
State	--	--	303	568	569	567
Local	--	--	344	428	1,154	1,150
Total	200	1,609	3,434	3,506	4,103	4,088
Total Subsidy[a]	518	3,510	7,139	10,425	13,371	13,880
Federal (%)	26	48	54	33	25	24
State & Local (%)	74	52	46	67	75	76
State (%)	--	--	16	26	26	27
Local (%)	--	--	30	41	49	49

Source: Pucher, Markstedt, and Hirshman (1983, p. 156); American Public Transit Association (1992); U.S. Department of Transportation (1982, 1987, and 1992).

Together with the increase in subsidies came an avalanche of government regulations that affected virtually every aspect of rail right-of-way and station construction, vehicle design, system operations, and financing. The growth in regulations was especially striking at the federal level, including stipulations about fare structure, service standards, accessibility for the elderly and handicapped, labor wages and work rules, environmental impacts, planning requirements, impacts on Blacks and Hispanics, community participation, and preference given to purchasing American-made vehicles.

To a significant extent, social, environmental, and political objectives superseded economic objectives in the planning and operating of public transport systems. Especially at the federal level, regulatory and funding decisions were sometimes totally unjustified by economic analysis, and subsidies were allocated to projects whose costs far exceeded their benefits. Even at the state and local level, the almost complete politicization of public transport often led to unrealistically low fares and excessive service expansion (Pucher et al., 1983).

Indeed, one of the most regrettable impacts of the sudden increase in government and subsidy during the 1970s was the tremendous increase in per-unit operating and capital costs in the public transport industry. Even when controlling for the declining value of the dollar during that decade, real, inflation-adjusted per-unit costs more than doubled! At the same time, productivity fell sharply in virtually every respect (Pucher et al., 1983). As a consequence, most of the ten-fold increase in real subsidy was dissipated by the explosion in costs. There were only small increases in vehicle-miles of service supplied, and although the quality of service improved and fares increased less than inflation, ridership grew by less than 10 percent. In general, there was great disappointment with the results of heavily subsidizing public transport, and that disappointment generated a quite different government policy in the 1980s.

4.3 Subsidy Stagnation and Cost Control

During the 12 years of the Reagan and Bush Republican Administrations, federal involvement in public transport decreased. Indeed, both presidents repeatedly tried to extract the federal government completely from the enormous subsidy program that had been built up in the 1970s. Those efforts were only partly successful because the Democratic-controlled Congress vigorously resisted subsidy cutbacks. Nevertheless, Reagan and Bush managed to reduce sharply the proportion of the total subsidy funded by the federal government (from 54 to 24 percent) and to curtail its subsidy contribution even in terms of deflated, nominal dollars (see Tables 6 and 7). Whereas federal subsidy had grown by an average annual rate of 54 percent from 1970 to 1975, and by 8.6 percent per year from 1975 to 1980, it actually fell by 3 to 5 percent per year from 1980 to 1991. State and local governments took up the slack left by federal subsidy reductions and provided substantial increases in their own subsidy contributions. The net result was continued growth in total subsidy, but the average annual rate of growth slowed down dramatically. As shown in Table 7, the overall public transport subsidy, for example, increased by only 4.2 percent per year from 1980 to 1985, by only 2.4 percent from 1985 to 1990, and by only 1.5 percent in 1991, in contrast to an average annual increase of 36 percent from 1970 to 1975. The percentage of total operating costs covered by passenger fares also stabilized during the 1980s, remaining between 56 and 59 percent over the entire decade (American Public Transit Association, 1992).

The slowdown in subsidy growth appears to have had some positive impacts on public transport finances. Since 1985, for example, labor productivity has increased substantially, and per-unit costs have increased by less than the rate of inflation (Federal Transit Administration, 1992). Thus, each subsidy dollar is going farther in producing more and better services. There can be little doubt that subsidy cutbacks and the reduced federal share of subsidies has increased the pressure on local governments to control costs. Public transport ridership remained almost constant during the 1980s, suggesting that the increased fiscal pressures on the industry did not have adverse impacts on public transport users.

TABLE 7

Average Annual Rates of Public Transport Subsidy Growth[a]

	1970-1975	1975-1980	1980-1985	1985-1990	1990-1991
Federal	53.8%	8.6%	-5.6%	-3.1%	-3.3%
State & Local	26.1	3.5	12.5	4.8	3.0
Total	35.6	6.1	4.2	2.4	1.5

Notes: [a]In inflation-adjusted constant dollars.

Source: Calculated on the basis of figures in Table 3.

4.4 The 1991 Federal Transportation Act (ISTEA)

Federal funding for public transport will probably increase considerably in the coming years. The Intermodal Surface Transportation Efficiency Act of 1991 (ISTEA) authorizes a total of $31.5 billion in federal subsidies explicitly for public transport for the six-year period from 1992 to 1997. That amounts to an average of over $5 billion a year, almost 50 percent more than the $3.3 billion per year of recent years. Moreover, the law permits the option of using an additional $58 billion in federal transportation funds for public transport, bicycle, and pedestrian facilities (Surface Transportation Policy Project 1991 and 1992). Of that $58 billion, $29.9 billion is explicitly designated as flexible funding. The Surface Transportation Program (STP) of ISTEA authorizes $23.9 billion in block grants to states and urban areas that can be spent on highways, bridges, public transport, carpool projects, bicycle and pedestrian facilities, safety, traffic management, pollution control, and planning. State and local governments and regional metropolitan planning agencies determine how the funds are spent. Likewise, the Congestion and Air Quality Improvement Program of ISTEA, which is authorized at a level of $6 billion over six years, can be used as a state and local option for a broad range of transportation programs, provided that they can be shown to improve air quality and reduce congestion. Finally, states have the option of shifting an additional $28 billion -- 50 percent of their federal highway funds and 40 percent of their federal bridge funds -- to projects that would improve public transport, carpooling, bicycling, or pedestrian facilities.

Not only is more funding being made available for public transport, but the federal matching rate has now been equalized at 80 percent for most federally assisted capital investments both for public transport and highways. Interstate highways still get funded at the 90-percent federal match, but that is somewhat offset by an equally generous 90-percent match for public transport vehicle costs incurred to comply with federal environmental standards (set by the 1990 Clean Air Act) and to provide mobility to the handicapped (as mandated by the Americans with Disabilities Act).

ISTEA is still in the first stages of being implemented, and it is not clear to what extent authorized funds will actually be appropriated by Congress. Moreover, statistics are not yet available on how states and local governments are deciding to allocate their block grants and flexible funds. Nevertheless, it seems certain that total public transport funding will indeed increase.

4.5 Increased Private Sector Involvement

At the same time that Presidents Reagan and Bush tried to reduce federal subsidies during the 1980s, they exerted pressure to increase private sector involvement in public transport. To some extent, the Republican policy shifts were based on ideological beliefs that the private sector is intrinsically better than the public sector, and that subsidies, especially from the federal government, are by their very nature bad. The new policy, however, was also a reaction to cost escalation, productivity decline, and the overall failure of public ownership and large subsidies to achieve any of the social, environmental, and economic objectives that had been used as justifications for increased public involvement.

Changes to the main federal transportation law in 1982, 1987, and 1991, and numerous executive orders and regulations which in fact implement the law, not only permitted private sector participation but mandated maximum possible private involvement in construction, ownership, and operation of public transport systems. Moreover, the Office of Private Sector Initiatives was established within the U.S. Department of Transportation in 1984 to assist private firms in competing with public systems for subsidy funds. In some instances, even services currently operated by public systems must be opened up to competitive bidding.

To date, however, the public transport industry in the United States remains very public indeed. As of 1992, only 3 percent of regularly scheduled, fixed-route bus and rail services was operated by private firms (Federal Transit Administration, 1992; American Public Transit Association, 1992). Not surprisingly, these public transport services tend to be the most unprofitable and have the least growth potential. In contrast, private contractors provided almost 70 percent of specialized paratransit services for the elderly and handicapped and 30 percent of school bus services. The large public transport monopolies in each metropolitan area have virtually no interest in providing such services; private firms have entered the market to fill the gap.

4.6 Prospects for Public Transport in the U.S.

In spite of increased federal funding in coming years, the future outlook for public transport in the United States remains rather bleak. Land use patterns and urban development continue to decentralize, and there is no reason to expect that suburbanization of residences and workplaces will slow down during this last decade of the 20th Century. The extremely low density suburban sprawl in the United States presents public transport with an insuperable obstacle to raising its modal split share of travel. Various attempts have been made to improve services to the suburbs in order to lure back middleclass commuters, but most such attempts have been either very expensive or had minor impacts. New heavy rail systems were built in Washington, San Francisco, Los Angeles, Atlanta, and Baltimore; and older systems in New York, Boston, Philadelphia, and Chicago have been expanded. Those large investments have given some hope to the industry as a whole and at least represent a visible government commitment to reviving the industry. Nevertheless, ridership generated by the additional services has been disappointingly low, far less than that necessary to justify the high costs.

Less visible, smaller scale attempts to adapt public transport services to changing travel patterns have been more successful, at least financially. Express bus routes to the suburbs have attracted ridership with minimal public subsidy. Likewise, experiments with specialized minibus and van services within suburban areas are improving the accessibility to conventional fixed-route public transport. These and other attempts to increase the effectiveness of public transport services by tailoring them more to market demand are, of course, laudable. Nevertheless, they are working against such massive trends toward decentralization and ever greater auto ownership and use that their overall impact is likely to be insignificant. No mode can really compete effectively with the automobile in low density suburbs.

4.7 Comparison with Europe

For at least the past five decades, public transport has been far more important in Europe than in the United States. In the mid-1980s, public transport accounted for a range of 10 to 25 percent of total urban travel in Western European countries, and from 50 to 80 percent of urban travel in Eastern European countries (Pucher, 1990b). By comparison, public transport's modal split for urban travel in the United States was only 3 percent.

European public transport has a longer history of public ownership and subsidization, but since the 1970s, American public transport has been even more subsidized than in most Western European countries (Pucher, 1988b), and 94 percent of public transport ridership in the United States is now on publicly owned systems (American Public Transit Association, 1992). Moreover, government regulation of public transport is even more complete in the United States than it is in Europe. In short, government involvement in public transport is at least as intense in the United States as in Europe, with high levels of public ownership, subsidies, and regulation.

In addition, the operations and finances of public transport in the United States seem to be headed in the same direction. On both continents, the decade of the 1970s was a period of rapid expansion in service, subsidy growth, and cost escalation. In contrast, the decade of the 1980s was a period of relative stagnation in service provision and ridership, and subsidies declined in real, inflation-adjusted terms in most countries. Both in Europe and the United States, government financial responsibility devolved from the central government to state/provincial and local/regional levels of government. In virtually all countries, general fiscal austerity in the public sector has put increased pressure on public transport systems to raise productivity and control costs.

Western European public transport is also facing problems due to rising living standards, suburbanization, and increasing levels of auto ownership and use. As in the United States, those developments put public transport at a competitive disadvantage that gets worse each year. Of course, the situation in Europe is not nearly so extreme as in the United States. Auto ownership rates remain much lower in Europe (see Table 4), and the costs of auto ownership and use in Europe are much higher than in the United States (see Table 5). Thus, the price of public transport use relative to the cost of auto use is much lower in Europe, an obvious incentive to choose public transport over the auto. Moreover, although European cities are increasingly spreading out into suburbs, Western European suburbs are on average four times as dense as American suburbs (Newman and Kenworthy, 1992). The more compact land use patterns in Europe ensure that public transport remains a viable alternative to the automobile for most of the population, whereas in the United States, most Americans do not really have any realistic choice except between the automobile and immobility.

If Europeans want to maintain a balanced transport system with viable alternatives to the automobile, they will have to avoid the many mistakes made in the United States. Above all, governments at every level must continue to enforce the strict land use controls that prevent unfocused, low density development in the suburbs. Moreover, taxation of auto ownership and use must be kept at high levels in order to internalize the social and environmental costs of auto use. Otherwise, auto use becomes possible at an artificially low price, thus putting public transport at an unfair competitive disadvantage. Finally, Europeans should probably intensify their efforts to limit the use of autos in cities. One of the most promising trends in European urban transport has been the spreading implementation of a whole range of policies to "tame" the automobile (Pucher and Clorer, 1992). An increasing number of cities have established large auto-free pedestrian zones and forced autos to be parked on the fringe of the city center. In addition, traffic-calming measures have restricted auto use in residential neighborhoods by narrowing streets, reducing speed limits, and placing obstacles and curves in streets to discourage through-traffic. Restricting auto use and raising its cost are probably the most effective ways to increase public transport use, more effective than heavily subsidizing public transport fares. At any rate, it is clear that public sector intervention is essential to the success of public transport and to improving the quality of urban life. The sort of laissez faire approach to auto use and urban/suburban development in the United States would spell disaster for Europe's cities.

5. Inter-city Rail and Bus Transport

Long distance passenger transport in the United States is dominated by automobile and air travel. Rail and bus services together carry less than 2 percent of total intercity passenger-miles of travel (U.S. Bureau of the Census, 1992, p. 600). By comparison, rail transport accounts for over 10 percent of inter-city passenger travel in most European countries. The current, minor role of passenger rail in the U.S. contrasts markedly with the situation at the end of WW II when rail, and to a lesser extent bus, were far more important. In 1945, for example, approximately 15 percent of inter-city passenger-miles were accounted for by the nation's railroads; 5 percent of inter-city passenger-miles were by bus.

Although only a fraction of inter-city travelers now use rail and bus transport, those modes continue to serve important market niches. In 1971, the federal government established the nation's first fully integrated passenger rail system. In the two decades since then, ridership has grown moderately, finances have improved, and the amount and quality of service have increased. With the exception of the heavily travelled corridor in the northeastern United States, however, the passenger rail network remains disjointed and service is sparse.

Inter-city rail may become more important in the future as increasing air and automobile traffic leads to greater congestion delays. There is little political support, however, for expanding the nationally operated long distance rail network beyond its present configuration, or for establishing a coordinated multi-modal inter-city transportation system. Instead, a few state governments in concert with private investors are pursuing a few isolated high speed rail developments.

5.1 Inter-city Rail Before 1971

During the last half of the 19th Century and the first half of the 20th Century, passenger rail dominated inter-city travel in the United States. In 1920, for example, rail logged nearly eight times as many inter-city rail passenger-miles as today, even though the population was much smaller and far less mobile (U.S. Bureau of the Census, 1975, p. 729). Railroading symbolized American private enterprise, with its colorful history of entrepreneurs and "robber barons". In the Progressive era, from 1900 to 1920, railroads increasingly became the target of federal reform activism. Various regulatory structures emerged, including federal control over freight rates, and separate rules governing labor relations and worker pensions. Until the mid-20th Century, freight and passenger railroads were profitable businesses. Even during the Great Depression of the 1930s, most of the major railroads managed to survive in spite of declining ridership, thanks in part to indirect assistance from federal New Deal programs (Armstrong, 1976, p. 147). By the end of World War II, ridership had climbed back to pre-Depression levels (U.S. Bureau of the Census, 1975, p. 729).

The long and precipitous decline of the nation's passenger rail system began almost immediately after World War II. Between 1945 and 1970, inter-city rail ridership fell by a staggering 93 percent (U.S. Bureau of the Census, 1975, p. 729). As with urban public transport, the post-War decline in rail ridership was partly a response to the increases in personal income enjoyed by most American households which, in turn, made auto and later air travel far more attractive and affordable. Public policies favoring competing modes reinforced the decline. Such policies included massive direct and indirect federal subsidies. In the 19th Century, railroads had benefitted from generous federal land grants intended to spur development in the western United States. In the 20th Century, however, direct government subsidies were not available for railroads prior to 1971. Automobile ownership and use were favored in the United States by low taxes on gasoline, massive highway construction, and land use and housing policies promoting decentralization. As a consequence, between 1950 and 1960, the auto's share of inter-city travel grew further from 86 to 90 percent. At the same time, rail's share declined from 6.4 percent, to below 3 percent (U.S. Bureau of the Census, 1975, p. 707).

After 1960, air travel assumed ever greater importance, especially over very long distances. Between 1960 and 1970, the modal split of air travel increased from 4 percent to 10 percent of inter-city passenger-miles, while rail's share continued to fall to less than 1 percent (U.S. Bureau of the Census, 1975, p. 707). Other ground transport modes also declined, including inter-city bus and auto. Since 1970, air travel has continued to gain market share.

Of course, the geography of the U.S., with its large land area and long distances between cities, gives air travel a natural economic advantage over ground transport. However, that advantage could not have been fully exploited without a major program of public support for airports and air traffic control systems, as well as public construction of urban highways, which greatly improved access to the new airports. Extensive federal assistance for airport development actually began during the 1930s, with the Great Depression. After World War II, federal and later state involvement expanded dramatically, and included not only major funding but also national planning for a system of airports, linked by a common air traffic control system (Armstrong, 1976, pp. 190-204).

5.2 The Amtrak Era

As inter-city rail ridership continued to decline, investment in rolling stock and infrastructure was neglected, further accelerating the losses in ridership. By 1971, most of the major railroads faced severe financial problems, and many were in the process of eliminating passenger service altogether. After considerable debate, the U.S. Congress acted to preserve a skeleton passenger rail system by creating the National Railroad Passenger Corporation, or Amtrak. Under the authorizing law, Amtrak acquired the inter-city passenger service components of most private railroads. Presently, Amtrak is the sole provider of inter-city rail transportation in the U.S.

Much of the early debate focused on system size and route selection. Economic analysts advocated eliminating most service, while maintaining routes in only a few corridors (e.g., New York City to Washington, D.C.). Due to political pressure, a more extensive network was eventually set up which included most major cities. However, with the exception of the Northeast Corridor (the Atlantic seaboard stretching from Boston, Massachusetts to Washington, D.C.), Chicago, and California, service to most areas was very infrequent. Most large cities, especially in the Midwest and South, were served by only one train per day.

Although Amtrak is nominally a private corporation, it more closely resembles a public enterprise. Amtrak is governed by a board of directors appointed by the President, and receives annual Congressional appropriations for operating and capital subsidies. While Amtrak issues "stock", most of its securities are held by the U.S. Department of Transportation. As a for-profit corporation, Amtrak has been given considerable discretion in managing its resources and setting fares. Yet, because Amtrak passenger fare revenues do not even cover its operating expenses, the overall size of both its capital and operating budgets is set by Congress.

Although government support for Amtrak has been important for its survival, subsidies have not been as generous or as consistent as those for other modes of transportation. Since the mid-1970s, total federal subsidies for Amtrak, including both operating and capital funds, have averaged only $700 million per year, amounting to $0.10 per passenger-mile (National Passenger Railroad Corporation, *Annual Reports*). By comparison, operating and capital subsidies for urban public transport were about $0.32 per passenger-mile in 1990 (American Public Transit Association, 1991). Subsidies for auto and air transport are even larger. Moreover, unlike highway, air, and urban public transport, Amtrak does not receive any funding from dedicated revenue sources. Instead, Amtrak's federal subsidies are derived from general appropriations and thus subject to cuts or even complete elimination in any given year. Finally, Amtrak has received only limited political support. Indeed, throughout its history, Amtrak has been singled out by conservative Republican administrations as a wasteful program, and there have been frequent threats to suspend funding.

Given the deteriorated condition of the passenger railroad system in 1971 and its sometimes perilous political fortunes, Amtrak's performance since 1971 must be considered at least a limited success. Passenger-miles of rail travel increased by 50 percent between 1972 and 1980 and by another 32 percent between 1980 and 1990 (National Passenger Railroad Corporation, *Annual Reports*). As a share of total inter-city passenger-miles, however, Amtrak remains at less than 1 percent.

Amtrak's ratio of operating revenues to operating expenses has increased gradually. Between 1975 and 1990, total operating revenues, including proceeds from passenger fares, real estate, mail, and contract services, increased from 45 percent to 65 percent of operating expenses. About 70 percent of Amtrak's operating revenues are from inter-city passenger fares.

Ridership gains have been induced to some extent by service and performance improvements, especially in the heavily traveled Northeast Corridor. Metroliner service between New York and Washington, D.C. is by far the most frequent and fastest service in the nation's rail system, with speeds averaging over 160 kilometers per hour. During its 20-year history, the vast majority of Amtrak's capital expenditures have been in the Northeast Corridor, including $2.5 billion for track upgrading, electrification, and station renovation.

The modest successes enjoyed by Amtrak over the last 15 years should not obscure the fact that the system has a very limited and specialized market. Amtrak's success has been mainly in the Northeast Corridor, especially between New York and Washington D.C., where premium service for business travel is offered. Indeed, approximately half of Amtrak's inter-city ridership is in the Northeast Corridor (National Passenger Railroad Corporation, 1992, p. 17). Within that market, Amtrak has been competitive with air transportation, having captured about 40 percent of the air-rail market between New York and Washington, D.C. and an even higher percentage of travel between intermediate cities such as Baltimore and Philadelphia (National Passenger Railroad Corporation, 1990, p. 7). Fares are about a third lower than the competing air shuttle services, but travel times are considerably longer. However, because this corridor is dominated by business travel, price elasticities are much lower than other inter-city markets. Consequently, marketing is based primarily on comfort, reliability, and avoidance of travel to and from airports.

Elsewhere, long distance rail service remains sparse, with few trains per week even in the largest cities. In many cases, there is no direct service between major cities within the same region. It is hardly surprising that Amtrak service in these "peripheral" areas is so limited. With the exception of city clusters on the East and West Coasts, most American cities are far apart. As a result, air travel is almost ten times faster for very long trips, even with air traffic congestion at airports. Moreover, since Amtrak has not been given adequate resources to construct new rail lines, connections between cities are often missing. Those discontinuities reflect post-War shrinkage in the passenger rail systems and a service pattern that predates the rise of many major cities, especially those in the South and West.

5.3 Future Prospects for Inter-city Rail

Inter-city rail is likely to become slightly more important in the United States as air travel grows increasingly crowded and inconvenient, and new high speed rail technologies emerge. Nevertheless, inter-city rail services are only competitive for travel corridors up to 500 miles, even at the highest practical rail speeds (Transportation Research Board, 1991, pp. 97-118). While that distance encompasses a large share of the inter-city market in Europe, it is a small fraction of the inter-city market in the U.S.

Amtrak will probably continue to maintain its monopoly in the Northeast Corridor. Improved comfort, dependability, and speed in the context of growing problems in the air travel system are likely to strengthen Amtrak ridership and financial performance. However, there appears to be little political support for expanding the nationally operated long distance rail network much beyond its present configuration. Indeed, many conservative economists and politicians advocate cutting back the Amtrak system. So far, however, they have not succeeded in gathering the necessary support for their position. In any event, the U.S. government's huge budget deficit makes unlikely a long term commitment to an expanded national system and more subsidy for inter-city rail. Large increases in federal subsidies would be required to improve existing rights-of-way and to construct new rail links, as well as for financing the additional operating costs.

High speed rail developments are being vigorously pursued, however, in isolated medium-distance corridors by a number of state governments in concert with private investors. Most such projects involve granting franchises to high speed rail development corporations or private joint ventures, sometimes with proprietary technology. In most proposals, state participation would include assembling and donating the right-of-way; authorizing subsidies from value capture taxes on adjacent property; state assumption of liability risk; and making available tax exempt government borrowing. States with high speed rail development programs include Florida, Ohio, New York, Virginia, Texas, Pennsylvania, and California. Multi-state cooperative proposals involve service between Chicago, Illinois and Milwaukee, Wisconsin; and between Los Angeles, California and Las Vegas, Nevada (Taylor, 1992b). Although the economic recession that began in 1989 has sidetracked many of these proposals, several have advanced. Most notable is the Texas high speed rail project, where a private joint venture including TGV technology has been selected, and private funding is being sought.

In fact, the federal government has become involved in high speed rail in general and magnetic levitation (maglev) technology in particular. Amtrak, for example, has begun testing the Swedish-built X-2000 high speed "tilt" train in the Northeast Corridor. Once electrification of the Northeast Corridor is complete, Amtrak anticipates high speed service at speeds of up to 240 kilometers per hour. Moreover, federal transportation legislation passed in 1992 provides large subsidies for research and demonstration programs. Those subsidies to high speed rail development do not, however, reflect a general commitment to national rail transportation. Instead, they are driven largely by industrial development considerations. The ultimate goal is to incubate new technologies in order to compete in domestic and world markets with the French, Japanese, and Germans.

In the more distant future, the inter-city rail system in the United States may become more fragmented and partially privatized, with most resources focused on a few high speed corridors of 500 miles or less. State involvement will become more important, although direct state funding will probably be limited. Within high speed corridors, one can expect premium service aimed primarily at business travellers, with prices approaching airline fares. The inter-city rail network will probably become more fragmented outside of these higher density corridors, especially if federal support for Amtrak dwindles, or if Amtrak is privatized. In either case, much of the existing national network would disappear.

5.4 Relevance for Europe

Differences between Europe and America in geography, history, government, political philosophy, and transportation priorities limit the relevance of American railroad practices and policies for Europe. For example, a major concern of inter-city transportation policy in Europe is integration of peripheral regions. That is not a key issue in the United States, since virtually all areas are well served by highways and air connections. Moreover, there is less regional disparity in levels of economic development within the U.S. than in Europe. Of course, Americans are interested in the impact of road and rail systems on regional development, but such concerns are usually state or local.

Privatization and deregulation of transport systems are key concerns in Europe. Due to its weak market potential, the passenger rail system in the United States is likely to remain a public corporation in the coming years. By contrast, privatization of certain European inter-city systems appears imminent. The Christian Democratic Government in Germany, for example, is planing to transform the federal railway system into three private corporations responsible for freight, passenger traffic, and system infrastructure, respectively. That privatization is scheduled for January 1, 1994. The Conservative Government of Britain is likewise committed to privatizing British Rail, but an exact timetable has not yet been established. In general, privatization efforts have been spurred by the desire to reduce the enormous public subsidies for unprofitable routes. Rail privatization in Europe appears to be more feasible than in the United States because of shorter travel distances between most major cities, a much better developed rail network, and the much higher user costs of the competing automobile and air transport modes. Moreover, European central governments will assume the accumulated debts of the former public systems.

If anything, the United States could benefit by adopting some aspects of past European inter-city transport policy. One of the crucial deficiencies in the American transport network, for example, is lack of centralized multi-modal coordination. In contrast, most major European countries have had both a national rail system and a national airline, which coordinate routes and schedules. Although a January 1993 EC ruling requires member nations to privatize their national airlines by 1995, there has been ample time under national ownership to nurture the development of comprehensive inter-city transport systems.

More generally, in European countries such as France and Germany, long distance transport policies are characterized by partnerships between the national railroad and airlines, the central government, and industry (Taylor, 1992a). In France and especially Germany, for instance, the central government supports private industry in developing high speed rail systems and thereafter provides both a domestic market and support for export of technology. The German experience in such partnerships is especially strong. There, the Lufthansa network includes rail services that link Frankfurt, the major Lufthansa hub, to Dusseldorf and Stuttgart. These rail connections are listed as flights in the airline's travel reservation system, and tickets are available through Lufthansa. Until now, no such broad-based action for high speed rail development has been proposed in the U.S.

5.5 Inter-city Bus

Although most of this section has focused on inter-city rail, inter-city buses carry twice as many passengers each year as inter-city and urban commuter rail systems combined. Because of much slower speeds, lower fares, and inferior service, the long distance inter-city bus market is limited, serving mainly low income travelers and remote rural areas where rail service is not available. Moreover, the prospects for the inter-city bus industry have become increasingly bleak with each passing decade, as personal incomes have risen. Increased auto ownership, reduced air fares, and depopulation of rural areas have steadily eroded the ridership base for inter-city bus service.

From about 1940 to 1980, the Greyhound and Trailways bus companies dominated the inter-city bus industry. Numerous smaller private bus firms competed with the two national carriers in certain regional markets. Presently, however, Greyhound is the only national carrier left, and even it is besieged by bankruptcy and labor difficulties. Greyhound continues to sell off its assets, including downtown real estate.

The U.S. inter-city bus network is almost completely private. Government regulation is limited to safety standards. With the decline of the once dominant national carriers and their divestiture of control over major urban bus terminals, opportunities for new entrants into regional markets have increased. Monopolistic pricing practices have thus been discouraged. However, since the size of the market is limited, one or two carriers, often operating exclusively in a region, can usually fulfill the entire market demand. In general, most regional markets are characterized by market contestability (see previous chapter by Banister, Berechman, and de Rus), with generally uniform pricing among the few carriers controlling a given market. On average, fares are 20 to 30 percent lower than for rail travel and much lower than air travel, but speed and comfort are inferior.

6. Air Passenger Transport

Whereas rail and bus services account for a very small proportion of inter-city passenger transport in the United States, air travel has expanded dramatically in recent years to become the principal common carrier over long distances. The rapid growth in air passenger travel has partly been the result of airline deregulation, which has been in effect since 1978. Deregulation has led to the more efficient operation of airline companies, causing substantially reduced costs. The cost savings in turn prompted decreases in fares and made airline travel an affordable mode of inter-city transportation for much of the population.

As described in the following sections, airline deregulation in the United States has not been an unqualified success. Repeated fare wars among the major airlines have led to financial instability in the industry. Bankruptcies, mergers, and leveraged buyouts have forced many carriers out of business, so that a small number of large airlines now control most of the market. In 1992 and 1993, almost all airline carriers in the United States suffered large operating losses, and their future is uncertain. The problems arising from deregulation in the United States suggest that Europeans should proceed cautiously with liberalization of the airline industry. They should consider not only the short term benefits but also the long term drawbacks.

6.1 Recent Trends in Passenger Air Transport

Air travel in the United States has grown rapidly over the last 40 years. Whereas air transport accounted for less than 2 percent of total inter-city travel within the United States in 1950, it had increased its share to 17.4 percent by 1990 (U.S. Bureau of the Census, 1992, p. 600). Passenger-miles flown by commercial airlines increased by almost 142 billion in absolute terms, an overall growth of 70 percent (see Table 1). During the 1980s, air travel by commercial airline was the fastest growing mode of transportation in the United States. Despite the impressive increase in passenger-miles flown by commercial airlines, general aviation travel (mostly small private planes) declined by 16 percent.

Corresponding to the increase in air travel demand, the supply of services also increased. Between 1980 and 1990, vehicle-miles flown by commercial airlines rose from 2,523 to 3,963 million, an increase of 57 percent (see Table 3). Vehicle-miles of air travel have not increased as fast as passenger-miles because of larger airplanes and higher seat occupancy rates. The proportion of occupied seating capacity on domestic flights rose from an average of 58 percent in 1980 to 60.4 percent in 1990 (U.S. Department of Transportation, 1992). Airline industry employment increased by 6 percent, from 354,264 in 1980 to 588,926 in 1990.

6.2 Public Sector Involvement and Regulation in the Airline Sector

Direct government involvement in the air transport sector has always been less in the United States than in other countries. The United States has never had a publicly owned or subsidized national airline similar to those in Europe. Instead, airlines in the United States have always been owned and managed by private corporations (Wheeler 1987).

Although direct public involvement in the airline industry has been minimal, federal, state, and local governments have planned and subsidized the construction of airports and related infrastructure. The most important federal laws in recent years were the 1970 Airport and Airways Development Act and the Airport and Airways Revenue Act. They authorized federal subsidies of $280 million a year over five years and established the Aviation Trust Fund, modelled on the Federal Highway Trust Fund. The Aviation Trust Fund is financed by an 8-percent tax on all domestic air fares and taxation of general aviation gasoline and jet fuel. In certain cases local authorities rely on landing fees and aircraft registration charges as an additional source of subsidy finance for their airport development. In addition, the Secretary of Transportation is entitled to make grants to public agencies for airport master planning projects.

Prior to 1978, public sector involvement in the airline industry was mainly through regulation, which began during the 1930s. There was a general feeling among the post-Depression policy makers that a lack of public sector control over airlines would generate an environment of cutthroat competition, ultimately resulting in fares well below the industry's operating costs (Fleming, 1991). Moreover, advocates of regulation believed that government control was necessary to coordinate integration of the fledgling air travel sector into the existing transportation system, and to ensure high safety standards. In fact, until the mid-1970s, they argued that removal of controls on industry would result in reduced safety standards as airlines cut their costs.

Regulation of the airline industry was established by the U.S. Civil Aeronautics Act of 1938. It created the Civil Aeronautics Board (CAB), which had sweeping powers over fare structures, regulated the entry or expansion of carriers in the industry, oversaw mergers and acquisitions, and granted direct, albeit limited, operating subsidies to the airlines (Button, 1989). In addition, the CAB was in charge of determining which airlines could operate in each city-pair market (Fleming, 1991). Although the CAB was initially also in charge of coordinating safety standards for the industry, the Federal Aviation Act of 1958 shifted this task to the Federal Aviation Authority (FAA).

6.3 Airline Deregulation: 1978 to the Present

Airline regulation in the United States lasted for 40 years, from 1938 to 1978. During that period, the CAB prohibited any new trunk airlines from entering the market. As a result, the air travel industry became highly concentrated and by 1977, the five largest carriers accounted for almost two-thirds of total air passenger revenues (Rakowski, 1990). The nearly monopolistic environment of air transportation, its inefficiency, and high fares eventually led to the end of airline regulation. During the 1970s, a growing number of economists had come to share the opinion that a tightly controlled airline industry did not serve the interests of consumers. In particular, they criticized the non-competitive environment arising from the CAB's refusal to allow new airlines to enter the market, which enabled existing carriers to charge high fares. Furthermore, many advocates of deregulation in the United States wanted airlines to be treated just as any other private industry, with maximum competition and minimal government intervention (Fleming, 1990). Those developments eventually led to the 1978 Airline Deregulation Act. It entirely phased out the barriers to entry of new airlines by 1981 and eliminated government regulation of passenger fares. Under deregulation, the CAB was scheduled to cease operations in 1984. The primary objective of the airline deregulators was to nurture a competitive atmosphere that would encourage airlines to operate more efficiently and thus reduce their costs. Liberalization of air transport in the United States, however, has not been an unqualified success. While consumers have generally benefitted through an overall reduction in fares, the airline industry has become increasingly unstable, especially in recent years, with many carriers making large losses, declaring bankruptcy, or ceasing operations altogether.

6.4 The Advantages and Drawbacks of Airline Deregulation

There is little doubt that the removal of barriers to new entrants encouraged carriers to enhance their efficiency in operation, management, and marketing, thus reducing their unit operating costs. In fact, airlines in the United States are now far more productive than they were in the mid-1970s (Wheatcroft and Lipman, 1990). Labor productivity of North American airlines exceeds that of European carriers even though average hourly wages are much lower in Europe (see chapter by Barrett in this volume). For example, the average staff productivity of carriers in the United States in 1990 was 164 ton-kilometers per 1,000 employees, whereas the equivalent for European airlines was 120 ton-kilometers.

One way US carriers successfully reduced their unit operating costs was through the fall in jet fuel prices during the 1980s. More importantly, the extensive adoption of hub-and-spoke systems enabled airlines to utilize their fleets more efficiently by increasing their seat occupancy rates. The hub-and-spoke system eliminated direct links for unprofitable routes. Instead, it enabled a single airline to combine passengers from one principle origin who are traveling to various smaller destinations with passengers from another origin who also have varying destinations (Button, 1989). This approach facilitated the use of fuel-efficient, wide-bodied aircraft such as the Boeing 767 and Airbus on principal routes linking hub cities. Airlines were also using their labor force more productively, employing two-man flight crews and extending flying hours.

Passengers benefitted from the more efficient operation of airlines. They could travel with a single carrier throughout their journey even though they often had to change planes. Furthermore, the hub-and-spoke system was intended to provide more frequent connections for travelers, especially those to and from smaller cities (Standard and Poor, 1992). Although in some instances routing was less direct, the overall amount and quality of service probably improved. Even more importantly from the consumers' point of view, the decrease in airline costs led to an overall reduction in fares. The average passenger fare (in constant 1980 dollars) fell from $84.55 in 1980 to only $67.83 in 1990, a decline of 19 percent (U.S. Department of Transportation, 1992a). Fare reductions resulted not only from increased productivity but also from various new marketing strategies used by the airlines, including a bewildering variety of discounting schemes. In 1987, approximately 92 percent of all travelers flew with discounted tickets, the average discount being 62 percent below regular coach fare (Button, 1989). As Barrett points out (see chapter in this volume), airline fares in North America are far lower than in Europe. For example, in September 1990, the average economy class fare per passenger-kilometer for a trip of 1000 kilometers was 19.6 cents in North America, whereas in Europe it was 38.4 cents.

Most of the burden of overall cost reduction in the airline industry has fallen on the employees (Wheatcroft and Lipman, 1990). Salaries and wages traditionally have accounted for as much as 38 percent of airline total operating costs. Shortly after deregulation took effect, the average salary for existing airlines was $42,000. By contrast, new entrants such as People's Express were able to operate at reduced costs by hiring non-union employees and paying the much lower average wage of $22,000 (Sorenson, 1991). In order to remain competitive, the established airlines eventually sought to reduce their operating costs by forcing labor concessions and introducing a two-tier wage system, whereby new employees were hired at a lower pay scale than old ones. Obviously, the transition towards a lower wage structure has not always taken place smoothly. In a number of cases, the most notable involving Eastern Airlines, it resulted in long and disruptive strikes. Since 1989, labor costs have begun to increase as labor unions have begun resisting the two-tier wage system (Standard and Poor, 1992).

Liberalization of the airline industry in the United States has not produced the expected competitive environment predicted by deregulation advocates. Until the mid-1980s, there was a rush of entries by new "low cost, no frills" airlines, the most notable one being People Express. By the end of the decade, however, the industry had reverted to its previous oligopolistic profile, where a few dominant airlines controlled most of the market. Furthermore, the largest carriers gained monopolistic control of certain key hubs, thus dominating air traffic. For instance, TWA now controls 82 percent of the St. Louis market, and USAir's share of the Pittsburgh market has risen to 84 percent. Most of the new entrant airlines relied on low fares to gain a foothold in the market. They were unable to survive the cutthroat competitive environment that prevailed during the mid-1980s. The larger, established carriers dominated the hub-and-spoke network and computerized reservation systems (CRS). They also profited from marketing advantages such as trademark image and were able to increase their operating efficiency. Thus, they were able to match the cost-cutting strategies of the new entrants, forcing them out of the market.

Over the last five years or so, fare wars among the various airlines have prevented carriers from generating enough revenues to cover costs. Frequent flyer programs, which offer large discounts to regular customers, have been used by airlines to generate customer loyalty. Although attractive to consumers, they have reduced revenues for most airlines. In addition, the Gulf War deterred much international travel and raised costs due to increased fuel prices (Standard and Poor, 1992). Those factors and the concomitant economic recession have caused financial instability in the American airline industry. Bankruptcies, mergers and acquisitions, and leveraged buyouts have become commonplace. Some of the most noticeable trends towards airline concentration include the absorption of Piedmont and PSA by USAir, TWA taking over Ozark, and American's acquisition of Air Cal. Even some of the giants of aviation such as PanAm and Eastern Airlines were forced into bankruptcy and ultimate demise. TWA has declared Chapter 11 bankruptcy, and its fate is uncertain.

All the major airlines now face dire economic troubles. In response, they have laid off workers and delayed orders for new equipment. Many are now trying to sell off their most unprofitable hubs and routes to small regional carriers (The New York Times, April

1, 1993, p. A1). The future of the U.S. airline industry is uncertain. The major airlines, especially American, Delta, and United, have turned their attention towards strengthening their position abroad, where competition is not as intense.

Table 8 indicates the increasing concentration that has taken place in the American airline industry between 1985 and 1991. By December 1991, the five largest U.S. carriers accounted for 77.8 percent of total passenger-miles flown, compared to their combined share of 54.4 percent in 1985. Together, the three largest carriers, American, United, and Delta, flew more than 55 percent of the total air passenger-miles and earned approximately 66 percent of the industry's total revenues.

TABLE 8

Market Shares of U.S. Airline Carriers as Percentage of Total Passenger Miles Flown, 1985 and 1991

Airline	Market Share 1991	Airline	Market Share 1985
American	20.2	American	13.3
United	18.7	United	12.5
Delta	16.8	Eastern	10.0
Northwest	2.4	TWA	9.6
Continental	9.7	Delta	9.0
USAir	8.0	Pan AM	8.1
TWA	6.7	NWA	6.7
America West	2.9	Continental	4.9
Southwest	2.6	People Express	3.3
Alaska	1.2	Republic	3.2
Others	0.8	Others	19.4

Source: Standard and Poor (1992, p. A-3).

The increasing level of market share concentration and hub airport domination has had a number of serious adverse consequences for both passengers and carriers. On average, fares tend to be highest on routes between two hub airports that are dominated by one airline (Standard and Poor, 1992). For instance, the General Accounting Office discovered that after TWA bought out Ozark, its principal competitor at the St. Louis hub, fares to and from St. Louis increased by as much as 39 percent (Rakowski, 1990). Dominant airlines at hub airports now have the freedom to set their own costs for landing slots, and can thus limit entry to prospective competitors.

The rapid growth of air passenger travel that arose from deregulation has caused severe congestion of runways and terminal buildings at most major airports. The main reason for congestion is that airlines seek to offer most of their services at peak times. Construction of new infrastructure has not kept up with the rapid growth of airline fleets. Indeed, although there are ample funds for providing new airport facilities through the Airport and Airways Trust Fund, there are construction plans for only one new major airport. Calls for imposing higher airport user costs for airlines to relieve congestion have been rejected because policy makers fear it would force smaller airlines out of business.

A final issue relating to airline deregulation concerns safety. Adversaries of deregulation have long contended that lack of control in the airline industry would lead to lax safety standards and thus raise the risk of accidents. The evidence since deregulation took effect does not support those assertions. In fact, in recent years there has been a decline in the number of accidents per 100,000 hours flown. Moreover, the number of reported near misses has roughly matched the increase in passenger-miles flown. Generally, safety has increased because carriers now spend more on aircraft maintenance than they did prior to deregulation (Button, 1989).

6.5 What Does Airline Deregulation Mean for Europe?

It is unlikely that deregulation of the European airline industry will lead to the phenomenal growth of inter-city air travel that has taken place in the United States since 1978. The average distance between European cities is much shorter than in the United States. Most European holiday travelers still travel to their destination by car or railroad. In contrast to the United States, Europe has a well-established network of inter-city rail connecting each of its major metropolitan areas as well as most smaller cities. Recent developments such as the construction of high speed rail lines and the impending opening of the Channel Tunnel will further reduce surface travel times between city centers, thus entrenching the train firmly as a strong competitor to the airplane for long distance travel within Europe. In addition, the European air corridors are already congested, and there is little room for further expansion of airline travel within the continent.

As Barrett points out (see his chapter in this volume), it is doubtful that unit costs in Europe will fall as sharply as they did in the United States because of factors such as higher fuel and landing costs. Moreover, much of the cost reduction achieved by American carriers resulted from wage cutbacks. In most European countries, well-organized labor unions will probably refuse to make such radical concessions in employee wages. Thus, the bargain fares enjoyed in America seem unlikely for European aviation.

However, the pattern of mergers and takeovers that have led to air market concentration in the United States will probably be repeated in Europe. Several of the largest European airlines, many of which were recently privatized, have already emerged as mega-carriers in their respective national markets. For example, British Airways is the dominant British carrier following the acquisition of British Caledonian and Dan Air. In the Netherlands, the national airline KLM has taken over Nederlines and is the major shareholder of Transavia. In Germany, Lufthansa has established itself as a virtual monopoly, controlling 98 percent of the market (Wheatcroft, 1990). Moves towards complete liberalization of air services within the European Community have already led to a number of cross-border takeovers such as British Airways' acquisition of 49 percent of TAT European Airways, a French company. A few European airlines are thus amassing an ever greater share of the market and establishing themselves as aviation giants. The smaller, least efficient nationally run carriers in the European community (e.g., Olympic Airways) face an uphill battle to stay in business.

At present, the most interesting development in the international airline industry has been the move towards global liberalization, particularly the transatlantic alliances between American and European carriers. The dominant carriers on both sides of the Atlantic have been expanding their international operations in an effort to meet the continued increase in demand for international travel. The U.S. Department of Transportation recently approved an agreement between the Dutch national carrier KLM and Northwest Airlines to combine their services and operate in effect as a single airline, thus paving the way for the first truly global airline. In March 1993, the U.S. Department of Transportation approved a bid by British Airways to purchase a 19- percent stake in USAir. While there is still considerable resistance by American and European politicians, similar agreements can probably be expected in the future. Alone the European airlines may find it difficult to compete with their more efficient, lower cost American counterparts.

7. Summary and Implications for Europe

In spite of all their differences, the United States and Europe have much in common that enables them to learn from each other. They face many of the same problems, such as congestion, pollution, traffic accidents, energy use, and infrastructure needs. In trying to solve those problems, they are subject to many of the same financial and environmental limitations. Moreover, the transport sector in both the United States and Europe is embedded in basically private, market-oriented economies and democratic societies where the preferences of individual consumers and voters strongly influence policies. Finally, Europeans and Americans enjoy roughly comparable, high standards of living that lead to demands for ever more mobility and correspondingly fast, dependable, and convenient transport services.

In both the United States and Europe, public policies are crucial in dealing with transportation problems. In the past, governments on both continents have guided the development of passenger transport systems and strongly influenced travel behavior. Although the United States may have a reputation for minimal government intervention in the economy, transportation is an important exception. Public regulation, ownership, operation, and subsidy have generally been greater in the European transport sector. Nevertheless, the American transport system is as much the outcome of public policy as its European counterparts. The main difference is not the degree but the type of government involvement and the modes of transport it has favored. Implicit policies, such as the failure to internalize social and environmental costs in the United States, have crucially affected transport. Differences in both explicit and implicit public policies explain much of the variation in the evolution of American and European transport systems and travel behavior over the past few decades.

Probably the biggest difference between Europe and the United States has been the longer history of private ownership in the United States. Until the 1970s, for example, most urban public transport services as well as long distance rail services were provided by private companies. Moreover, long distance bus service and air transport are still provided exclusively by privately owned firms. By contrast, public ownership has long dominated virtually all passenger transport modes in most European countries.

Public regulation of transportation has a longer history in Europe. Moreover, there is an additional, multi-national level of government regulation in Europe on top of national, state, and local regulations. The European Community imposes a wide array of laws, regulations, and guidelines that affect virtually every aspect of transportation. On a national level as well, regulation is generally more extensive in Europe than in the United States. For example, automobile use in the United States has been far less regulated than in Europe; in particular, American governments at all levels have been less willing to control auto use and to internalize its social and environmental costs. Likewise, deregulation of air travel went into effect in the United States almost a decade before European countries even began considering it.

Public subsidies to passenger transport have been enormous both in the United States and in Europe. The main difference is that roadways and automobile use have been massively subsidized in the United States at every government level, both directly and indirectly. Auto users pay an artificially low price that reflects virtually none of the auto's enormous social and environmental costs. Moreover, roadway user taxes in the United States cover only 60 percent of the direct economic costs of roadway provision. By comparison, auto users in European countries pay roadway user taxes four to ten times as high as in the United States, and those taxes generate public sector revenues that are roughly two to four times higher than government roadway expenditures.

The overwhelming government support for automobile use in the United States has placed all forms of public transport at an unfair competitive disadvantage. Urban public transport as well as long distance bus and rail transport suffer from the artificially low price of auto use. The currently high level of urban public transport subsidies is necessary to offset even partially the enormous direct and indirect subsidies to auto use. Government financing of public transport in Europe is also considerable and has a much longer history than in the United States. Moreover, subsidies have been far more effective at maintaining public transport's modal split share in Europe because they are complemented by high taxes on all aspects of auto ownership and use.

Whatever the differences between Europe and the United States, transport policies generally appear to be moving in the same direction and for similar reasons. Government fiscal austerity since the mid-1980s has, for example, curtailed growth in transport subsidies on both continents, thereby increasing pressures for productivity gains and cost control in all transport sectors. Just as the rapid subsidy growth during the 1970s led to alarming increases in costs and falling productivity, the much slower subsidy growth during the 1980s appears to have improved productivity and reduced costs. In Europe as well as the United States, there has been a trend toward devolution of policy decision making and financial responsibility from central to state and local governments. The shift of subsidy finance to lower government levels also increases pressure for cost control and has prodded state and local governments in some countries to examine the potential efficiency advantages of privatization. So far, there has been a great deal of talk about privatization but very little action, with the exception of bus transport in Great Britain. The contracting out of bus services to private operators in Scandinavia, and to a lesser extent in the United States, offers the possibility of increasing efficiency while maintaining public control. That intermediate form of privatization probably has more potential than complete privatization of ownership, operation, and financing, especially in the deficit-ridden public transport sector.

In the past, Europe has often followed the societal and economic developments in the United States. It seems unlikely, however, that the evolving passenger transport system in Europe will or should more closely resemble the auto- and air-oriented system in the United States. Even with their much lower levels of auto ownership and use, European countries are suffering severe social and environmental problems. The greater population densities and restricted possibilities for roadway expansion in Europe sharply limit the feasibility of increased auto use. Similarly, the already severely congested air traffic corridors and airports in Europe leave little room for increases in air travel. In contrast, improvement of the passenger rail network would avoid many of the social and environmental problems of auto and air travel. Moreover, unlike the United States, the relatively short distances between European cities make rail transport, especially high speed rail, an attractive alternative to both auto and air travel. In this respect, government policies in the United States almost certainly would be inappropriate in the very different European context.

References

Altshuler, A., Womack, J., and Pucher, J., 1979, *The Urban Transportation System*, MIT Press, Cambridge.

American Public Transit Association, Annual, *Transit Fact Book*, American Public Transit Association, Washington, D.C.

Amstrong, E. (ed.), 1976. *History of Public Works in the United States*, American Public Works Association, Chicago.

Button, K., 1989. The Deregulation of U.S. Interstate Aviation; An Assessment of Causes and Consequences, *Transport Reviews*, 9(2&3), 99-118, 189-215.

European Conference of the Ministers of Transport, 1990, *Transport Policy and the Environment*, OECD, Paris.

Federal Highway Administration, 1973, 1978, and 1992, *Nationwide Personal Trends*, Department of Transportation, Washington, D.C.

Federal Highway Administration, 1991, *Highway Statistics, Personal Transportation Survey*, U.S. Department of Transportation, Washington, D.C.

Federal Transit Administration, 1992, *National Transit Summaries and Trends*, Department of Transportation, Washington, D.C.

Fleming, D.K., 1991, Competition in the U.S. Airline Industry, *Transportation Quarterly,* 45(2), 181-210.

German Ministry of Transport, 1992, *Verkehr in Zahlen*, Deutsches Institut fuer Wirtschaftsforschung, Berlin.

International Roadway Federation, 1990, *World Road Statistics*, International Roadway Federation, Geneva.

Klein, D. and Fielding, G., 1992, Private Toll Roads: Learning from the Nineteenth Century, *Transportation Quarterly*, 46(3), 321-341.

National Passenger Railroad Corporation, *Annual Reports,* National Passenger Railroad Corporation, Washington, D.C.

Newman, P. and Kenworthy, J., 1992, Is There a Role for Physical Planners?, *Journal of the American Planning Association*, 58(3), 353-362.

The New York Times, April 1, 1993, *Hurt in Expansion, Airlines Cut Back and May Sell Hubs*, A1 and D6.

Nice, D.C., 1991, Passenger Train Ridership in the Amtrak System, *Transportation Quarterly*, 45(1), 121-132.

Organization for Economic Cooperation and Development, 1992, *Energy Prices and Taxes*, No. 3., International Energy Agency, Paris.

Pucher, J., Markstedt, A., and Hirschman, I., 1983. Impacts of Subsidies on the Costs of Urban Public Transport, *Journal of Transport Economics and Policy*, 27(2), 155-176.

Pucher, J., 1988a, Urban Travel Behavior as the Outcome of Public Policy: The Example of Modal Split in Western Europe and North America, *Journal of the American Planning Association*, 54(4), 509-520.

Pucher, J., 1988b, Subsidies to Urban Public Transport in Western Europe and North America, *Transportation Quarterly*, 42(3), 377-402.

Pucher, J., 1990a, Capitalism, Socialism, and Urban Transportation, *Journal of the American Planning Association*, 56(3), 278-296.

Pucher, J., 1990b, The East-West Transportation Spectrum, *Transportation Quarterly*, 44(3), 441-466.

Pucher, J. and Clorer, S., 1992. Taming the Automobile in Germany, *Transportation Quarterly*, 46(3), 383-396.

Rakowski, J.P., 1990, Marketing Myopia Meets Marketing Economies: Expected Results of U.S. Airline and Trucking Deregulation, *Transportation Quarterly*, 44(4), 499-516.

Saltzman, A., 1979, Public Transportation in the 20th Century, in Gray, G. and Hoel, L. (eds.), *Public Transportation*, Englewood Cliffs, Prentice-Hall.

Sorenson, N., 1991, The Impact of Geographic Scale and Traffic Density on Airline Production Costs: The Decline of the No-Frills Airlines, *Economic Geography*, 67, 333-345.

Standard and Poor, 1992, *Industry Surveys: Aerospace and Air Transport*, Standard and Poor Corp., New York.

Taylor, P., 1992a, National Strategies for Implementing High Speed Rail in France and Germany, *Parsons Brinckerhoff Network*, 6(54), 32-33.

Taylor, P., 1992b, Cooperation and Risk Sharing: Defining Public and Private Sector Roles in Developing U.S. High Speed Rail, *Parsons Brinckerhoff Network*, 6(54), 34-40.

Transportation Research Board, 1991, *In Pursuit of Speed: New Options for Inter-city Passenger Transport*, National Research Council, Washington D.C.

Urban Mass Transportation Administration, Annual, National Urban Mass Transportation Statistics, U.S. Department of Transportation, Washington, D.C.

U.S. Bureau of the Census, 1975, *Historical Statistics of the United States: Colonial Times to 1970*, Department of Commerce, Washington D.C.

U.S. Bureau of the Census, 1992, Statistical Abstract of the United States, Department of Commerce, Washington, D.C.

U.S. Department of Transportation, 1992a, National Transportation Statistics, Research and Special Programs Administration, Washington, D.C.

U.S. Department of Transportation, 1992b, *Intermodal Surface Transportation Efficiency Act of 1991: A Summary*, U.S. Department of Transportation, Washington, D.C.

Wheatcroft, S., 1990, Towards Transnational Airlines, *Tourism Management*, December, 353-358.

Wheatcroft, S. and Lipman, G., 1990, *European Liberalization and World Air Transport. Towards a Transnational Industry*, The Economist Intelligence Unit, London.

Wheeler, A., 1987, The Role of the Air Carrier, in Hodgson, A. (ed.), *The Travel and Tourism Industry*, Pergamon Press, Oxford.

CONTRIBUTORS

Bjorn Andersen is Associate Professor at More and Romsdal College in Molde, Norway.

David Banister is Reader in Transport Planning at University College London, United Kingdom.

Sean Barrett is Senior Lecturer in the Department of Economics at Trinity College, Dublin, Ireland.

Joseph Berechman is Professor in the Public Policy Program at Tel Aviv University, Israel.

Ulrich Blum is Professor of Economic Policy and Research at the Technical University of Dresden, Germany.

Kenneth Button is Professor of Applied Economics and Transport at Loughborough University, United Kingdom.

Vlasta Dugonjic is the Economic Affairs Officer in the Transport Division of the UN Economic Commission for Europe in Geneva, Switzerland.

Bernard Gerardin is Director of Research at INRETS and Technical Adviser to the European Investment Bank, Luxembourg.

Maria Giaoutzi is Professor in the Department of Geography and Regional Planning at the Technical University of Athens, Greece.

Gerold Hauser is Professor and Director of the Socioeconomic Institute at Zurich University, Switzerland.

Veli Himanen is a Senior Research Scientist at the Technical Research Center of Finland at Espoo, Finland.

Ira Hirschman is Principal Economist for the New York-based transportation and planning firm of Parsons, Brinckerhoff Inc., The United States.

Dimitri Ioannides is a Ph.D. candidate in the Department of Urban Planning at Rutgers University, the United States.

Peter Jones is Professor and Director of the Transport Studies Group at the University of Westminster, London, United Kingdom.

Jorgen Kristiansen is Associate Professor in the Department of Development and Planning at Aalborg University, Denmark.

Frank Leibbrand is with the Faculty of Economic Sciences at the Technical University of Dresden, Germany.

Rico Maggi is Professor at the Socioeconomic Institute at Zurich University, Switzerland.

Gines de Rus Mendoza is Professor in the Department of Applied Sciences and Economics at the University of Las Palmas in the Grand Canaries, Spain.

Peter Nijkamp is Professor in the Department of Economics at the Free University of Amsterdam, The Netherlands.

Juraj Padjen is Professor in the Institute of Economics at the University of Zagreb, Croatia.

John Pucher is Associate Professor in the Department of Urban Planning at Rutgers University, The United States.

Jose Viegas is Professor of Transportation at the Instituto Superior Tecnico in the Technical University of Lisbon, Portugal.

SUBJECT INDEX